Oh!great

TRANSLATED AND ADAPTED BY
Makoto Yukon

LETTERED BY
Janice Chiang

BALLANTINE BOOKS • NEW YORK

A Del Rey Trade Paperback Original

Air Gear, volume 3 Copyright © 2003 by Oh!great
English translation copyright © 2007 by Oh!great
Emblem design copyright © 2003 by Kai Machida

Published in the United States by Del Rey Books, an imprint of The Random House Publishing Group, a division of Random House, Inc., New York.

Publication rights arranged through Kodansha Ltd.

First published in Japan in 2003 by Kodansha Ltd., Tokyo

ISBN 978-0-345-49280-7

Printed in the United States of America

www.delreymanga.com

9 8 7 6 5 4 3 2 1

Translator and Adaptor—Makoto Yukon
Lettering—Janice Chiang

Honorifics Explained

Throughout the Del Rey Manga books, you will find Japanese honorifics left intact in the translations. For those not familiar with how the Japanese use honorifics and, more important, how they differ from American honorifics, we present this brief overview.

Politeness has always been a critical facet of Japanese culture. Ever since the feudal era, when Japan was a highly stratified society, use of honorifics—which can be defined as polite speech that indicates relationship or status—has played an essential role in the Japanese language. When addressing someone in Japanese, an honorific usually takes the form of a suffix attached to one's name (example: "Asuna-san"), is used as a title at the end of one's name, or appears in place of the name itself (example: "Negi-sensei," or simply "Sensei!").

Honorifics can be expressions of respect or endearment. In the context of manga and anime, honorifics give insight into the nature of the relationship between characters. Many translations into English leave out these important honorifics and therefore distort the feel of the original Japanese. Because Japanese honorifics contain nuances that English honorifics lack, it is our policy at Del Rey not to translate them. Here, instead, is a guide to some of the honorifics you may encounter in Del Rey Manga.

-san: This is the most common honorific and is equivalent to Mr., Miss, Ms., or Mrs. It is the all-purpose honorific and can be used in any situation where politeness is required.

-sama: This is one level higher than "-san." It is used to confer great respect.

-dono: This comes from the word "tono," which means "lord." It is an even higher level than "-sama" and confers utmost respect.

-kun: This suffix is used at the end of boys' names to express familiarity or endearment. It is also sometimes used by men among friends, or when addressing someone younger or of a lower station.

-chan: This is used to express endearment, mostly toward girls. It is also used for little boys, pets, and even among lovers. It gives a sense of childish cuteness.

Bozu: This is an informal way to refer to a boy, similar to the English terms "kid" or "squirt."

Sempai/
Senpai: This title suggests that the addressee is one's senior in a group or organization. It is most often used in a school setting, where underclassmen refer to their upperclassmen as "sempai." It can also be used in the workplace, such as when a newer employee addresses an employee who has seniority in the company.

Kohai: This is the opposite of "sempai" and is used toward underclassmen in school or newcomers in the workplace. It connotes that the addressee is of a lower station.

Sensei: Literally meaning "one who has come before," this title is used for teachers, doctors, or masters of any profession or art.

[blank]: Usually forgotten in these lists, but perhaps the most significant difference between Japanese and English. The lack of honorific means that the speaker has permission to address the person in a very intimate way. Usually, only family, spouses, or very close friends have this kind of permission. Known as *yobisute,* it can be gratifying when someone who has earned the intimacy starts to call one by one's name without an honorific. But when that intimacy hasn't been earned, it can be very insulting.

AIR GEAR

大暮維人 3
Oh!great

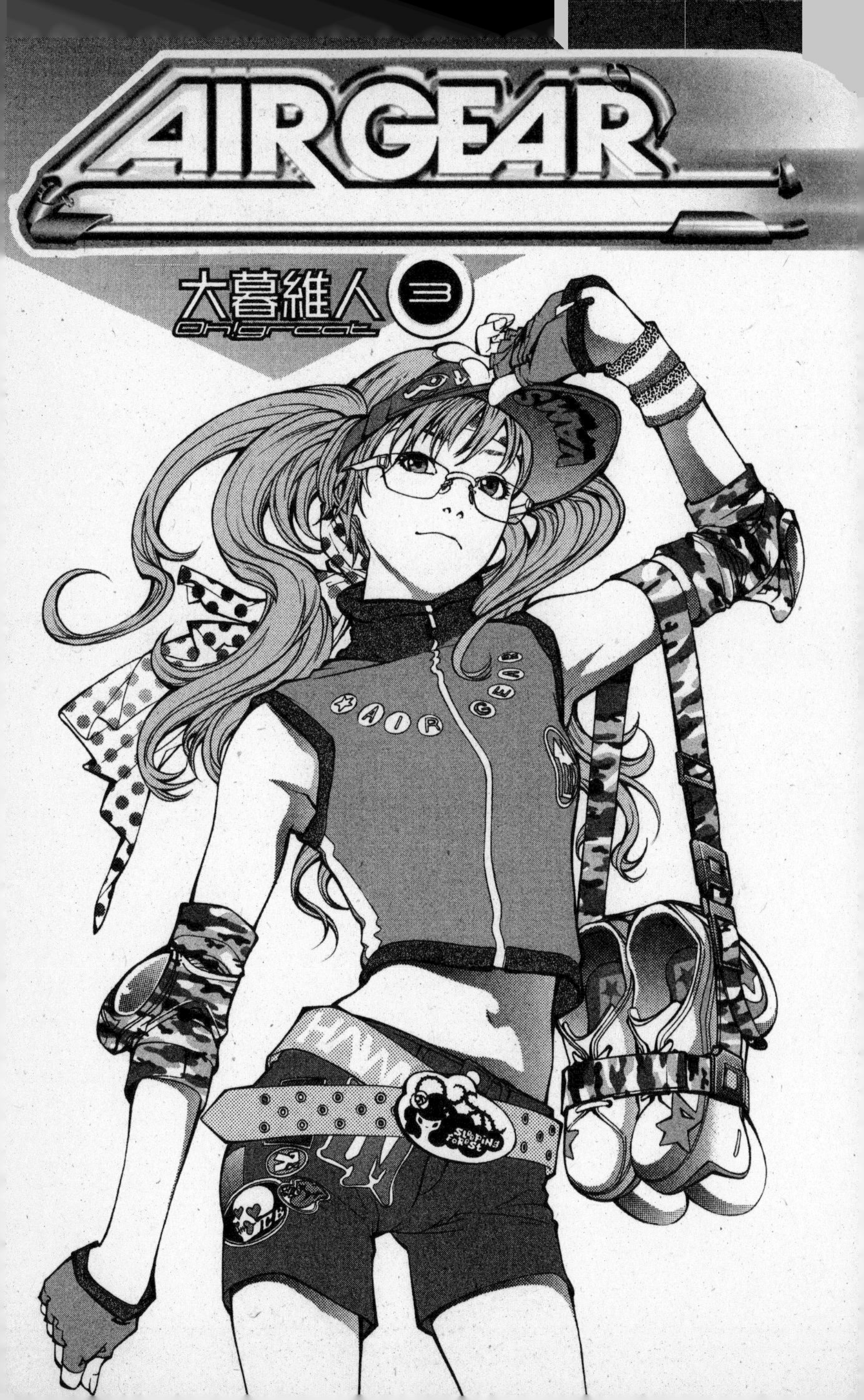
AIR GEAR
SLEEPING FOREST

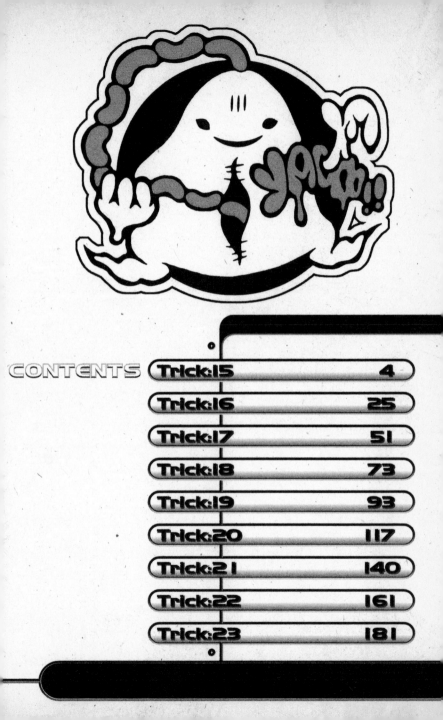

CONTENTS

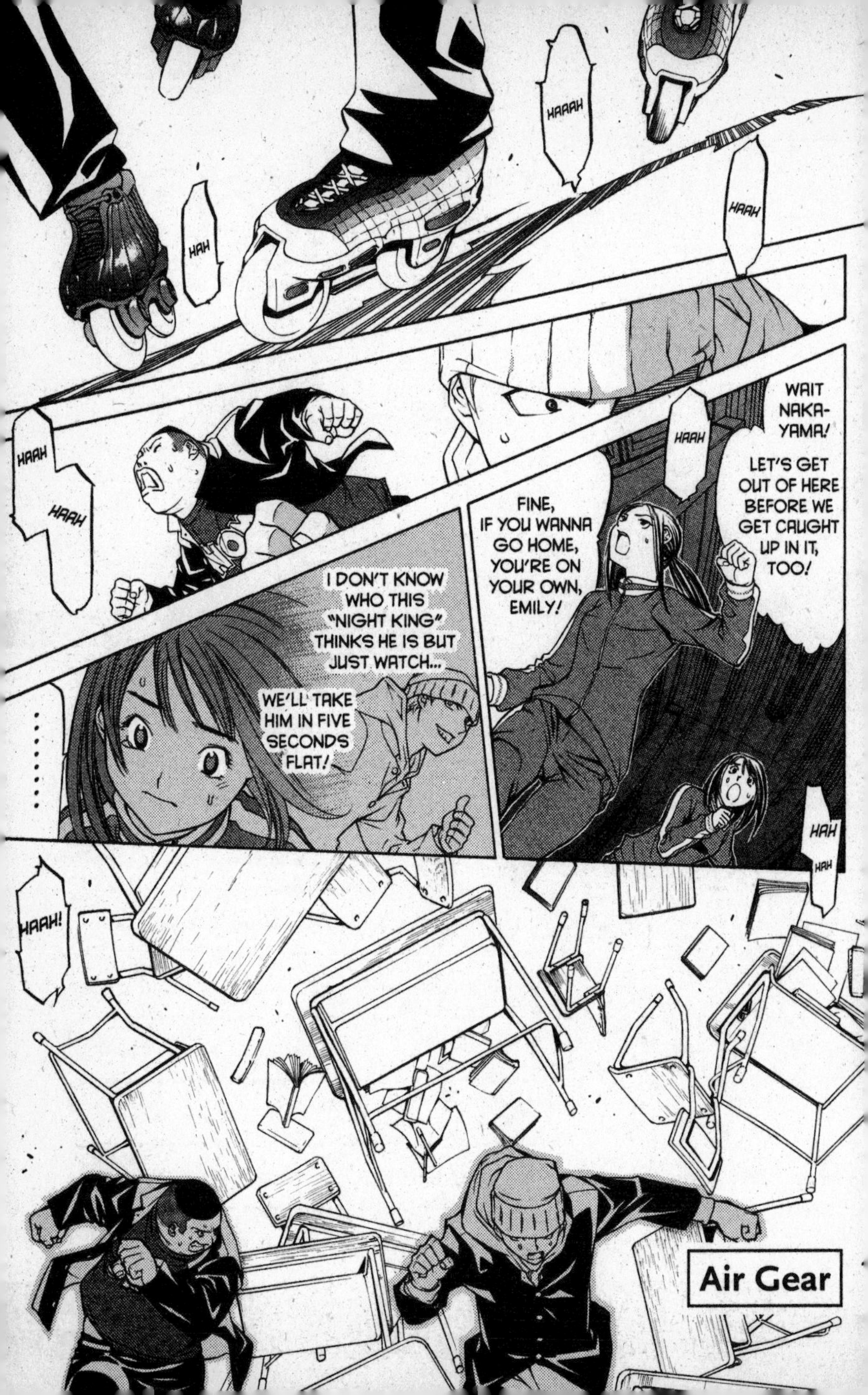

HAAH
HAAAH
HAH
WAIT NAKA-YAMA!
LET'S GET OUT OF HERE BEFORE WE GET CAUGHT UP IN IT, TOO!
HAAH
HAAH
HAAH
FINE, IF YOU WANNA GO HOME, YOU'RE ON YOUR OWN, EMILY!
HAH
HAH
I DON'T KNOW WHO THIS "NIGHT KING" THINKS HE IS BUT JUST WATCH...
WE'LL TAKE HIM IN FIVE SECONDS FLAT!
......
HAAH!

Air Gear

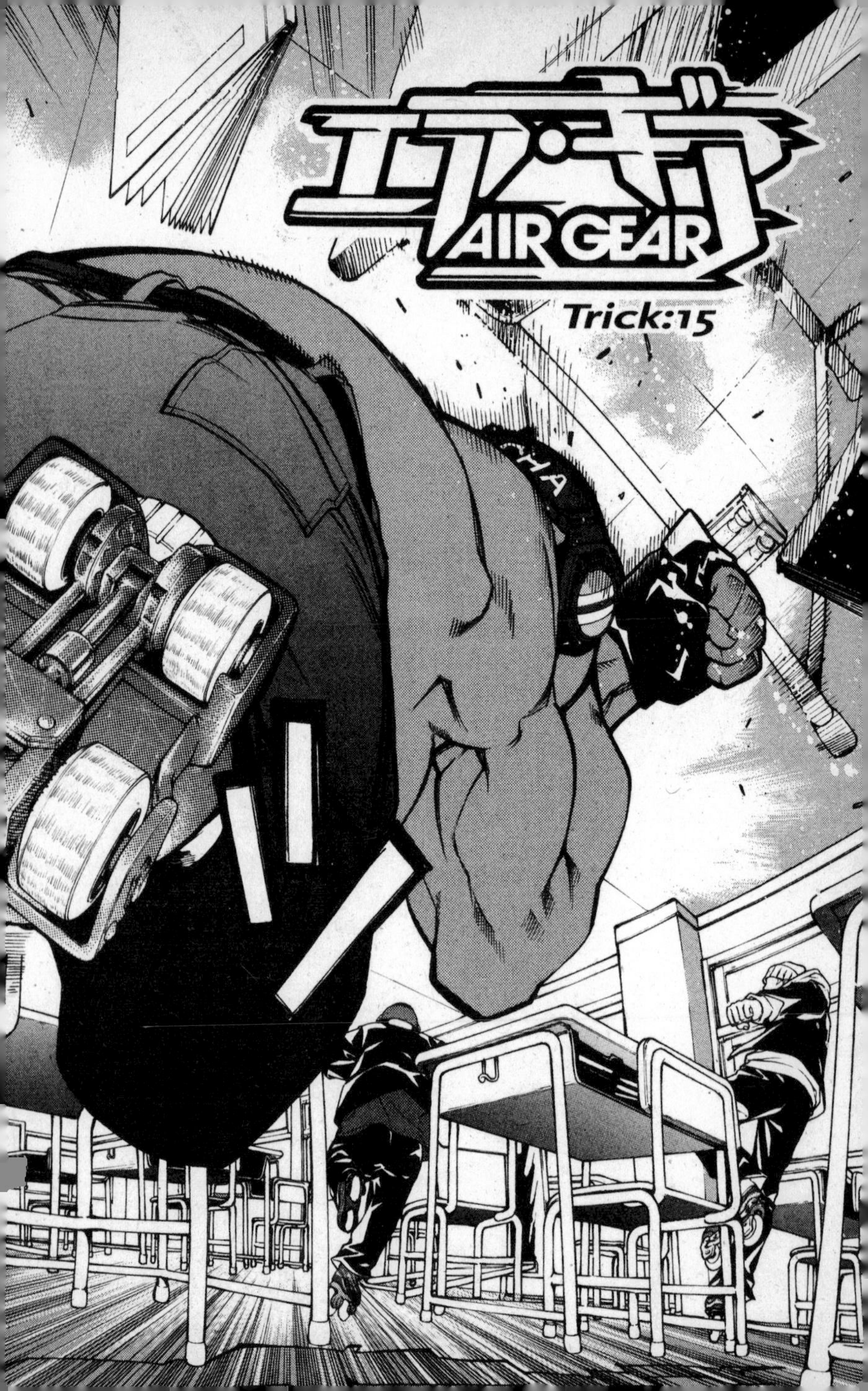
エア・ギア
AIR GEAR
Trick:15

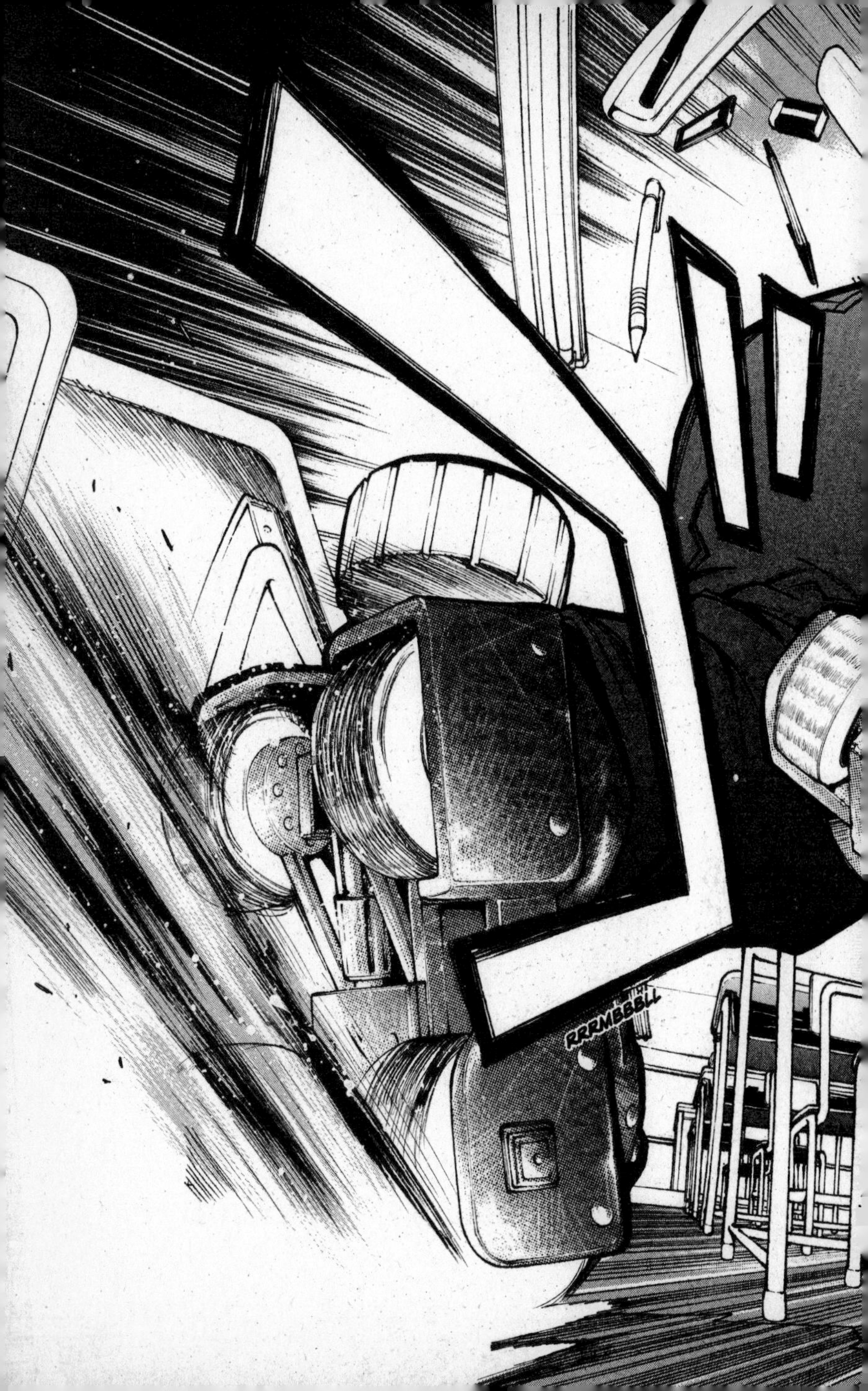
RRRMBBBLL

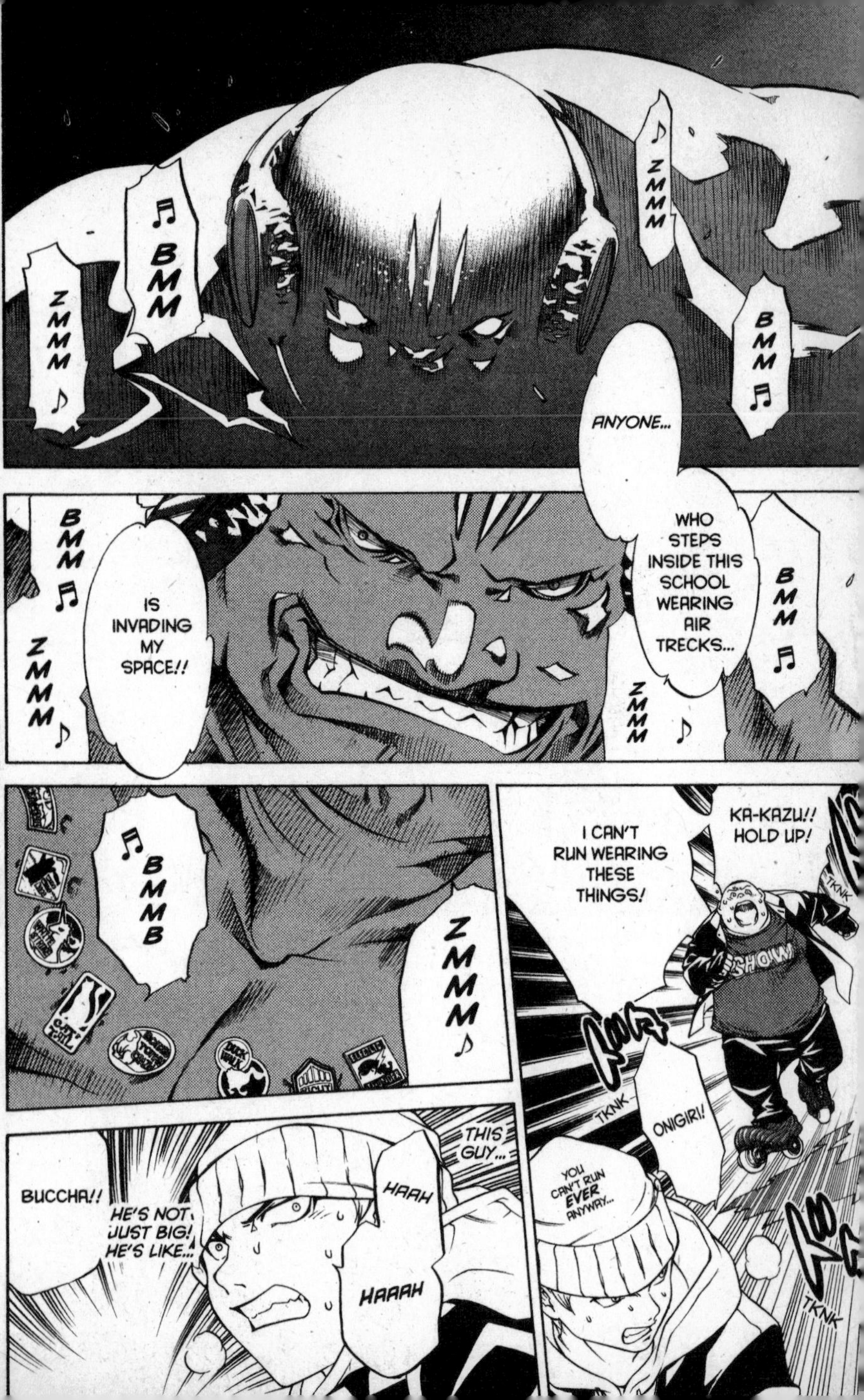
BMM ♫
ZMMM ♪
ANYONE...
♫ BMM
ZMMM ♪
WHO STEPS INSIDE THIS SCHOOL WEARING AIR TRECKS...
BMM ♫
ZMMM ♪
IS INVADING MY SPACE!!
BMM ♫
ZMMM ♪
KA-KAZU!! HOLD UP!
I CAN'T RUN WEARING THESE THINGS!
TKNK
TKNK
ONIGIRI!
YOU CAN'T RUN EVER ANYWAY...
TKNK
ZMMM ♪
♫ BMMB
THIS GUY...
HAAH
BUCCHA!!
HE'S NOT JUST BIG! HE'S LIKE...
HAAAH

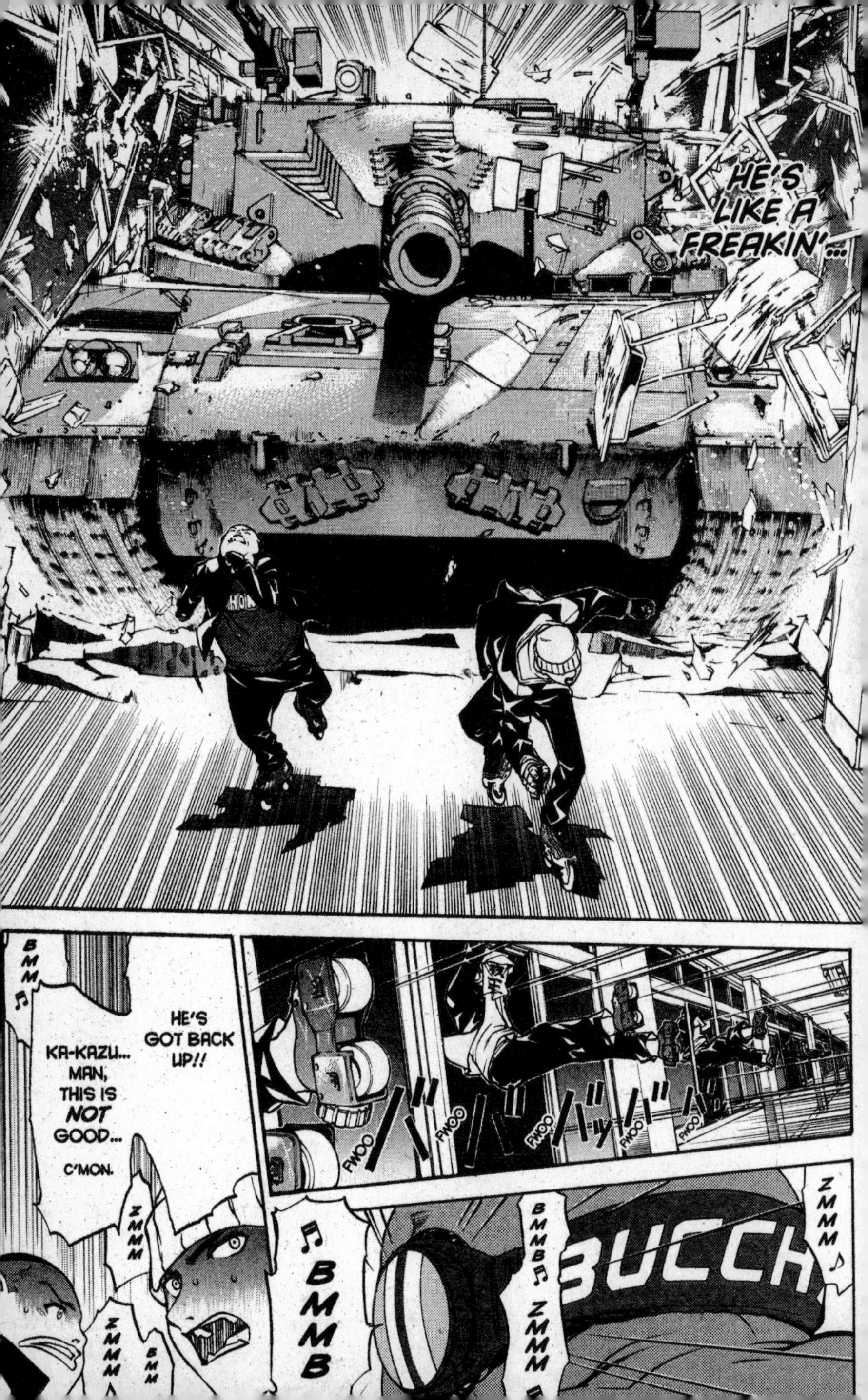
HE'S LIKE A FREAKIN'...
FWOO
FWOO
FWOO
FWOO
FWOO
ZMMM♪
BUCCH
BMMB♪
ZMMM
♪ BMMB
BMM♪
HE'S GOT BACK UP!!
KA-KAZU... MAN, THIS IS NOT GOOD...
C'MON.
ZMMM
ZMMM
BMM

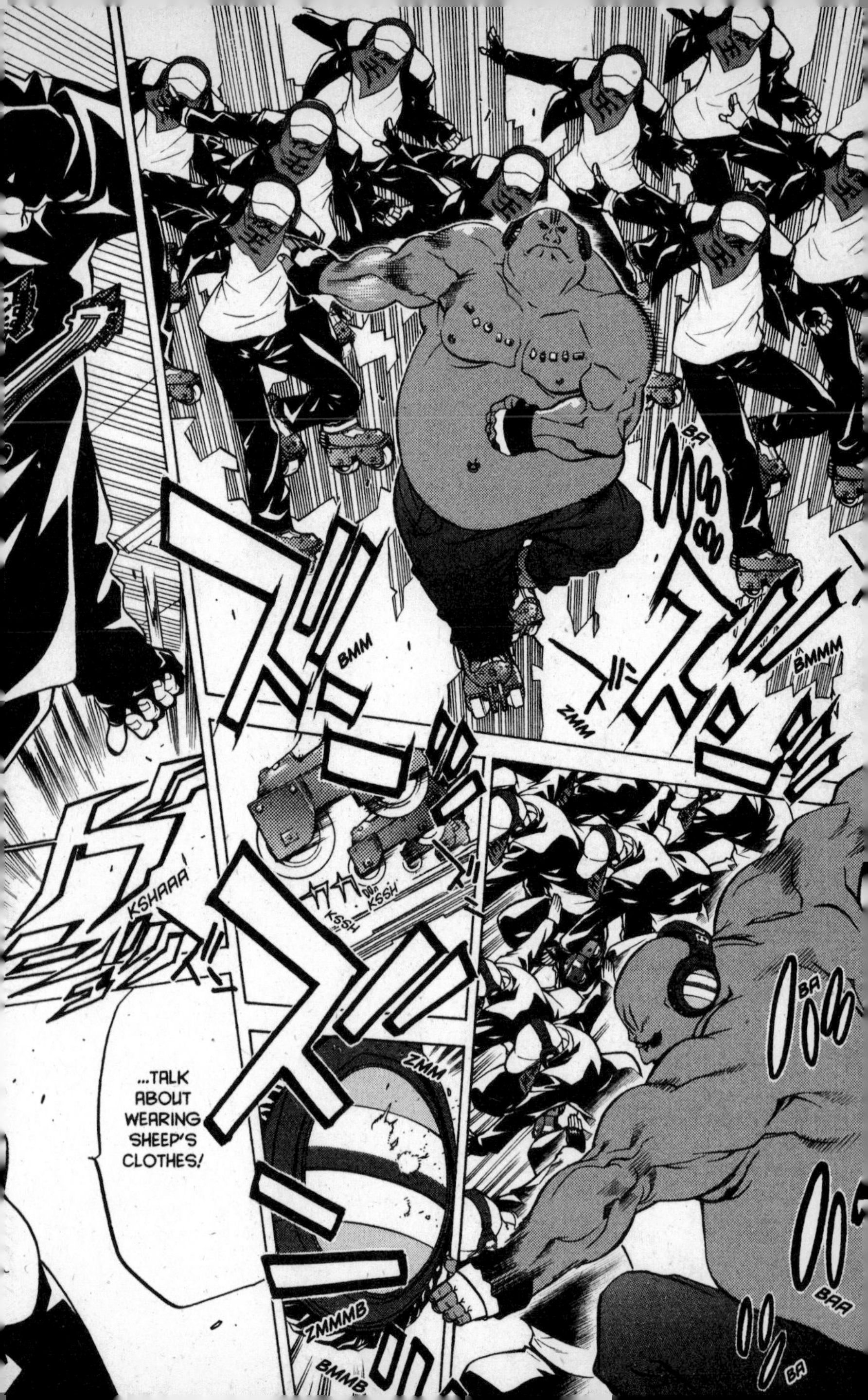
BA
BMMM
ZMM
BMM
BA
BAA
BA
KSSH
KSSH
ZMM
ZMMMB
BMMB
KSHAAA
...TALK ABOUT WEARING SHEEP'S CLOTHES!

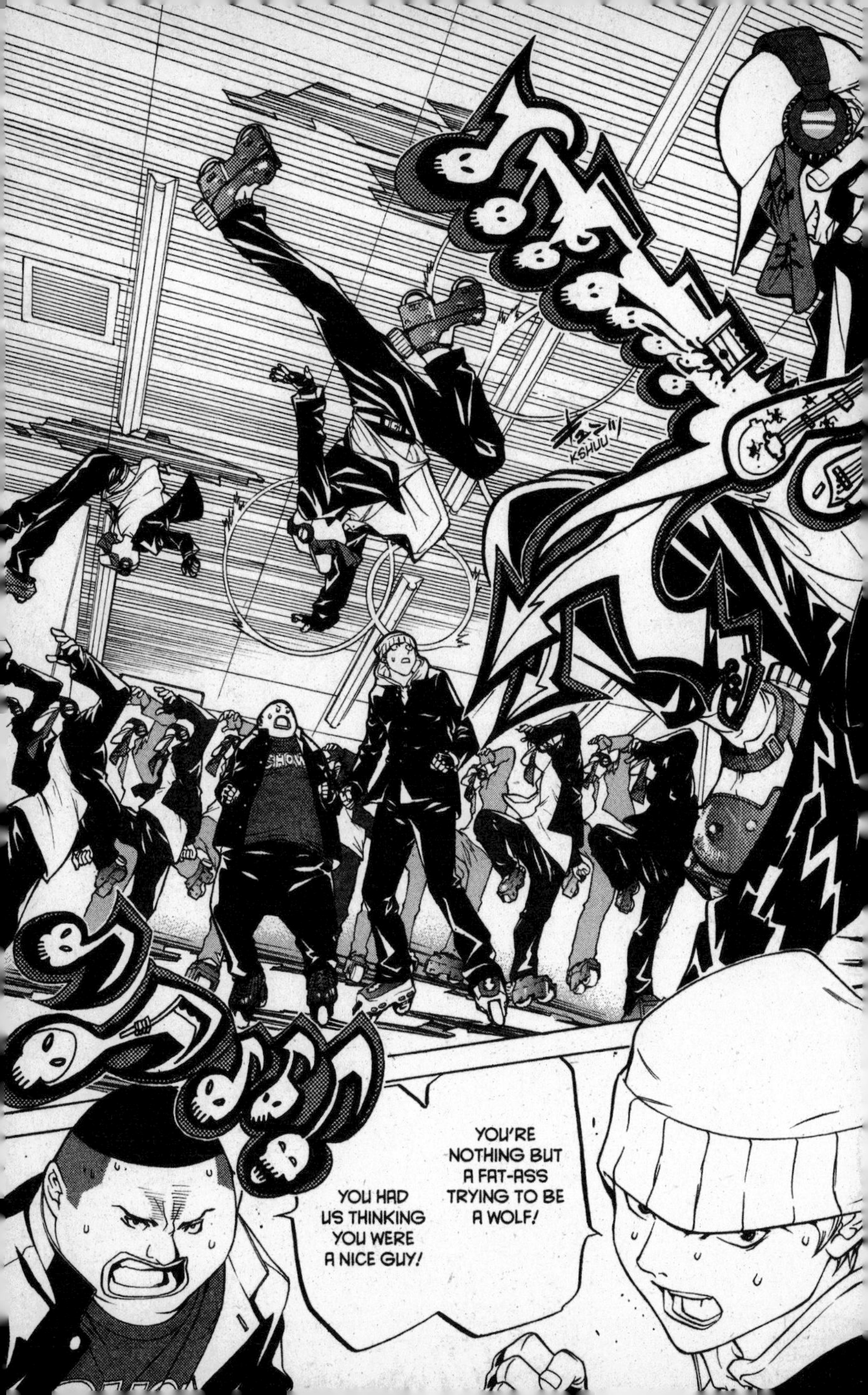
KSHUU
YOU'RE NOTHING BUT A FAT-ASS TRYING TO BE A WOLF!
YOU HAD US THINKING YOU WERE A NICE GUY!

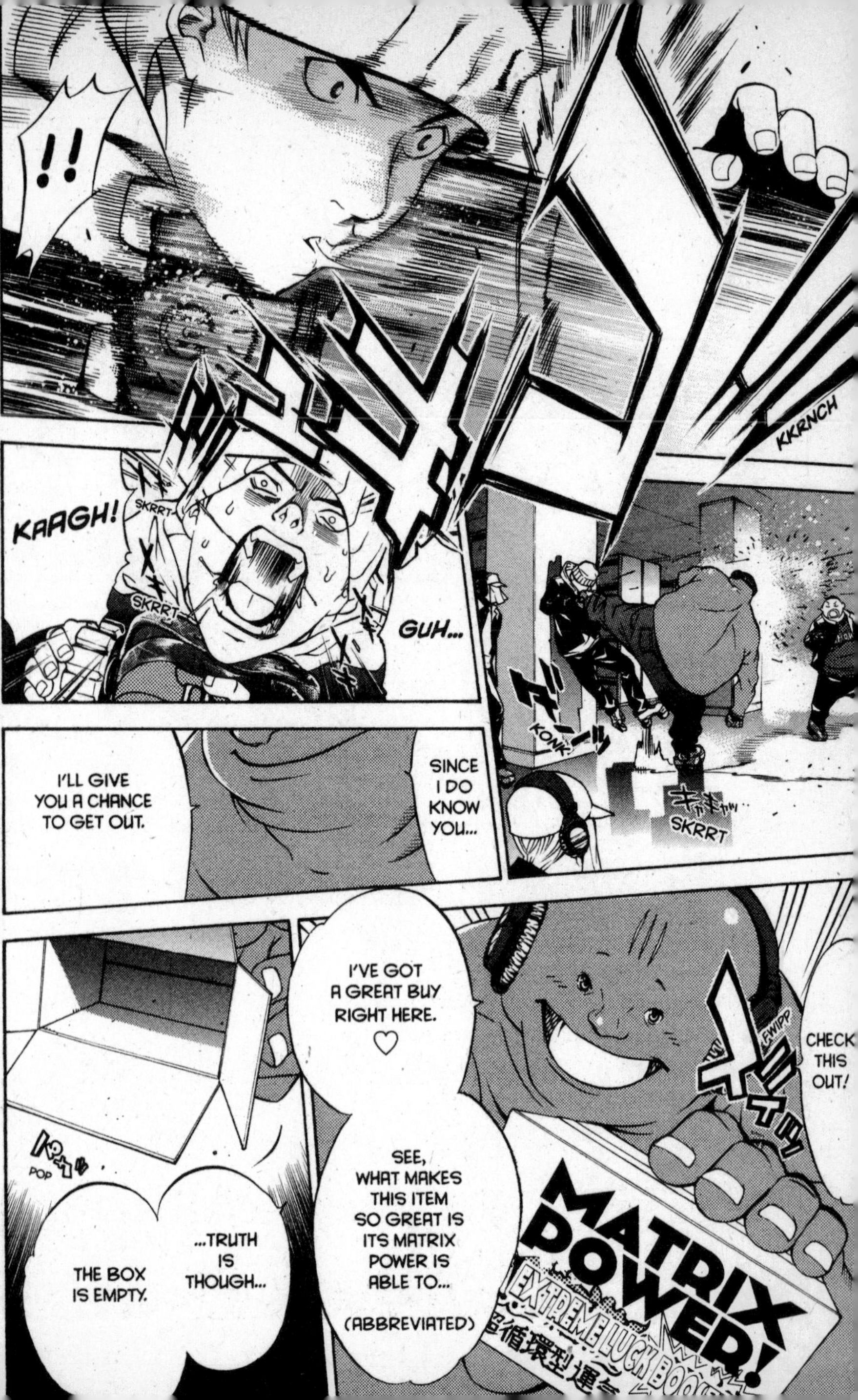
!!
KKRNCH
KONK
SKRRT
KAAGH!
SKRRT
SKRRT
GUH...
SINCE I DO KNOW YOU...
I'LL GIVE YOU A CHANCE TO GET OUT.
CHECK THIS OUT!
FWIPP
I'VE GOT A GREAT BUY RIGHT HERE. ♡
MATRIX POWER!
EXTREME LUCK
SEE, WHAT MAKES THIS ITEM SO GREAT IS ITS MATRIX POWER IS ABLE TO...
(ABBREVIATED)
...TRUTH IS THOUGH...
THE BOX IS EMPTY.
POP

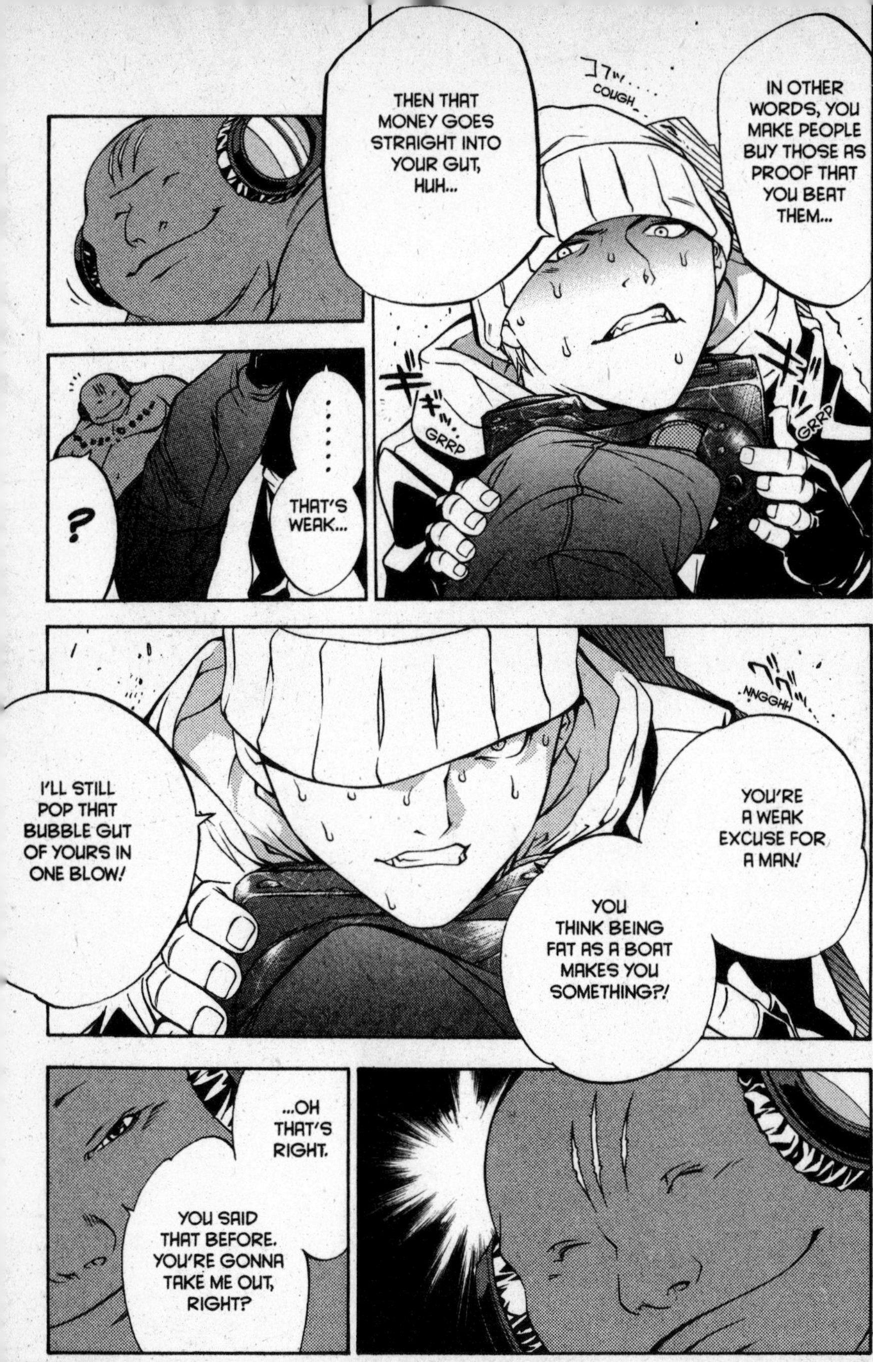
IN OTHER WORDS, YOU MAKE PEOPLE BUY THOSE AS PROOF THAT YOU BEAT THEM...
COUGH...
THEN THAT MONEY GOES STRAIGHT INTO YOUR GUT, HUH...
GRRP
GRRP
......
THAT'S WEAK...
?
NNGGHH...
YOU'RE A WEAK EXCUSE FOR A MAN!
YOU THINK BEING FAT AS A BOAT MAKES YOU SOMETHING?!
I'LL STILL POP THAT BUBBLE GUT OF YOURS IN ONE BLOW!
...OH THAT'S RIGHT.
YOU SAID THAT BEFORE. YOU'RE GONNA TAKE ME OUT, RIGHT?

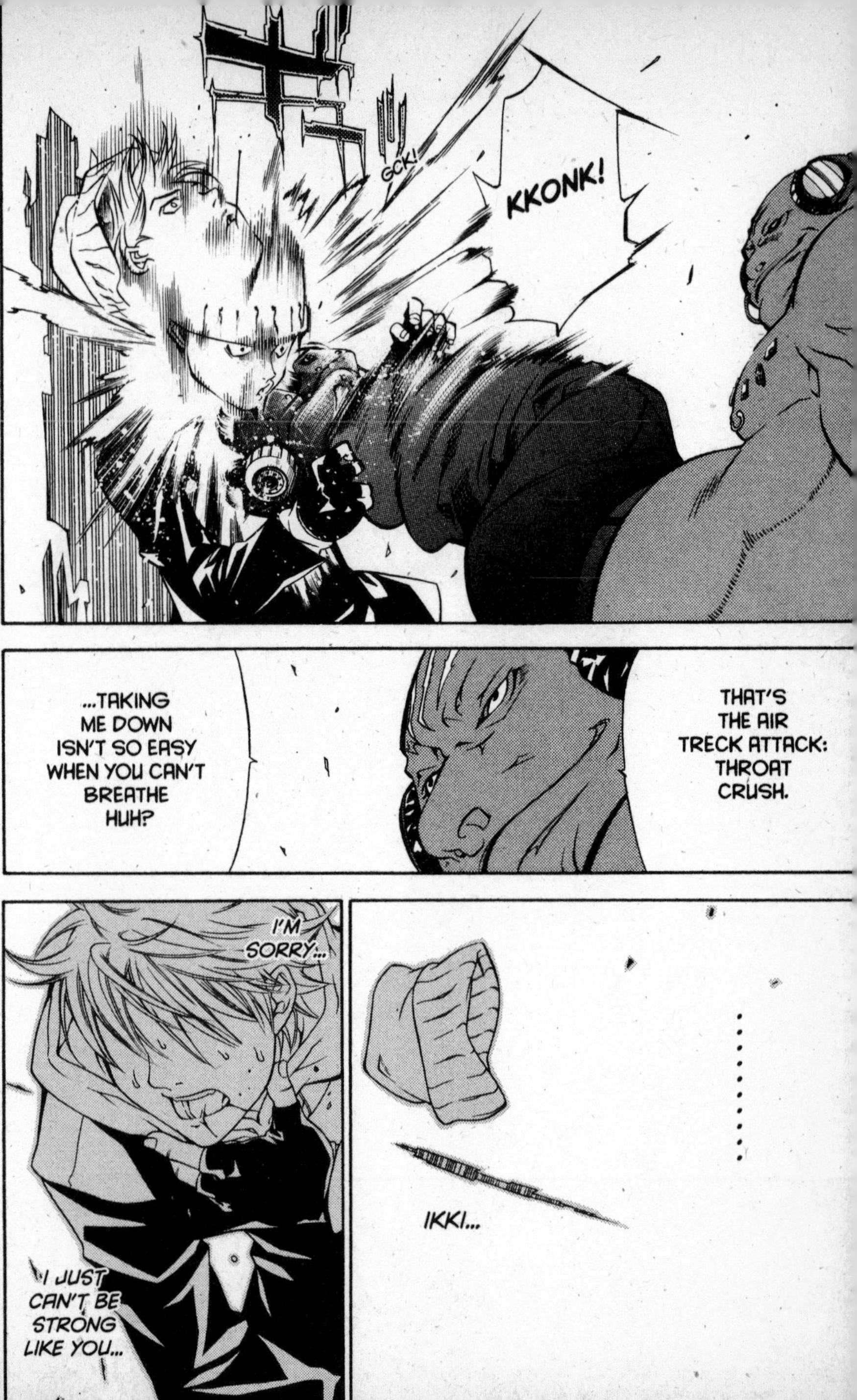

KKONK!
GCK!
THAT'S THE AIR TRECK ATTACK: THROAT CRUSH.
...TAKING ME DOWN ISN'T SO EASY WHEN YOU CAN'T BREATHE HUH?
......
IKKI...
I'M SORRY...
I JUST CAN'T BE STRONG LIKE YOU...

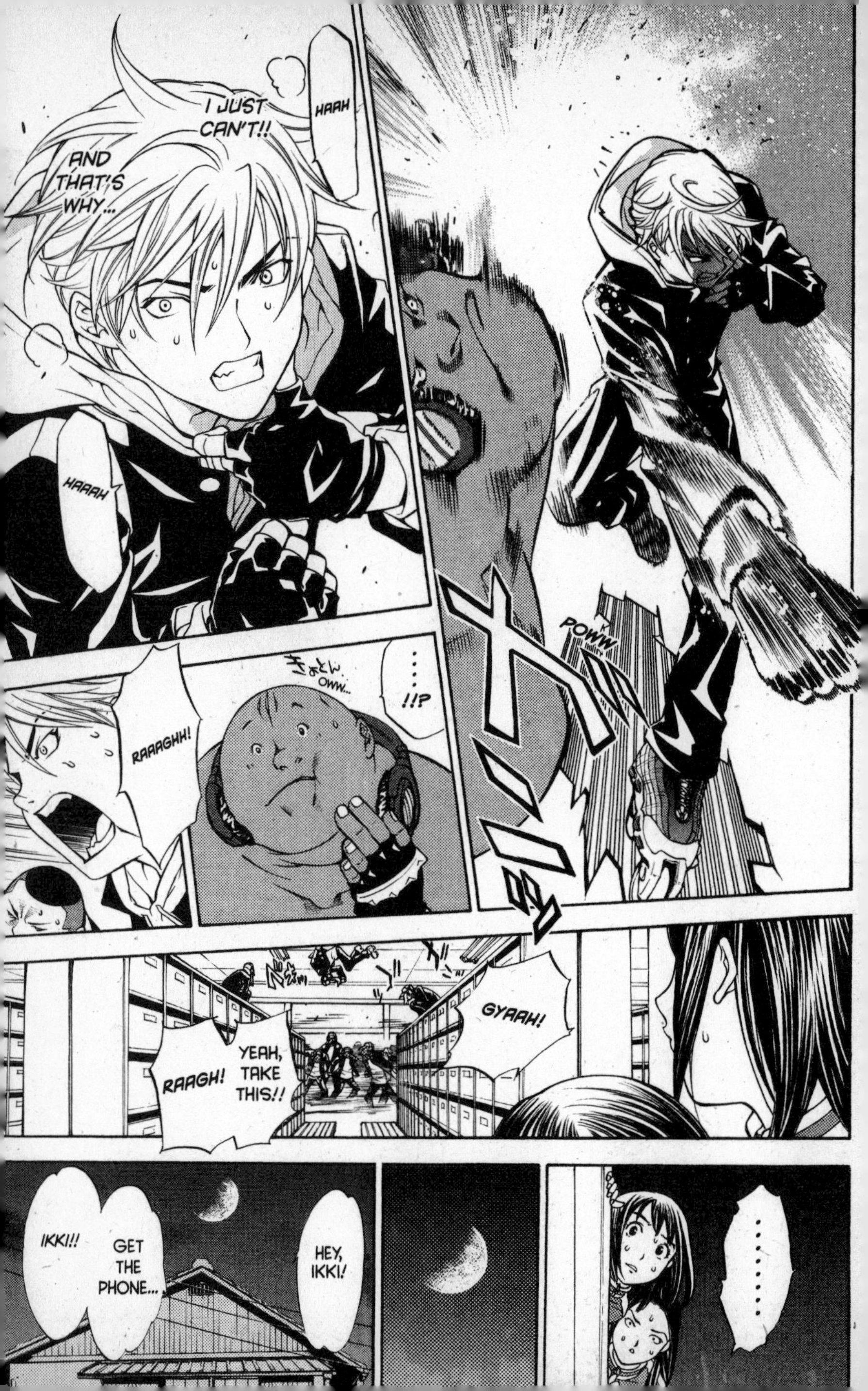
POWW
HAAH
I JUST CAN'T!!
AND THAT'S WHY...
HAAAH
......
!!?
OWW...
RAAAGHH!
GYAAH!
YEAH, TAKE THIS!!
RAAGH!
....
HEY, IKKI!
GET THE PHONE...
IKKI!!

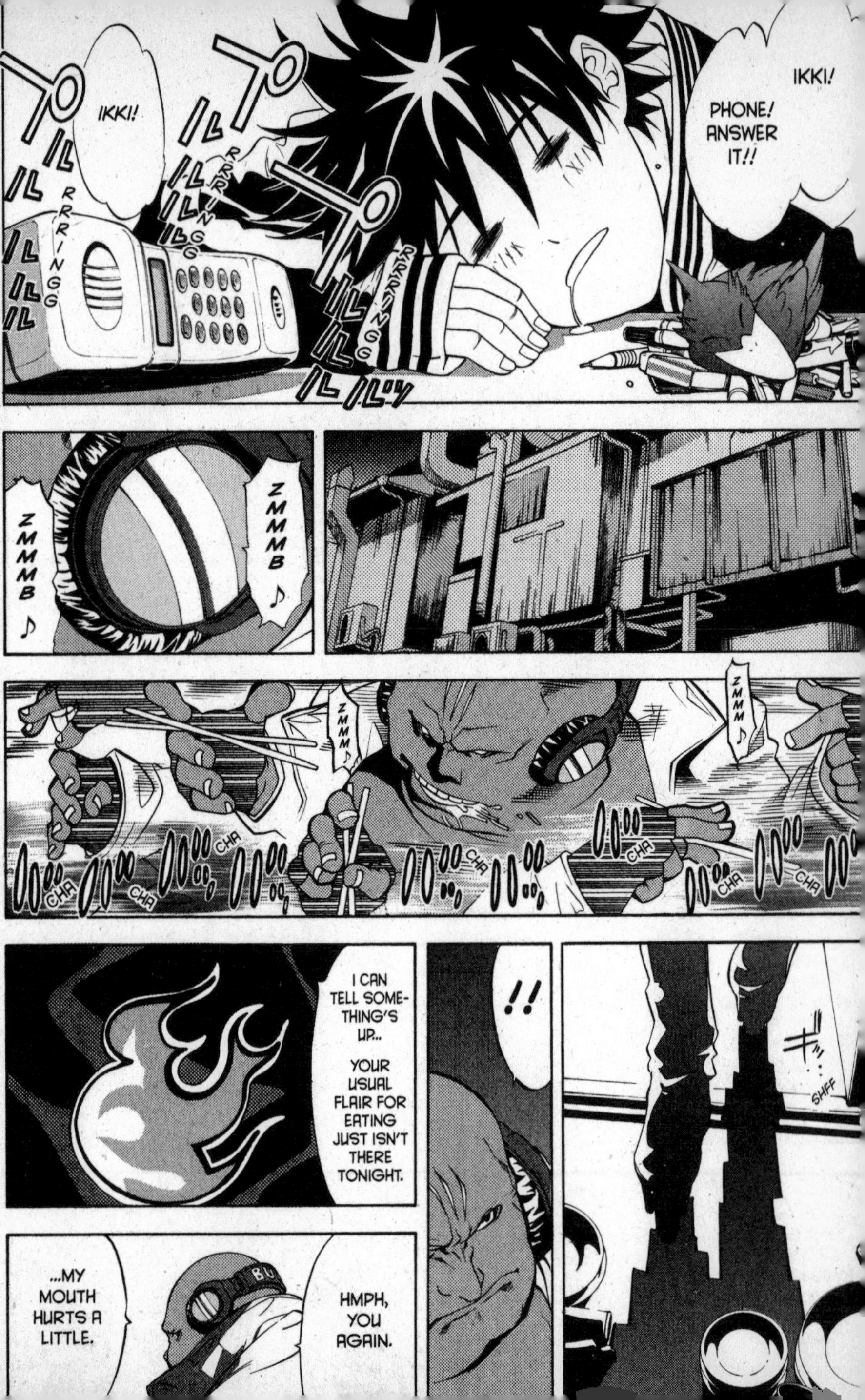
IKKI! PHONE! ANSWER IT!!
RRRRINGG
IKKI!
RRRRINGG
RRRINGG
ZMMMB ♪
ZMMMB ♪
ZMMM ♪
ZMMM ♪
CHA CHA CHA CHA CHA CHA CHA
SHFF
!!
I CAN TELL SOME-THING'S UP... YOUR USUAL FLAIR FOR EATING JUST ISN'T THERE TONIGHT.
HMPH, YOU AGAIN.
...MY MOUTH HURTS A LITTLE.

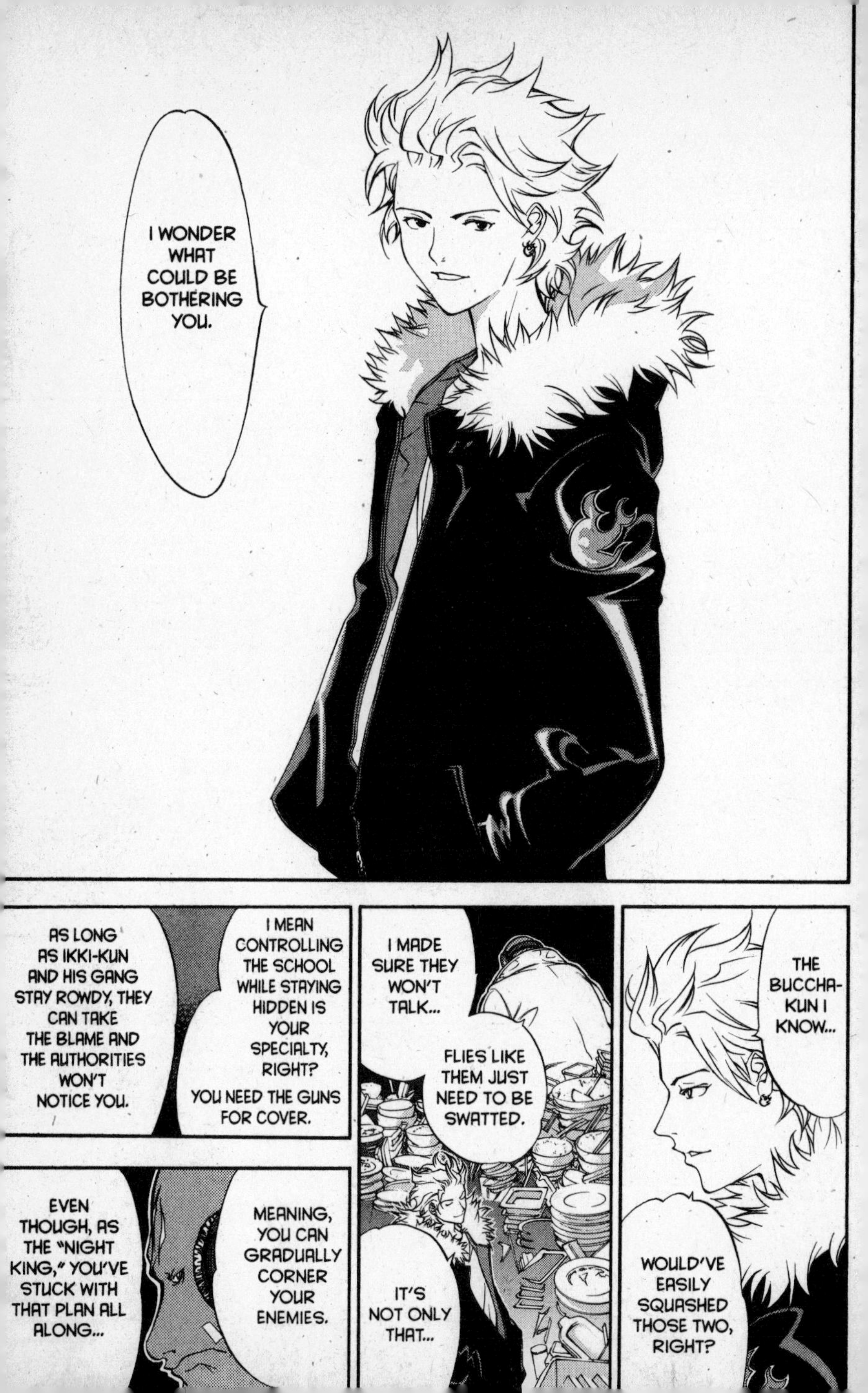
I WONDER WHAT COULD BE BOTHERING YOU.
THE BUCCHA-KUN I KNOW...
WOULD'VE EASILY SQUASHED THOSE TWO, RIGHT?
I MADE SURE THEY WON'T TALK...
FLIES LIKE THEM JUST NEED TO BE SWATTED.
IT'S NOT ONLY THAT...
I MEAN CONTROLLING THE SCHOOL WHILE STAYING HIDDEN IS YOUR SPECIALTY, RIGHT?
YOU NEED THE GUNS FOR COVER.
AS LONG AS IKKI-KUN AND HIS GANG STAY ROWDY, THEY CAN TAKE THE BLAME AND THE AUTHORITIES WON'T NOTICE YOU.
MEANING, YOU CAN GRADUALLY CORNER YOUR ENEMIES.
EVEN THOUGH, AS THE "NIGHT KING," YOU'VE STUCK WITH THAT PLAN ALL ALONG...

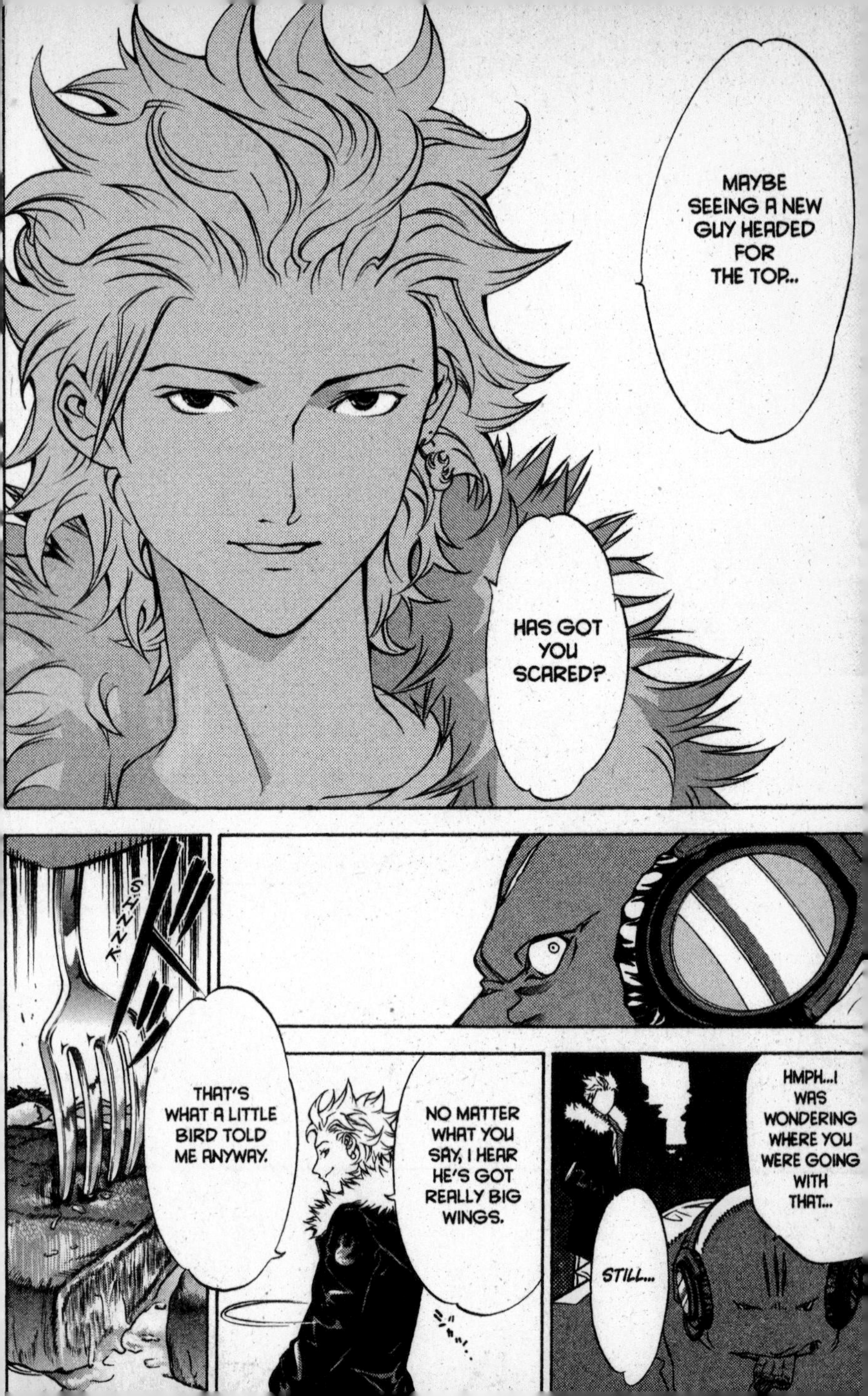
MAYBE SEEING A NEW GUY HEADED FOR THE TOP...
HAS GOT YOU SCARED?
HMPH...I WAS WONDERING WHERE YOU WERE GOING WITH THAT...
STILL...
NO MATTER WHAT YOU SAY, I HEAR HE'S GOT REALLY BIG WINGS.
SHNNK
THAT'S WHAT A LITTLE BIRD TOLD ME ANYWAY.

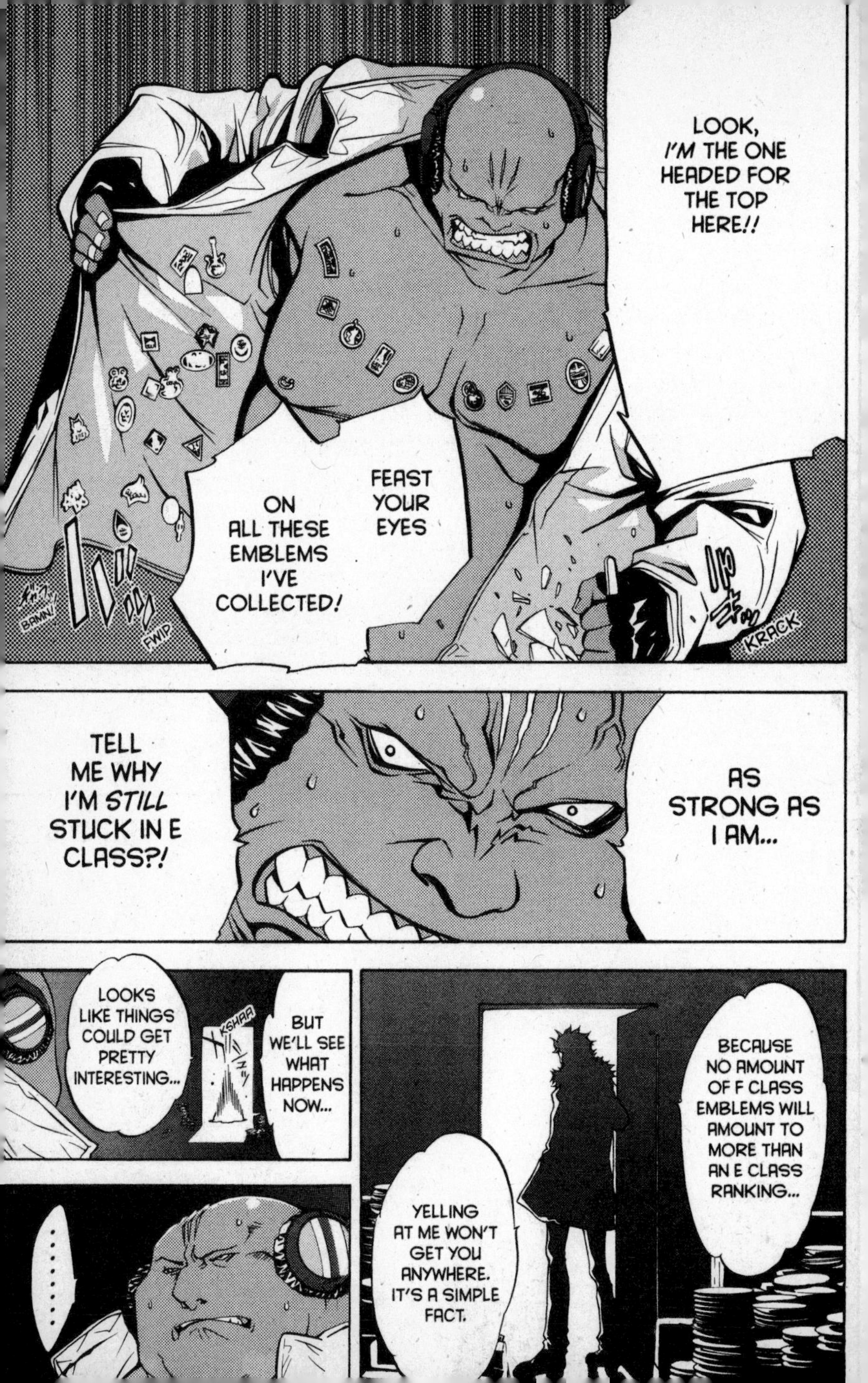
LOOK, *I'M* THE ONE HEADED FOR THE TOP HERE!!
FEAST YOUR EYES
ON ALL THESE EMBLEMS I'VE COLLECTED!
KRACK
FWIP
BAMN!
AS STRONG AS I AM...
TELL ME WHY I'M *STILL* STUCK IN E CLASS?!
BECAUSE NO AMOUNT OF F CLASS EMBLEMS WILL AMOUNT TO MORE THAN AN E CLASS RANKING...
YELLING AT ME WON'T GET YOU ANYWHERE. IT'S A SIMPLE FACT.
BUT WE'LL SEE WHAT HAPPENS NOW...
KSHAA
LOOKS LIKE THINGS COULD GET PRETTY INTERESTING...
......

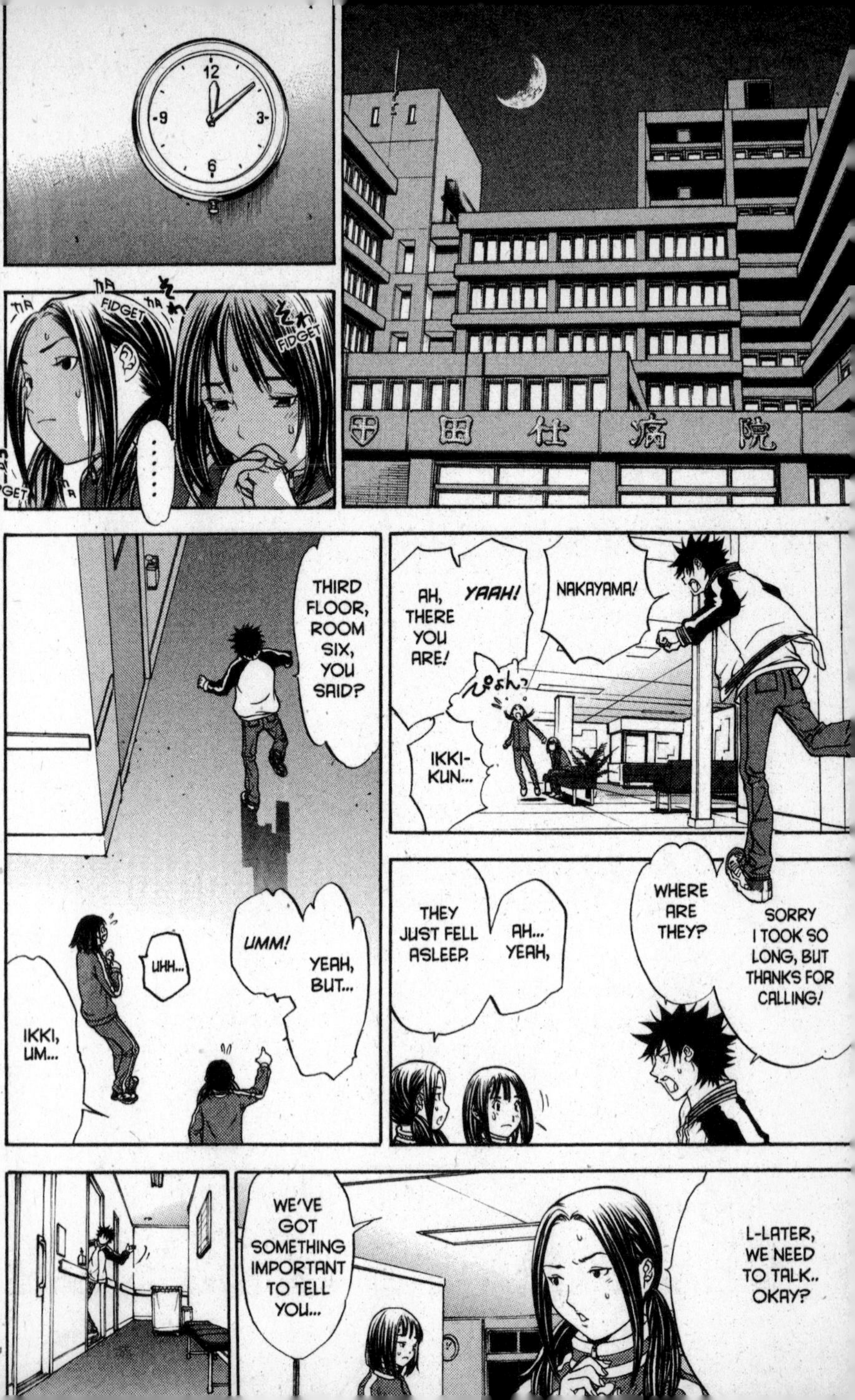

FIDGET
FIDGET
FIDGET
......
NAKAYAMA!
AH, THERE YOU ARE!
YAAH!
ぴょん
IKKI-KUN...
SORRY I TOOK SO LONG, BUT THANKS FOR CALLING!
WHERE ARE THEY?
AH... YEAH,
THEY JUST FELL ASLEEP.
THIRD FLOOR, ROOM SIX, YOU SAID?
UMM!
YEAH, BUT...
UHH...
IKKI, UM...
L-LATER, WE NEED TO TALK.. OKAY?
WE'VE GOT SOMETHING IMPORTANT TO TELL YOU...

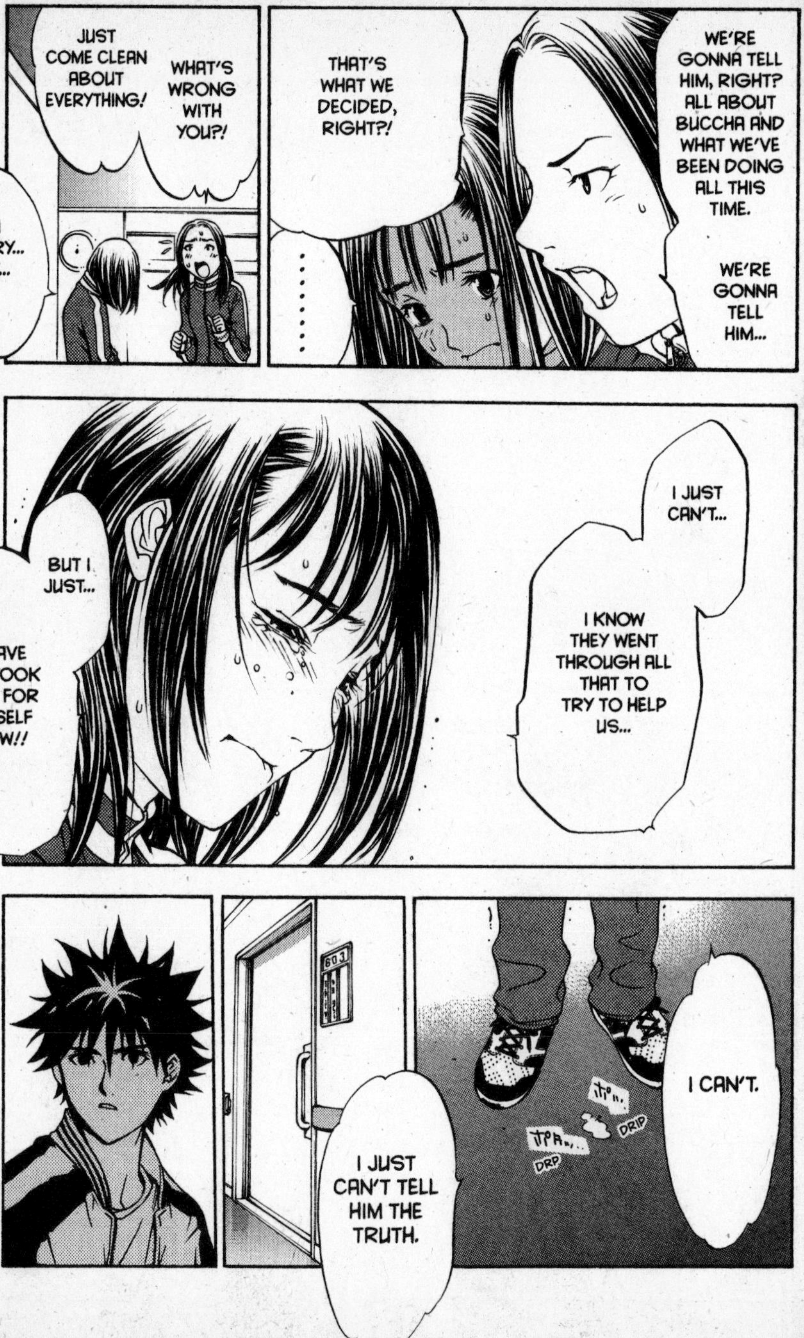

WE'RE GONNA TELL HIM, RIGHT? ALL ABOUT BUCCHA AND WHAT WE'VE BEEN DOING ALL THIS TIME.
WE'RE GONNA TELL HIM...
THAT'S WHAT WE DECIDED, RIGHT?!
......
WHAT'S WRONG WITH YOU?!
JUST COME CLEAN ABOUT EVERYTHING!
I'M SORRY... BUT...
I JUST CAN'T...
I KNOW THEY WENT THROUGH ALL THAT TO TRY TO HELP US...
BUT I JUST...
I HAVE TO LOOK OUT FOR MYSELF NOW!!
I CAN'T.
DRIP
DRP
603
I JUST CAN'T TELL HIM THE TRUTH.

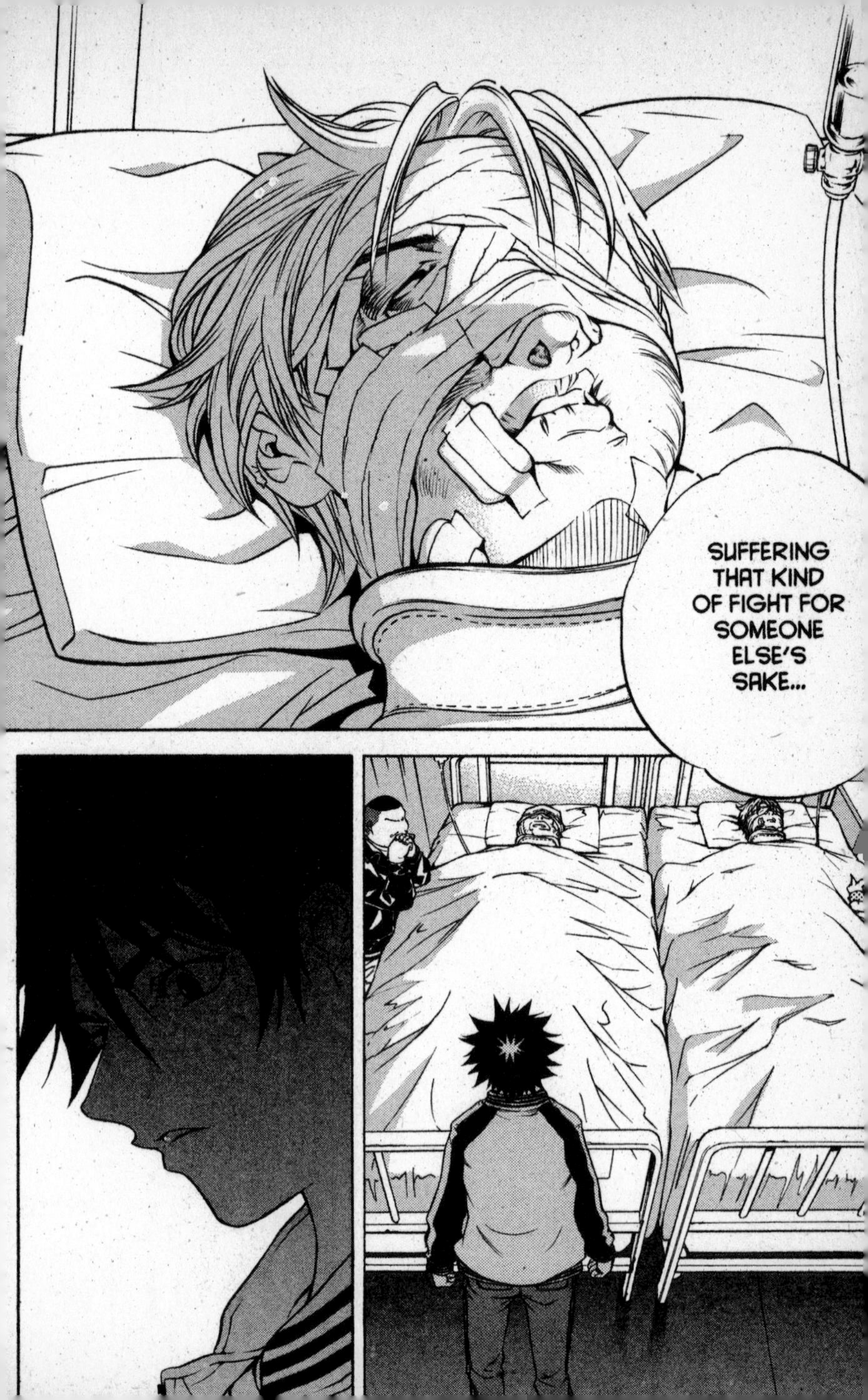
SUFFERING THAT KIND OF FIGHT FOR SOMEONE ELSE'S SAKE...

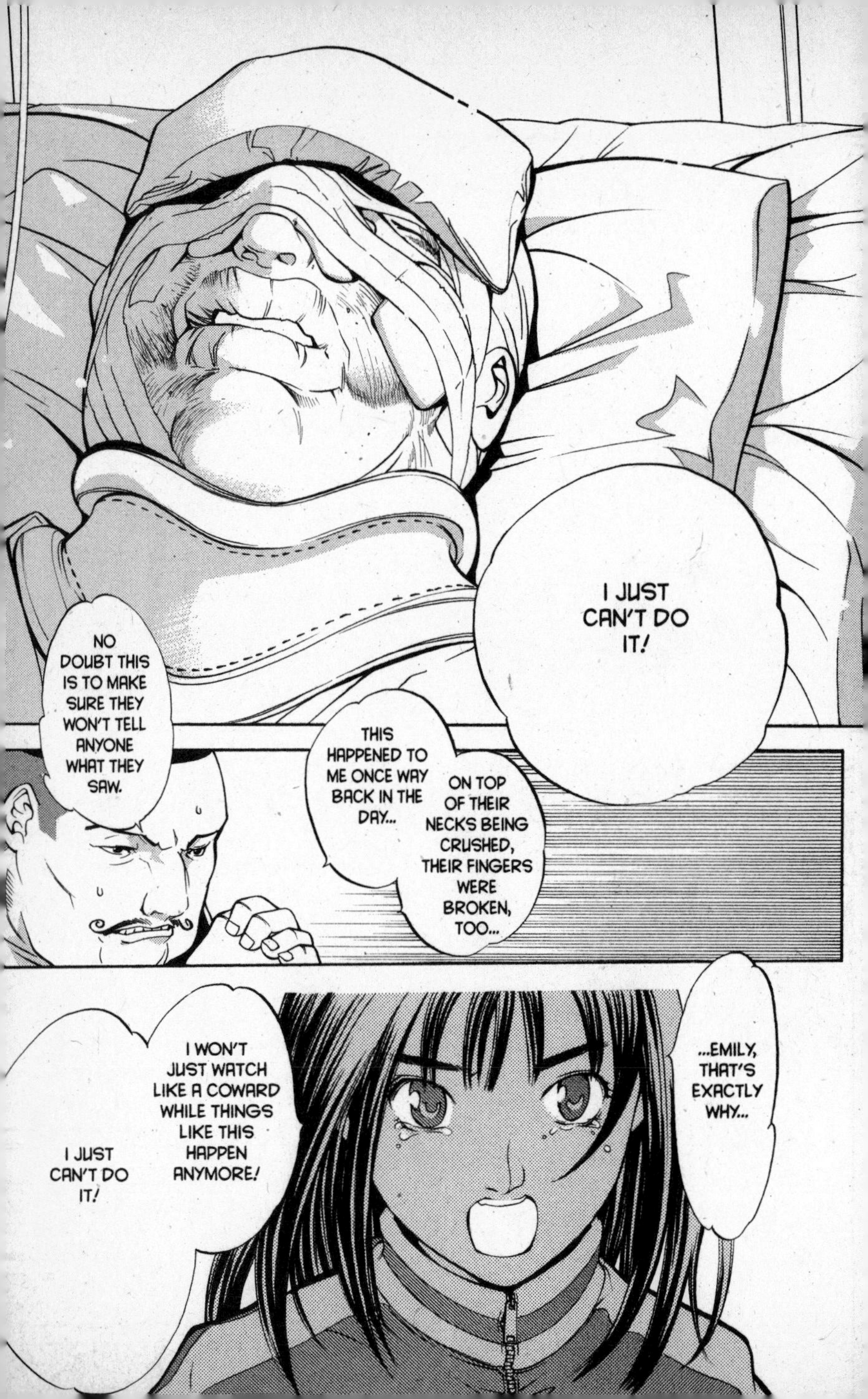
I JUST CAN'T DO IT!
THIS HAPPENED TO ME ONCE WAY BACK IN THE DAY...
ON TOP OF THEIR NECKS BEING CRUSHED, THEIR FINGERS WERE BROKEN, TOO...
NO DOUBT THIS IS TO MAKE SURE THEY WON'T TELL ANYONE WHAT THEY SAW.
...EMILY, THAT'S EXACTLY WHY...
I WON'T JUST WATCH LIKE A COWARD WHILE THINGS LIKE THIS HAPPEN ANYMORE!
I JUST CAN'T DO IT!

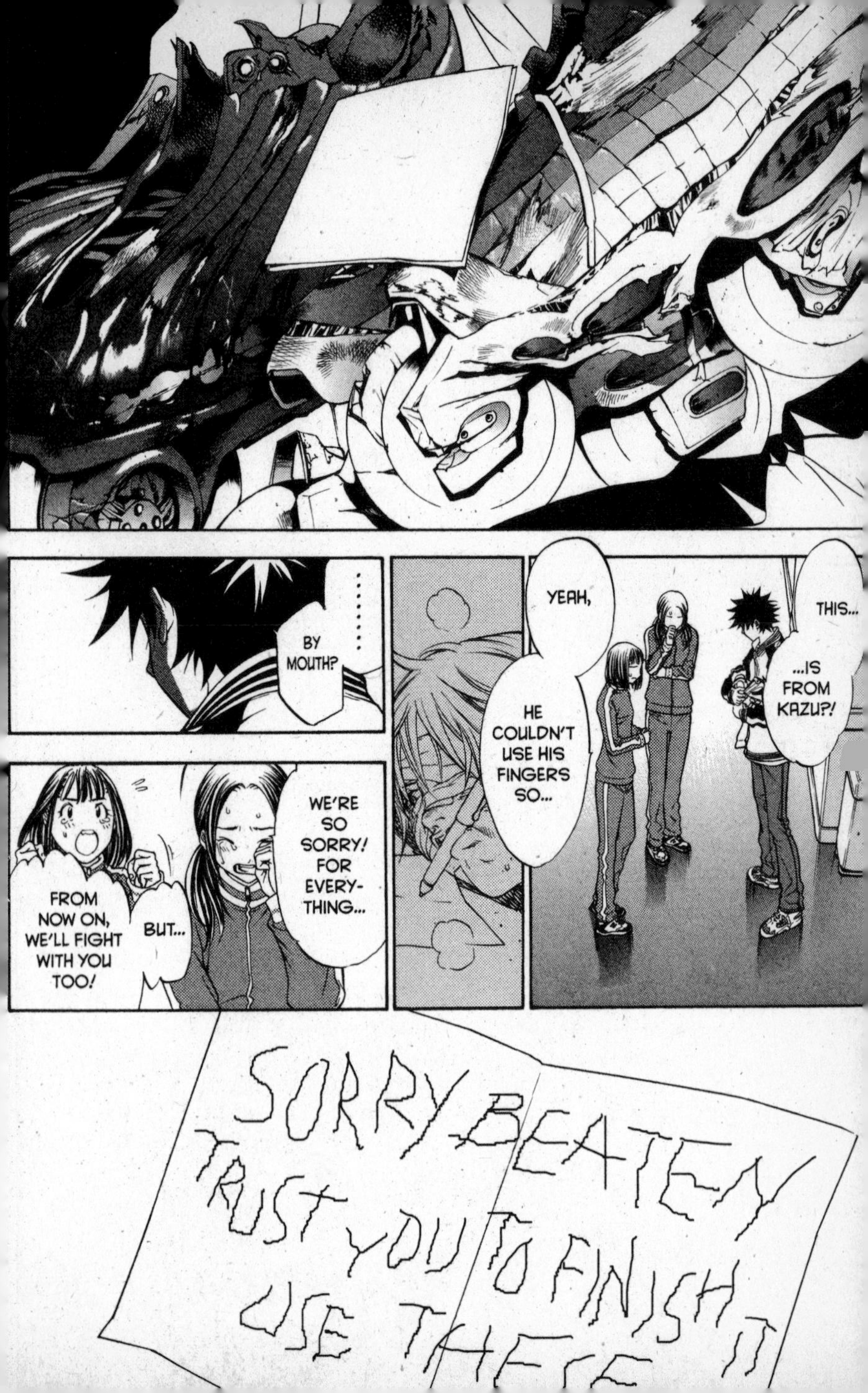
THIS...
...IS FROM KAZU?!
YEAH,
HE COULDN'T USE HIS FINGERS SO...
......
BY MOUTH?
WE'RE SO SORRY! FOR EVERYTHING...
BUT...
FROM NOW ON, WE'LL FIGHT WITH YOU TOO!
SORRY BEATEN
TRUST YOU TO FINISH IT
USE THESE

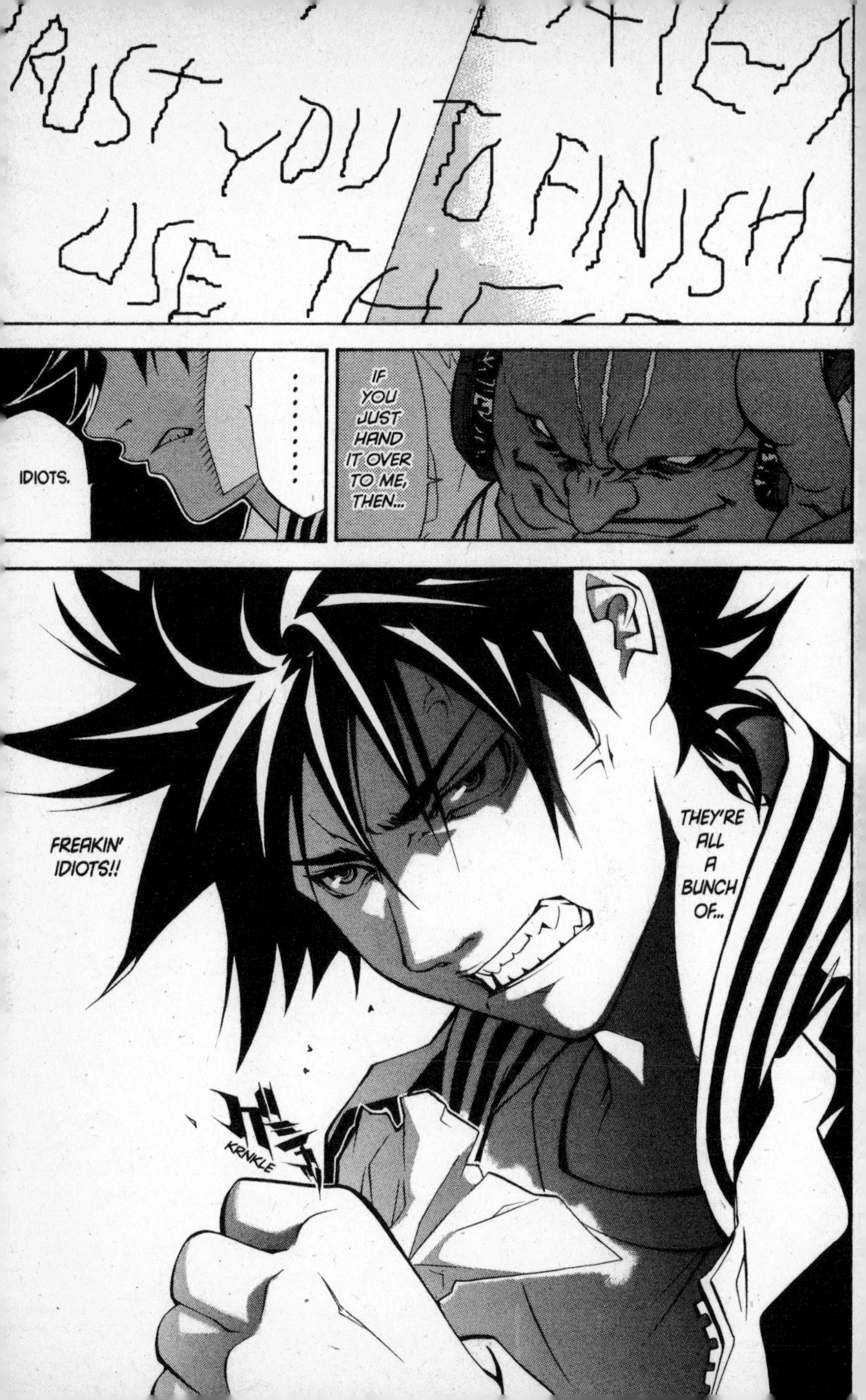
O FINISH
RUST YOU
IF YOU JUST HAND IT OVER TO ME, THEN...
......
IDIOTS.
THEY'RE ALL A BUNCH OF...
FREAKIN' IDIOTS!!
KRNKLE

FORMER WRESTLING STAR ENCYCLOPEDIA ARTICLE 1

AH-POH!
DNN
FORK
THE "BUCCHA" OF OLD DAYS HAD THIS SPECIAL UPPERCUT SKILL
SHAA
THIS IS GIANT BABA

WHEN THESE TWO HAD A MATCH, THEY MADE THE RING SEEM TINY...

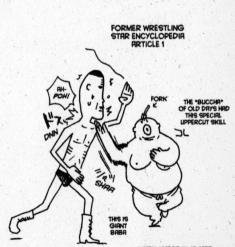

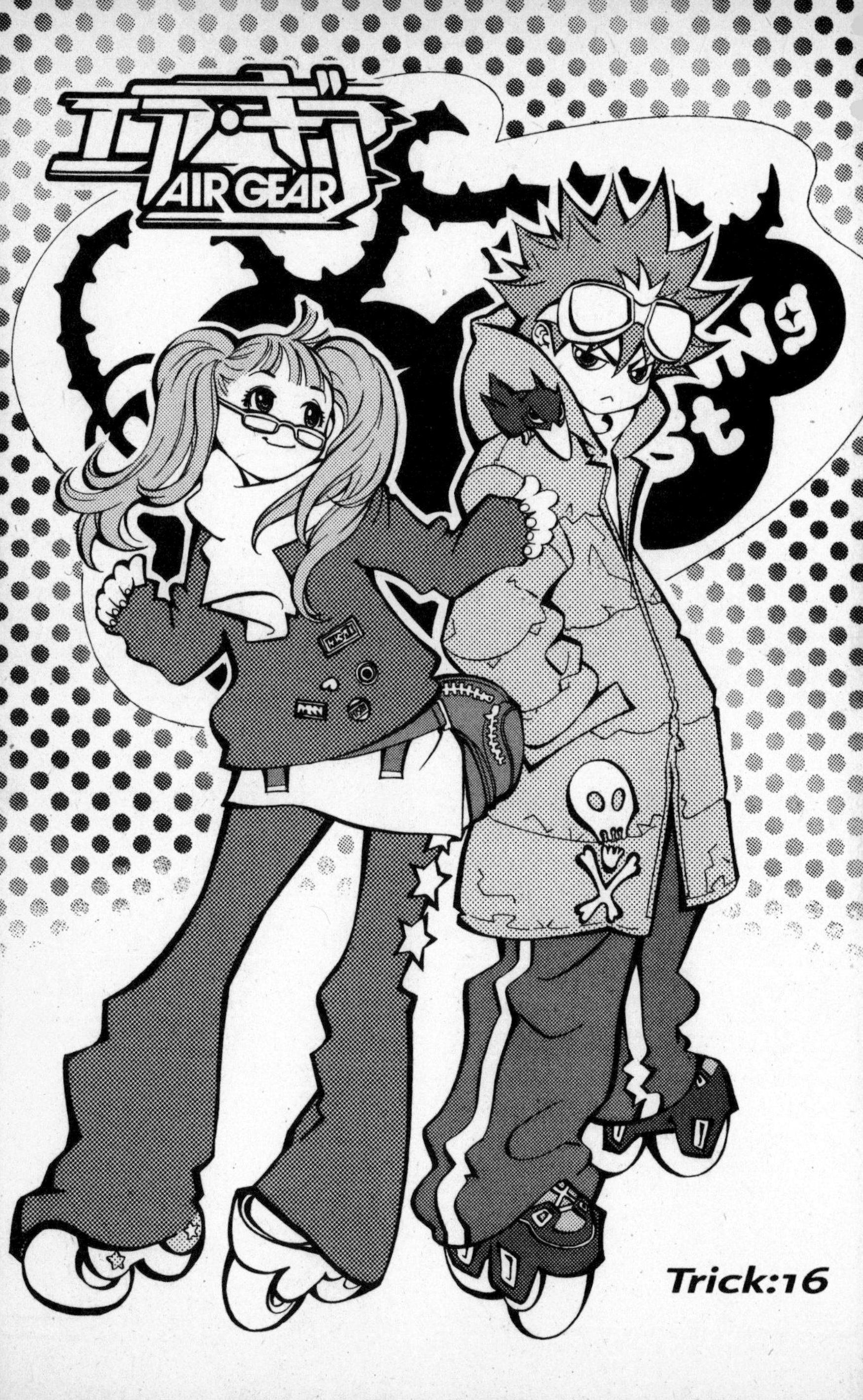
エア・ギア
AIR GEAR
Trick:16

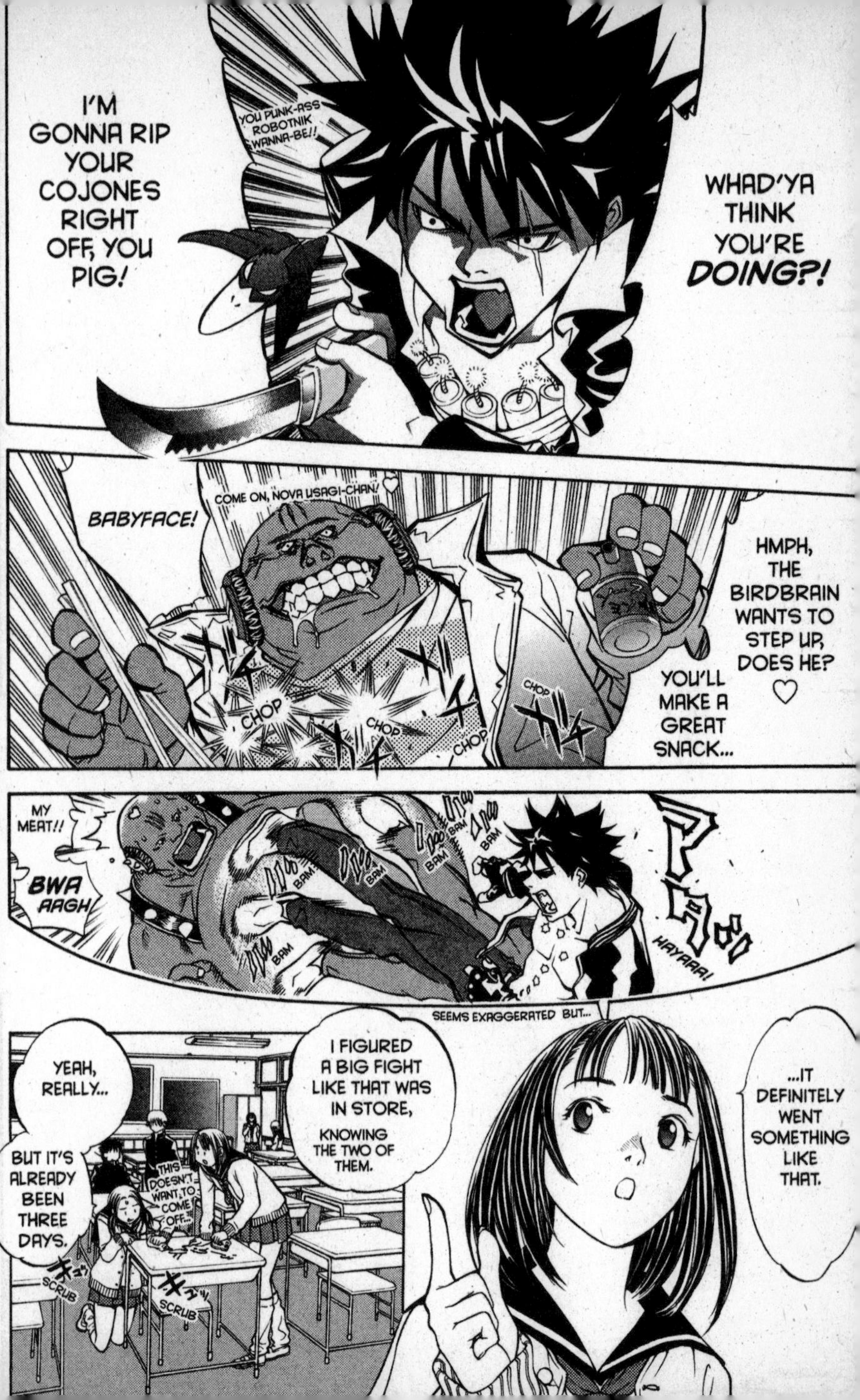

WHAD'YA THINK YOU'RE DOING?!
YOU PUNK-ASS ROBOTNIK WANNA-BE!!
I'M GONNA RIP YOUR COJONES RIGHT OFF, YOU PIG!
HMPH, THE BIRDBRAIN WANTS TO STEP UP, DOES HE? ♡
YOU'LL MAKE A GREAT SNACK...
COME ON, NOVA USAGI-CHAN! ♡
BABYFACE!
CHOP
CHOP
CHOP
CHOP
HAYAAA!
BAM
BAM
BAM
BAM
BAM
BAM
MY MEAT!!
BWA AAGH
...IT DEFINITELY WENT SOMETHING LIKE THAT.
SEEMS EXAGGERATED BUT...
I FIGURED A BIG FIGHT LIKE THAT WAS IN STORE,
KNOWING THE TWO OF THEM.
YEAH, REALLY...
BUT IT'S ALREADY BEEN THREE DAYS.
THIS DOESN'T WANT TO COME OFF...
SCRUB
SCRUB

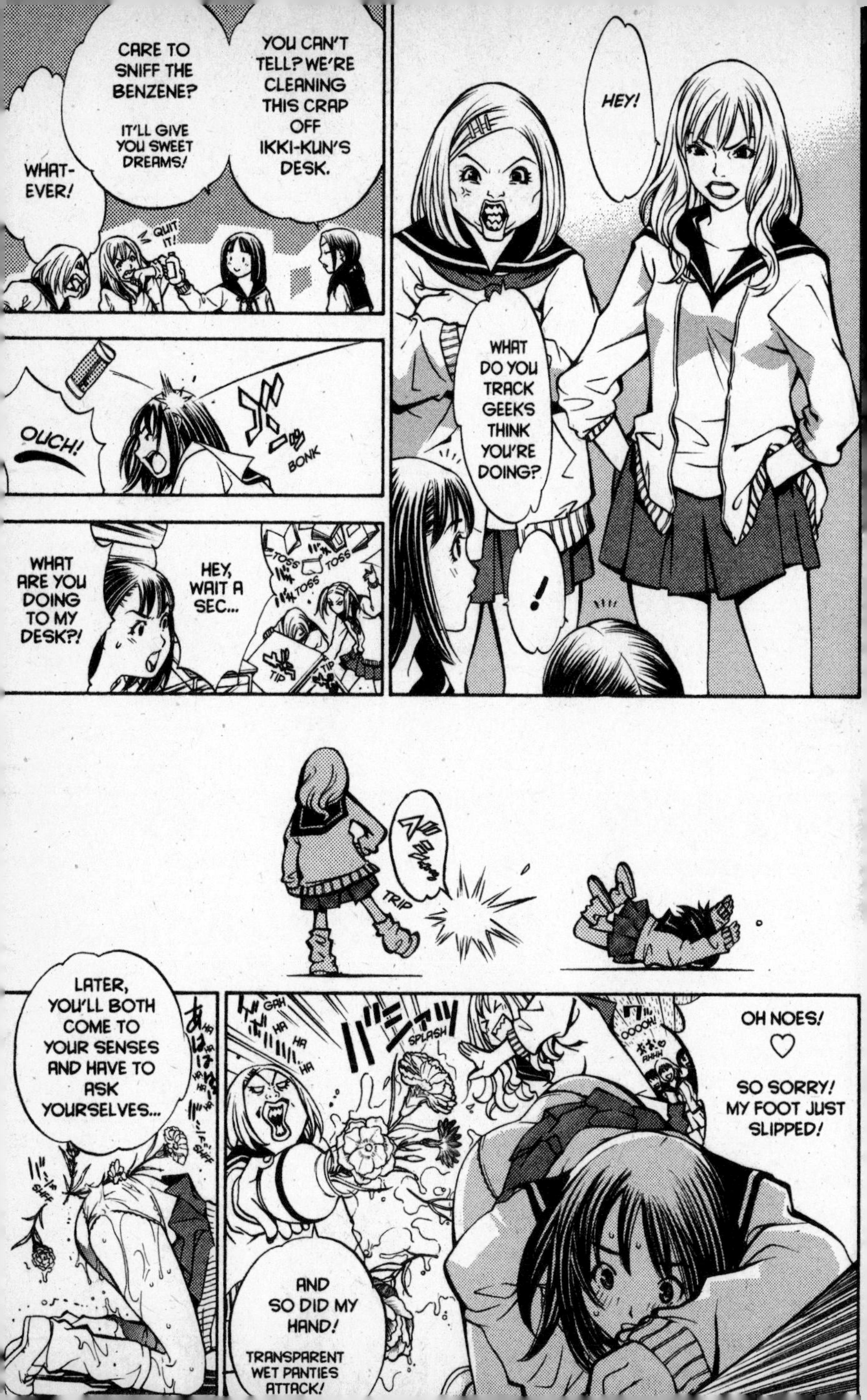
HEY!
WHAT DO YOU TRACK GEEKS THINK YOU'RE DOING?
!
YOU CAN'T TELL? WE'RE CLEANING THIS CRAP OFF IKKI-KUN'S DESK.
CARE TO SNIFF THE BENZENE?
IT'LL GIVE YOU SWEET DREAMS!
QUIT IT!
WHAT-EVER!
BONK
OUCH!
TOSS
TOSS
TOSS
TIP
TIP
HEY, WAIT A SEC...
WHAT ARE YOU DOING TO MY DESK?!
TRIP
OH NOES! ♡
SO SORRY! MY FOOT JUST SLIPPED!
OOOOH!
AHHH
SPLASH
GAH
HA
HA
HA
AND SO DID MY HAND!
TRANSPARENT WET PANTIES ATTACK!
HA
HA
HA
HA
SNIFF
SNIFF
LATER, YOU'LL BOTH COME TO YOUR SENSES AND HAVE TO ASK YOURSELVES...

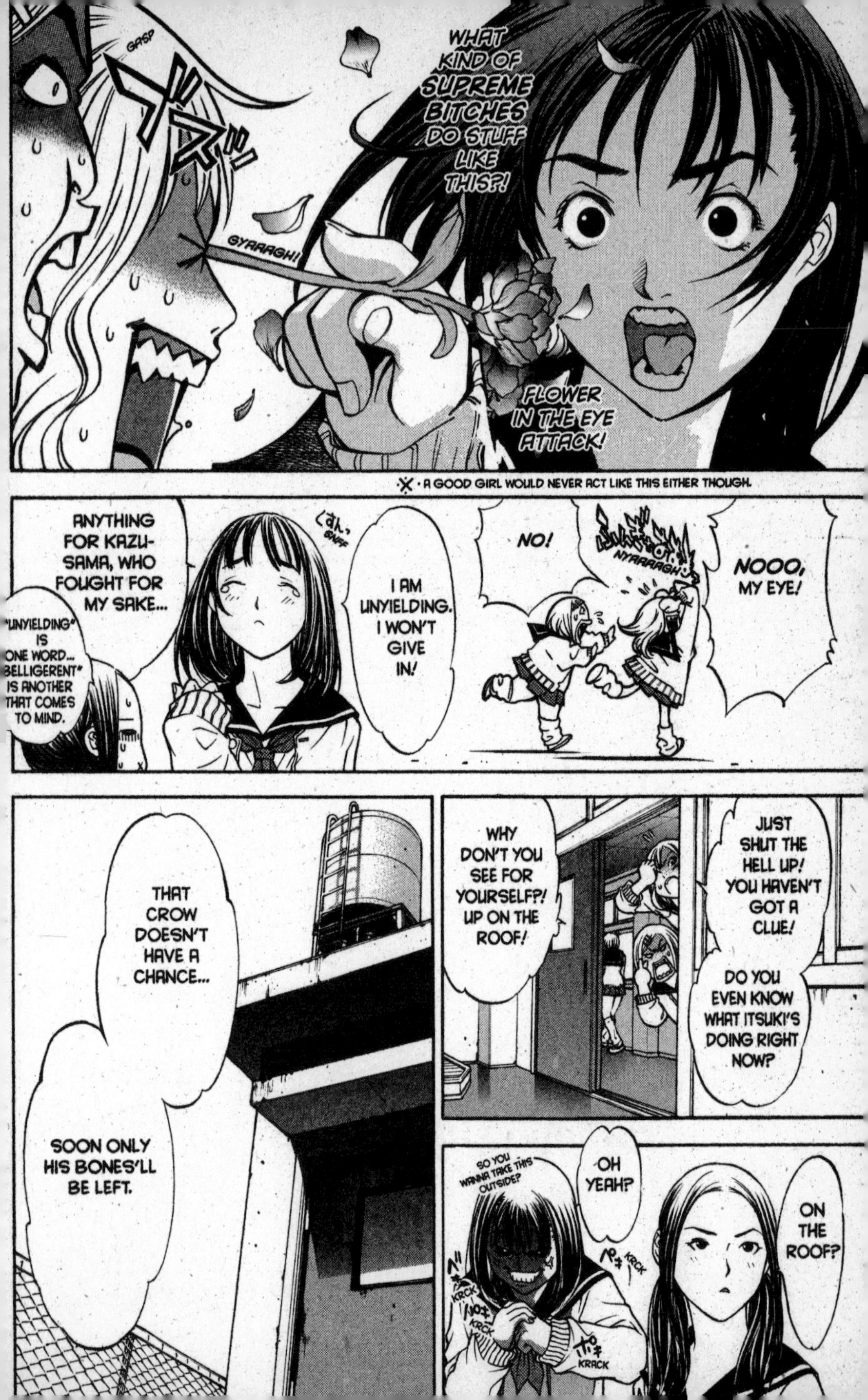
WHAT KIND OF SUPREME BITCHES DO STUFF LIKE THIS?!
GASP
GYARRAGH!
FLOWER IN THE EYE ATTACK!
※ A GOOD GIRL WOULD NEVER ACT LIKE THIS EITHER THOUGH.
NOOO, MY EYE!
NYARRAGH
NO!
I AM UNYIELDING. I WON'T GIVE IN!
SNIFF
ANYTHING FOR KAZU-SAMA, WHO FOUGHT FOR MY SAKE...
"UNYIELDING" IS ONE WORD... "BELLIGERENT" IS ANOTHER THAT COMES TO MIND.
JUST SHUT THE HELL UP! YOU HAVEN'T GOT A CLUE!
DO YOU EVEN KNOW WHAT ITSUKI'S DOING RIGHT NOW?
WHY DON'T YOU SEE FOR YOURSELF?! UP ON THE ROOF!
ON THE ROOF?
OH YEAH?
SO YOU WANNA TAKE THIS OUTSIDE?
KRCK
KRCK
KRCK
KRCK
THAT CROW DOESN'T HAVE A CHANCE...
SOON ONLY HIS BONES'LL BE LEFT.

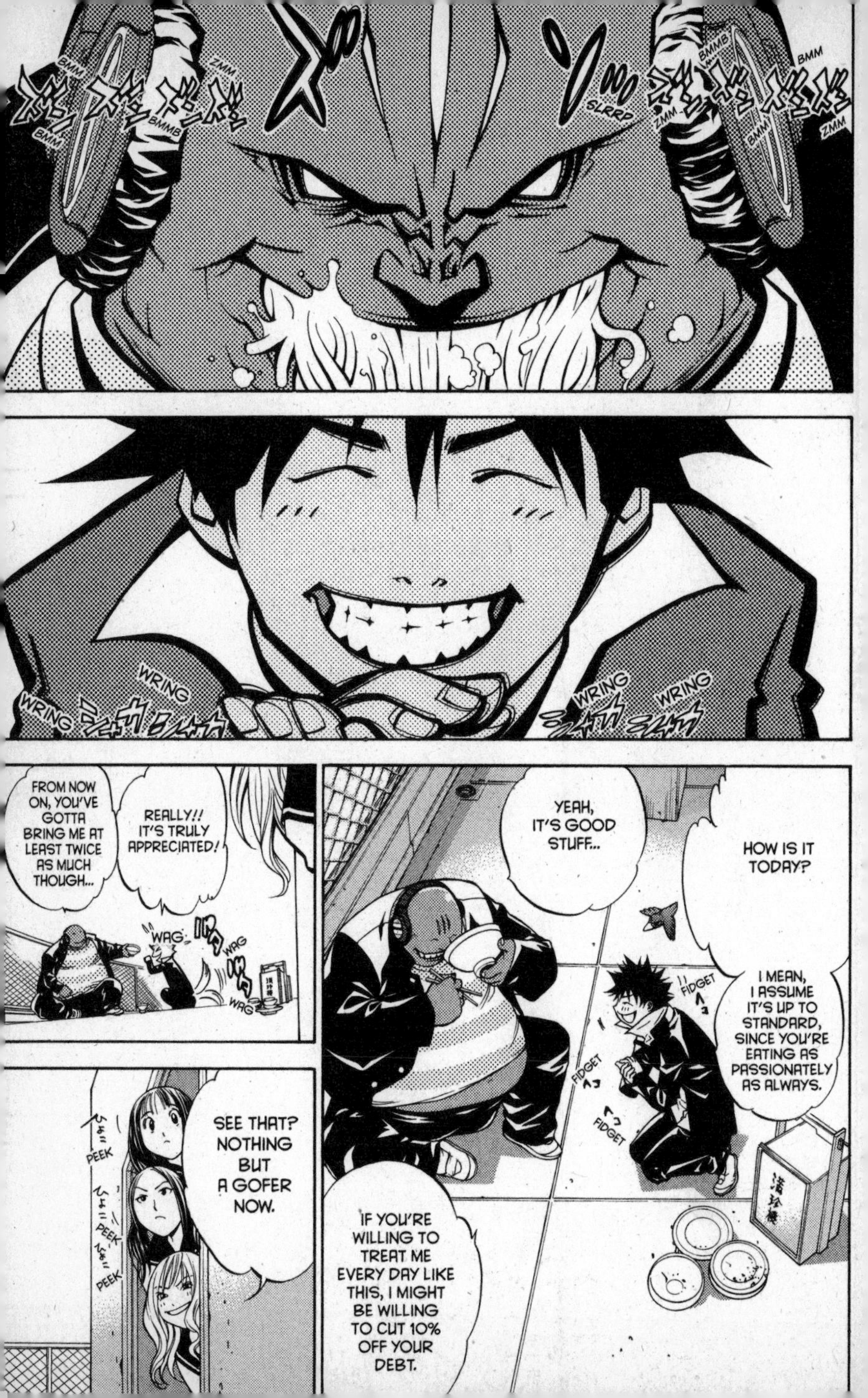
BMM
BMMB
ZMM
BMM
ZMM
SLRRP
ZMM
BMMB
BMM
BMM
WRING
WRING
WRING
WRING
HOW IS IT TODAY?
I MEAN, I ASSUME IT'S UP TO STANDARD, SINCE YOU'RE EATING AS PASSIONATELY AS ALWAYS.
YEAH, IT'S GOOD STUFF...
FIDGET
FIDGET
FIDGET
IF YOU'RE WILLING TO TREAT ME EVERY DAY LIKE THIS, I MIGHT BE WILLING TO CUT 10% OFF YOUR DEBT.
REALLY!! IT'S TRULY APPRECIATED!
FROM NOW ON, YOU'VE GOTTA BRING ME AT LEAST TWICE AS MUCH THOUGH...
WAG
WAG
WAG
SEE THAT? NOTHING BUT A GOFER NOW.
PEEK
PEEK
PEEK

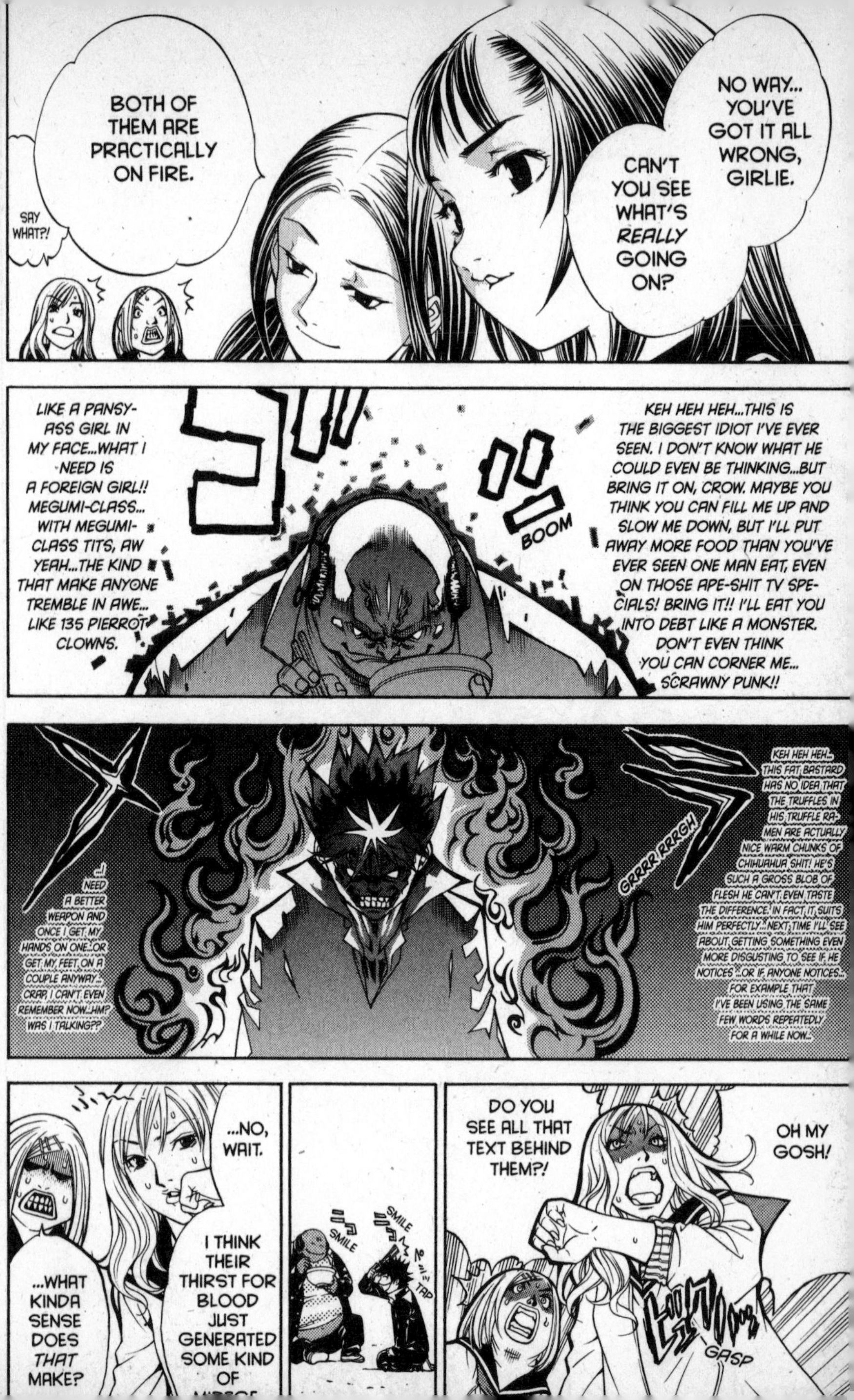
NO WAY... YOU'VE GOT IT ALL WRONG, GIRLIE.
CAN'T YOU SEE WHAT'S REALLY GOING ON?
BOTH OF THEM ARE PRACTICALLY ON FIRE.
SAY WHAT?!
KEH HEH HEH...THIS IS THE BIGGEST IDIOT I'VE EVER SEEN. I DON'T KNOW WHAT HE COULD EVEN BE THINKING...BUT BRING IT ON, CROW. MAYBE YOU THINK YOU CAN FILL ME UP AND SLOW ME DOWN, BUT I'LL PUT AWAY MORE FOOD THAN YOU'VE EVER SEEN ONE MAN EAT, EVEN ON THOSE APE-SHIT TV SPECIALS! BRING IT!! I'LL EAT YOU INTO DEBT LIKE A MONSTER. DON'T EVEN THINK YOU CAN CORNER ME... SCRAWNY PUNK!!
BOOM
LIKE A PANSY-ASS GIRL IN MY FACE...WHAT I NEED IS A FOREIGN GIRL!! MEGUMI-CLASS... WITH MEGUMI-CLASS TITS, AW YEAH...THE KIND THAT MAKE ANYONE TREMBLE IN AWE... LIKE 135 PIERROT CLOWNS.
KEH HEH HEH... THIS FAT BASTARD HAS NO IDEA THAT THE TRUFFLES IN HIS TRUFFLE RAMEN ARE ACTUALLY NICE WARM CHUNKS OF CHIHUAHUA SHIT! HE'S SUCH A GROSS BLOB OF FLESH HE CAN'T EVEN TASTE THE DIFFERENCE. IN FACT IT SUITS HIM PERFECTLY... NEXT TIME I'LL SEE ABOUT GETTING SOMETHING EVEN MORE DISGUSTING TO SEE IF HE NOTICES ...OR IF ANYONE NOTICES... FOR EXAMPLE THAT I'VE BEEN USING THE SAME FEW WORDS REPEATEDLY FOR A WHILE NOW...
GRRRR RRRGH
I NEED A BETTER WEAPON AND ONCE I GET MY HANDS ON ONE...OR GET MY FEET ON A COUPLE ANYWAY... CRAP, I CAN'T EVEN REMEMBER NOW...HM? WAS I TALKING??
OH MY GOSH!
DO YOU SEE ALL THAT TEXT BEHIND THEM?!
GASP
SMILE
SMILE
TAP
...NO, WAIT.
I THINK THEIR THIRST FOR BLOOD JUST GENERATED SOME KIND OF
...WHAT KINDA SENSE DOES THAT MAKE?

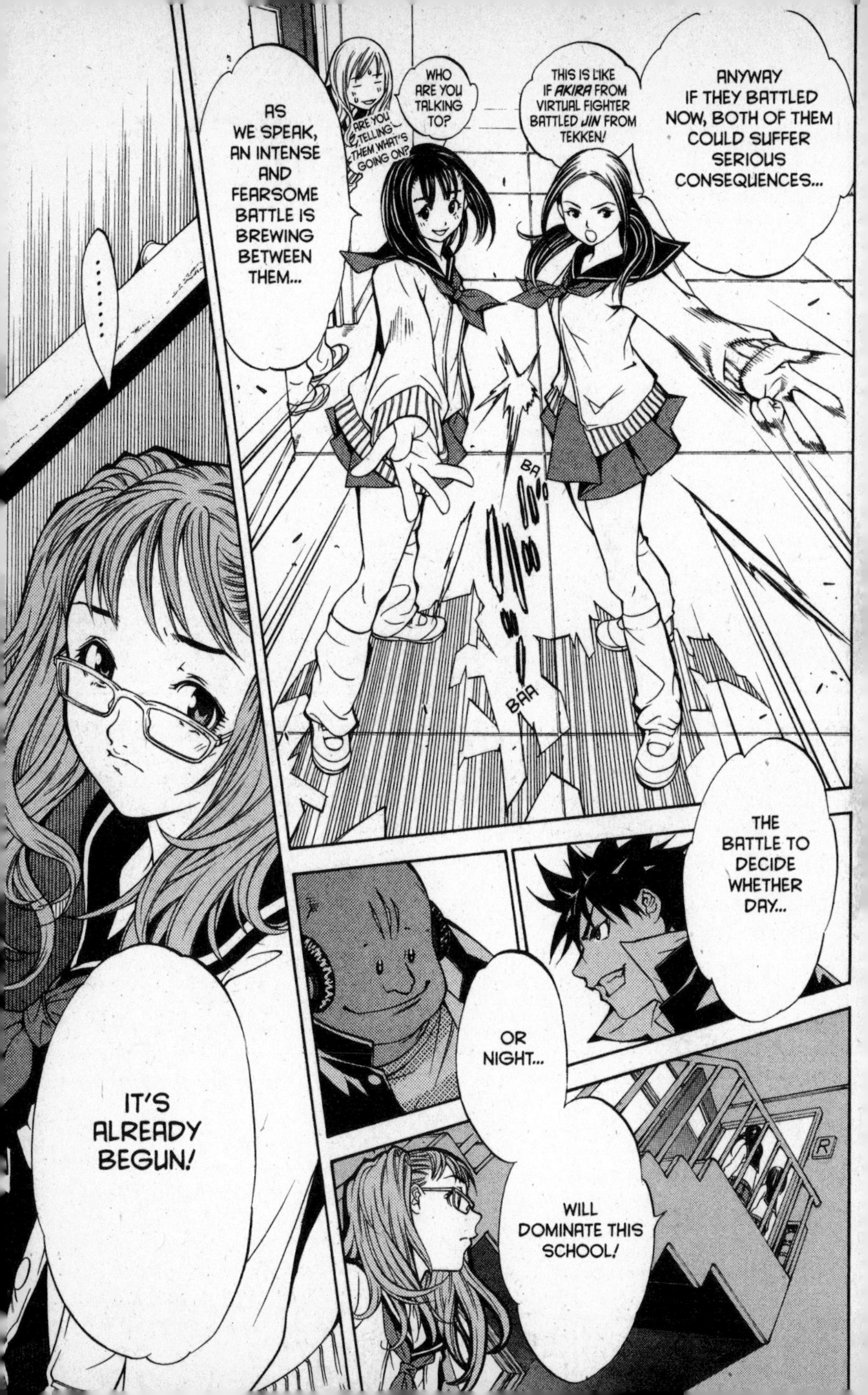

ANYWAY IF THEY BATTLED NOW, BOTH OF THEM COULD SUFFER SERIOUS CONSEQUENCES...
THIS IS LIKE IF AKIRA FROM VIRTUAL FIGHTER BATTLED JIN FROM TEKKEN!
WHO ARE YOU TALKING TO?
ARE YOU TELLING THEM WHAT'S GOING ON?
AS WE SPEAK, AN INTENSE AND FEARSOME BATTLE IS BREWING BETWEEN THEM...
BA
BAA
THE BATTLE TO DECIDE WHETHER DAY...
OR NIGHT...
WILL DOMINATE THIS SCHOOL!
R
......
IT'S ALREADY BEGUN!

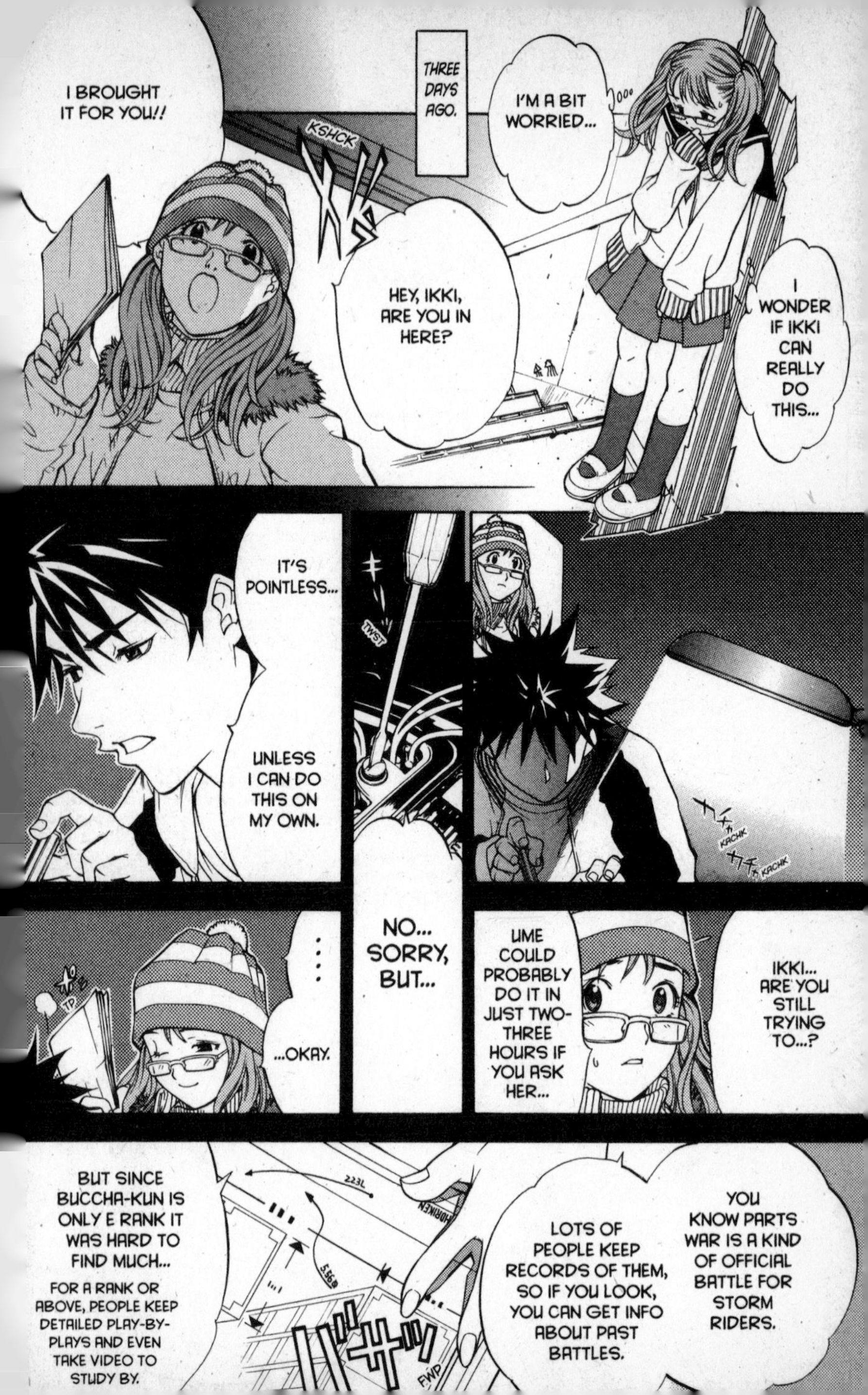

THREE DAYS AGO.
I'M A BIT WORRIED...
I WONDER IF IKKI CAN REALLY DO THIS...
KSHCK
HEY, IKKI, ARE YOU IN HERE?
I BROUGHT IT FOR YOU!!
KACHK
KACHK
TWST
IT'S POINTLESS...
UNLESS I CAN DO THIS ON MY OWN.
IKKI... ARE YOU STILL TRYING TO...?
UME COULD PROBABLY DO IT IN JUST TWO-THREE HOURS IF YOU ASK HER...
NO... SORRY, BUT...
....
...OKAY.
TP
YOU KNOW PARTS WAR IS A KIND OF OFFICIAL BATTLE FOR STORM RIDERS.
LOTS OF PEOPLE KEEP RECORDS OF THEM, SO IF YOU LOOK, YOU CAN GET INFO ABOUT PAST BATTLES.
BUT SINCE BUCCHA-KUN IS ONLY E RANK IT WAS HARD TO FIND MUCH...
FOR A RANK OR ABOVE, PEOPLE KEEP DETAILED PLAY-BY-PLAYS AND EVEN TAKE VIDEO TO STUDY BY.
FWP

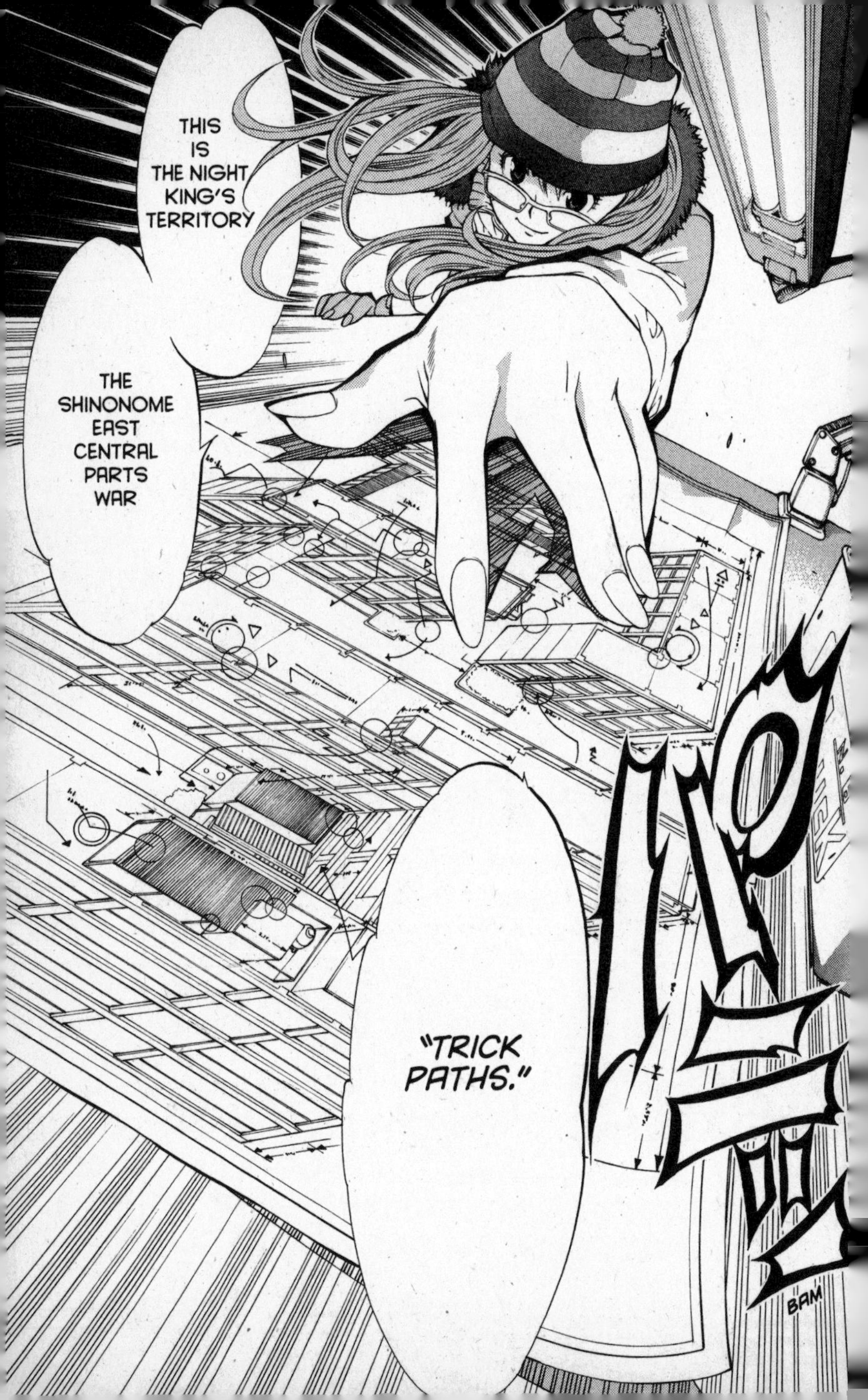
THIS IS THE NIGHT KING'S TERRITORY
THE SHINONOME EAST CENTRAL PARTS WAR
"TRICK PATHS."
BAM

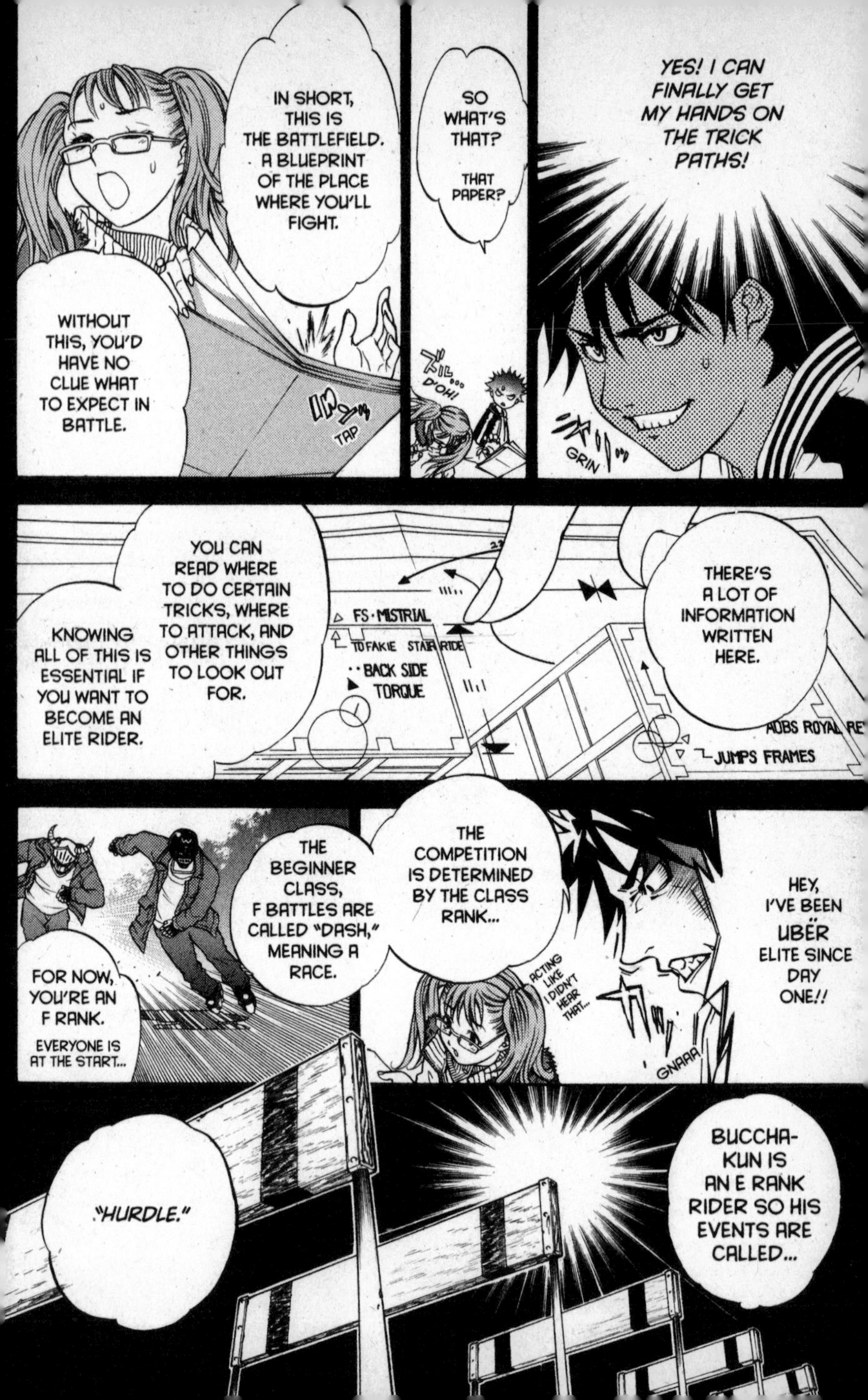

YES! I CAN FINALLY GET MY HANDS ON THE TRICK PATHS!
GRIN
SO WHAT'S THAT?
THAT PAPER?
D'OH!
IN SHORT, THIS IS THE BATTLEFIELD. A BLUEPRINT OF THE PLACE WHERE YOU'LL FIGHT.
WITHOUT THIS, YOU'D HAVE NO CLUE WHAT TO EXPECT IN BATTLE.
TAP
THERE'S A LOT OF INFORMATION WRITTEN HERE.
YOU CAN READ WHERE TO DO CERTAIN TRICKS, WHERE TO ATTACK, AND OTHER THINGS TO LOOK OUT FOR.
KNOWING ALL OF THIS IS ESSENTIAL IF YOU WANT TO BECOME AN ELITE RIDER.
FS·MISTRIAL
TOFAKIE STAIR RIDE
BACK SIDE
TORQUE
ADBS ROYAL RE
JUMPS FRAMES
THE COMPETITION IS DETERMINED BY THE CLASS RANK...
HEY, I'VE BEEN UBËR ELITE SINCE DAY ONE!!
ACTING LIKE I DIDN'T HEAR THAT...
GNAAR
THE BEGINNER CLASS, F BATTLES ARE CALLED "DASH," MEANING A RACE.
FOR NOW, YOU'RE AN F RANK.
EVERYONE IS AT THE START...
BUCCHA-KUN IS AN E RANK RIDER SO HIS EVENTS ARE CALLED...
"HURDLE."

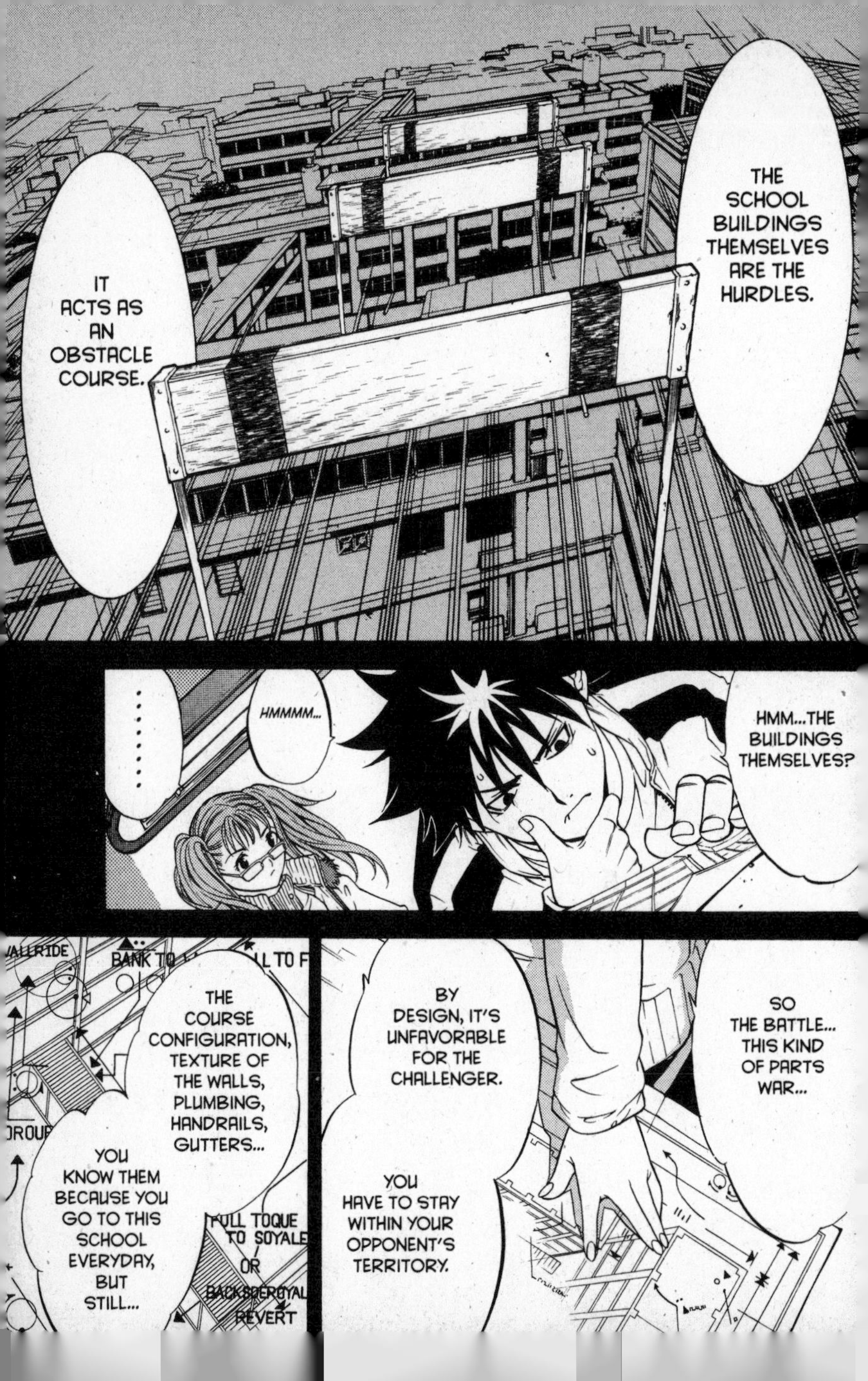
THE SCHOOL BUILDINGS THEMSELVES ARE THE HURDLES.
IT ACTS AS AN OBSTACLE COURSE.
HMM...THE BUILDINGS THEMSELVES?
HMMMM...
......
SO THE BATTLE... THIS KIND OF PARTS WAR...
BY DESIGN, IT'S UNFAVORABLE FOR THE CHALLENGER.
YOU HAVE TO STAY WITHIN YOUR OPPONENT'S TERRITORY.
THE COURSE CONFIGURATION, TEXTURE OF THE WALLS, PLUMBING, HANDRAILS, GUTTERS...
YOU KNOW THEM BECAUSE YOU GO TO THIS SCHOOL EVERYDAY, BUT STILL...
FULL TOQUE TO SOYALE
OR
REVERT

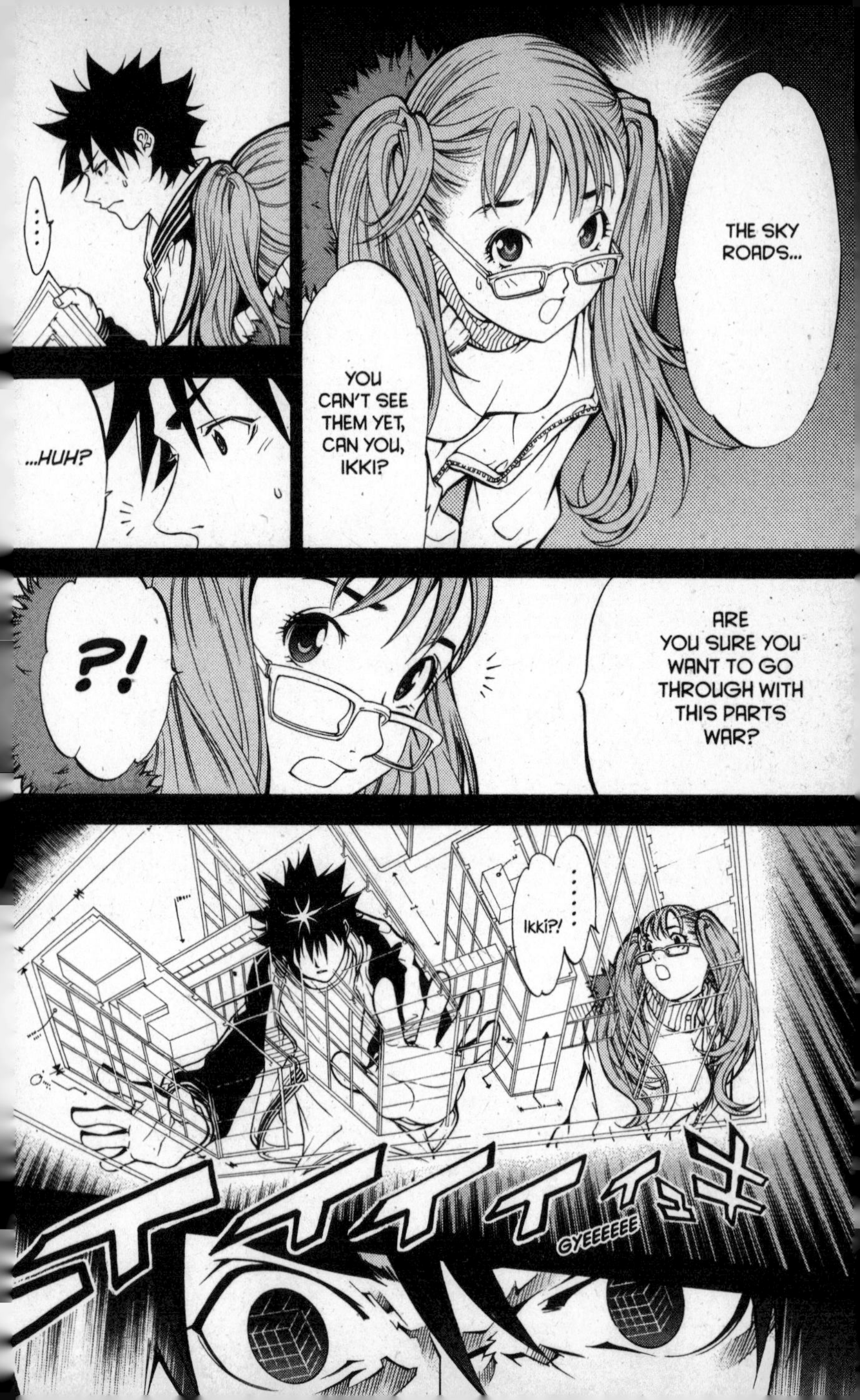

THE SKY ROADS...
YOU CAN'T SEE THEM YET, CAN YOU, IKKI?
...
...HUH?
ARE YOU SURE YOU WANT TO GO THROUGH WITH THIS PARTS WAR?
?!
......
IKKI?!
GYEEEEEE

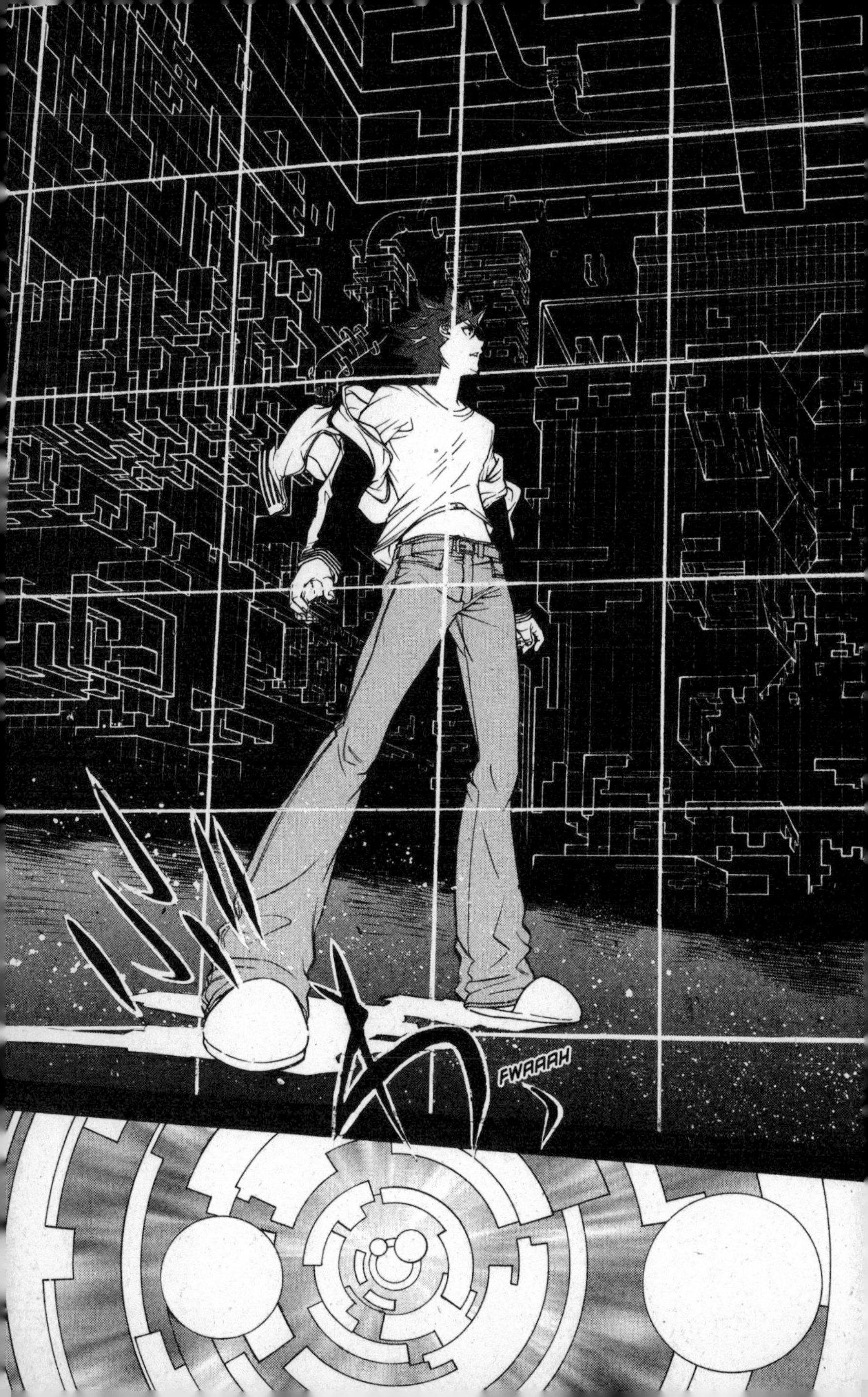
FWAAAH

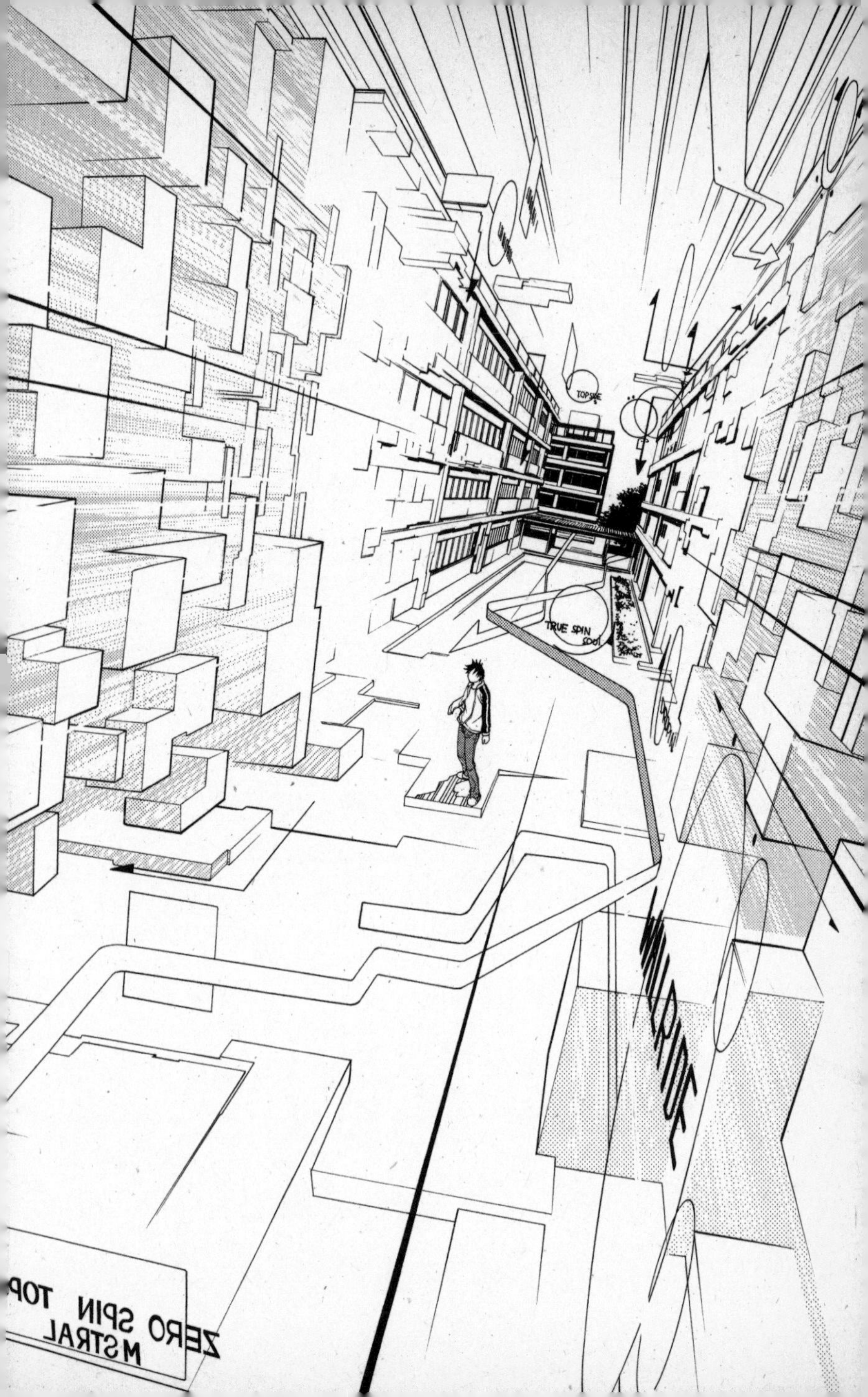
TOPSIDE
TRUE SPIN
WALLRIDE

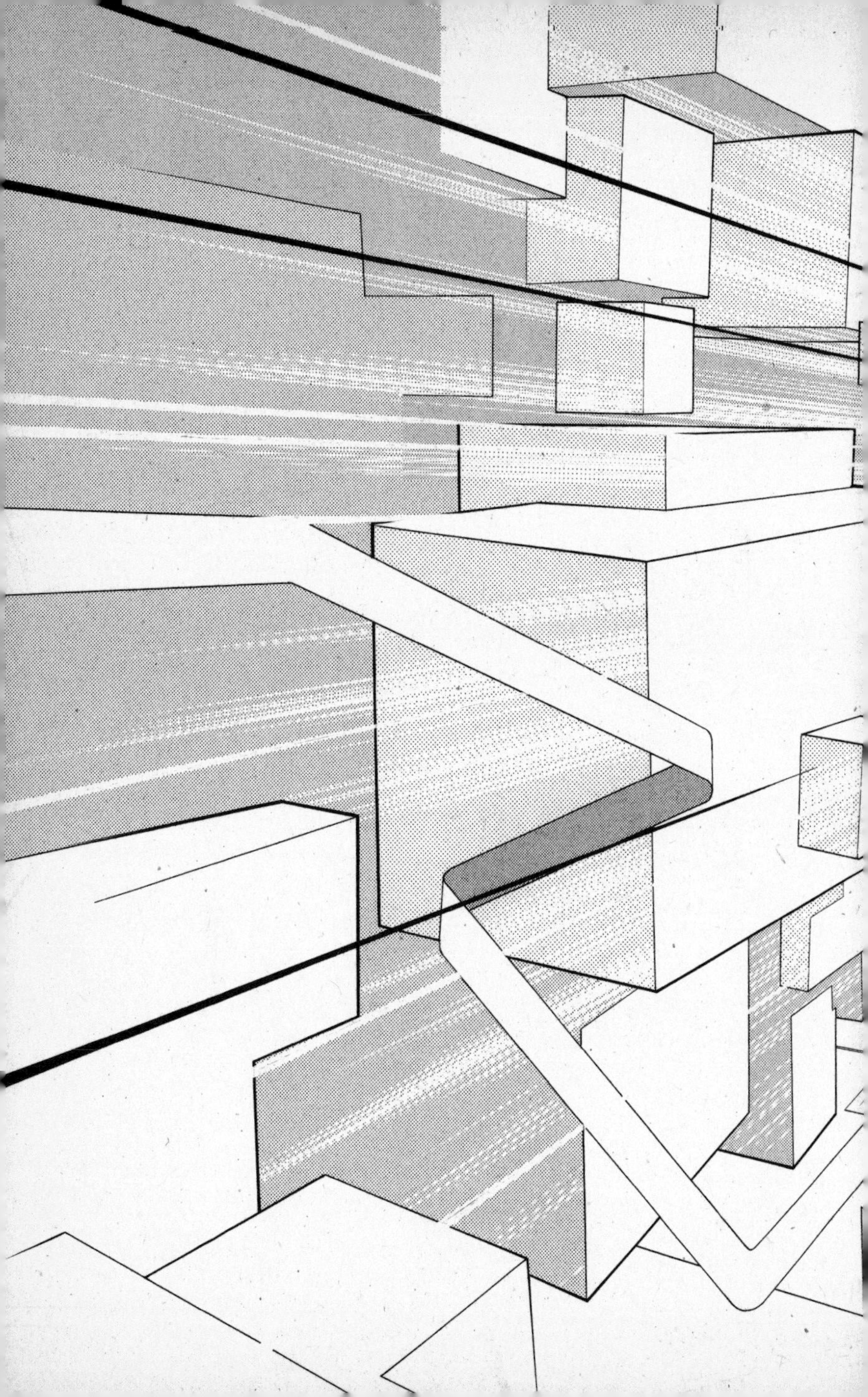

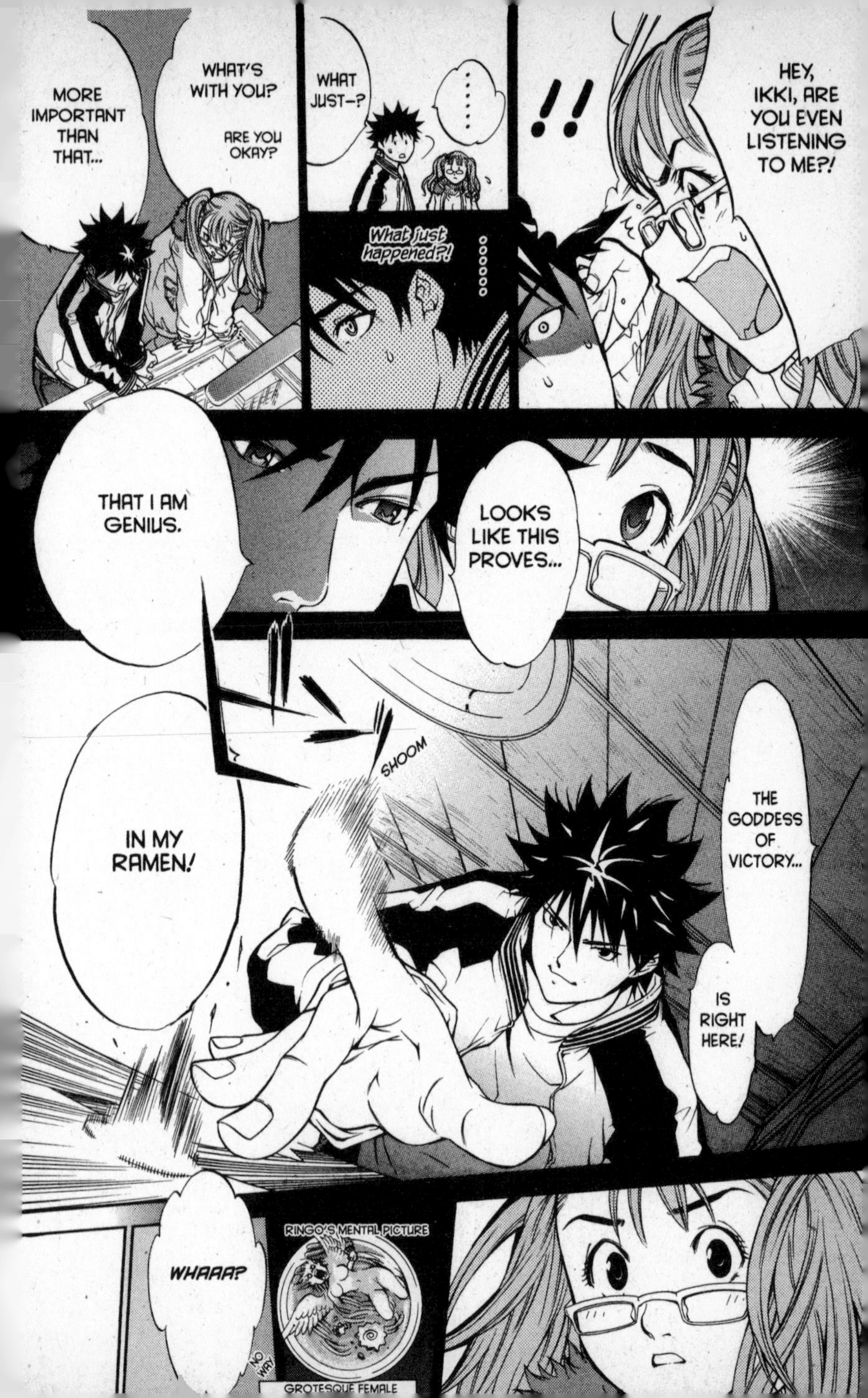
!!
HEY, IKKI, ARE YOU EVEN LISTENING TO ME?!
WHAT JUST-?
......
What just happened?!
oooooo
WHAT'S WITH YOU?
ARE YOU OKAY?
MORE IMPORTANT THAN THAT...
LOOKS LIKE THIS PROVES...
THAT I AM GENIUS.
THE GODDESS OF VICTORY...
IS RIGHT HERE!
SHOOM
IN MY RAMEN!
RINGO'S MENTAL PICTURE
NO WAY
GROTESQUE FEMALE
WHAAA?

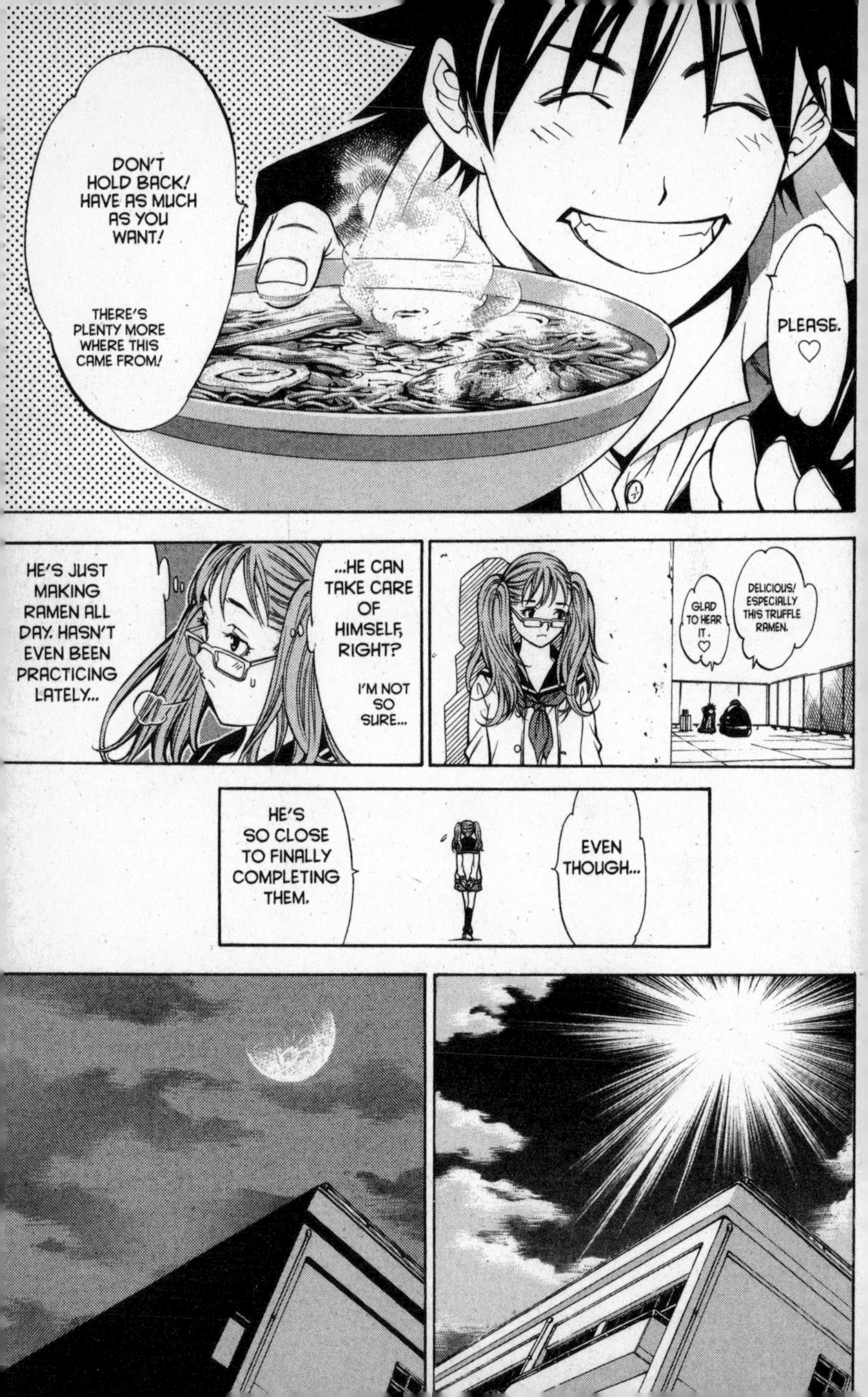
PLEASE. ♡
DON'T HOLD BACK! HAVE AS MUCH AS YOU WANT!
THERE'S PLENTY MORE WHERE THIS CAME FROM!
DELICIOUS! ESPECIALLY THIS TRUFFLE RAMEN.
GLAD TO HEAR IT. ♡
...HE CAN TAKE CARE OF HIMSELF, RIGHT?
I'M NOT SO SURE...
HE'S JUST MAKING RAMEN ALL DAY. HASN'T EVEN BEEN PRACTICING LATELY...
EVEN THOUGH...
HE'S SO CLOSE TO FINALLY COMPLETING THEM.

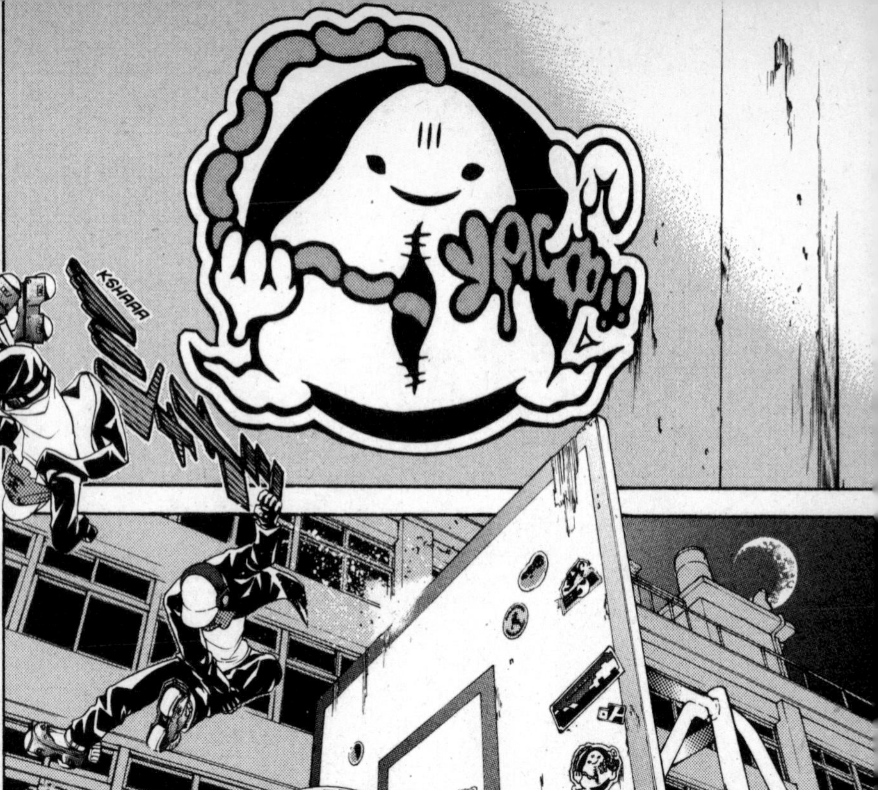
KSHAAA

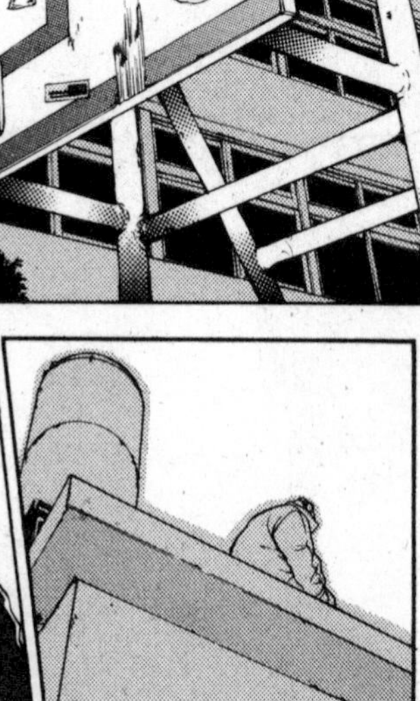

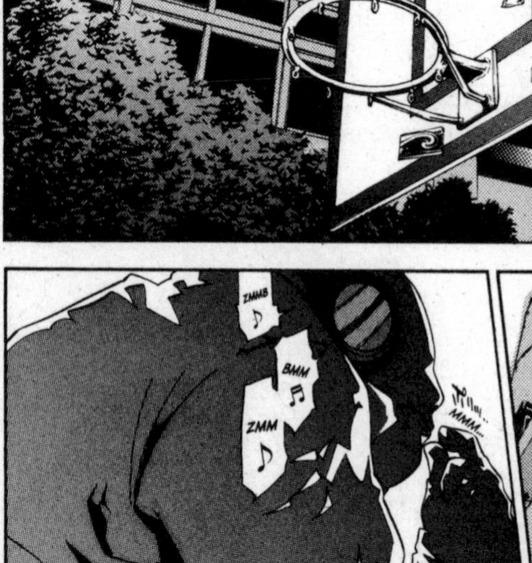
ZMMB ♪
BMM ♫
ZMM ♪
MMM...

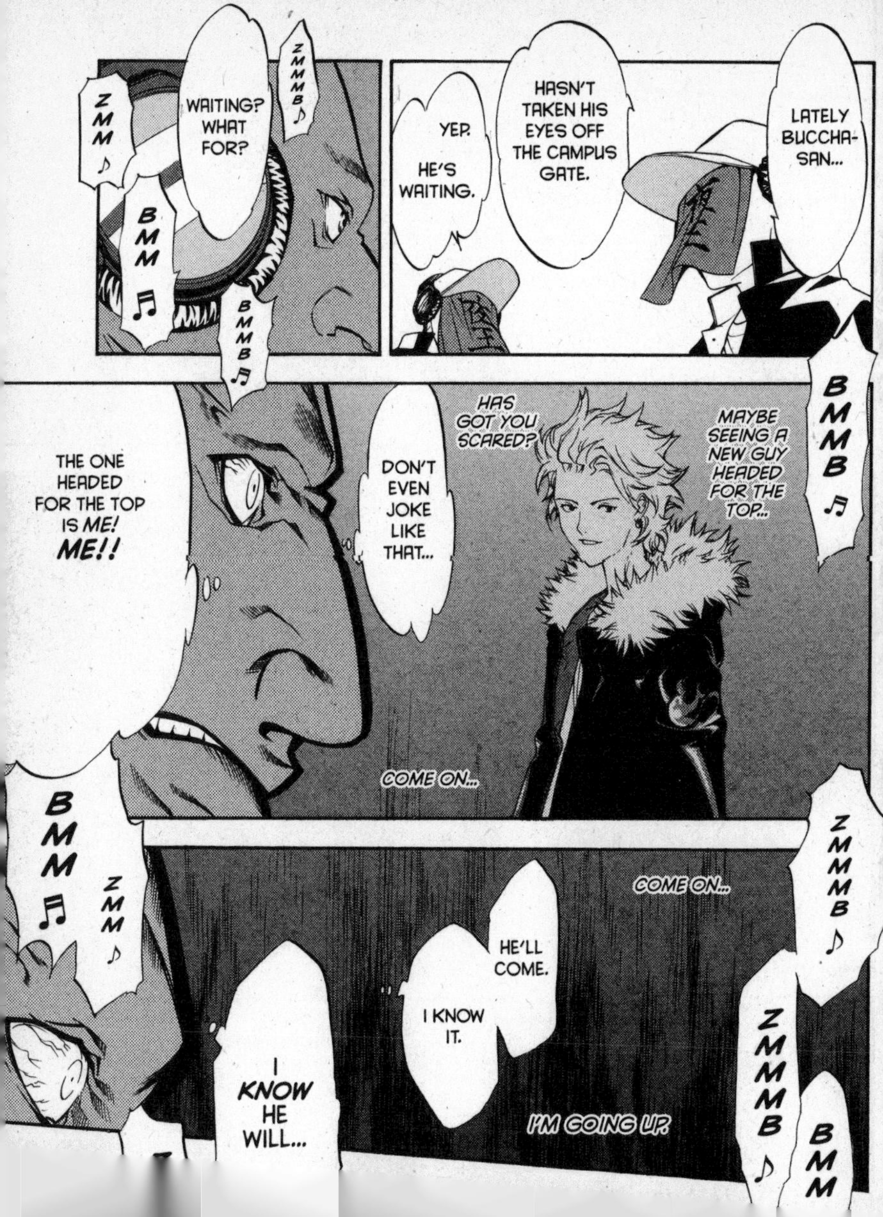
LATELY BUCCHA-SAN...
HASN'T TAKEN HIS EYES OFF THE CAMPUS GATE.
YEP.
HE'S WAITING.
ZMMMB
WAITING? WHAT FOR?
ZMM
BMM
BMMB
BMMB
MAYBE SEEING A NEW GUY HEADED FOR THE TOP...
HAS GOT YOU SCARED?
DON'T EVEN JOKE LIKE THAT...
COME ON...
THE ONE HEADED FOR THE TOP IS ME! ME!!
ZMMMB
COME ON...
HE'LL COME.
I KNOW IT.
I'M GOING UP.
I KNOW HE WILL...
ZMMMB
BMM
BMM
ZMM

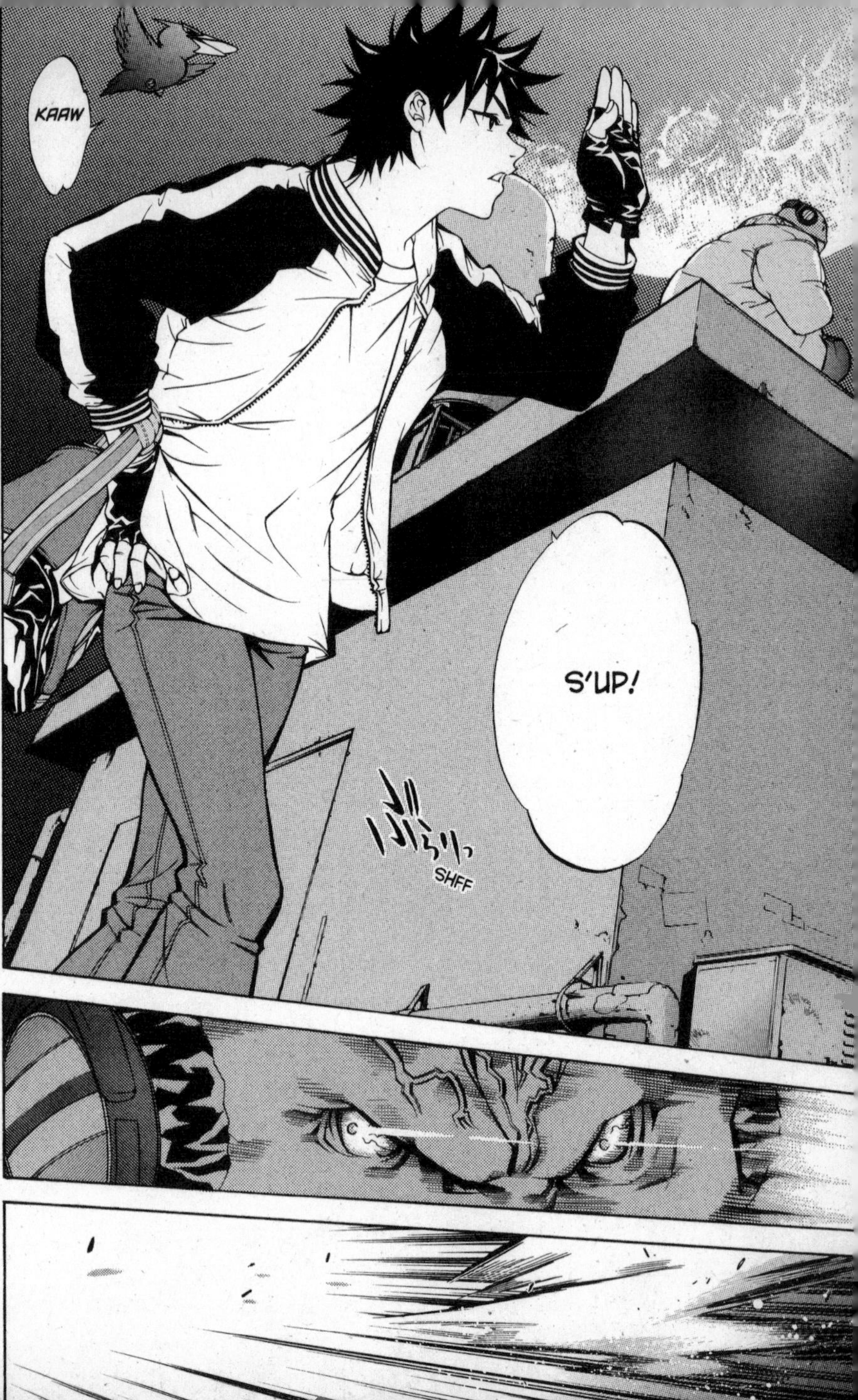
KAAW
S'UP!
SHFF

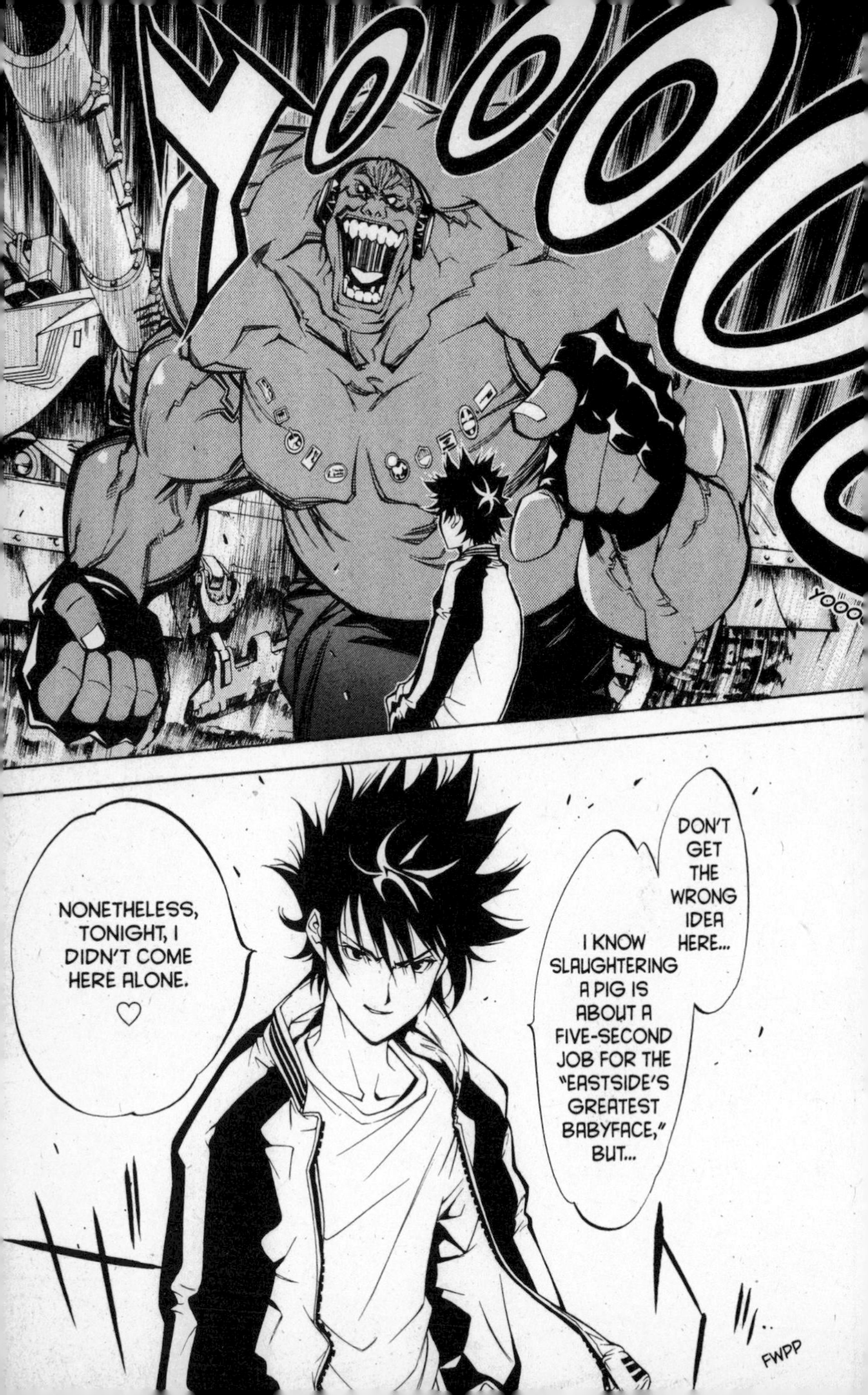
YOOO
DON'T GET THE WRONG IDEA HERE...
I KNOW SLAUGHTERING A PIG IS ABOUT A FIVE-SECOND JOB FOR THE "EASTSIDE'S GREATEST BABYFACE," BUT...
NONETHELESS, TONIGHT, I DIDN'T COME HERE ALONE. ♡
FWPP

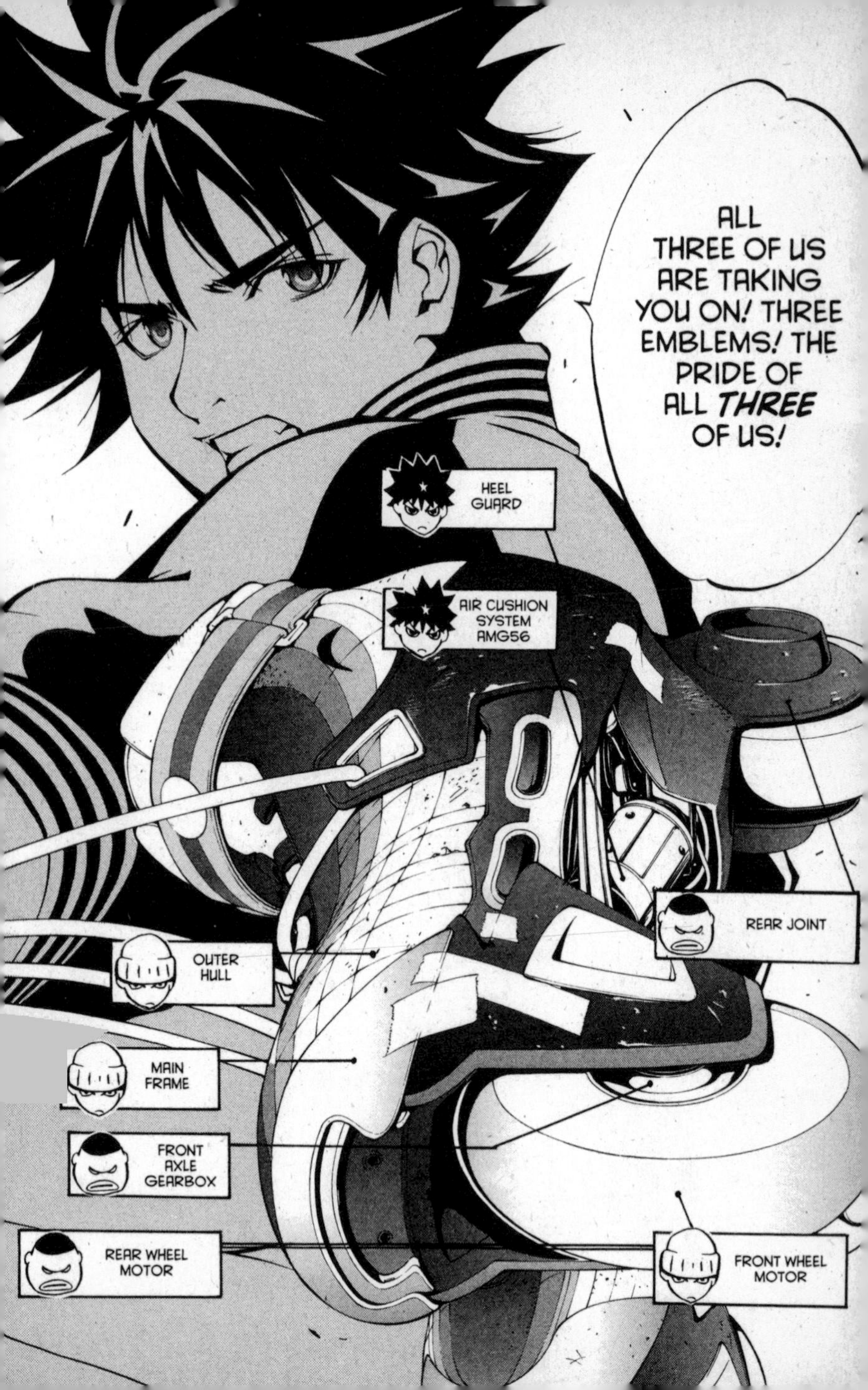
ALL THREE OF US ARE TAKING YOU ON! THREE EMBLEMS! THE PRIDE OF ALL *THREE* OF US!
HEEL GUARD
AIR CUSHION SYSTEM AMG56
REAR JOINT
OUTER HULL
MAIN FRAME
FRONT AXLE GEARBOX
FRONT WHEEL MOTOR
REAR WHEEL MOTOR

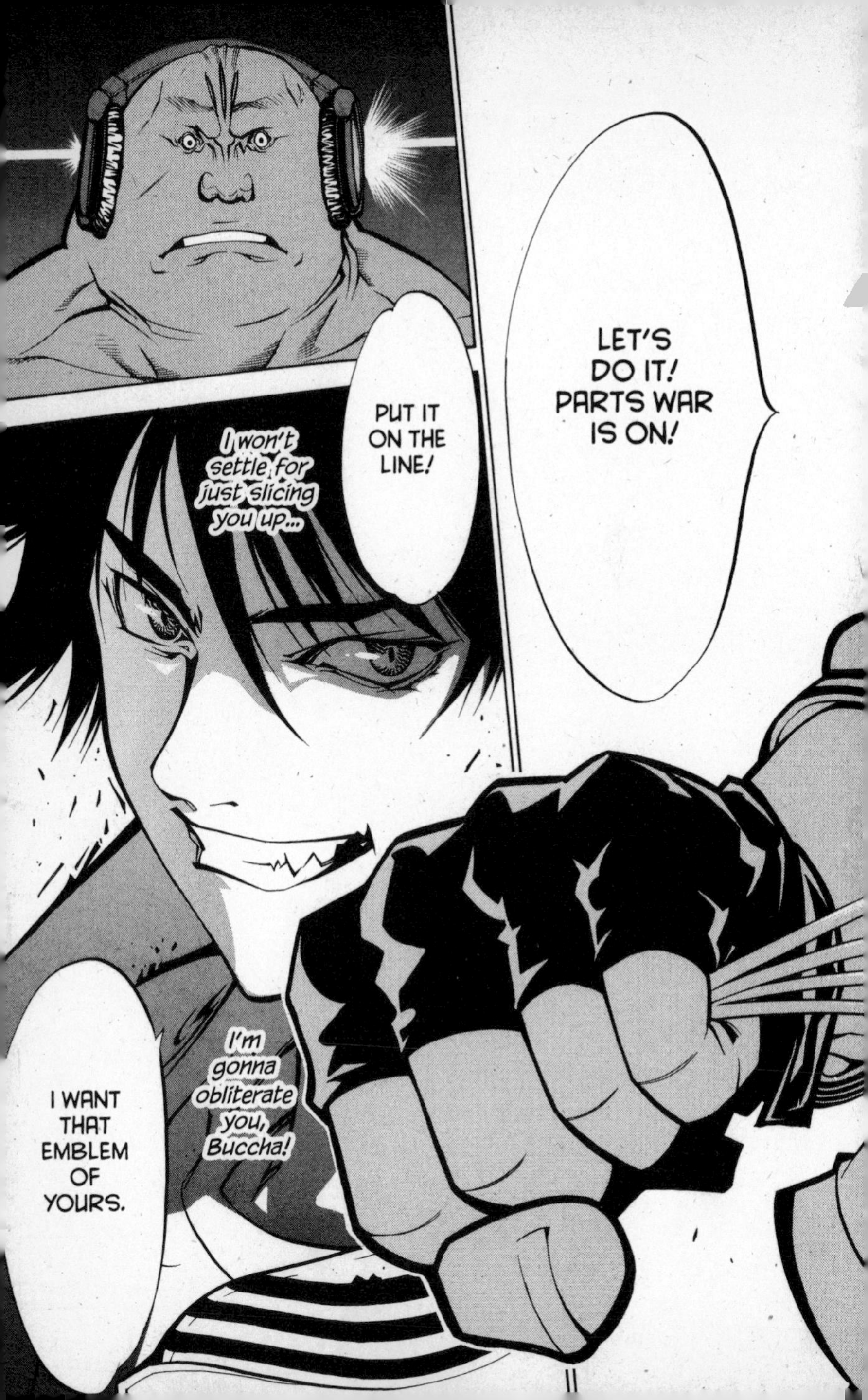
LET'S DO IT! PARTS WAR IS ON!
PUT IT ON THE LINE!
I won't settle for just slicing you up...
I'm gonna obliterate you, Buccha!
I WANT THAT EMBLEM OF YOURS.

I'VE EATEN ACTUAL TRUFFLE
RAMEN ONCE BEFORE...

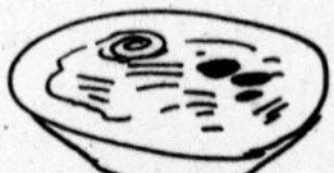

AND IT WAS
NASTY.

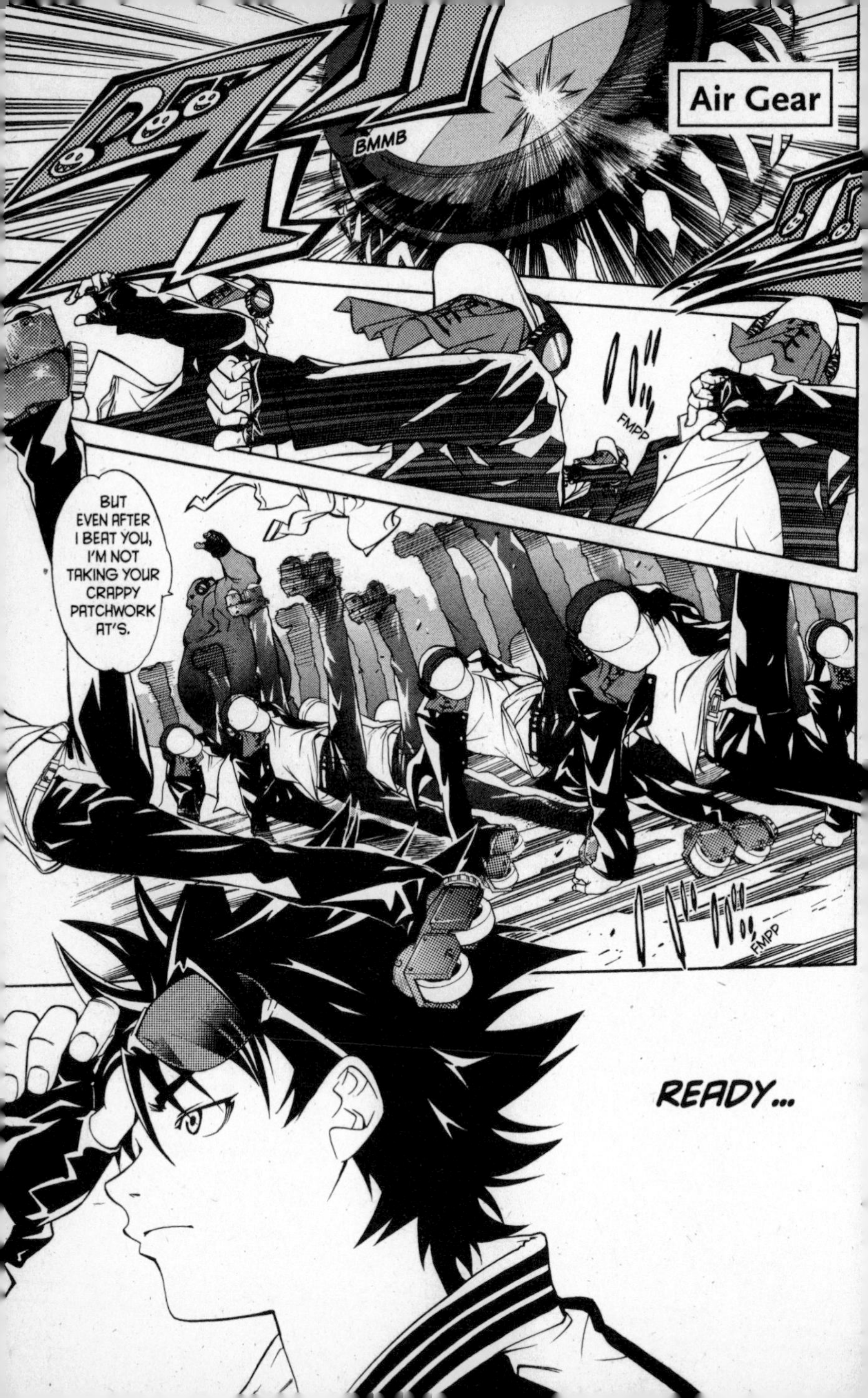
Air Gear
BMMB
FMPP
BUT EVEN AFTER I BEAT YOU, I'M NOT TAKING YOUR CRAPPY PATCHWORK AT'S.
FMPP
READY...

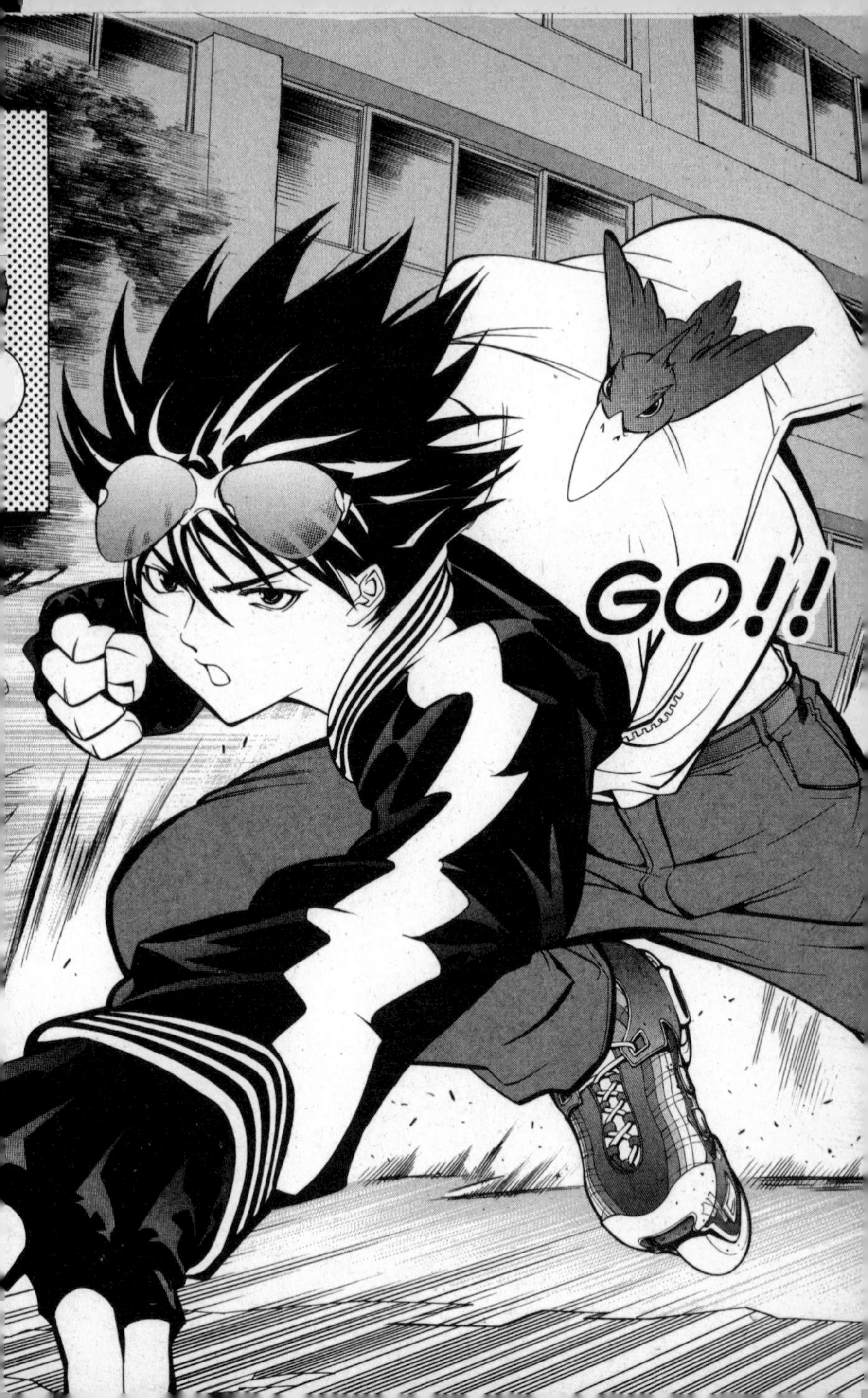
GO!!

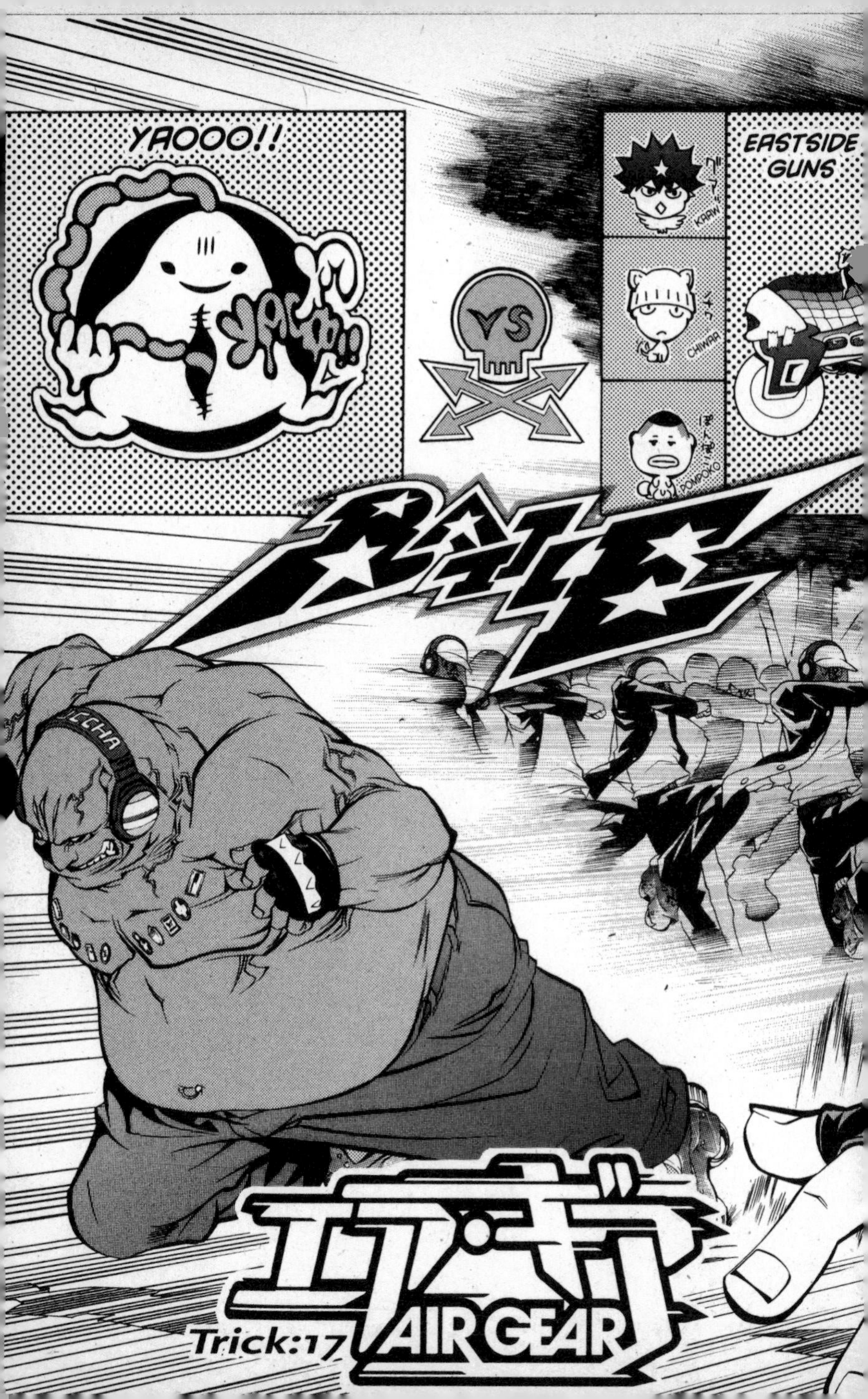
EASTSIDE GUNS
KRAW
CHIWAA
POMPOKO
VS
YAOOO!!
Trick:17
エア・ギア
AIR GEAR

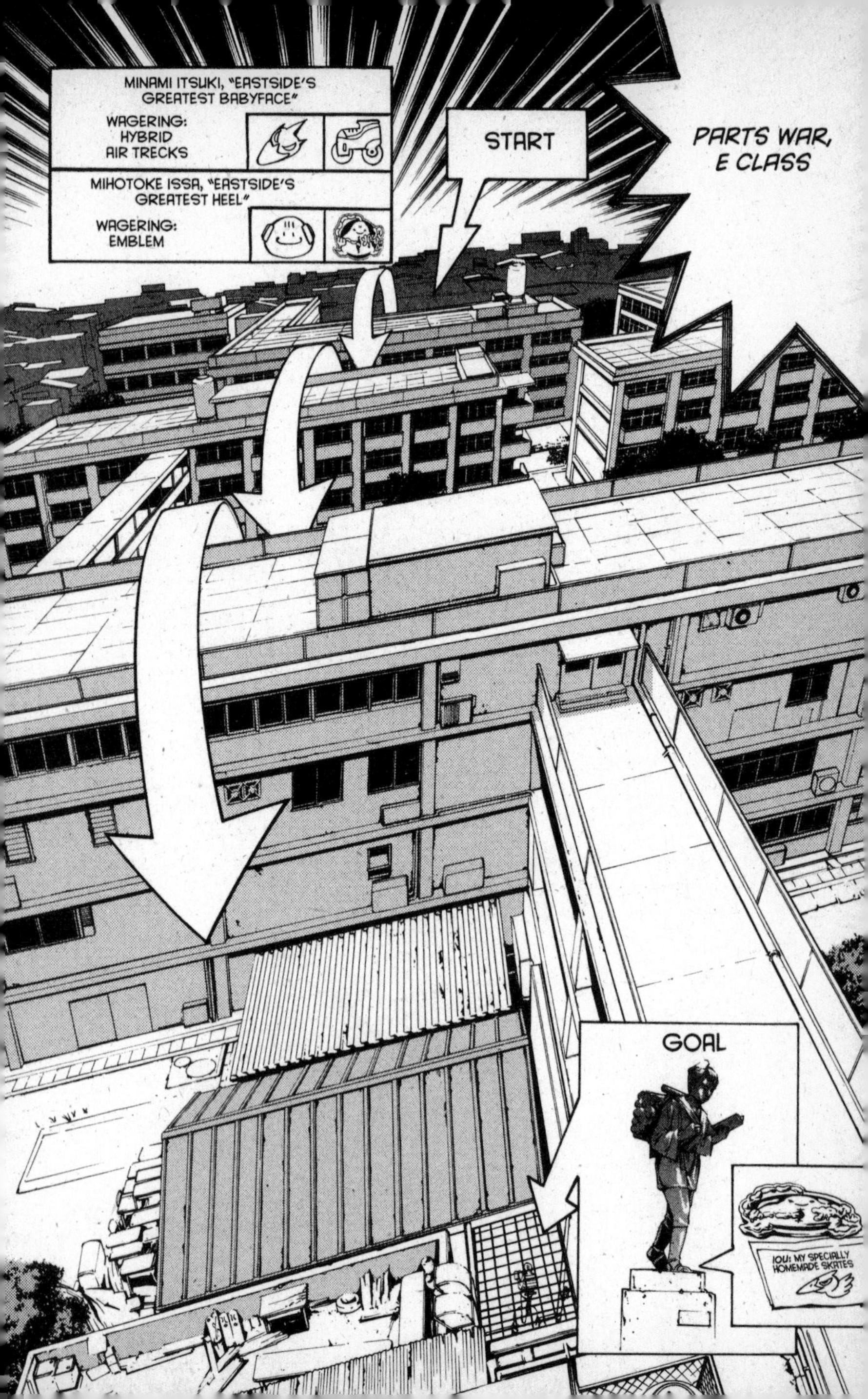
PARTS WAR, E CLASS
START
MINAMI ITSUKI, "EASTSIDE'S GREATEST BABYFACE"
WAGERING: HYBRID AIR TRECKS
MIHOTOKE ISSA, "EASTSIDE'S GREATEST HEEL"
WAGERING: EMBLEM
GOAL
IOU: MY SPECIALLY HOMEMADE SKATES

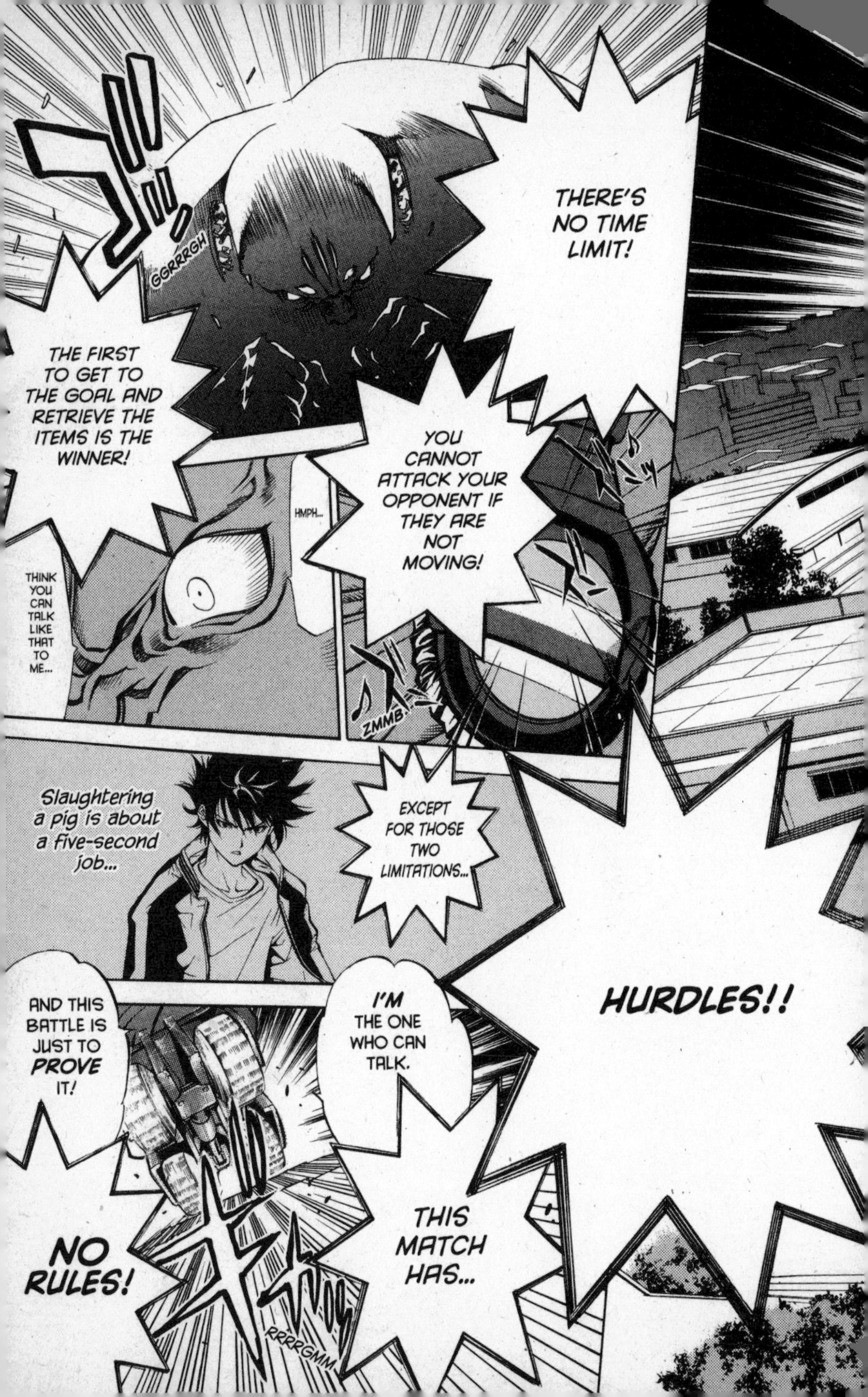
THERE'S NO TIME LIMIT!
YOU CANNOT ATTACK YOUR OPPONENT IF THEY ARE NOT MOVING!
THE FIRST TO GET TO THE GOAL AND RETRIEVE THE ITEMS IS THE WINNER!
GGRRRGH
HMPH...
THINK YOU CAN TALK LIKE THAT TO ME...
ZMMB
EXCEPT FOR THOSE TWO LIMITATIONS...
Slaughtering a pig is about a five-second job...
I'M THE ONE WHO CAN TALK.
AND THIS BATTLE IS JUST TO PROVE IT!
THIS MATCH HAS...
NO RULES!
HURDLES!!
RRRRGMM

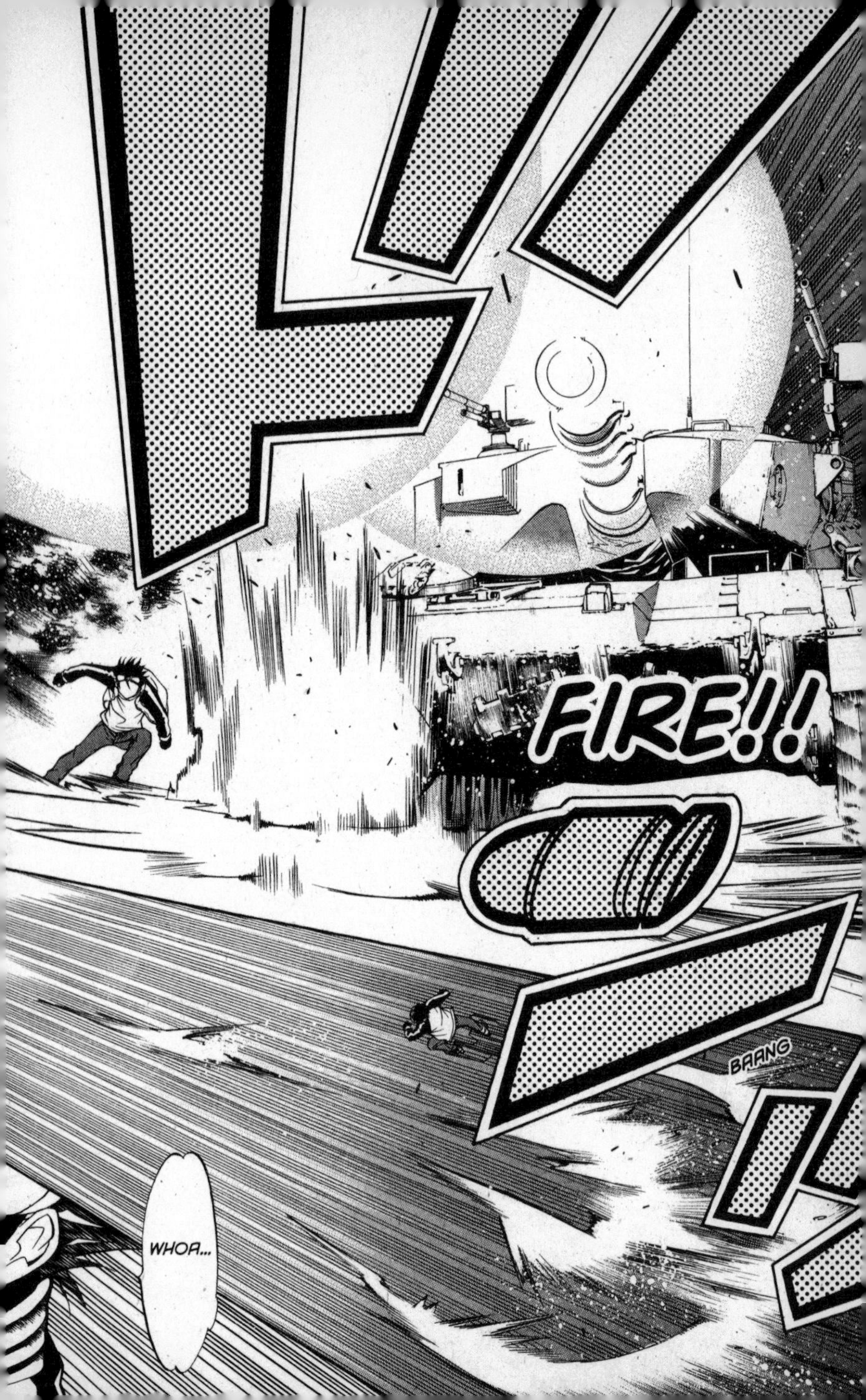
FIRE!!
BAANG
WHOA...

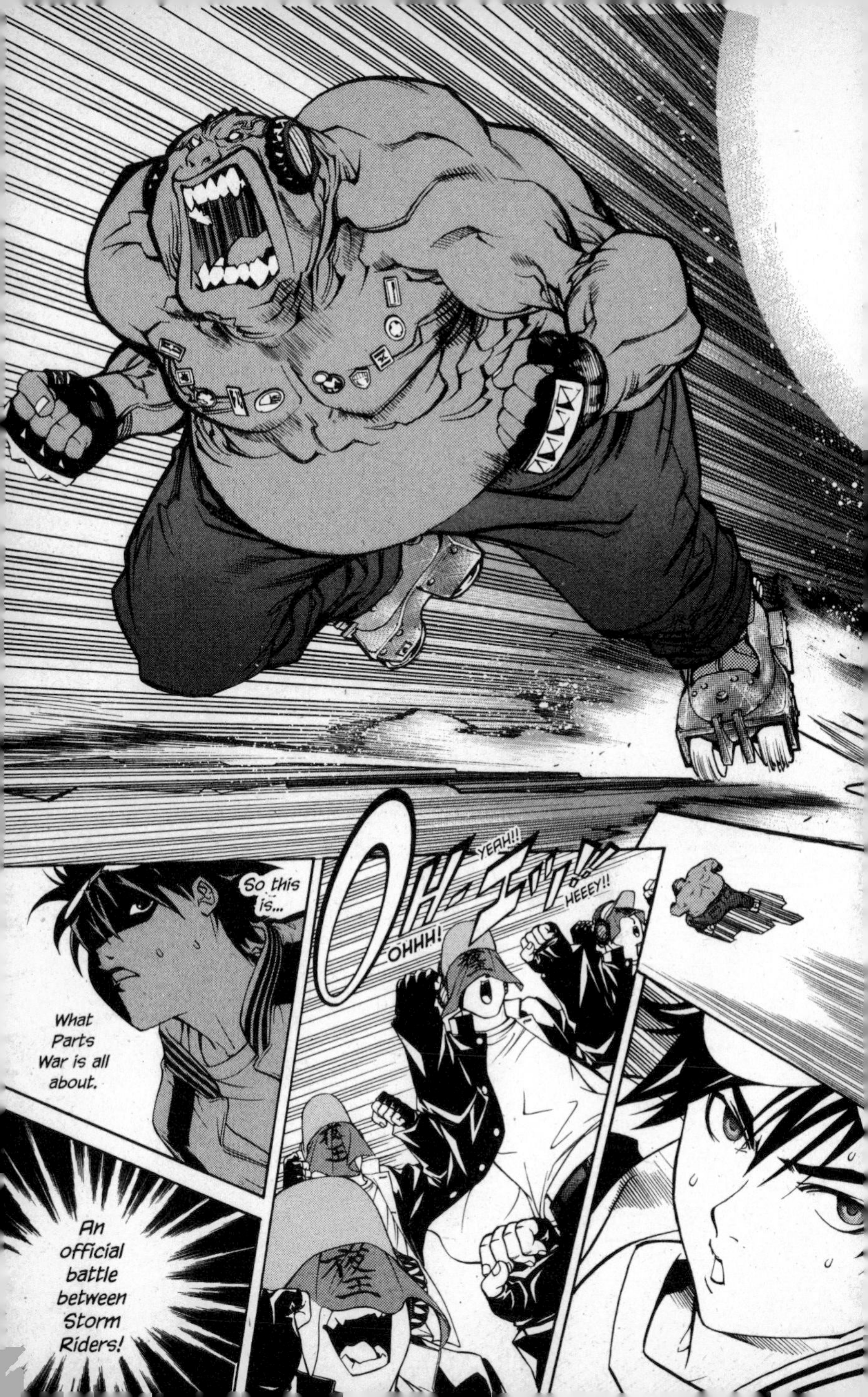
YEAH!!
HEEEY!!
OHHH!
So this is...
What Parts War is all about.
An official battle between Storm Riders!

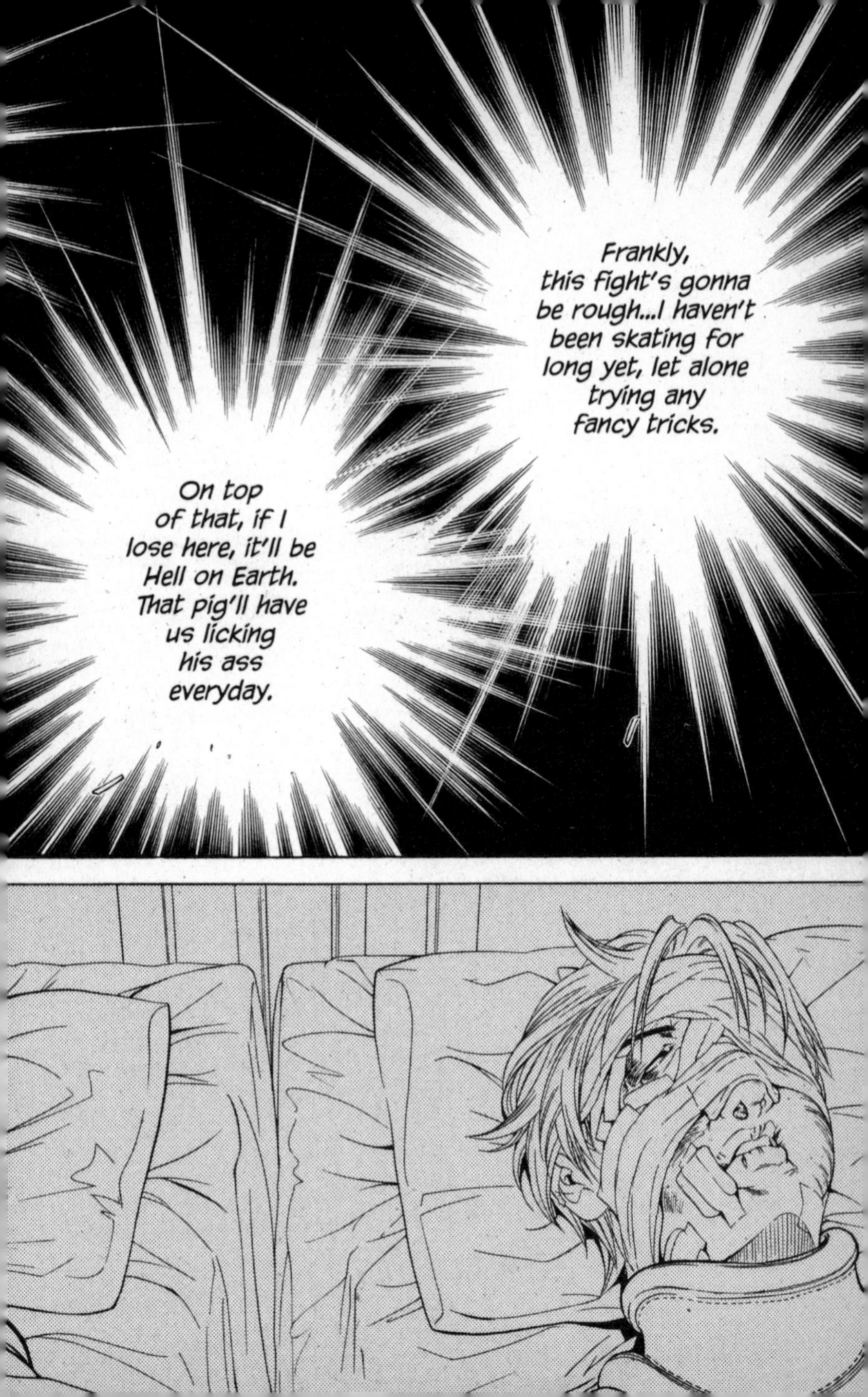
Frankly, this fight's gonna be rough...I haven't been skating for long yet, let alone trying any fancy tricks.
On top of that, if I lose here, it'll be Hell on Earth. That pig'll have us licking his ass everyday.

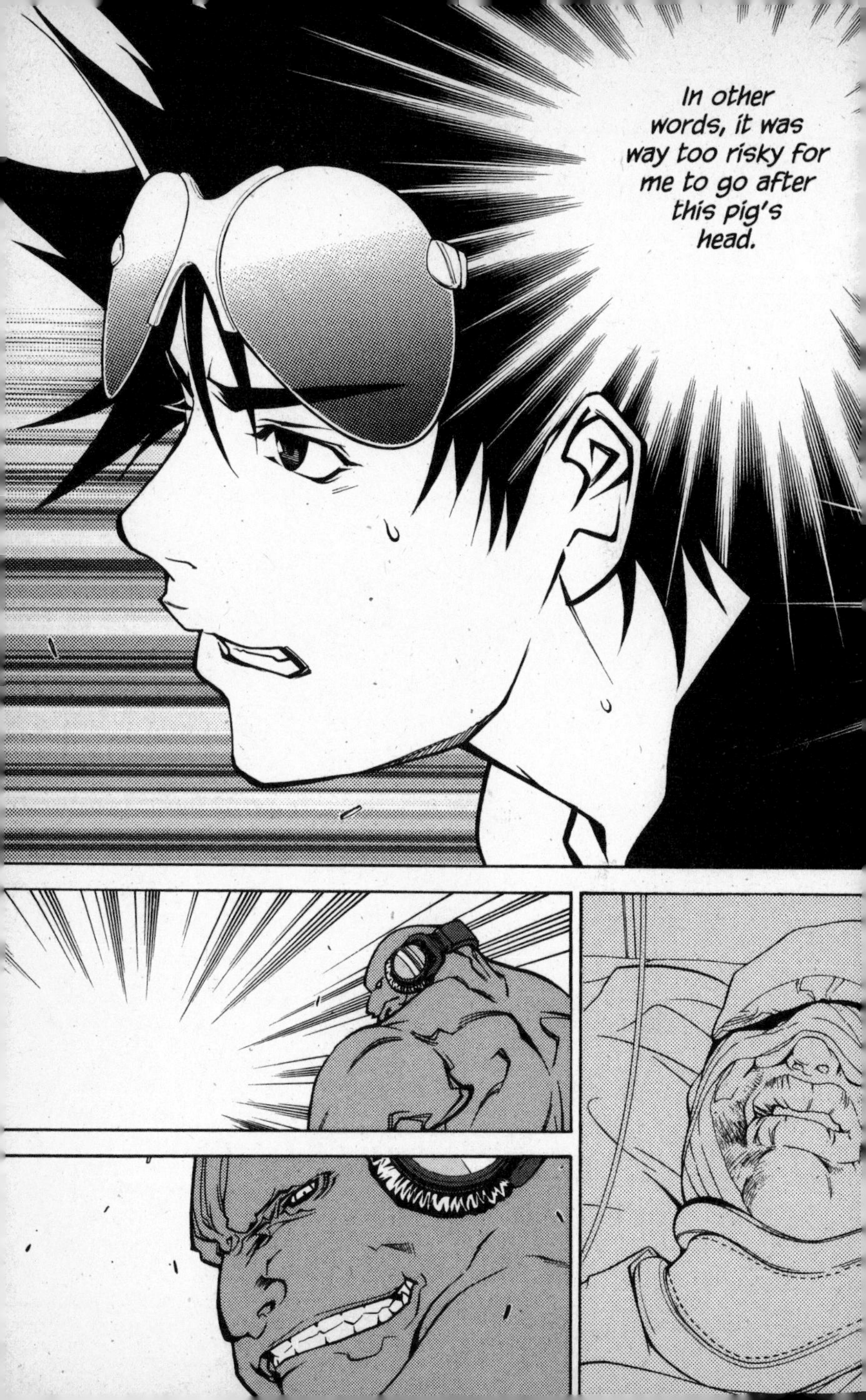
In other words, it was way too risky for me to go after this pig's head.

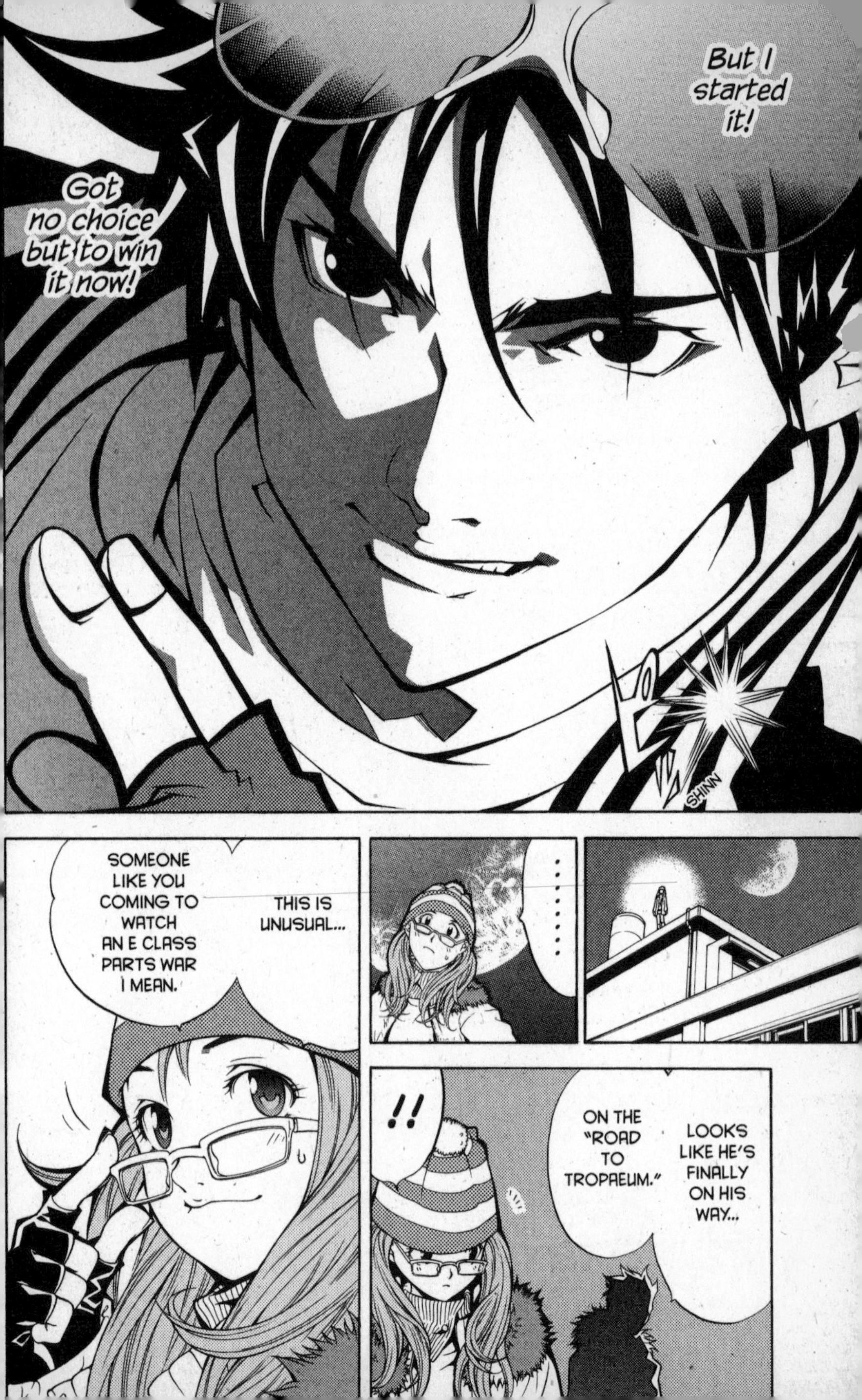
But I started it!
Got no choice but to win it now!
SHINN
......
!!
LOOKS LIKE HE'S FINALLY ON HIS WAY...
ON THE "ROAD TO TROPAEUM."
THIS IS UNUSUAL...
SOMEONE LIKE YOU COMING TO WATCH AN E CLASS PARTS WAR I MEAN.

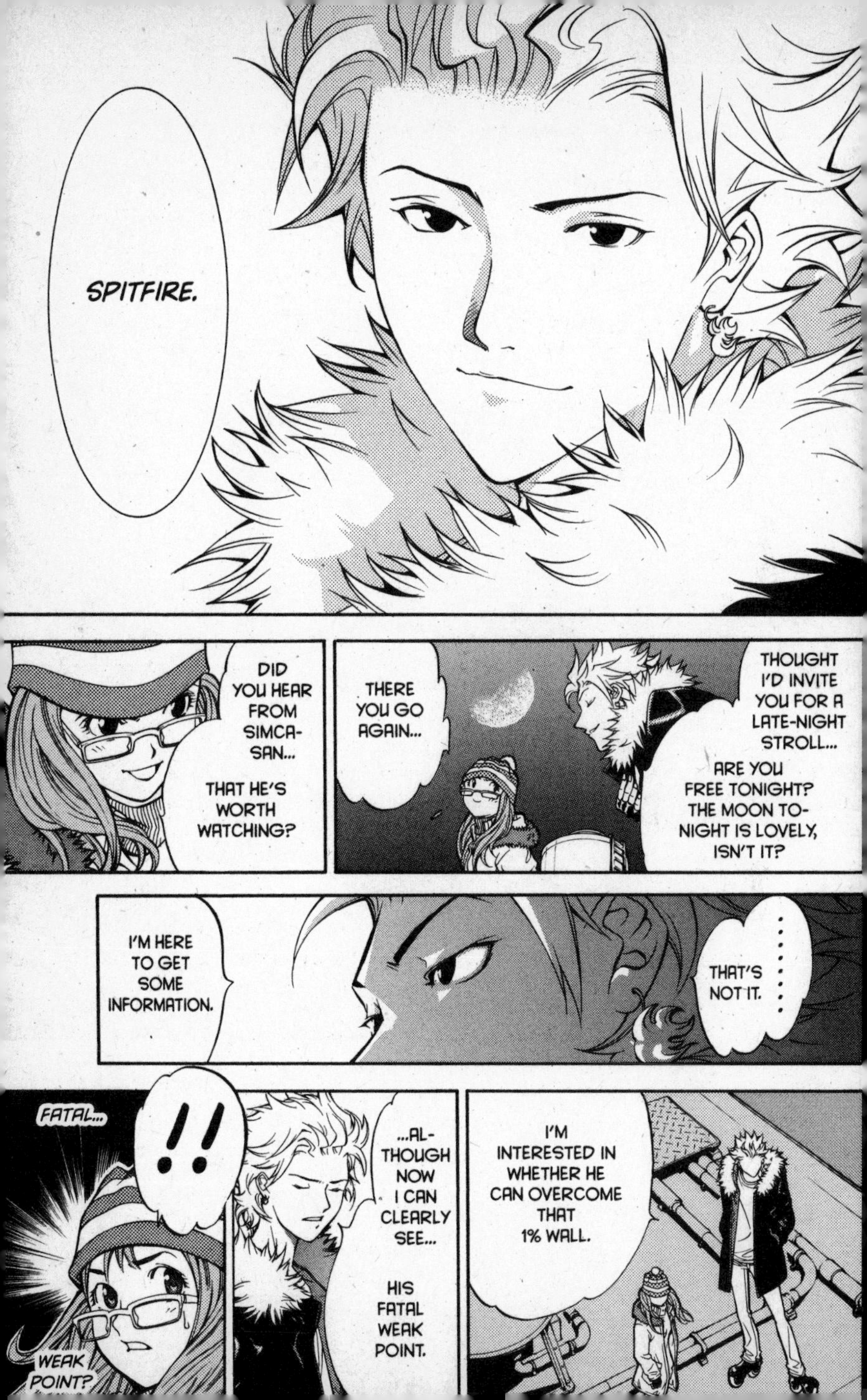
SPITFIRE.
THOUGHT I'D INVITE YOU FOR A LATE-NIGHT STROLL...
ARE YOU FREE TONIGHT? THE MOON TO-NIGHT IS LOVELY, ISN'T IT?
THERE YOU GO AGAIN...
DID YOU HEAR FROM SIMCA-SAN...
THAT HE'S WORTH WATCHING?
......
THAT'S NOT IT.
I'M HERE TO GET SOME INFORMATION.
I'M INTERESTED IN WHETHER HE CAN OVERCOME THAT 1% WALL.
...AL-THOUGH NOW I CAN CLEARLY SEE...
HIS FATAL WEAK POINT.
!!
FATAL...
WEAK POINT?

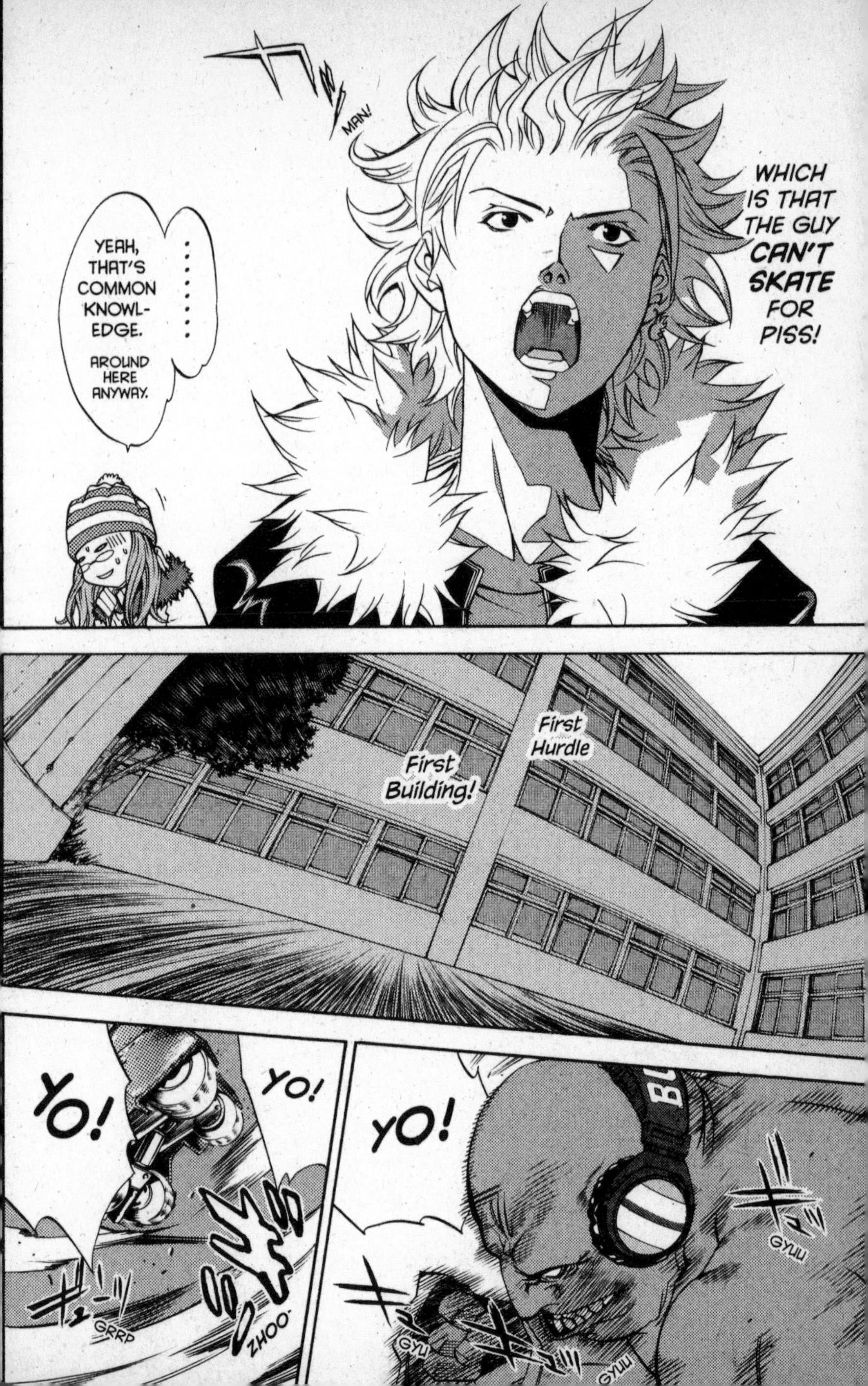
MAN!
WHICH IS THAT THE GUY CAN'T SKATE FOR PISS!
......
YEAH, THAT'S COMMON KNOWL-EDGE.
AROUND HERE ANYWAY.
First Hurdle
First Building!
yO!
GYUU
GYUU
GYU
YO!
YO!
ZHOO
GRRP

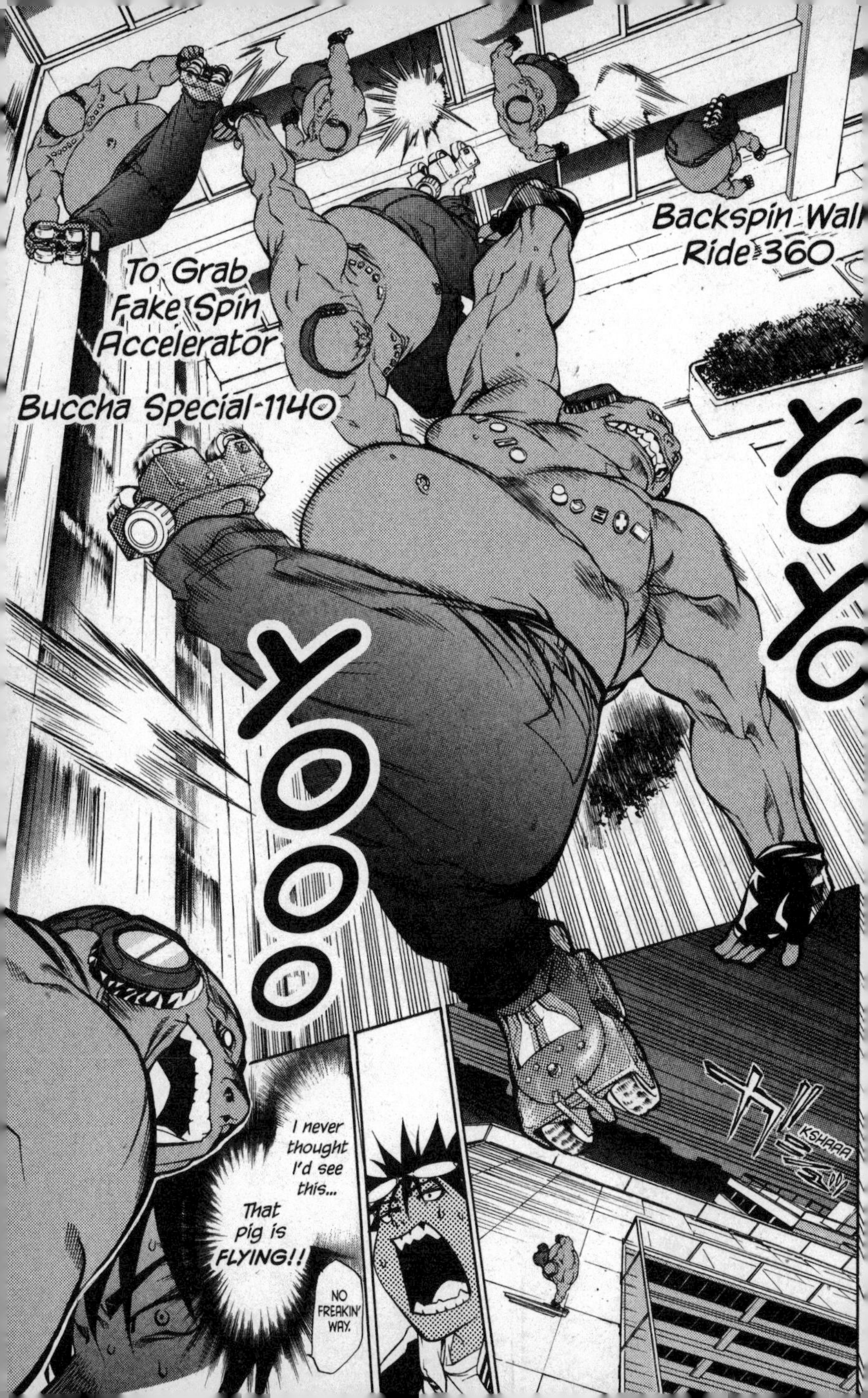
Backspin Wall Ride 360
To Grab Fake Spin Accelerator
Buccha Special 1140
YOOO
YO YO
KSHAAA
I never thought I'd see this...
That pig is FLYING!!
NO FREAKIN' WAY.

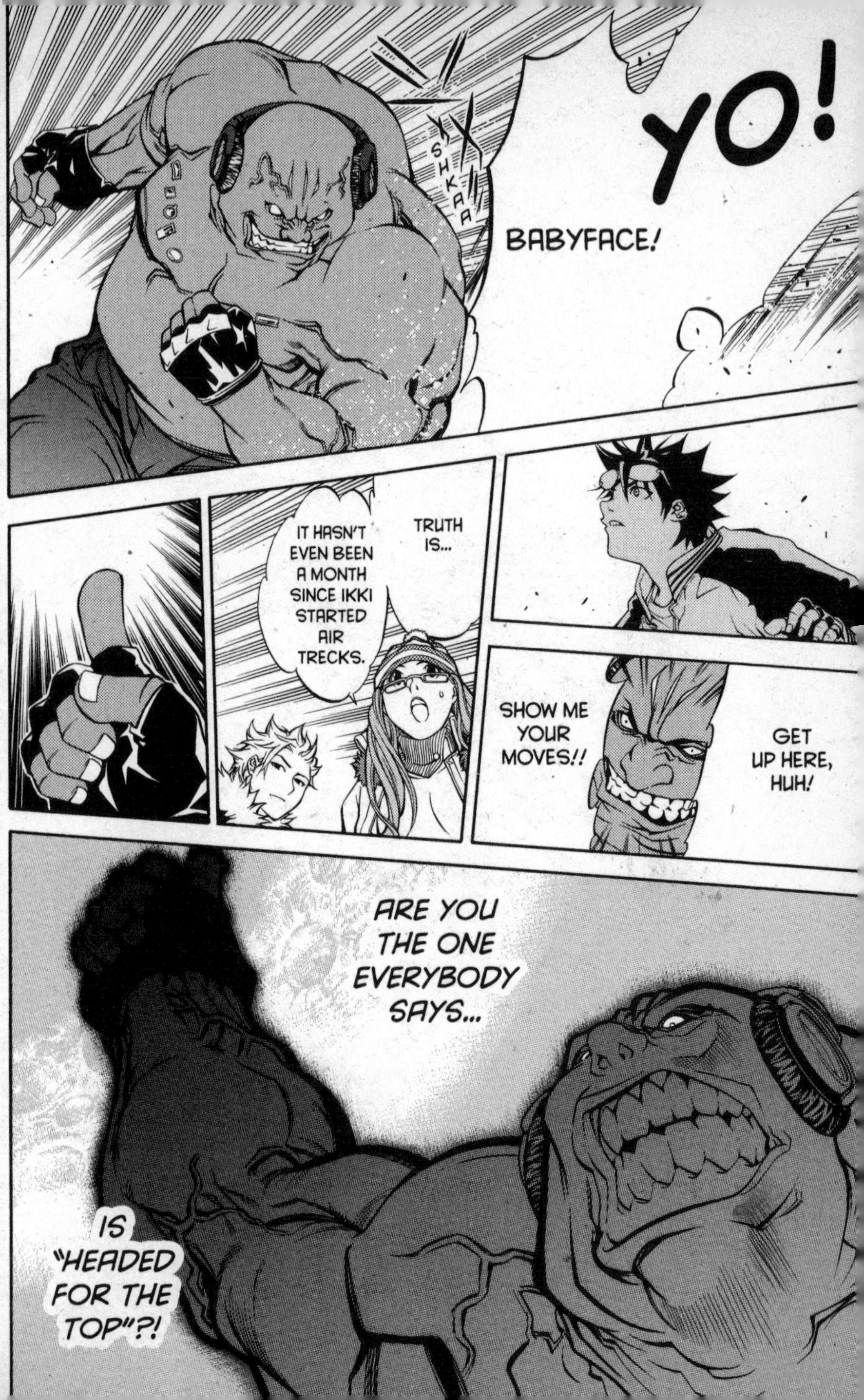
YO!
BABYFACE!
SHKAA
GET UP HERE, HUH!
SHOW ME YOUR MOVES!!
TRUTH IS...
IT HASN'T EVEN BEEN A MONTH SINCE IKKI STARTED AIR TRECKS.
ARE YOU THE ONE EVERYBODY SAYS...
IS "HEADED FOR THE TOP"?!

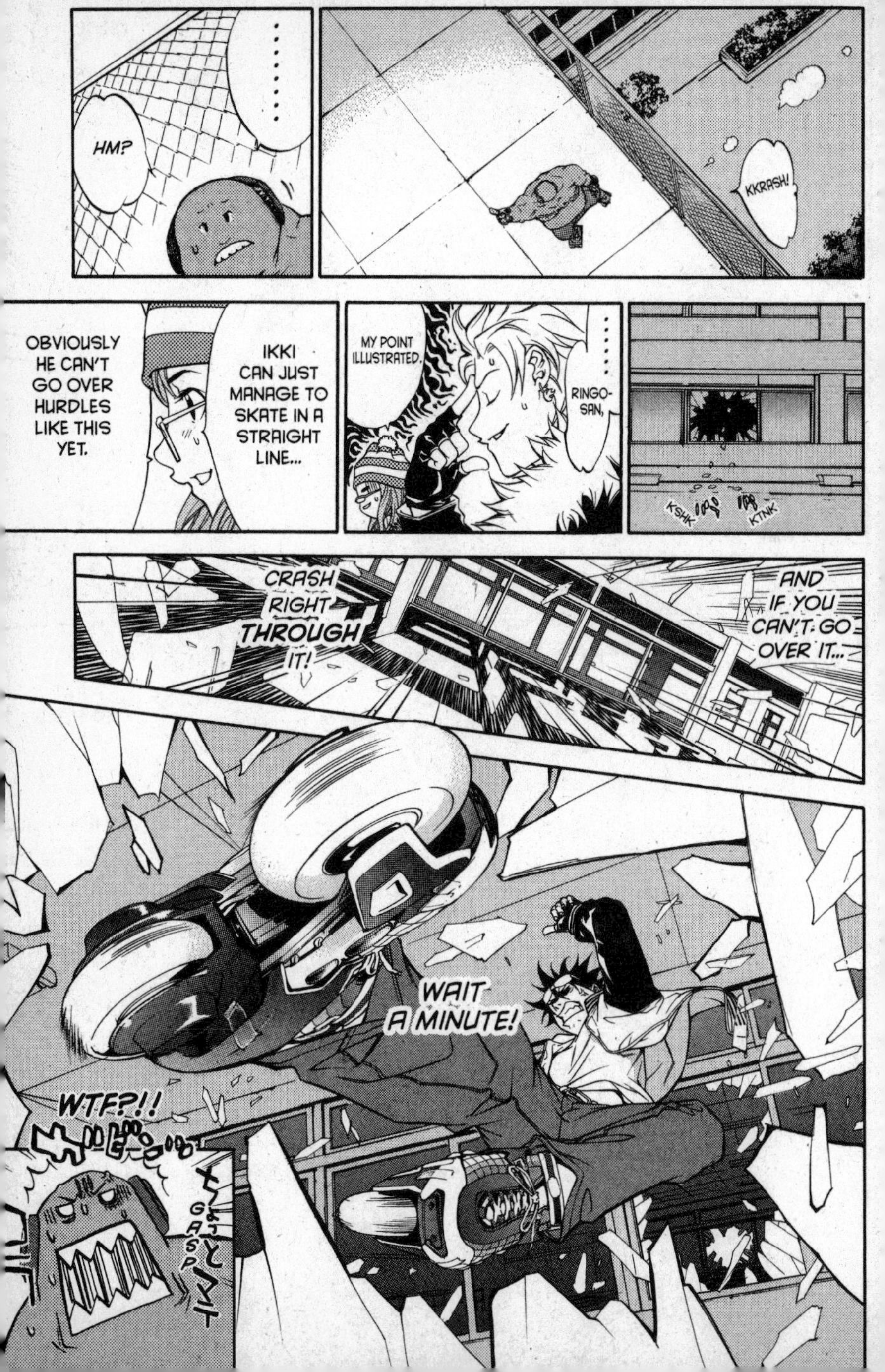
KKRASH!
......
HM?
KSHK
KTNK
......
RINGO-SAN,
MY POINT ILLUSTRATED.
IKKI CAN JUST MANAGE TO SKATE IN A STRAIGHT LINE...
OBVIOUSLY HE CAN'T GO OVER HURDLES LIKE THIS YET.
AND IF YOU CAN'T GO OVER IT...
CRASH RIGHT THROUGH IT!
WAIT A MINUTE!
GASP
WTF?!!

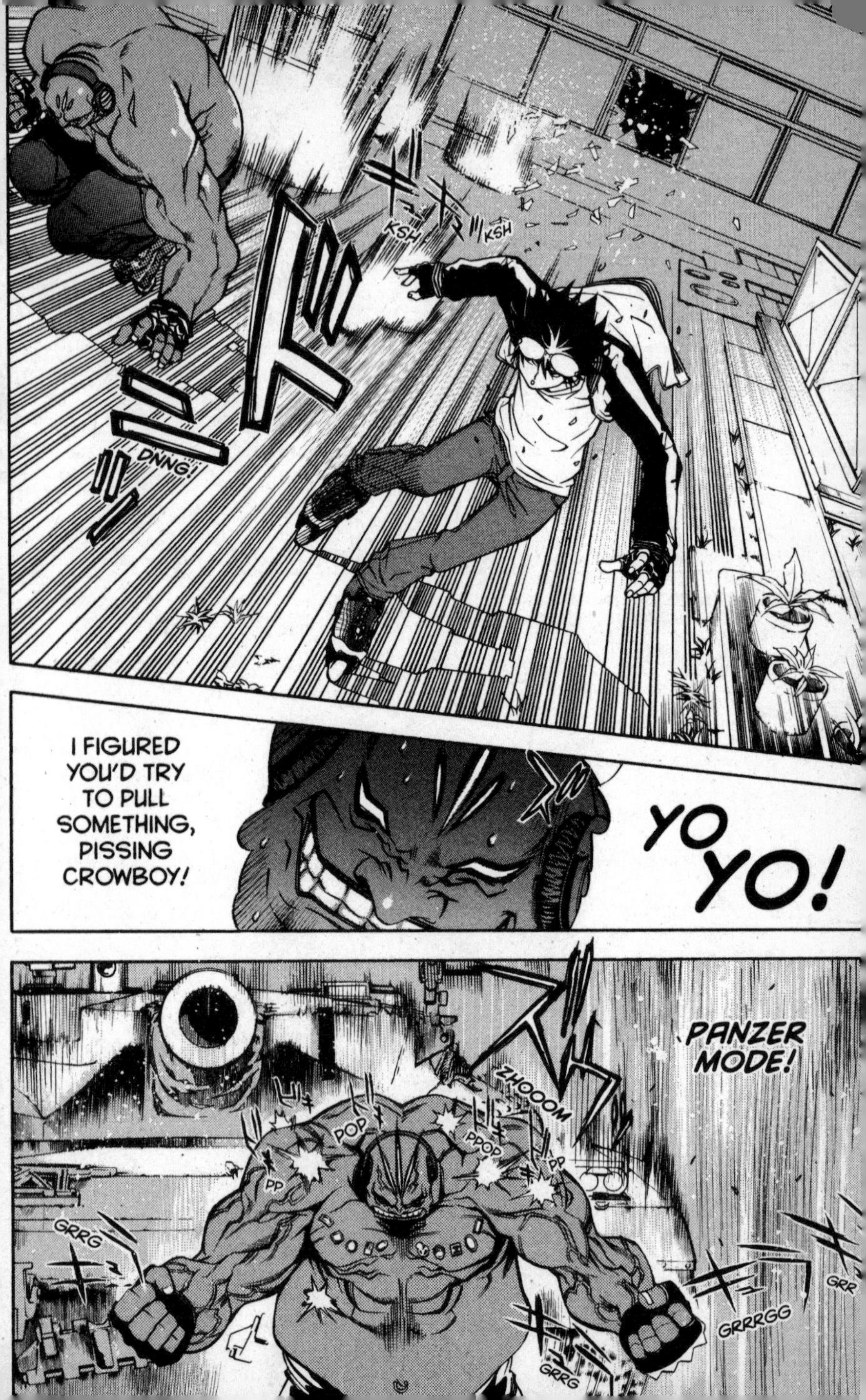
KSH
KSH
DNNG!
YO YO!
I FIGURED YOU'D TRY TO PULL SOMETHING, PISSING CROWBOY!
PANZER MODE!
ZHOOOOM
POP
PPOP
PP
PP
GRRG
GRR
GRRRGG
GRRG

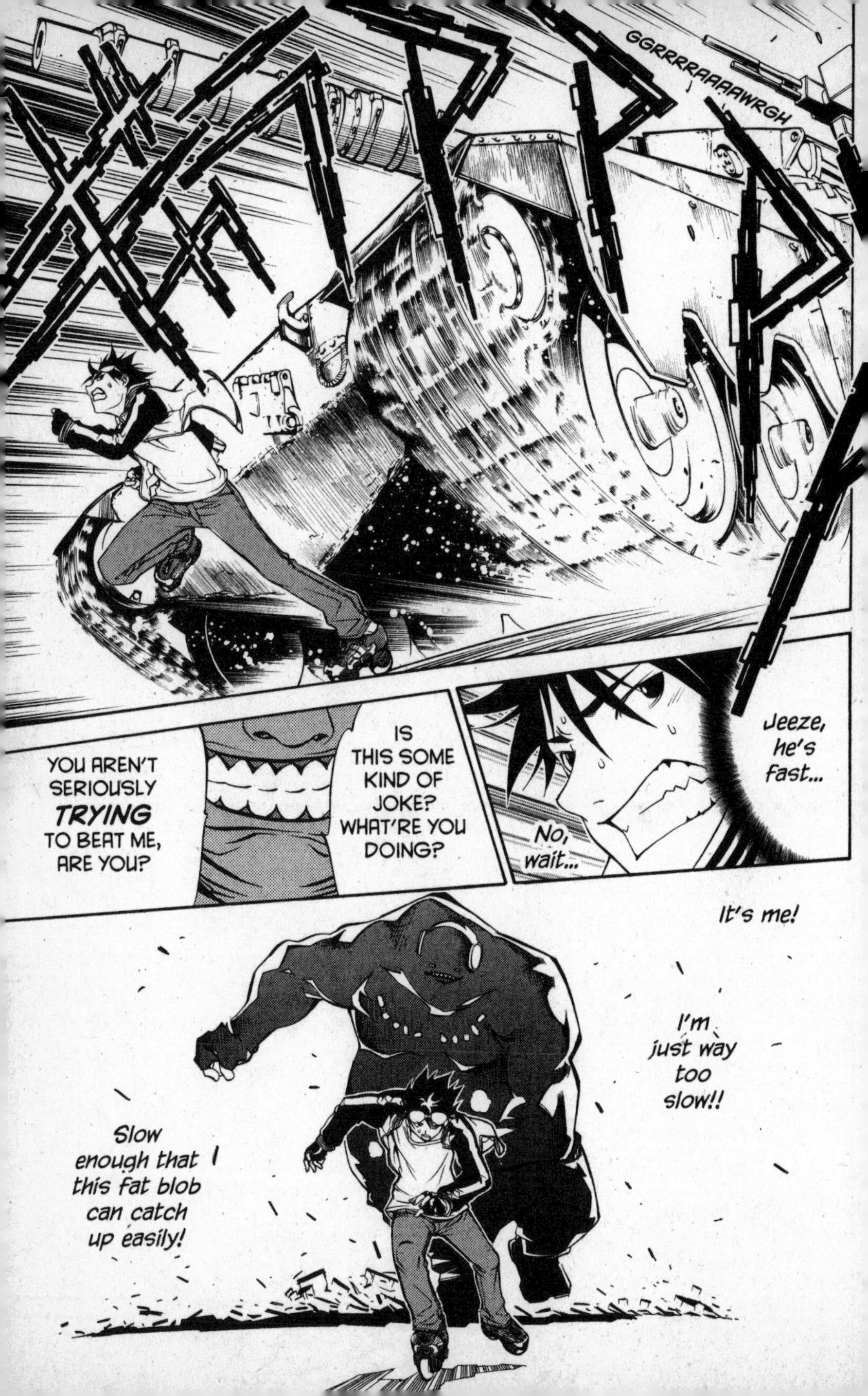
GGRRRRAAAAAWRGH
Jeeze, he's fast...
No, wait...
IS THIS SOME KIND OF JOKE? WHAT'RE YOU DOING?
YOU AREN'T SERIOUSLY *TRYING* TO BEAT ME, ARE YOU?
It's me!
I'm just way too slow!!
Slow enough that this fat blob can catch up easily!

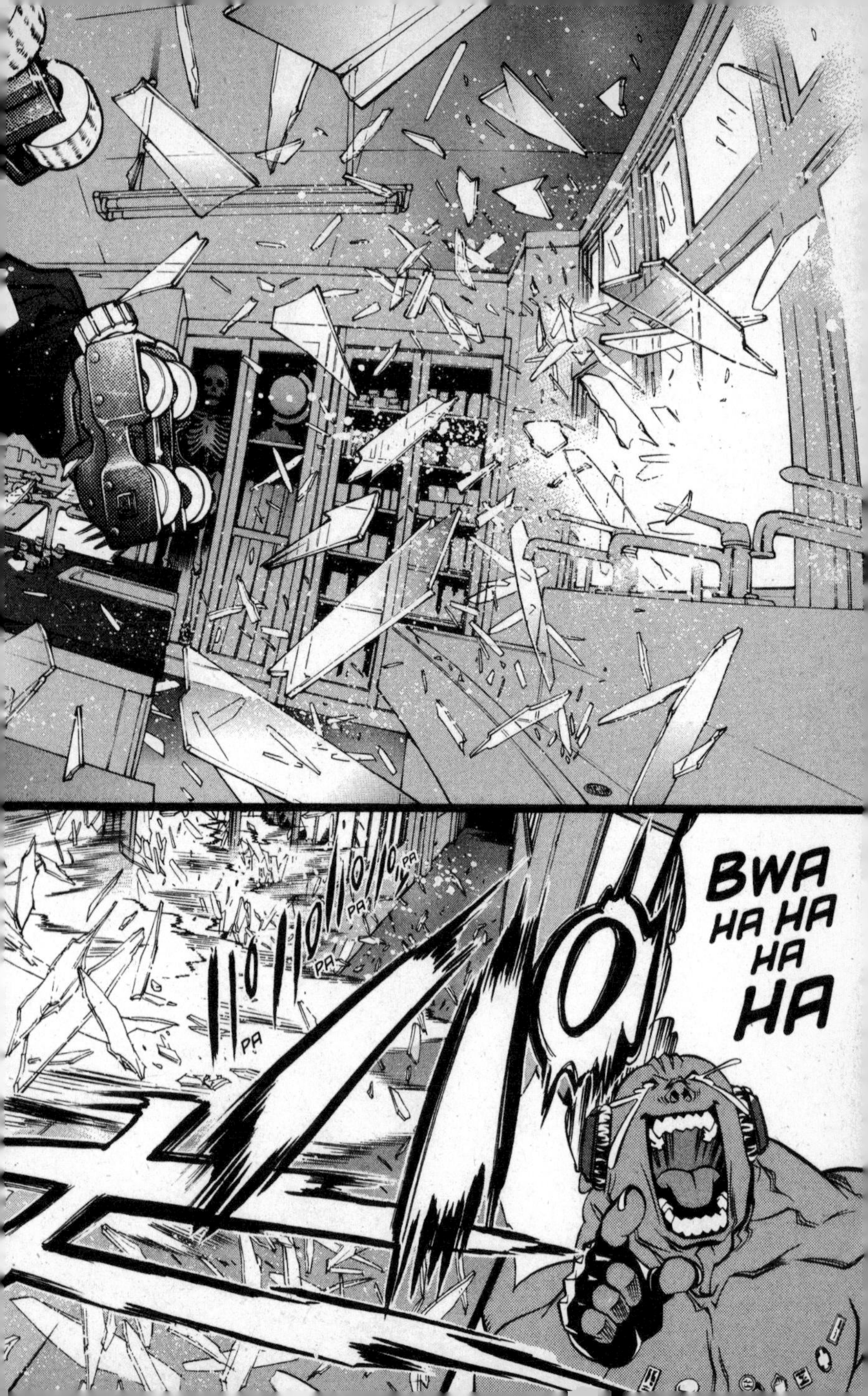
BWA HA HA HA HA
PA
PA
PA
PA

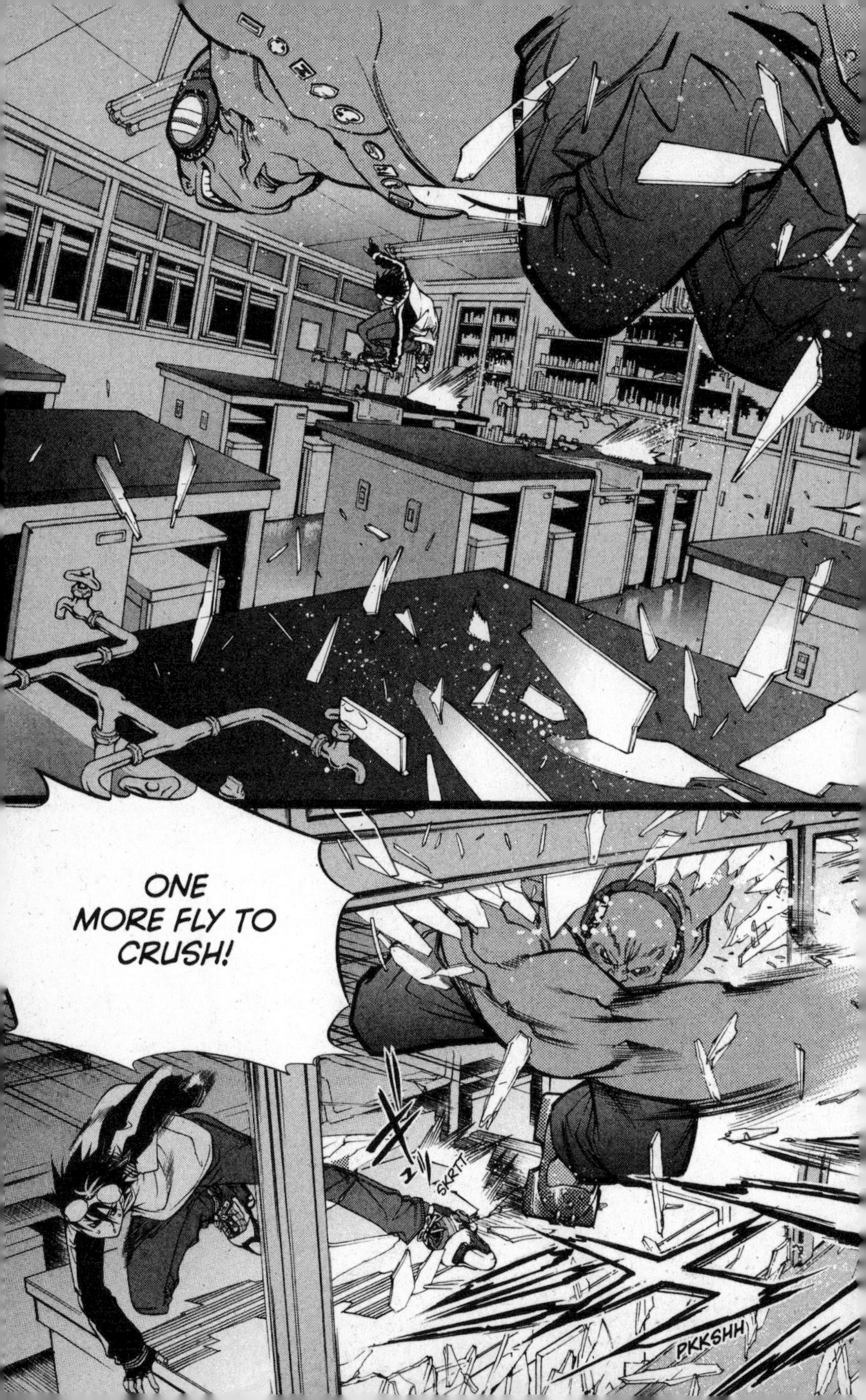
ONE MORE FLY TO CRUSH!
SKRT-T
PKKSHH

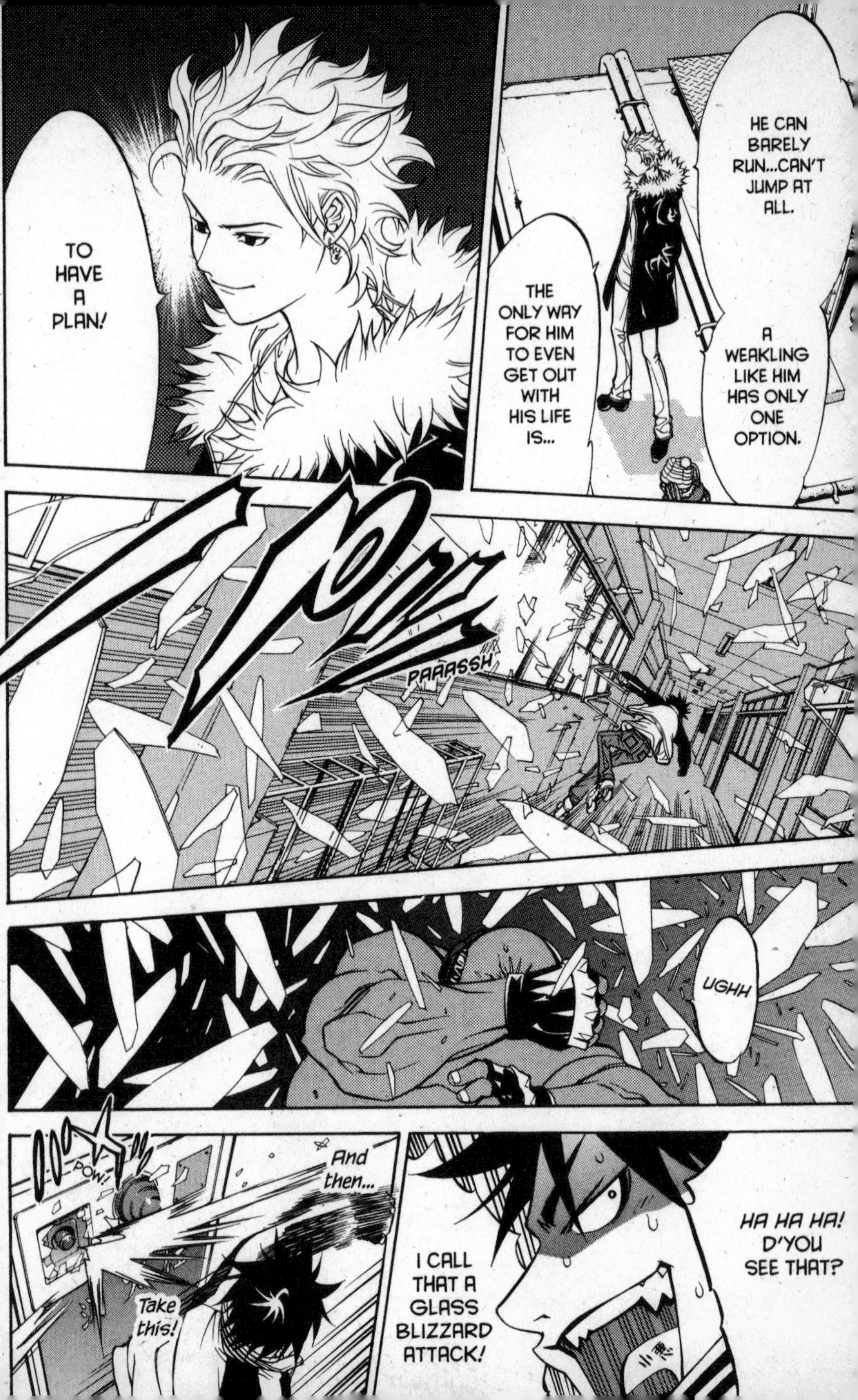
HE CAN BARELY RUN...CAN'T JUMP AT ALL.
A WEAKLING LIKE HIM HAS ONLY ONE OPTION.
THE ONLY WAY FOR HIM TO EVEN GET OUT WITH HIS LIFE IS...
TO HAVE A PLAN!
PAAASSH
UGHH
HA HA HA! D'YOU SEE THAT?
I CALL THAT A GLASS BLIZZARD ATTACK!
And then...
POW!
Take this!

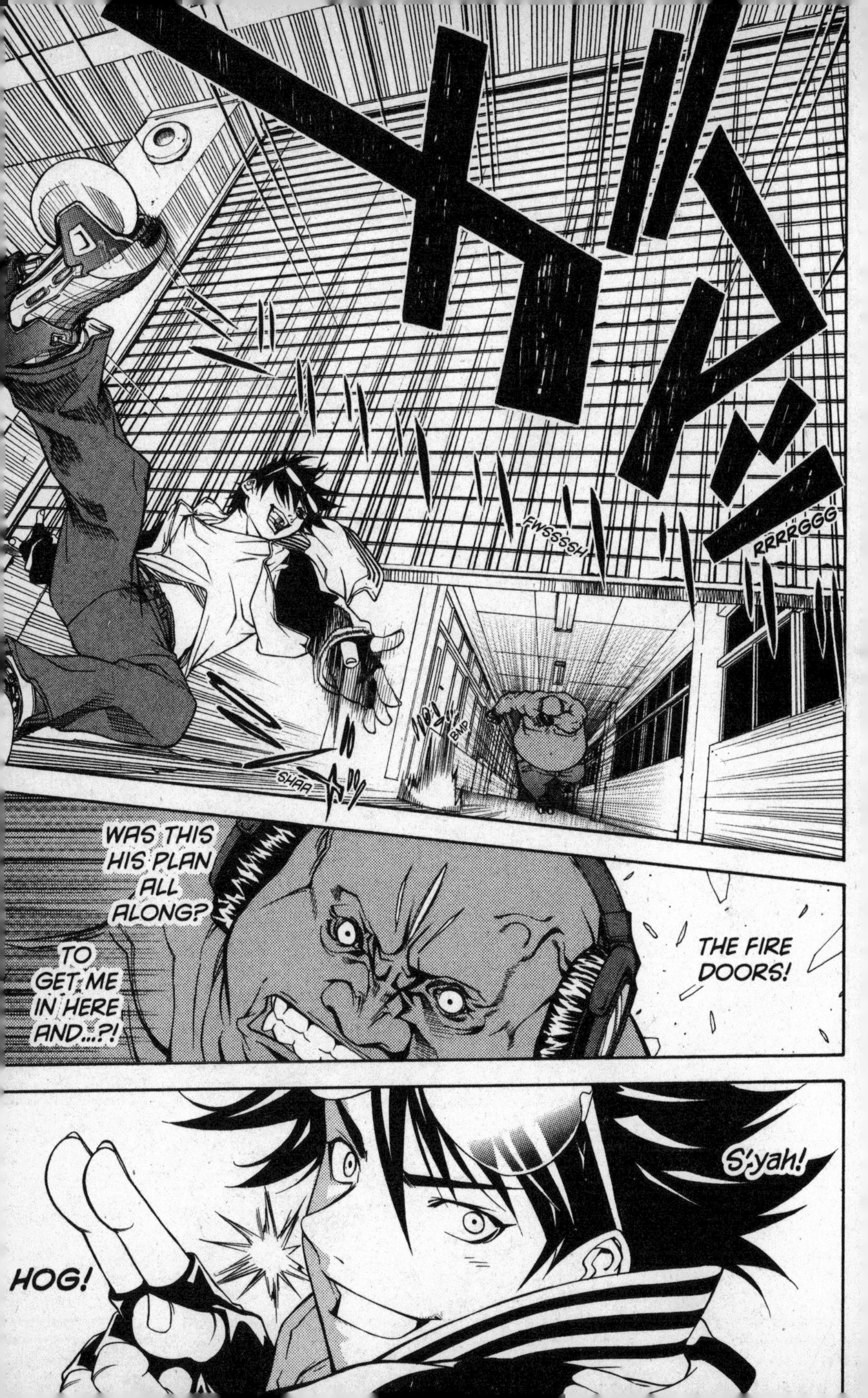
RRRRGGG
FWSSSSH
BMP
SHAA
THE FIRE DOORS!
WAS THIS HIS PLAN ALL ALONG?
TO GET ME IN HERE AND...?!
S'yah!
HOG!

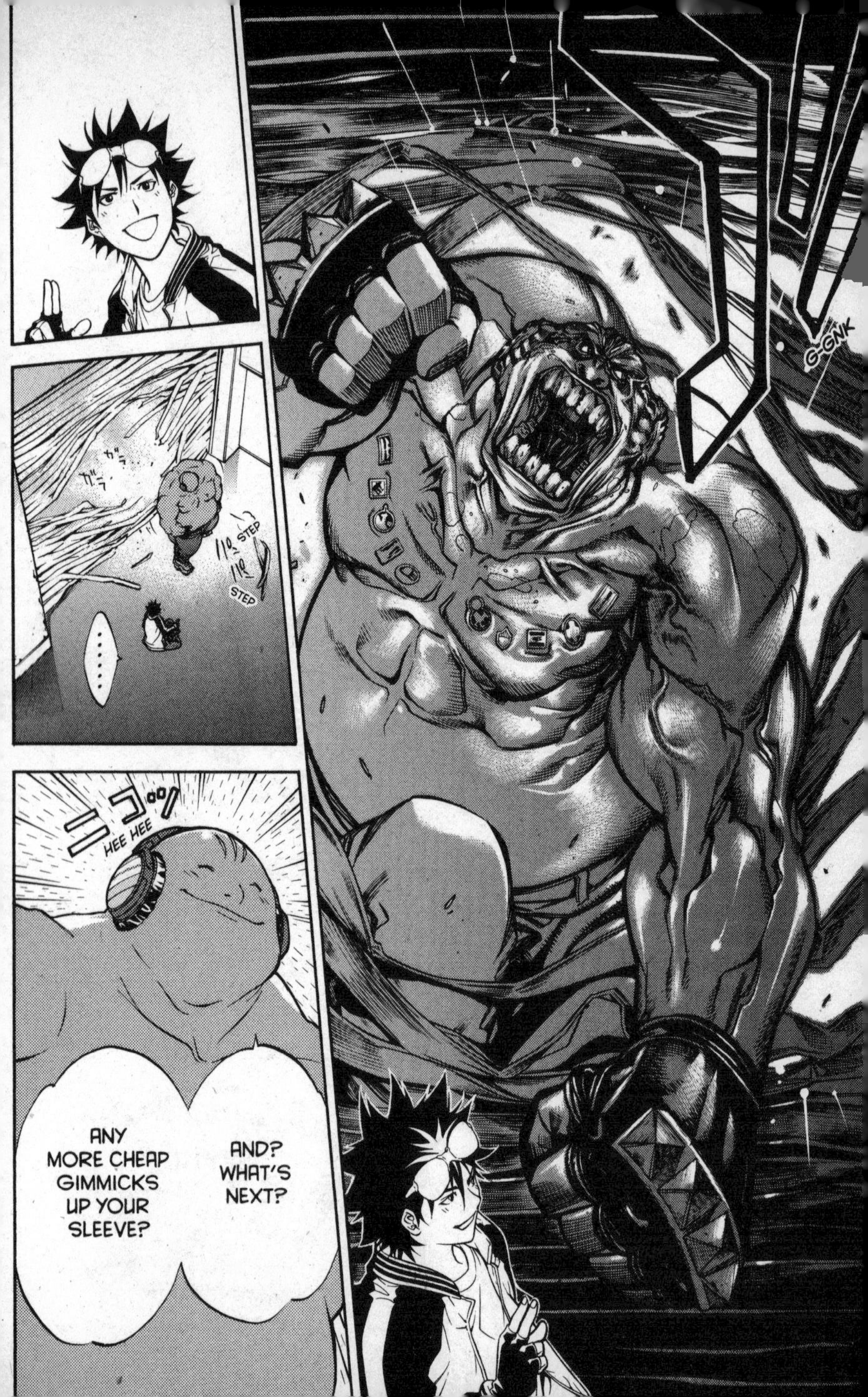
G-GNK
STEP
STEP
……
HEE HEE
AND? WHAT'S NEXT?
ANY MORE CHEAP GIMMICKS UP YOUR SLEEVE?

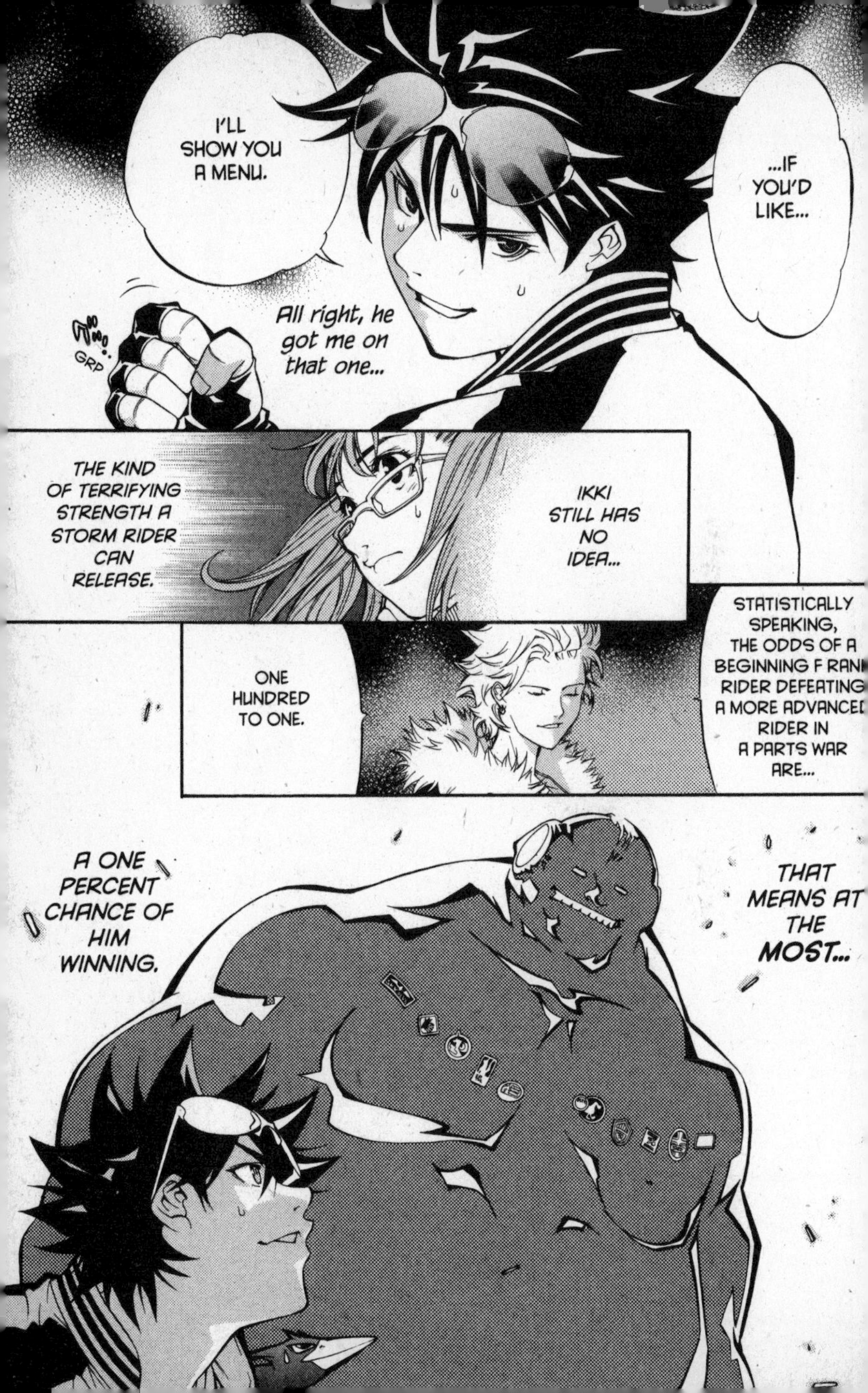
...IF YOU'D LIKE...
I'LL SHOW YOU A MENU.
All right, he got me on that one...
GRP
IKKI STILL HAS NO IDEA...
THE KIND OF TERRIFYING STRENGTH A STORM RIDER CAN RELEASE.
STATISTICALLY SPEAKING, THE ODDS OF A BEGINNING F RANK RIDER DEFEATING A MORE ADVANCED RIDER IN A PARTS WAR ARE...
ONE HUNDRED TO ONE.
THAT MEANS AT THE MOST...
A ONE PERCENT CHANCE OF HIM WINNING.

BACKSPIN WALL RIDE THREE SIXTY TO GRAB FAKE...
SPIN ACCELERATOR BUCCHA SPECIAL ONE THOUSAND FOUR HUNDR--
OUCH! BIT MY TONGUE!!
....

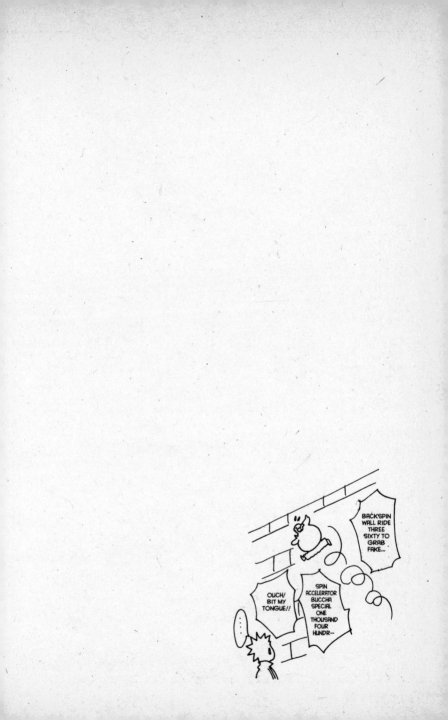

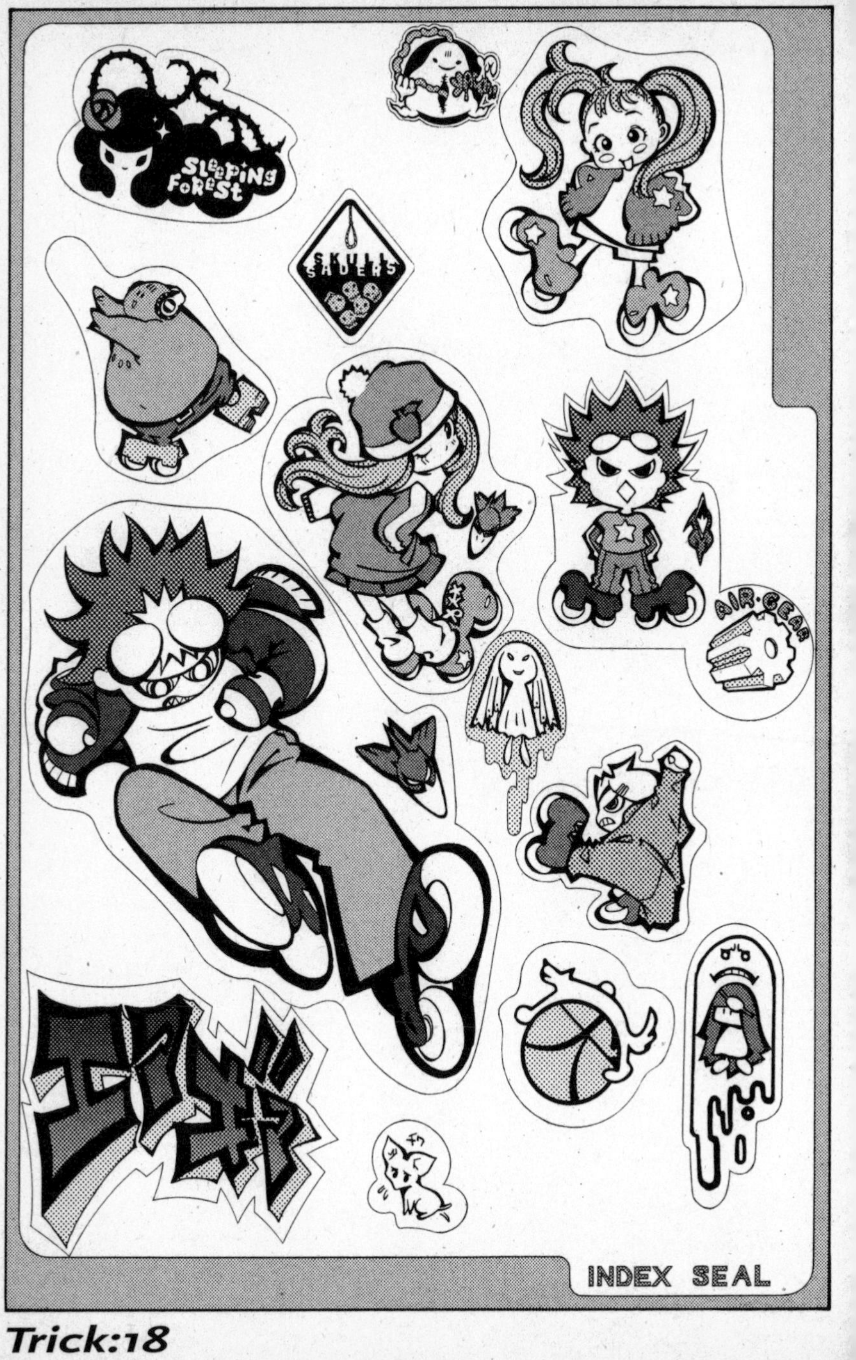
SLEEPING FOREST
SKULL SADERS
AIR·GEAR
INDEX SEAL

Trick:18

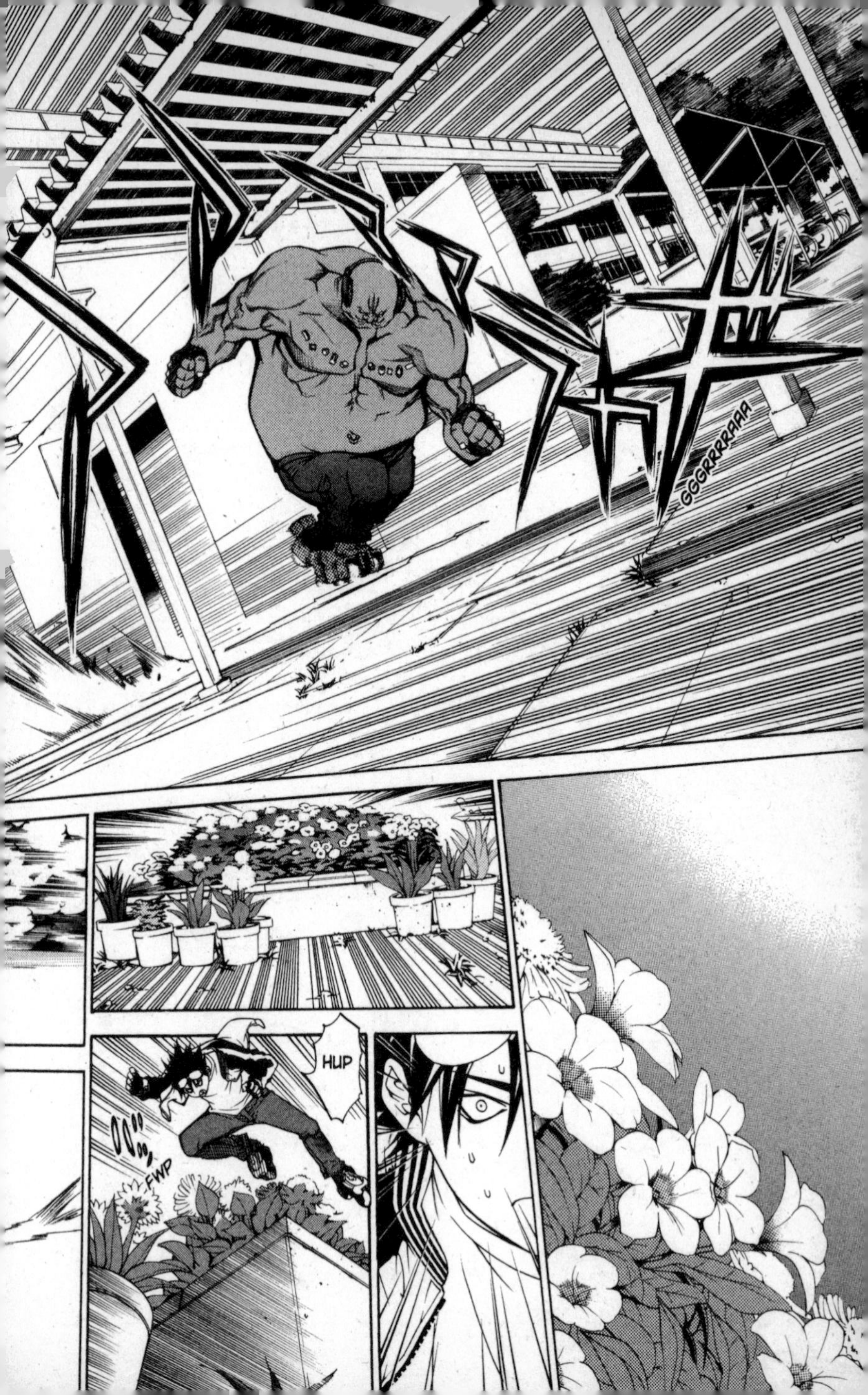
GGGRRRRAAA
HUP
FWP

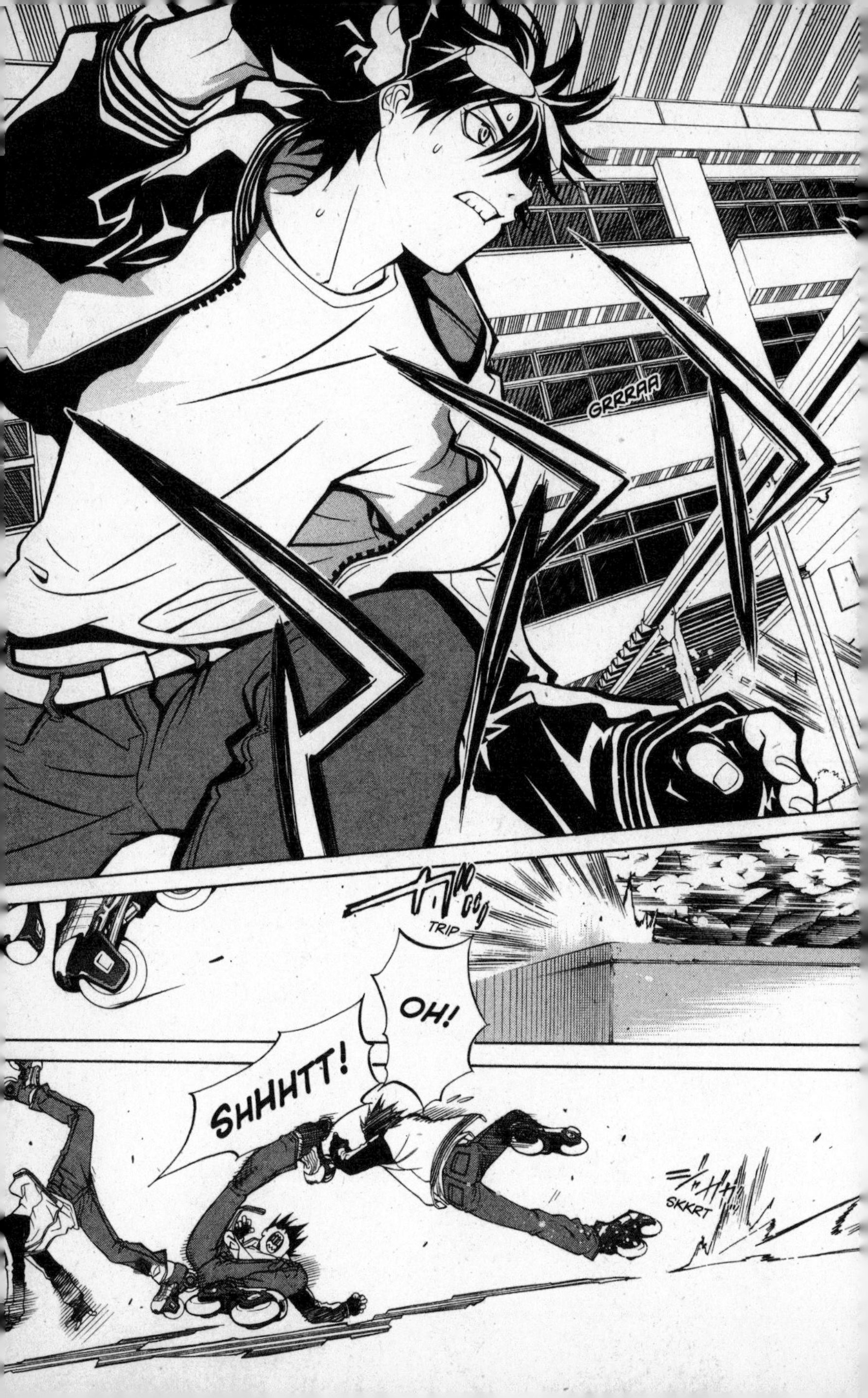
GRRRAA
TRIP
OH!
SHHHTT!
SKKRT

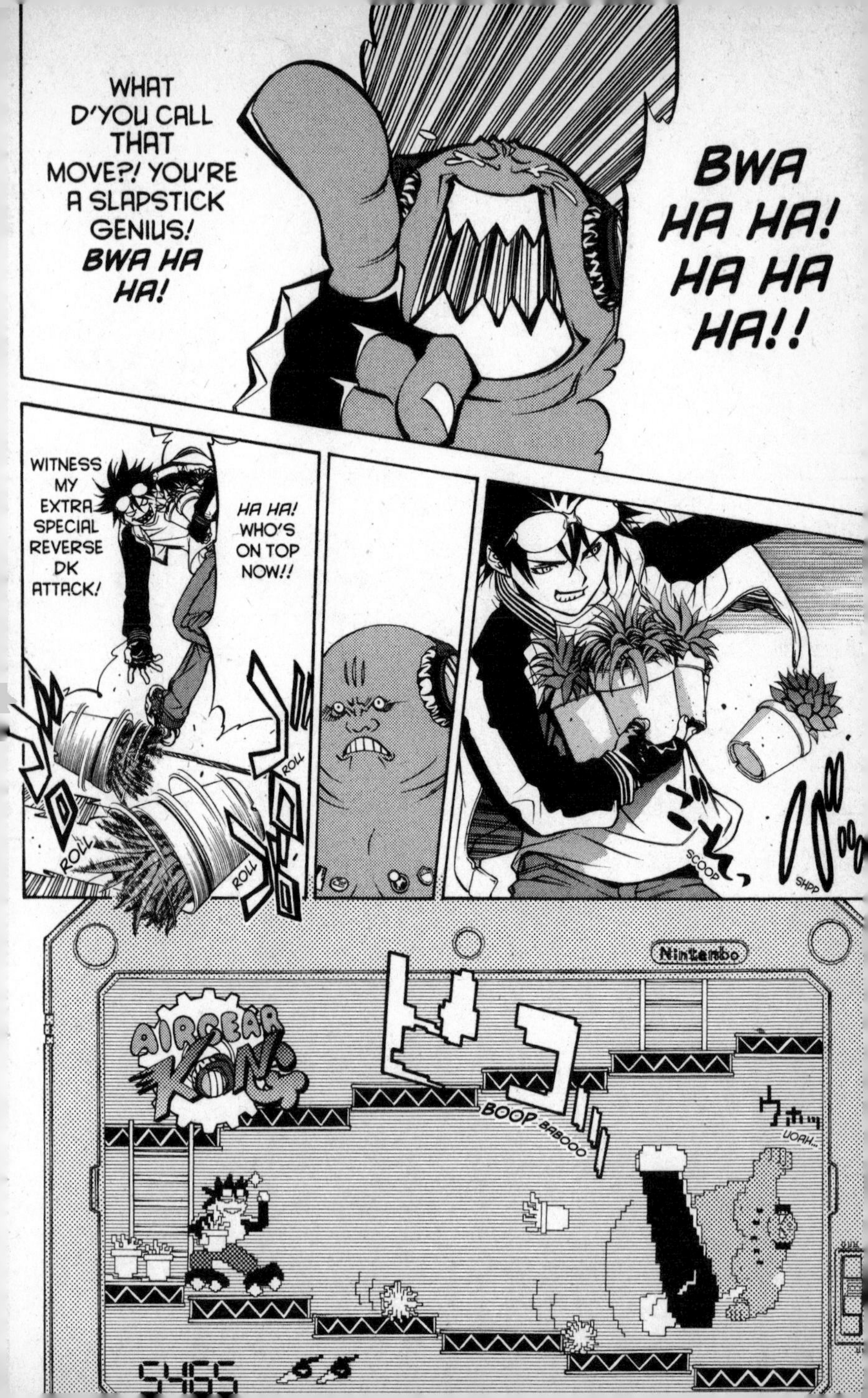
BWA HA HA! HA HA HA!!
WHAT D'YOU CALL THAT MOVE?! YOU'RE A SLAPSTICK GENIUS! BWA HA HA!
SCOOP
SHPP
HA HA! WHO'S ON TOP NOW!!
WITNESS MY EXTRA SPECIAL REVERSE DK ATTACK!
ROLL
ROLL
ROLL
Nintenbo
BOOP BABOOO
UOAH...
AIRGEAR KONG
5465

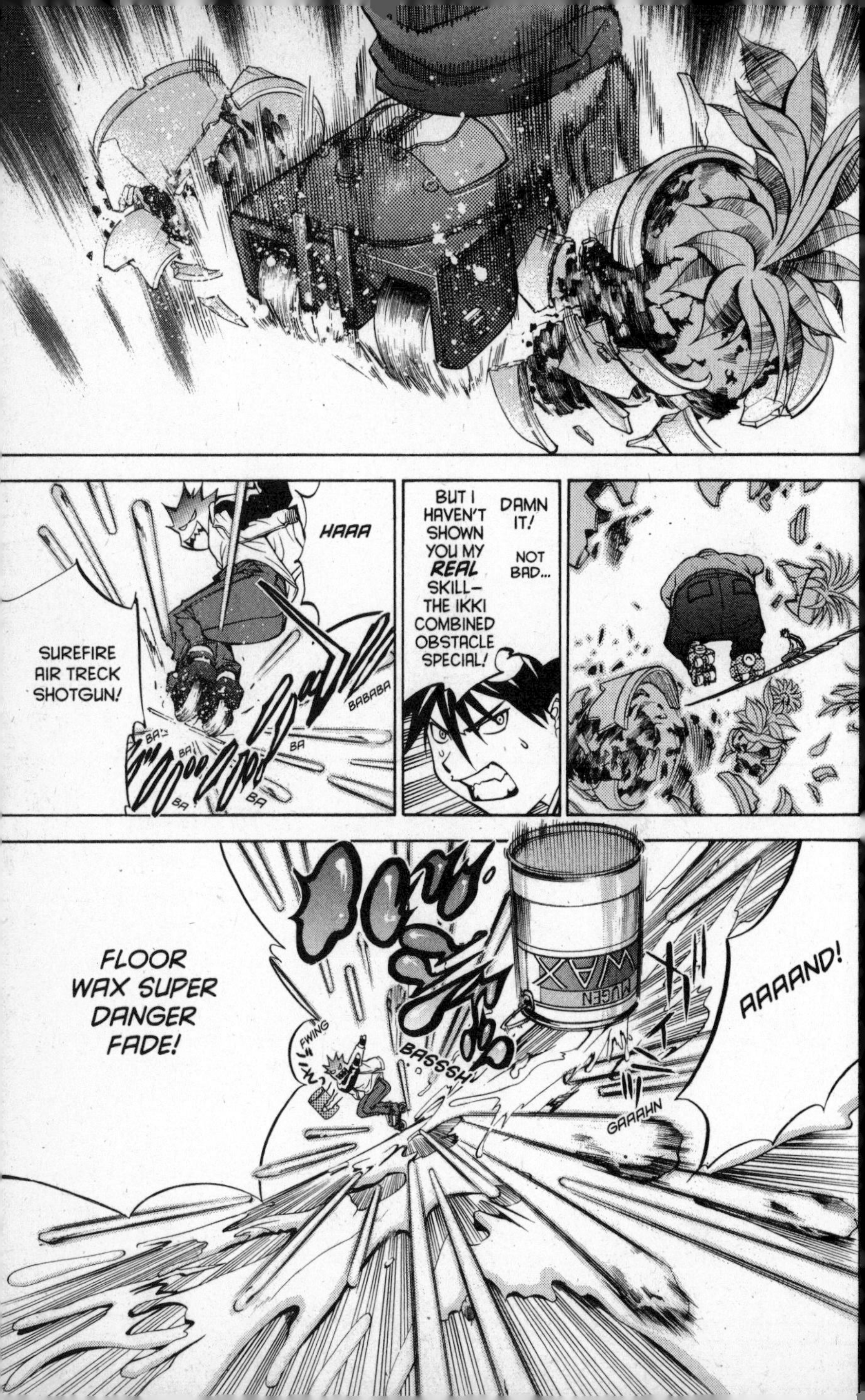
DAMN IT!
NOT BAD...
BUT I HAVEN'T SHOWN YOU MY REAL SKILL— THE IKKI COMBINED OBSTACLE SPECIAL!
HAAA
SUREFIRE AIR TRECK SHOTGUN!
BABABA
BA
BA
BA
BA
BA
AAAAND!
WAX
MUGEN
BASSSH
FWING
GAAAHN
FLOOR WAX SUPER DANGER FADE!

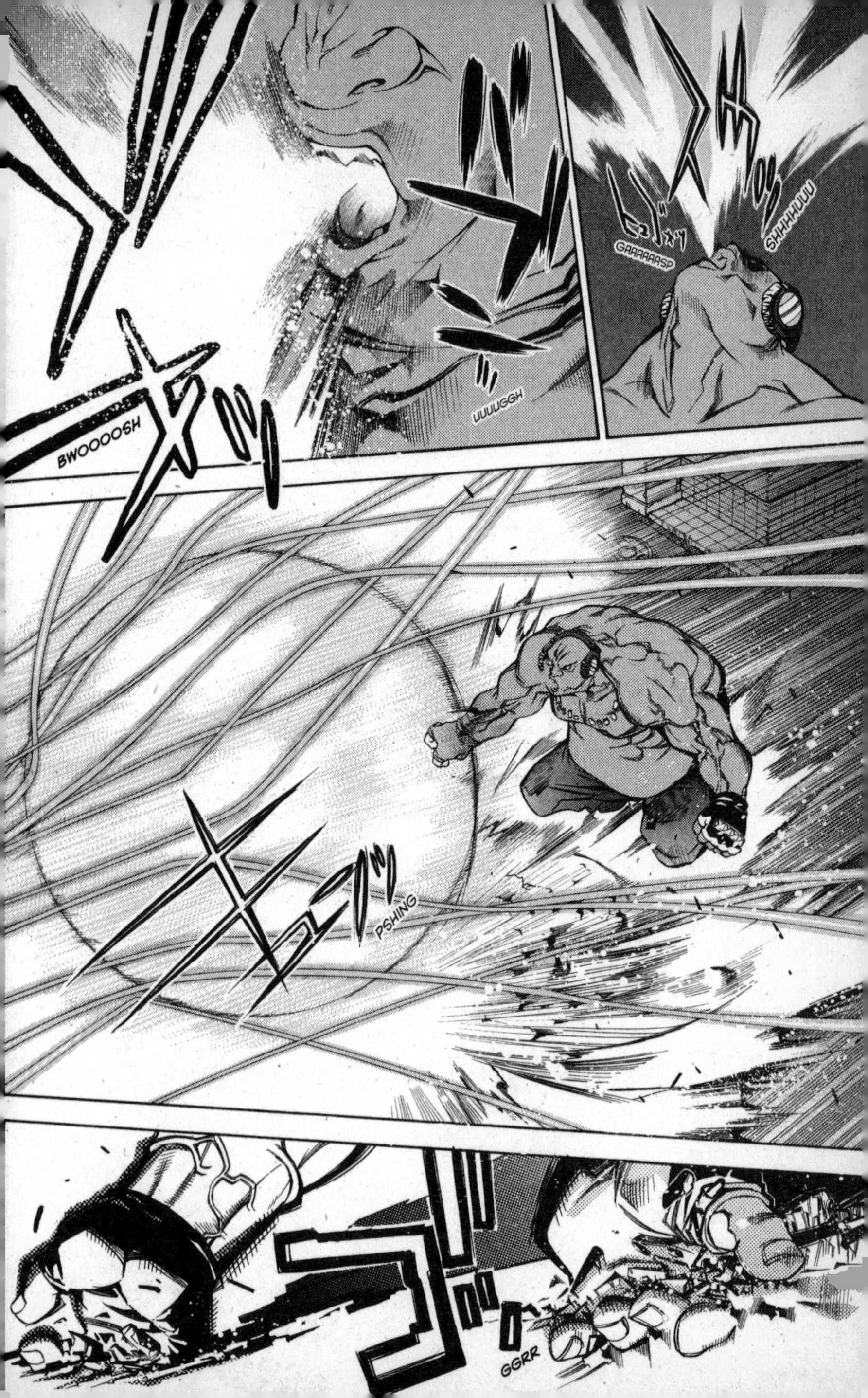
SHHHHUUU
GAAAAAASP
UUUUGGH
BWOOOOSH
PSHING
GGRR

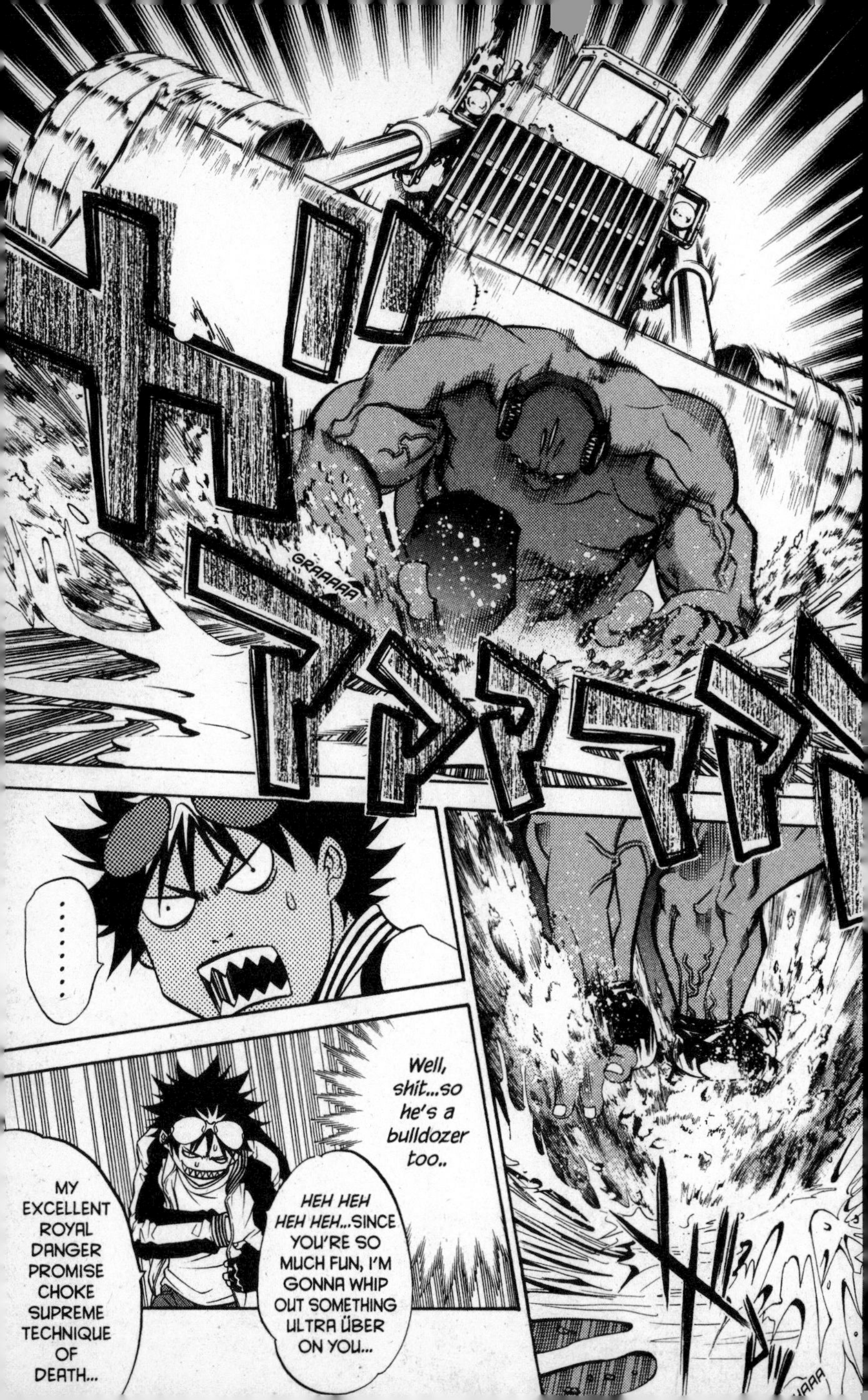
GRAAAAA
......
Well, shit...so he's a bulldozer too..
HEH HEH HEH HEH...SINCE YOU'RE SO MUCH FUN, I'M GONNA WHIP OUT SOMETHING ULTRA ÜBER ON YOU...
MY EXCELLENT ROYAL DANGER PROMISE CHOKE SUPREME TECHNIQUE OF DEATH...

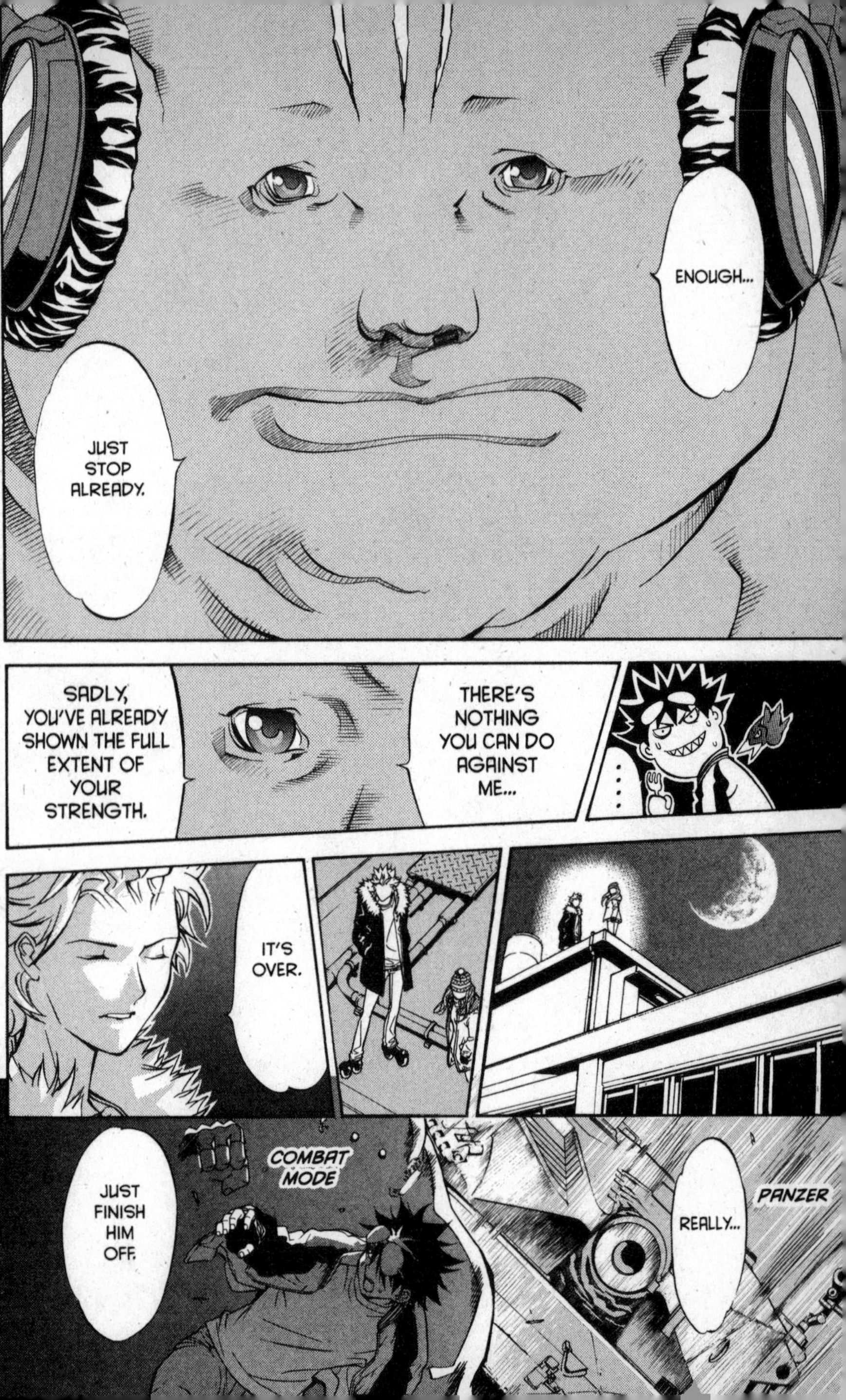
ENOUGH...
JUST STOP ALREADY.
....
THERE'S NOTHING YOU CAN DO AGAINST ME...
SADLY, YOU'VE ALREADY SHOWN THE FULL EXTENT OF YOUR STRENGTH.
IT'S OVER.
PANZER
REALLY...
COMBAT MODE
JUST FINISH HIM OFF.

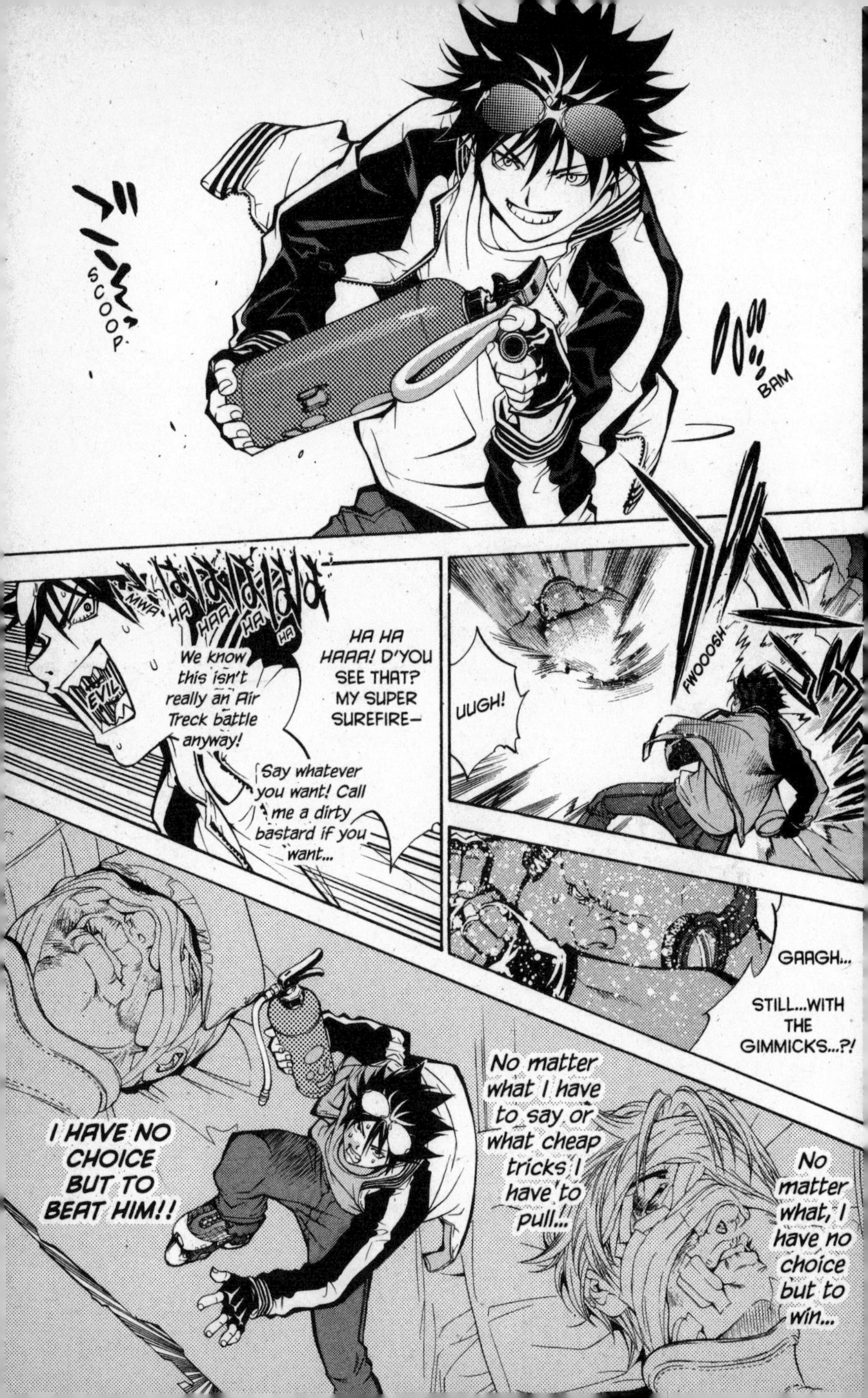
BAM
SCOOOP
FWOOOSH
UUGH!
MWA HA HAA HA HA
HA HA HAAA! D'YOU SEE THAT? MY SUPER SUREFIRE—
We know this isn't really an Air Treck battle anyway!
EVIL
Say whatever you want! Call me a dirty bastard if you want...
GAAGH...
STILL...WITH THE GIMMICKS...?!
No matter what, I have no choice but to win...
No matter what I have to say or what cheap tricks I have to pull...
I HAVE NO CHOICE BUT TO BEAT HIM!!

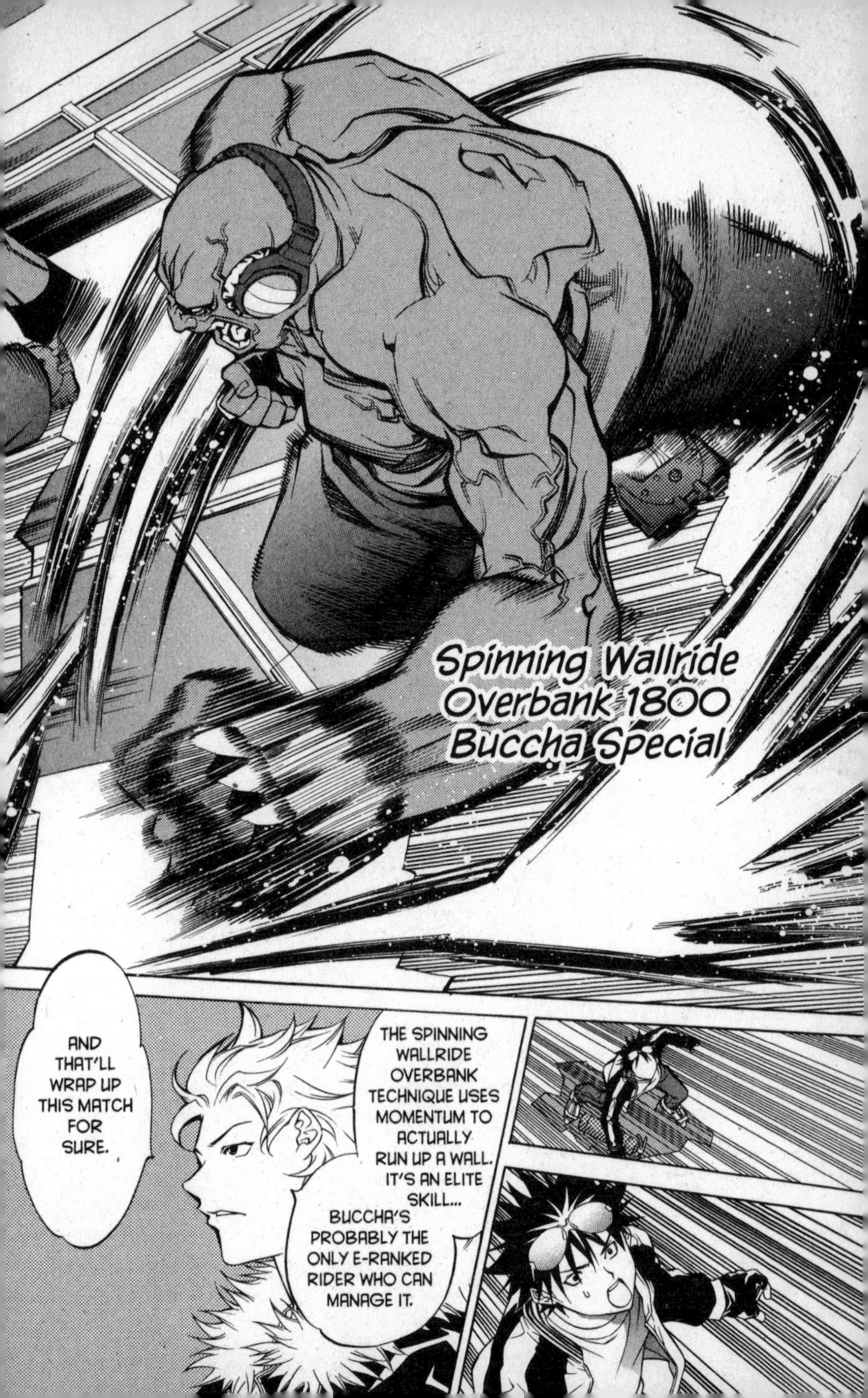
Spinning Wallride Overbank 1800 Buccha Special
THE SPINNING WALLRIDE OVERBANK TECHNIQUE USES MOMENTUM TO ACTUALLY RUN UP A WALL. IT'S AN ELITE SKILL...
BUCCHA'S PROBABLY THE ONLY E-RANKED RIDER WHO CAN MANAGE IT.
AND THAT'LL WRAP UP THIS MATCH FOR SURE.

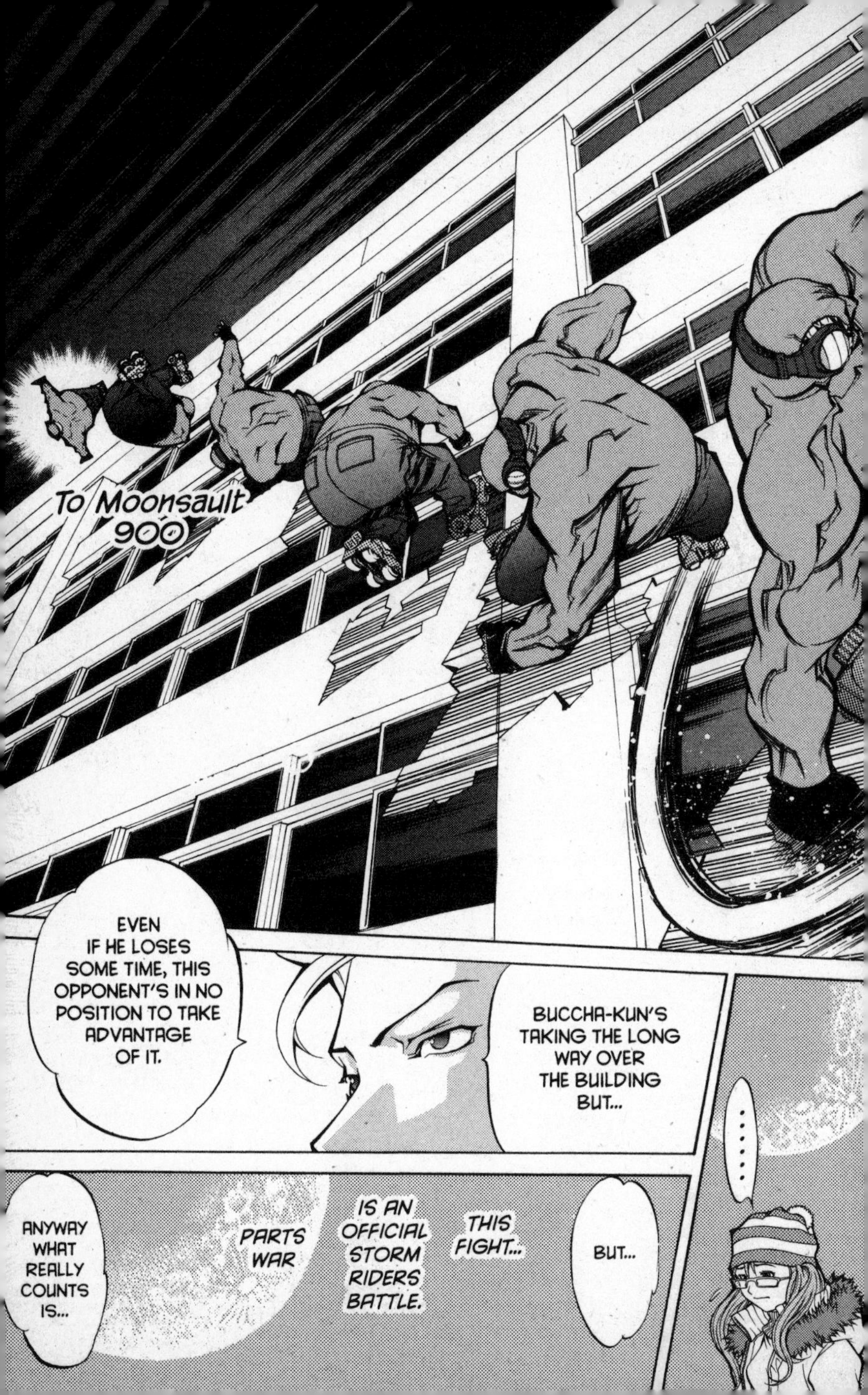
To Moonsault 900
.....
BUCCHA-KUN'S TAKING THE LONG WAY OVER THE BUILDING BUT...
EVEN IF HE LOSES SOME TIME, THIS OPPONENT'S IN NO POSITION TO TAKE ADVANTAGE OF IT.
BUT...
THIS FIGHT...
IS AN OFFICIAL STORM RIDERS BATTLE.
PARTS WAR
ANYWAY WHAT REALLY COUNTS IS...

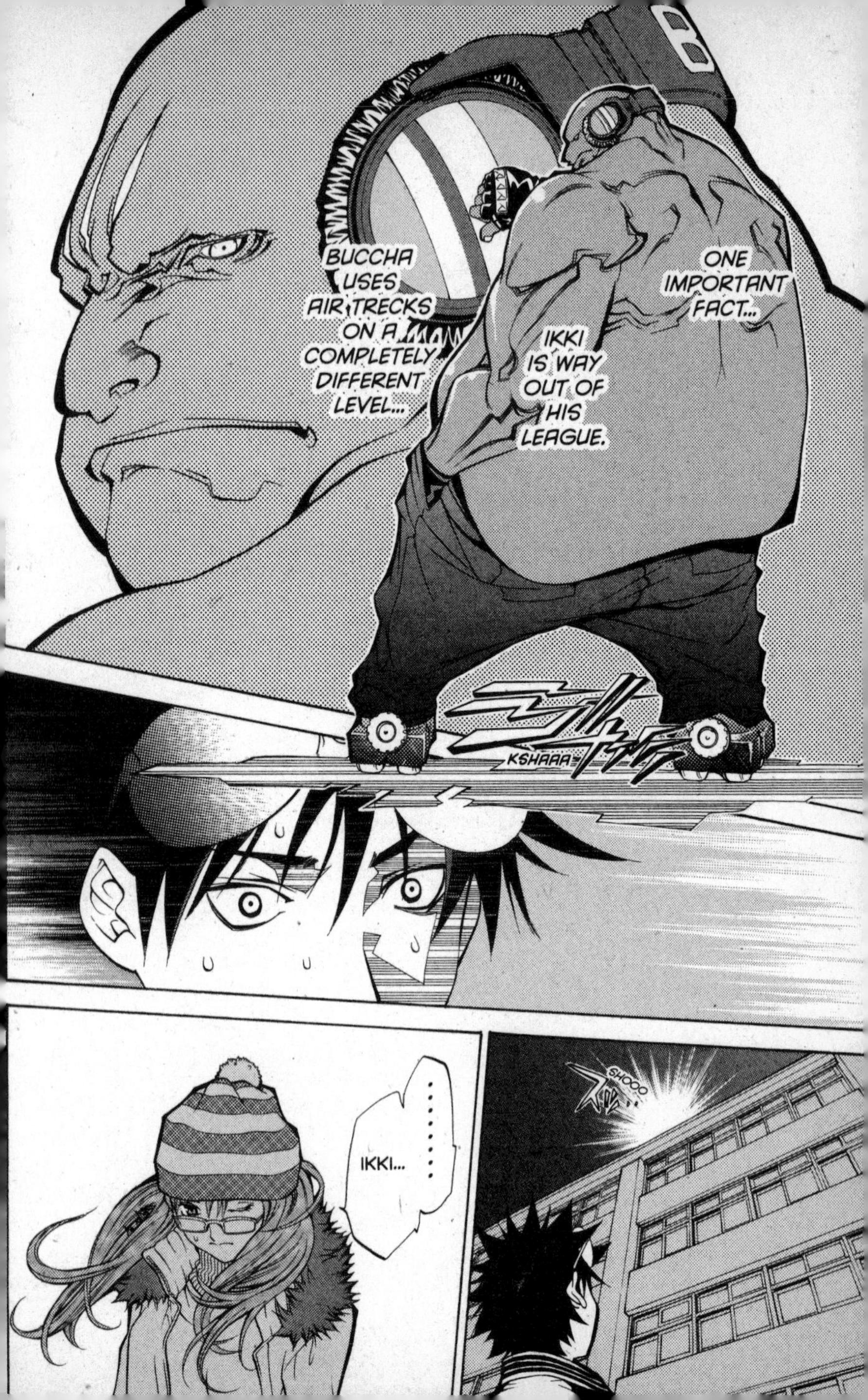
ONE IMPORTANT FACT...
BUCCHA USES AIR TRECKS ON A COMPLETELY DIFFERENT LEVEL...
IKKI IS WAY OUT OF HIS LEAGUE.
KSHAAA
SHOOO
......
IKKI...

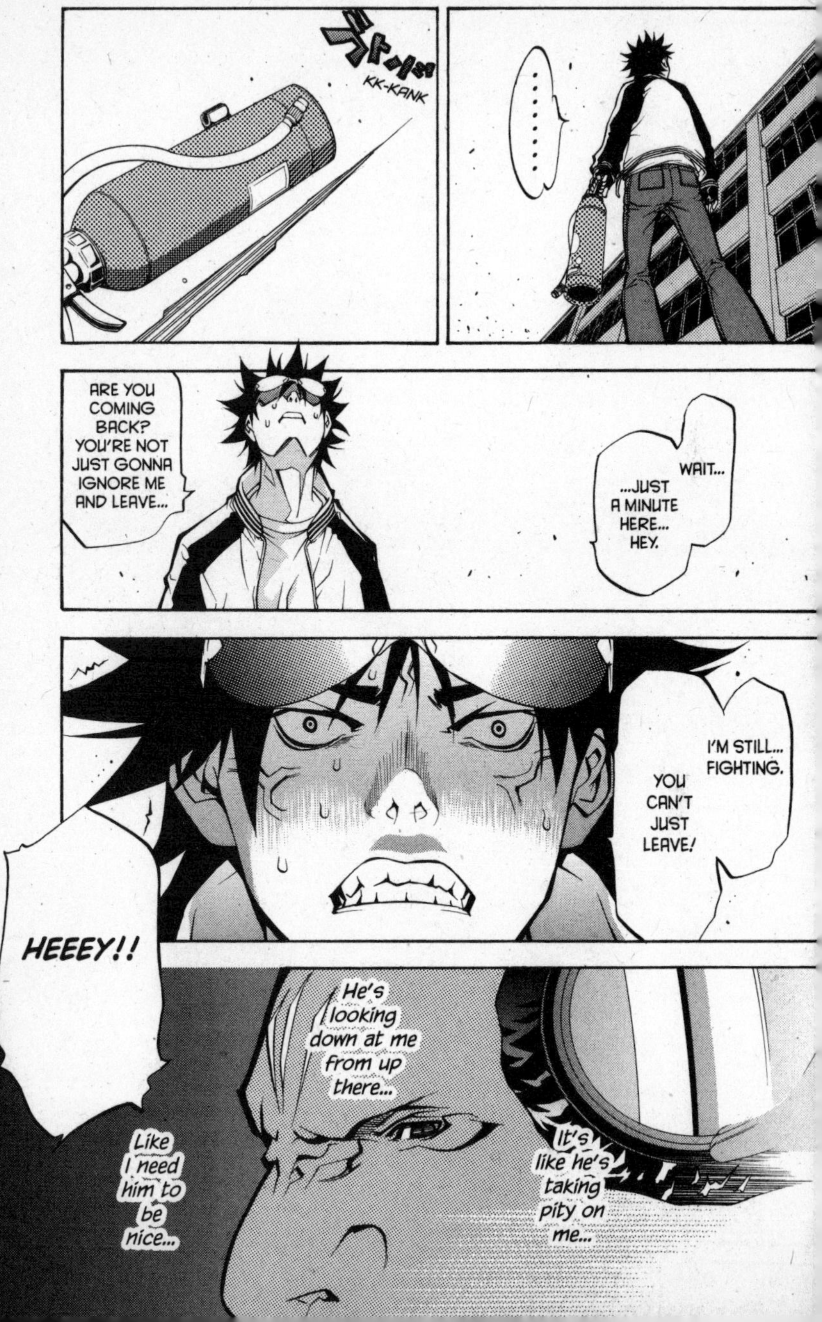
. . . . . .
KK-KANK
WAIT... ...JUST A MINUTE HERE... HEY.
ARE YOU COMING BACK? YOU'RE NOT JUST GONNA IGNORE ME AND LEAVE...
I'M STILL... FIGHTING.
YOU CAN'T JUST LEAVE!
HEEEY!!
He's looking down at me from up there...
It's like he's taking pity on me...
Like I need him to be nice...

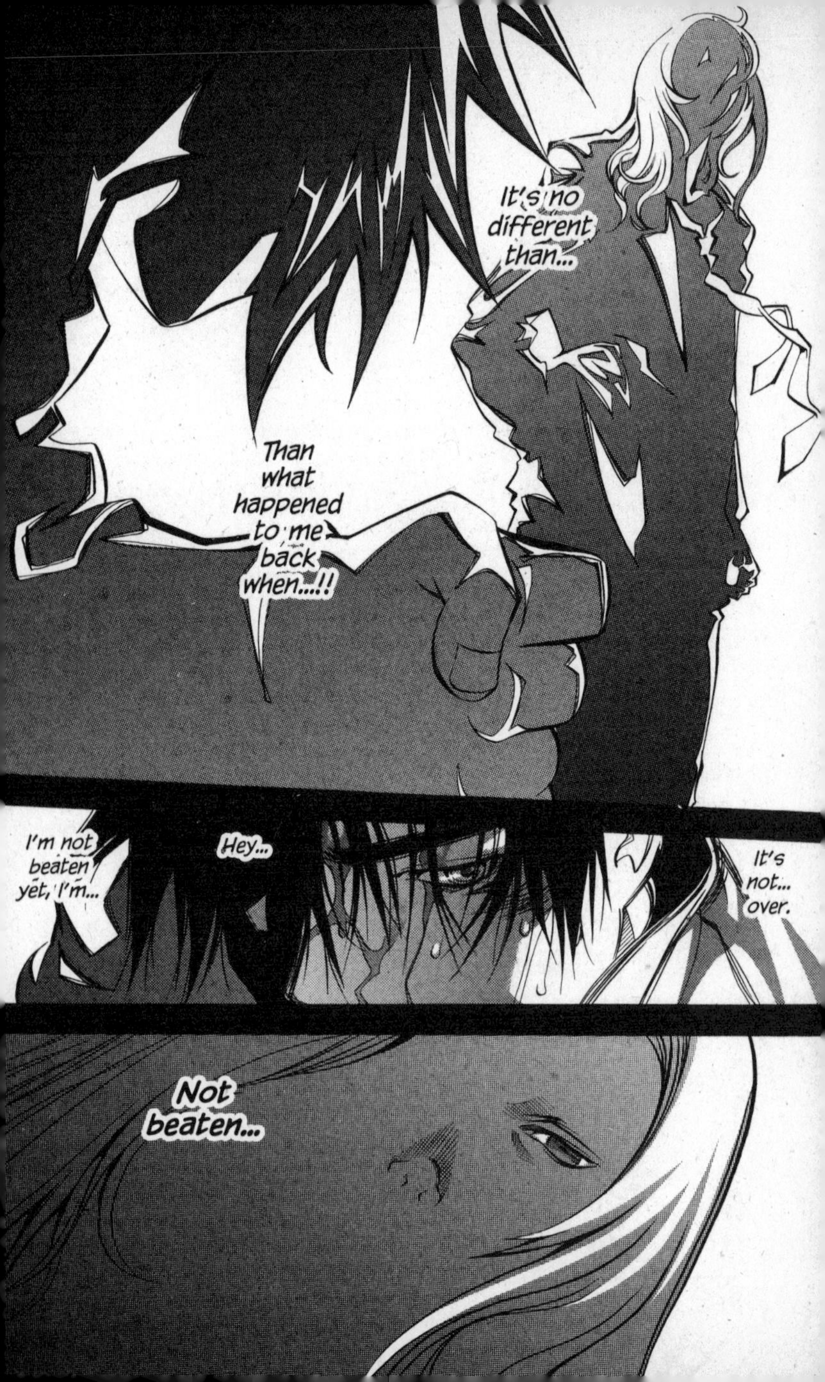
It's no different than...
Than what happened to me back when...!!
It's not... over.
Hey...
I'm not beaten yet, I'm...
Not beaten...

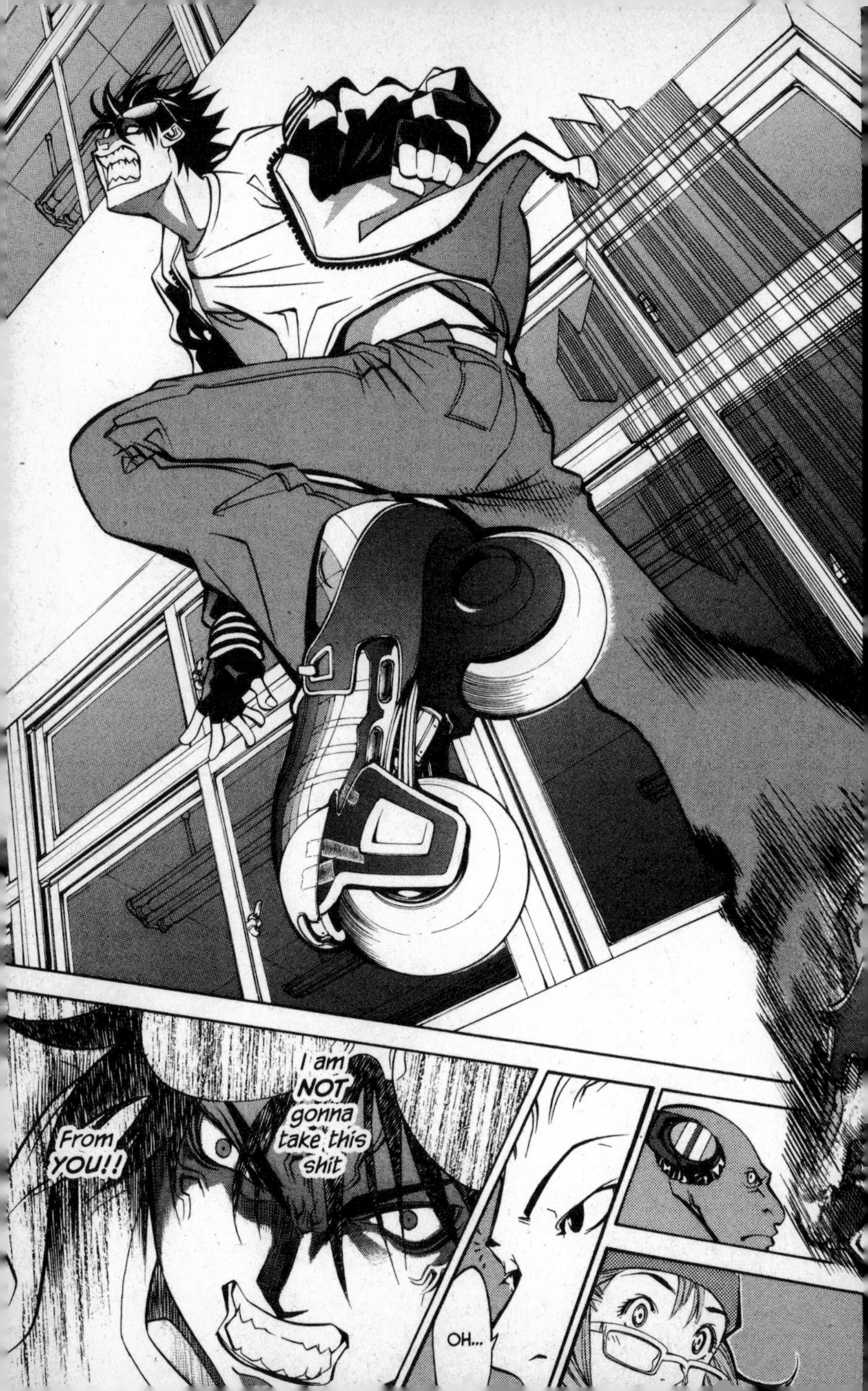
OH...
I am NOT gonna take this shit
From YOU!!

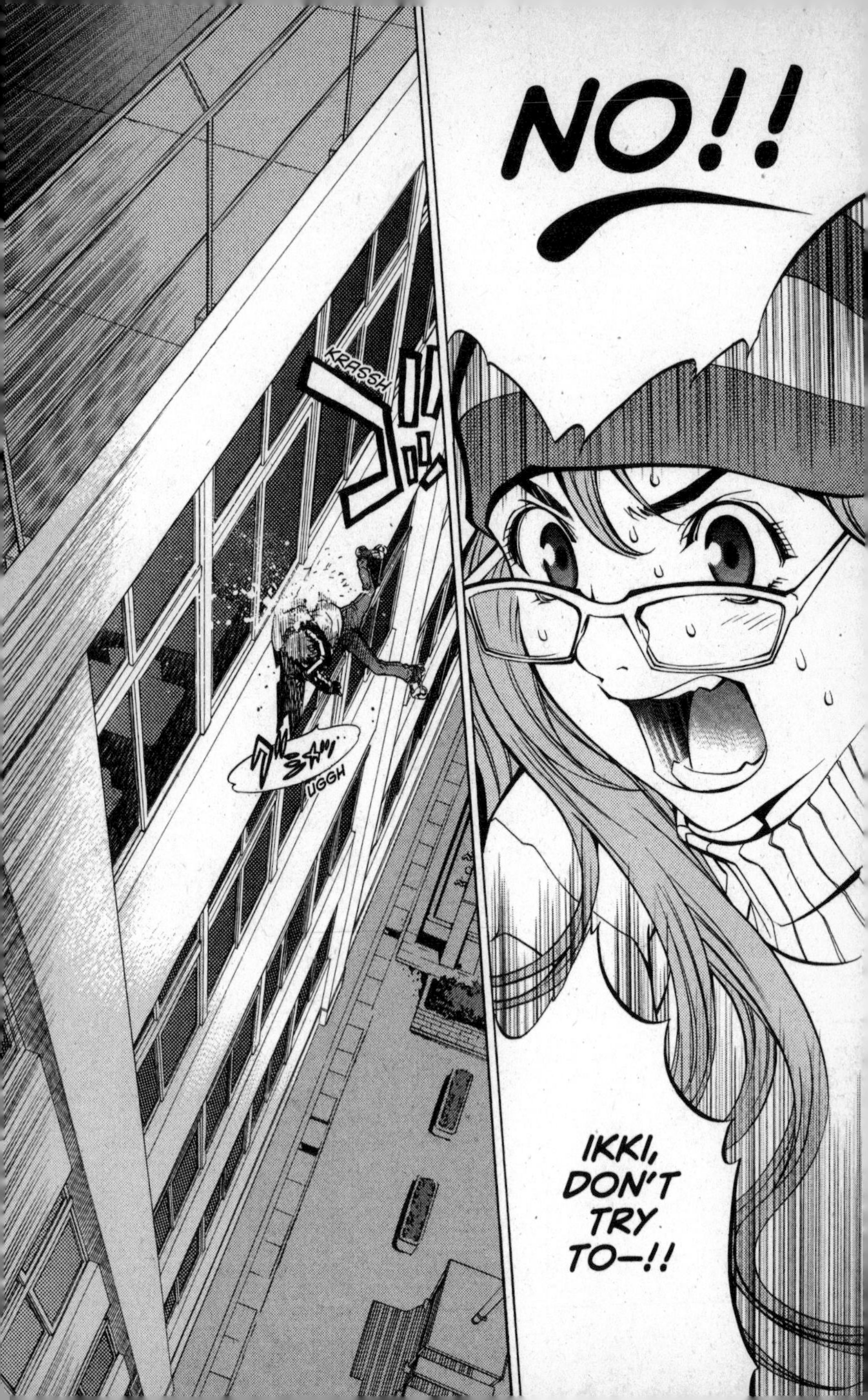
NO!!
IKKI, DON'T TRY TO–!!
KRASSH
UGGH

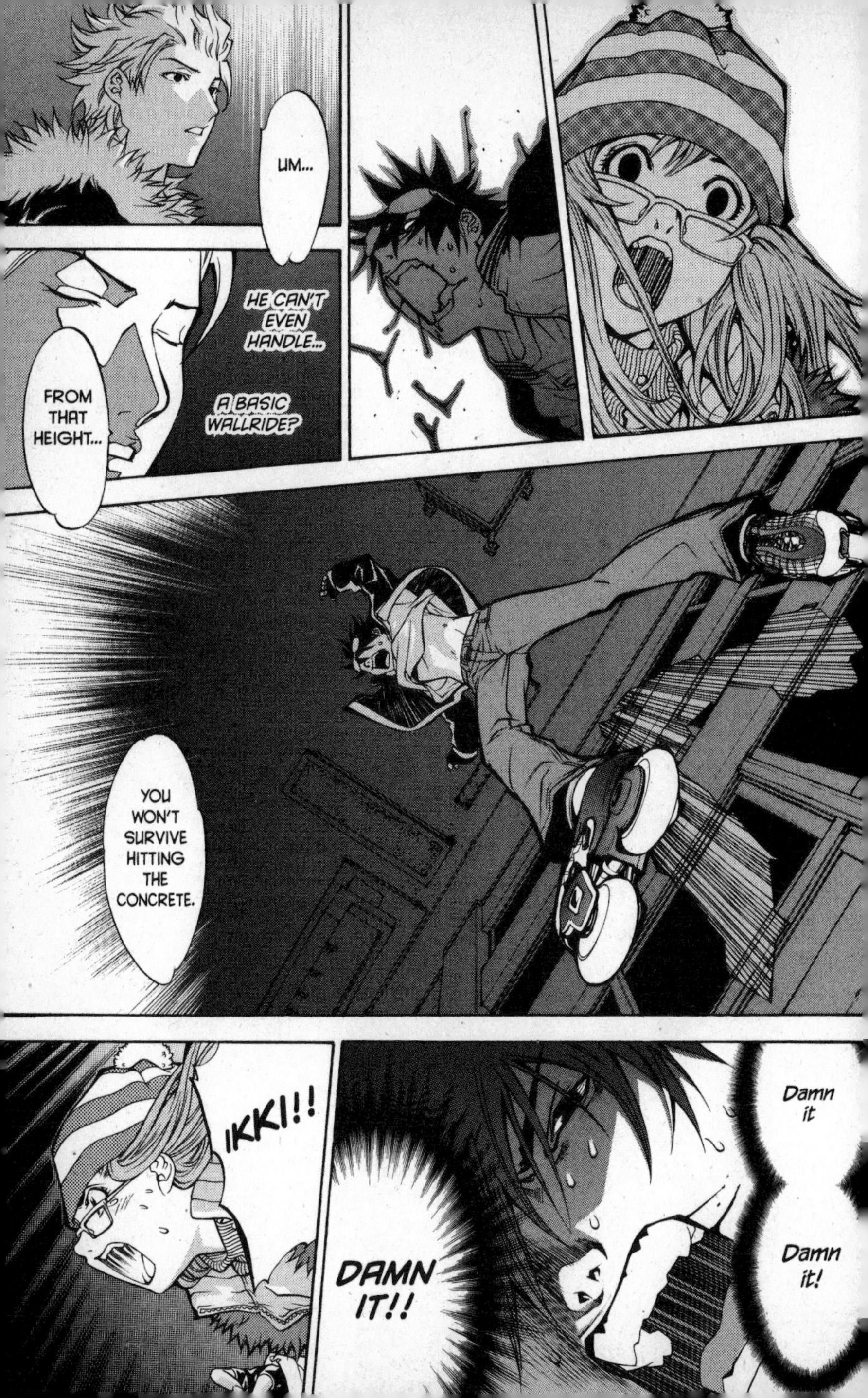
UM...
HE CAN'T EVEN HANDLE...
A BASIC WALLRIDE?
FROM THAT HEIGHT...
YOU WON'T SURVIVE HITTING THE CONCRETE.
Damn it
Damn it!
DAMN IT!!
IKKI!!

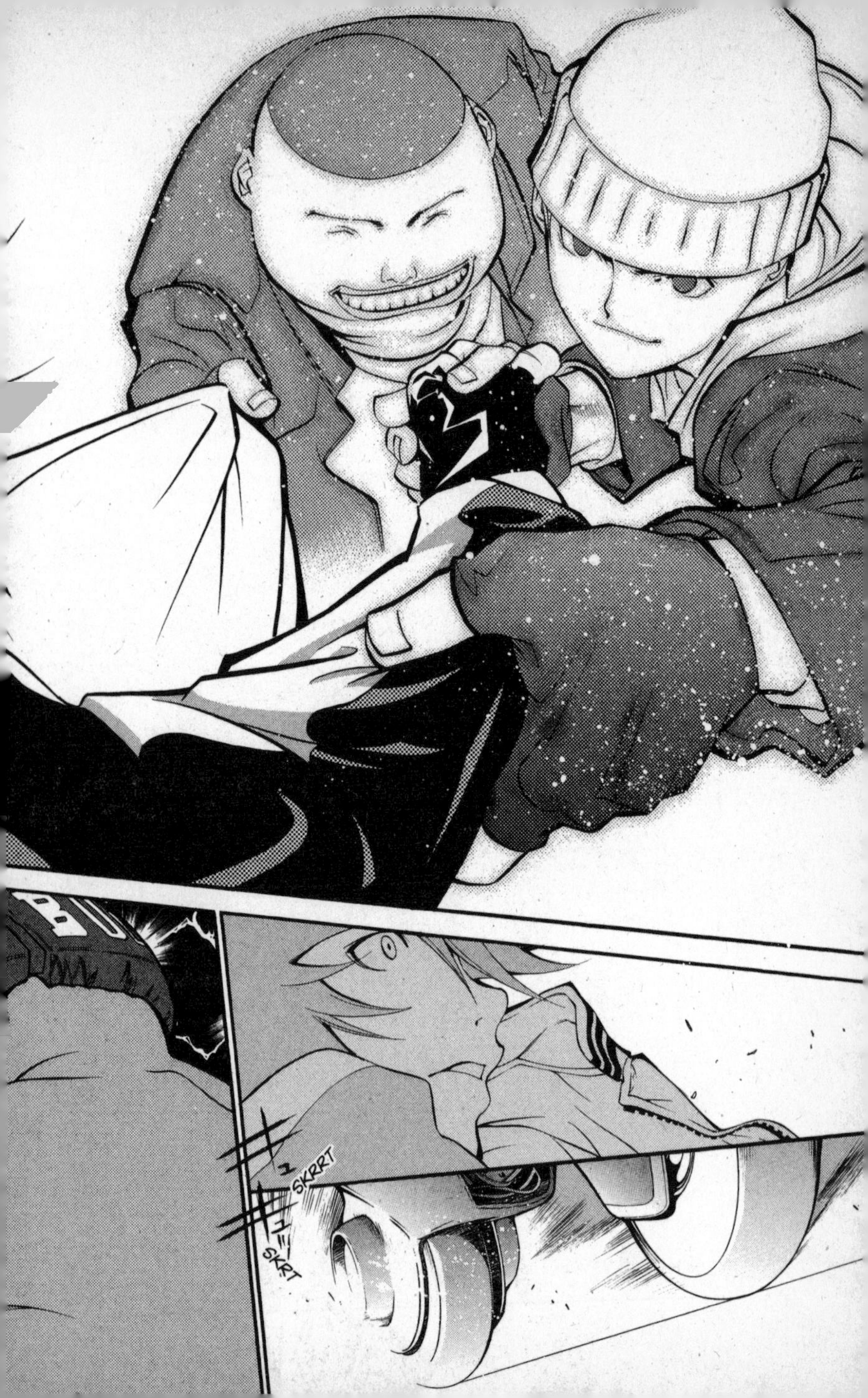
SKRRT
SKRT

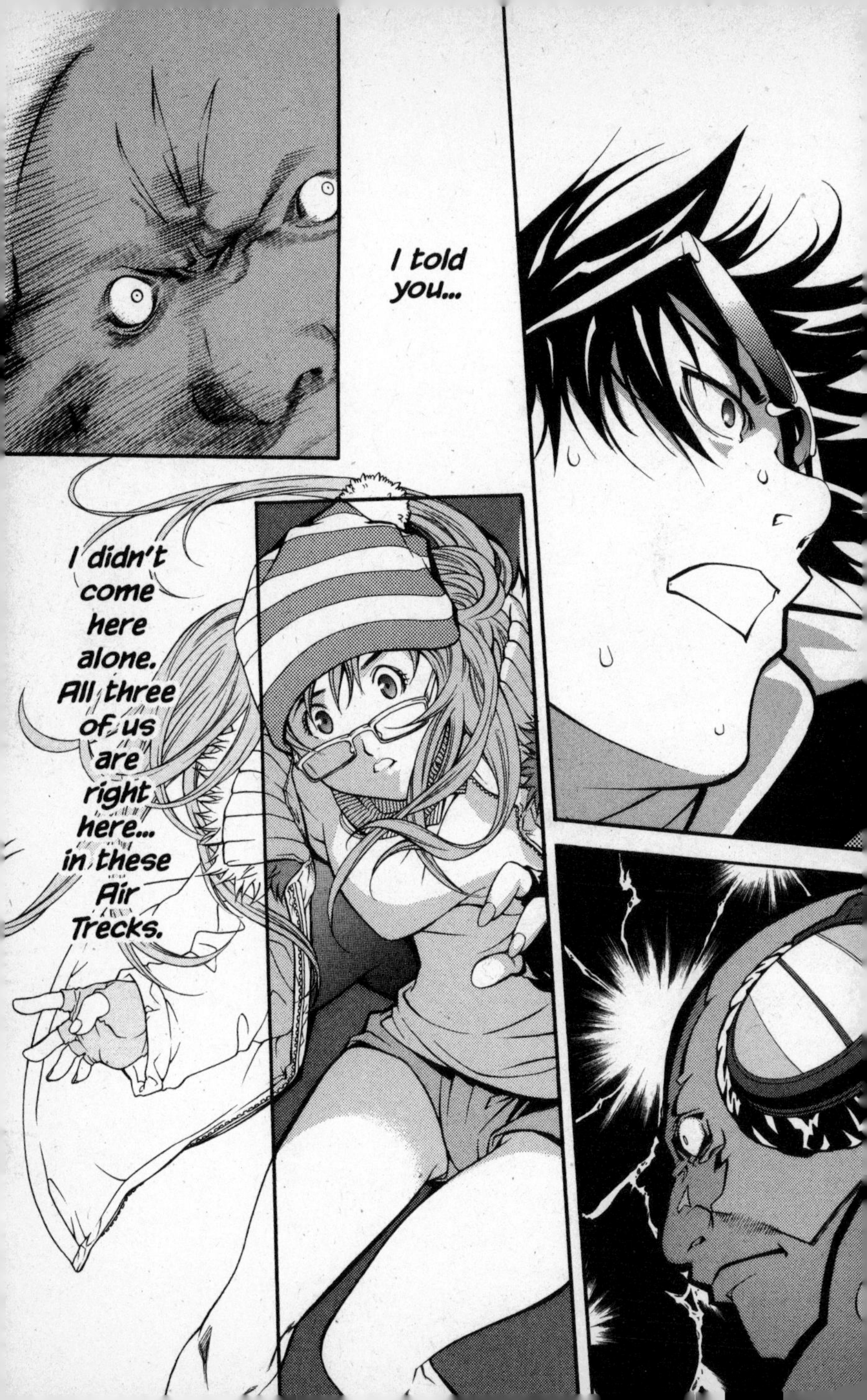
I told you...
I didn't come here alone. All three of us are right here... in these Air Trecks.

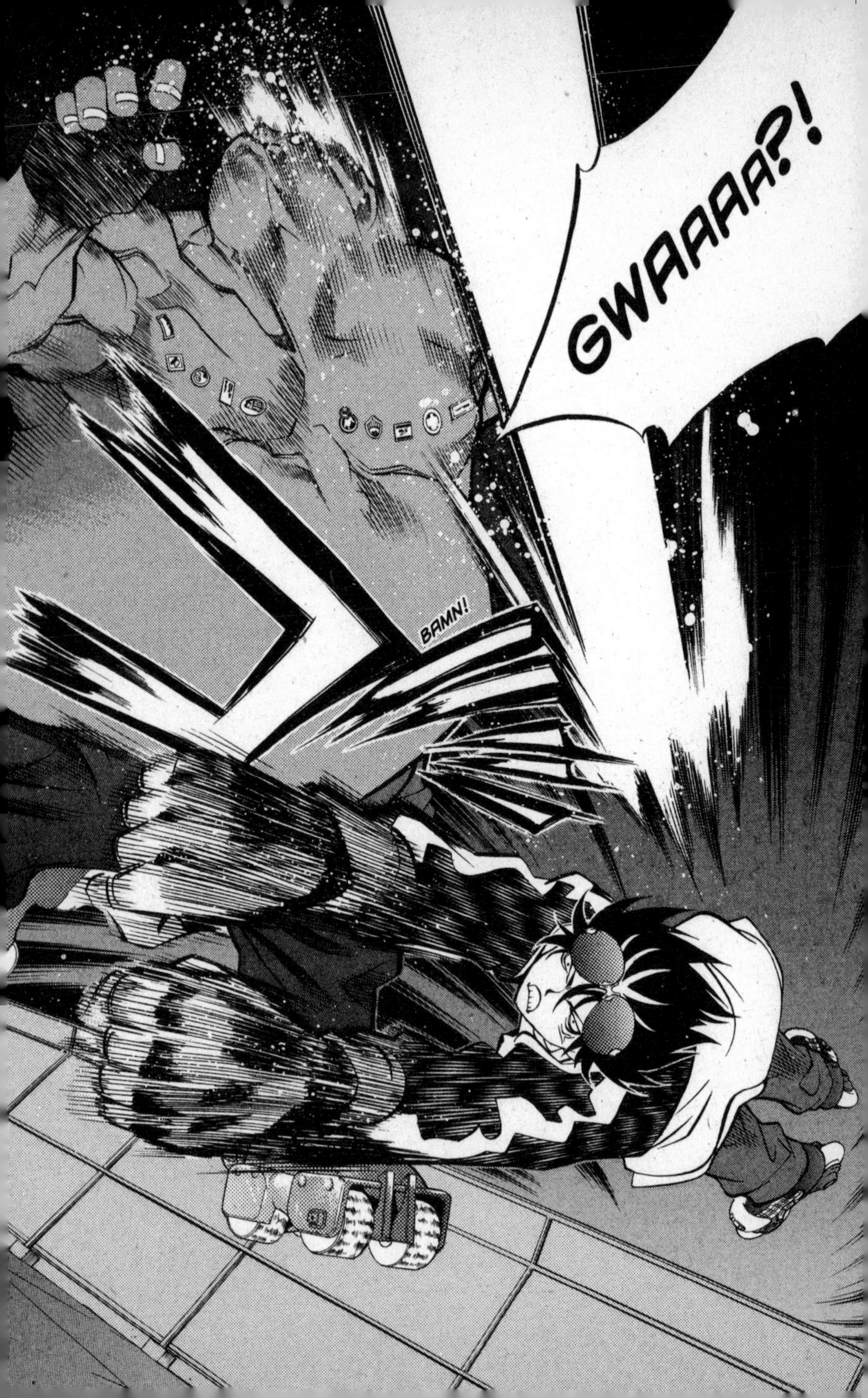
GWAAAA?!
BAMN!

エア・ギア
AIR GEAR

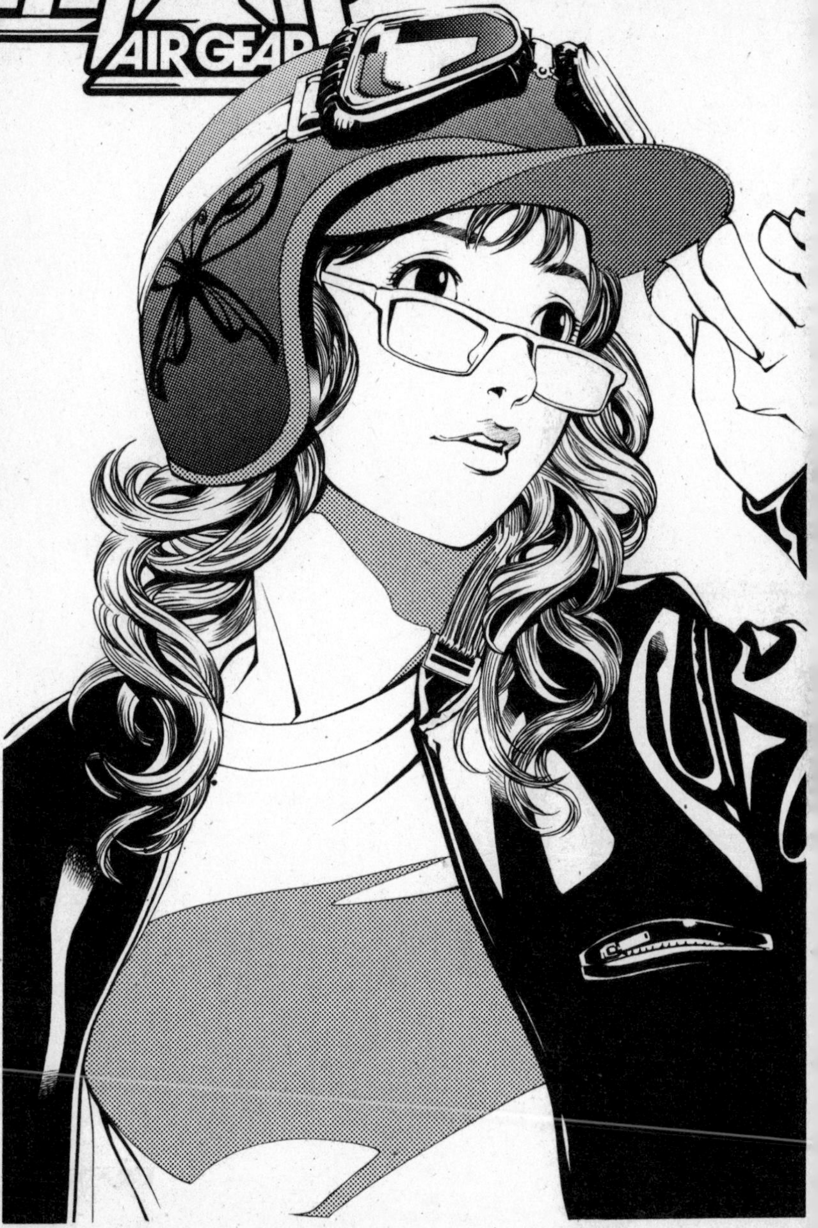

Trick:19

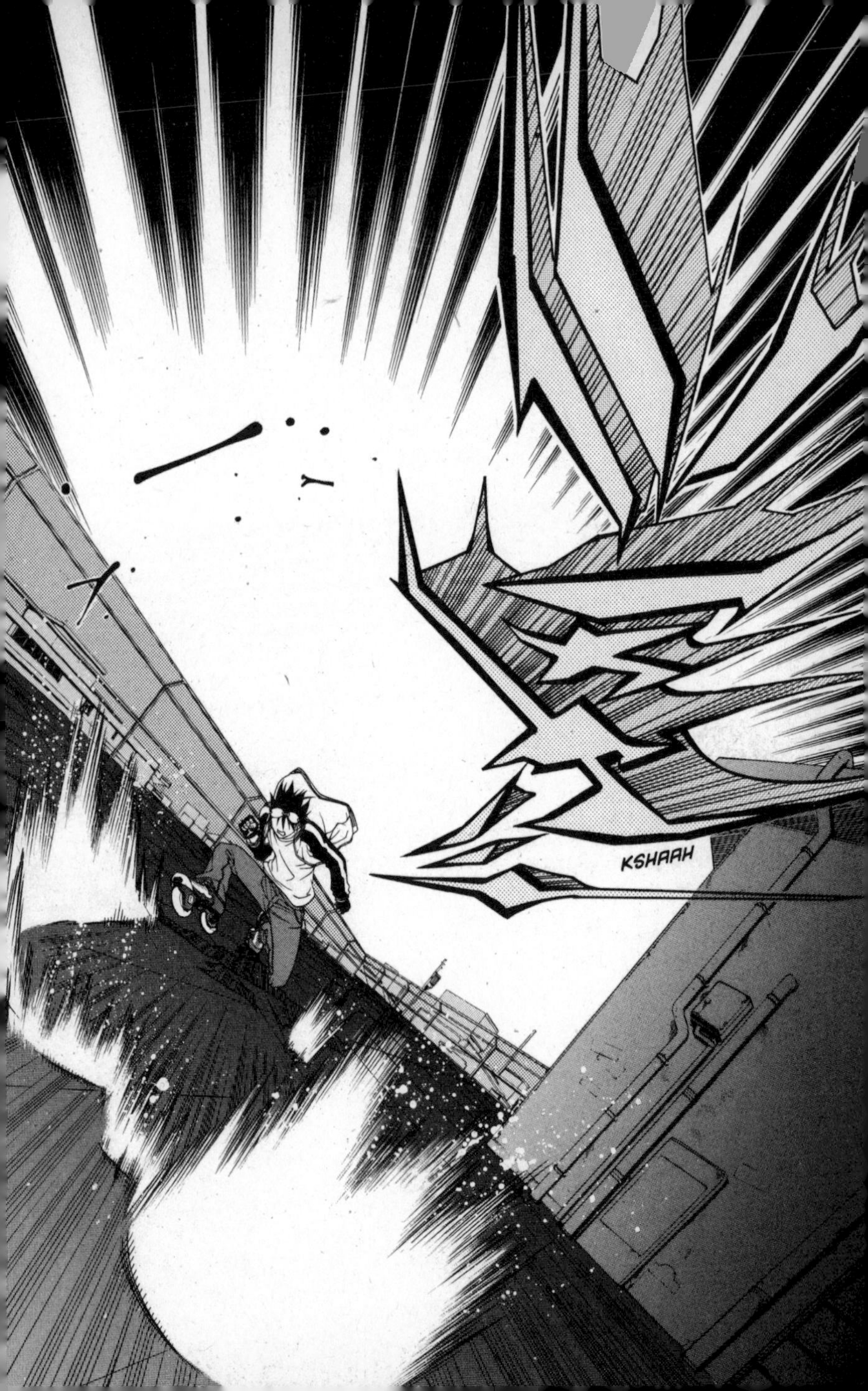
KSHAAH

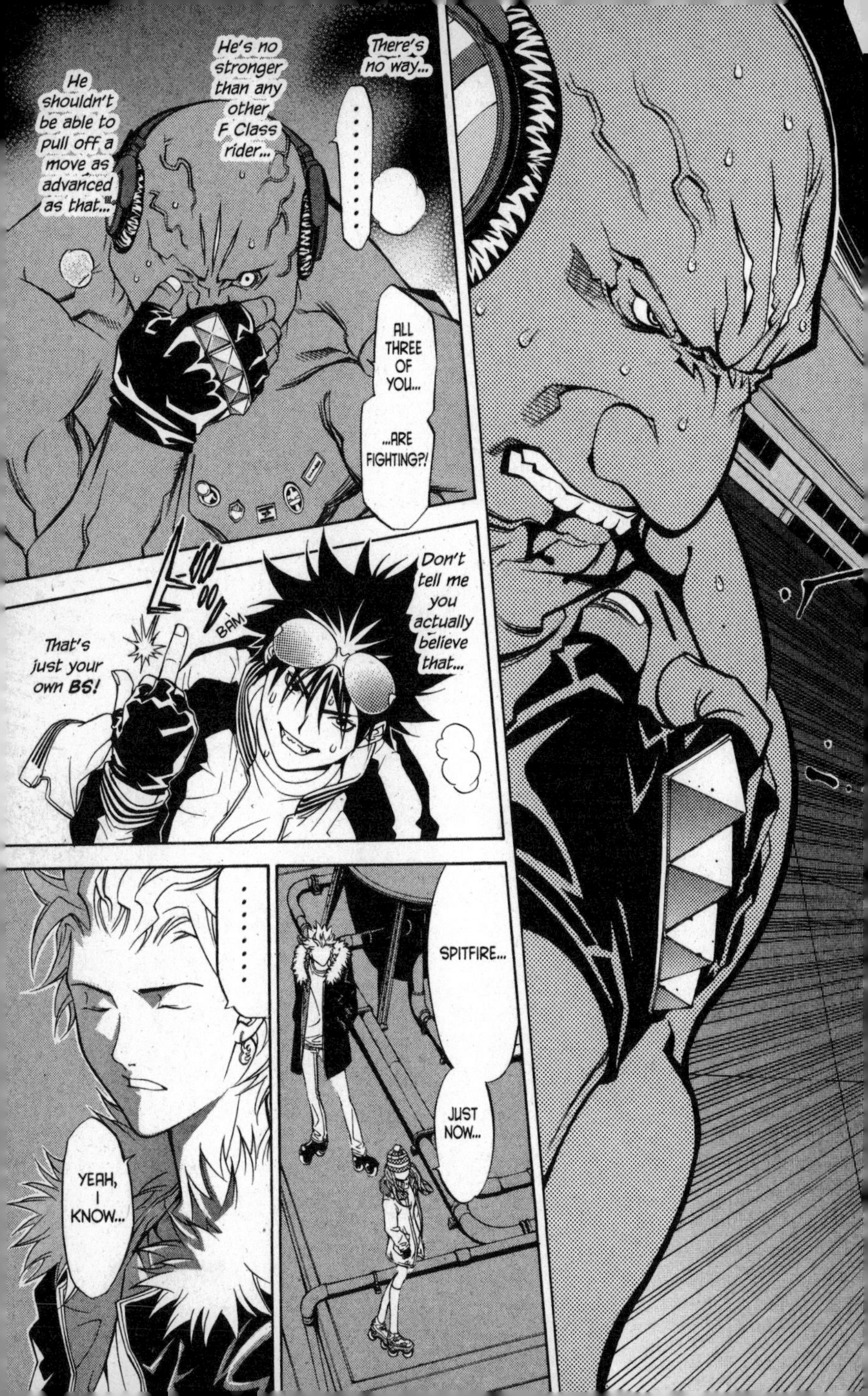
There's no way...
......
He's no stronger than any other F Class rider...
He shouldn't be able to pull off a move as advanced as that...
ALL THREE OF YOU... ...ARE FIGHTING?!
Don't tell me you actually believe that...
BAM
That's just your own BS!
SPITFIRE...
JUST NOW...
......
YEAH, I KNOW...

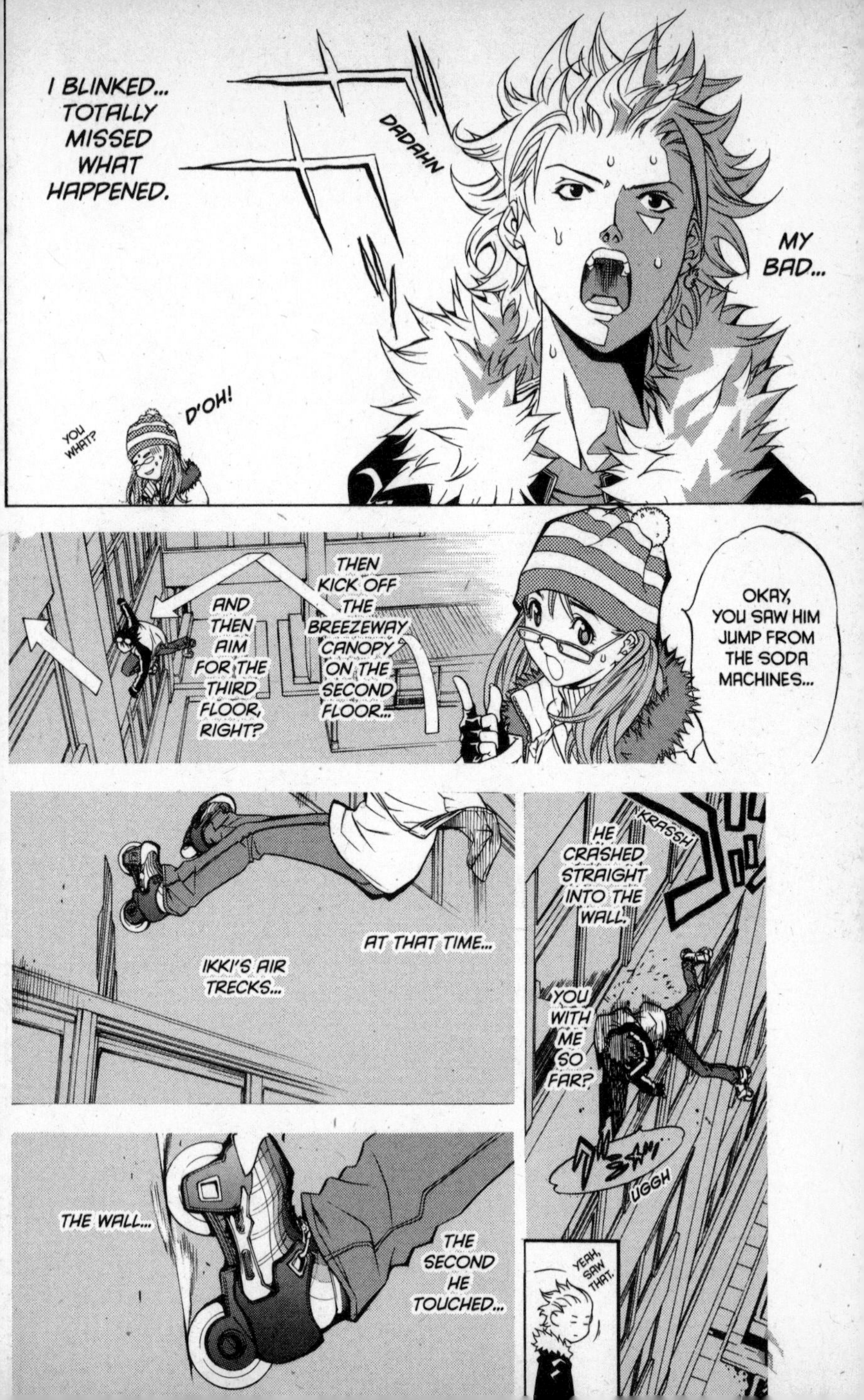
MY BAD...
DADAHN
I BLINKED... TOTALLY MISSED WHAT HAPPENED.
D'OH!
YOU WHAT?
OKAY, YOU SAW HIM JUMP FROM THE SODA MACHINES...
THEN KICK OFF THE BREEZEWAY CANOPY ON THE SECOND FLOOR...
AND THEN AIM FOR THE THIRD FLOOR, RIGHT?
KRASSH
HE CRASHED STRAIGHT INTO THE WALL.
YOU WITH ME SO FAR?
UGGH
YEAH, SAW THAT.
AT THAT TIME...
IKKI'S AIR TRECKS...
THE SECOND HE TOUCHED...
THE WALL...

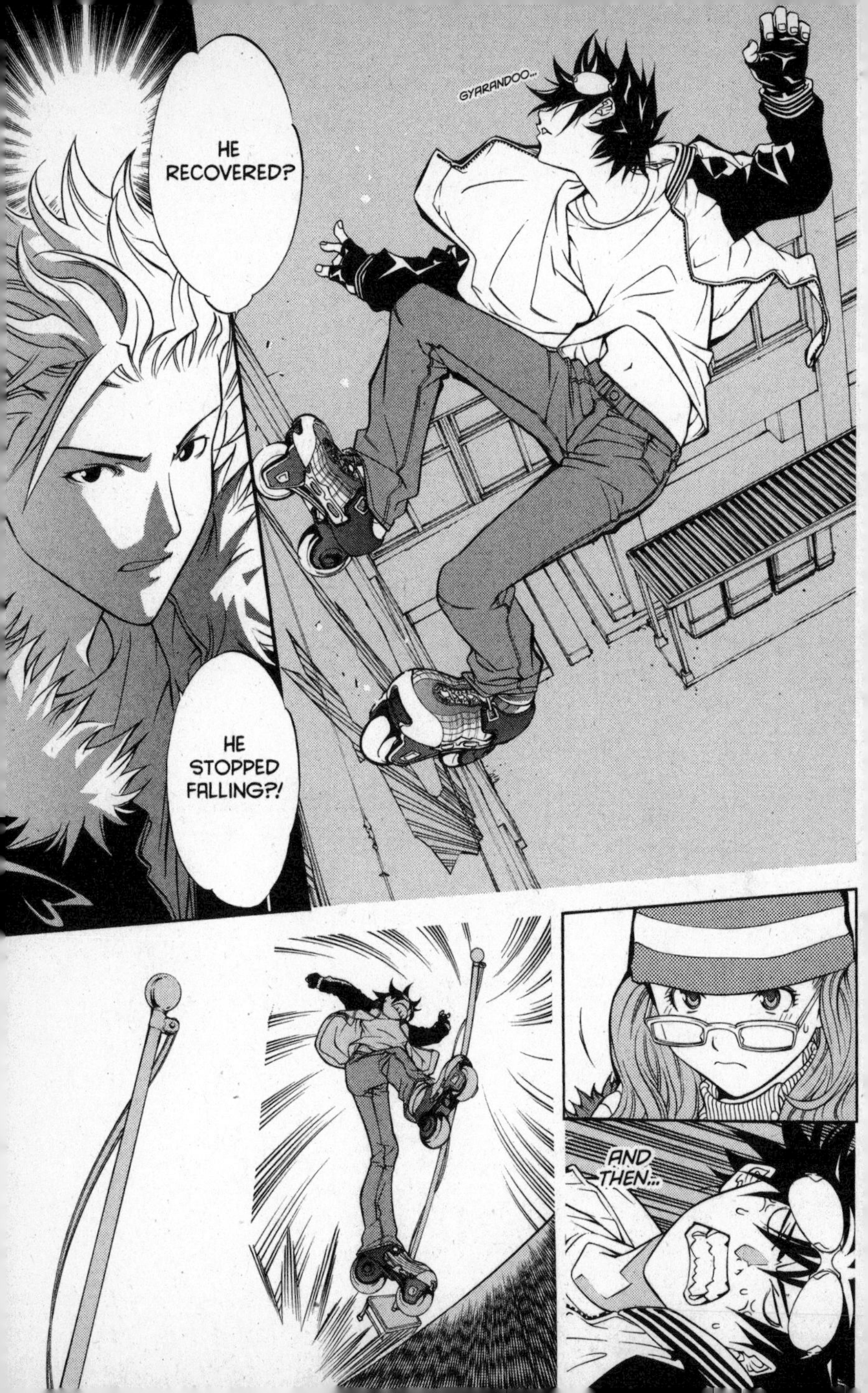
GYARANDOO...
HE RECOVERED?
HE STOPPED FALLING?!
AND THEN...

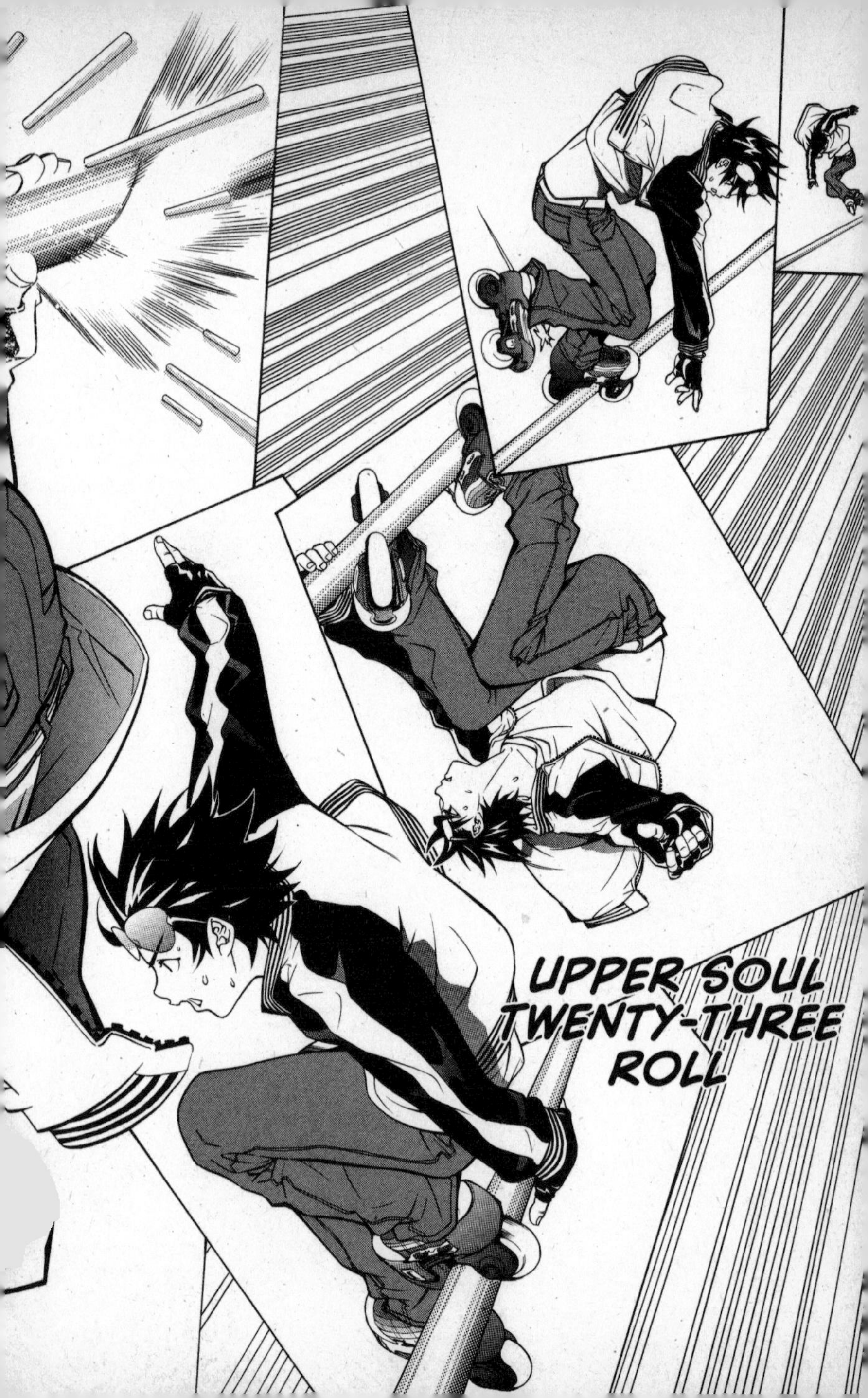
UPPER SOUL
TWENTY-THREE
ROLL

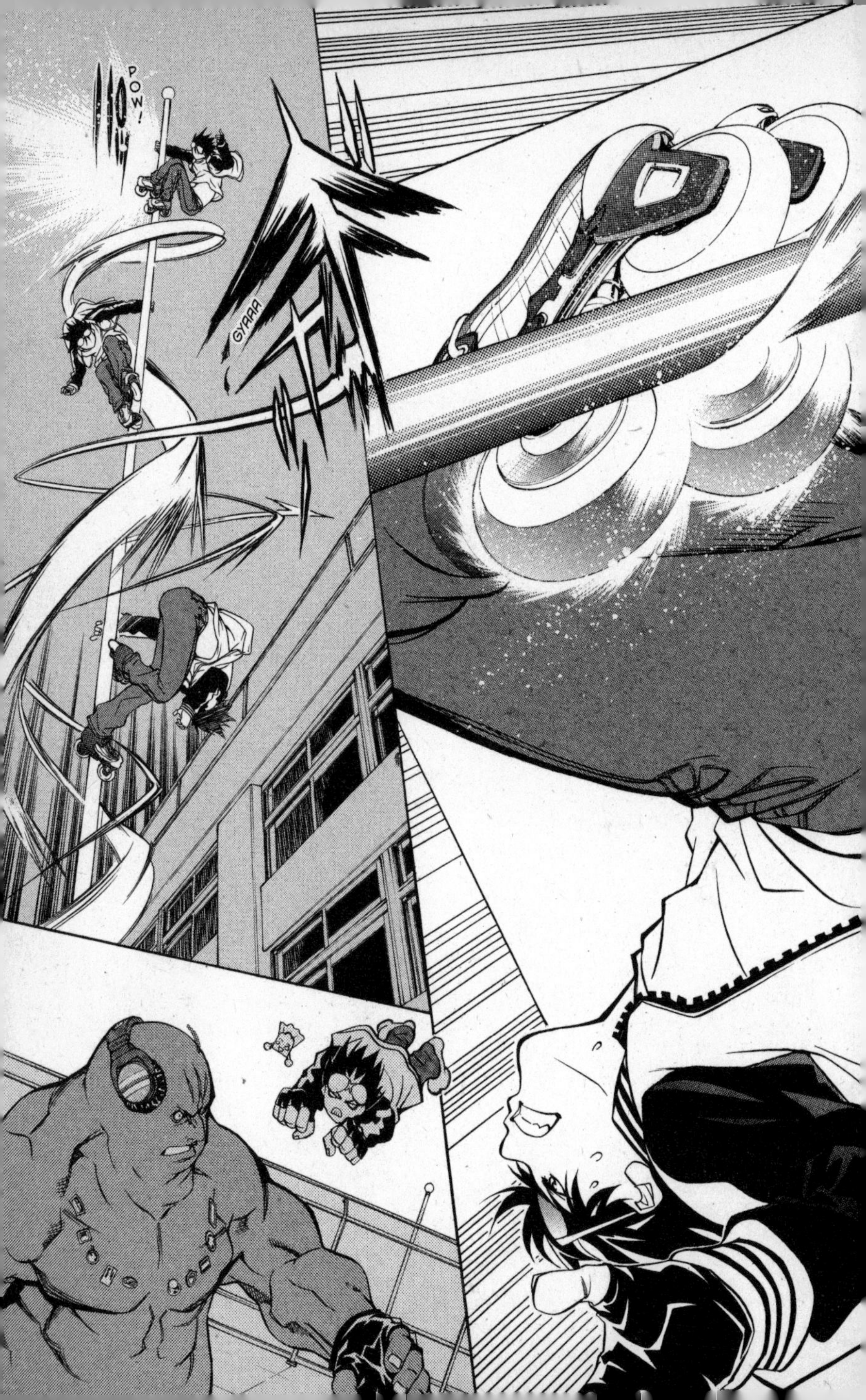
POW!
GYAAA

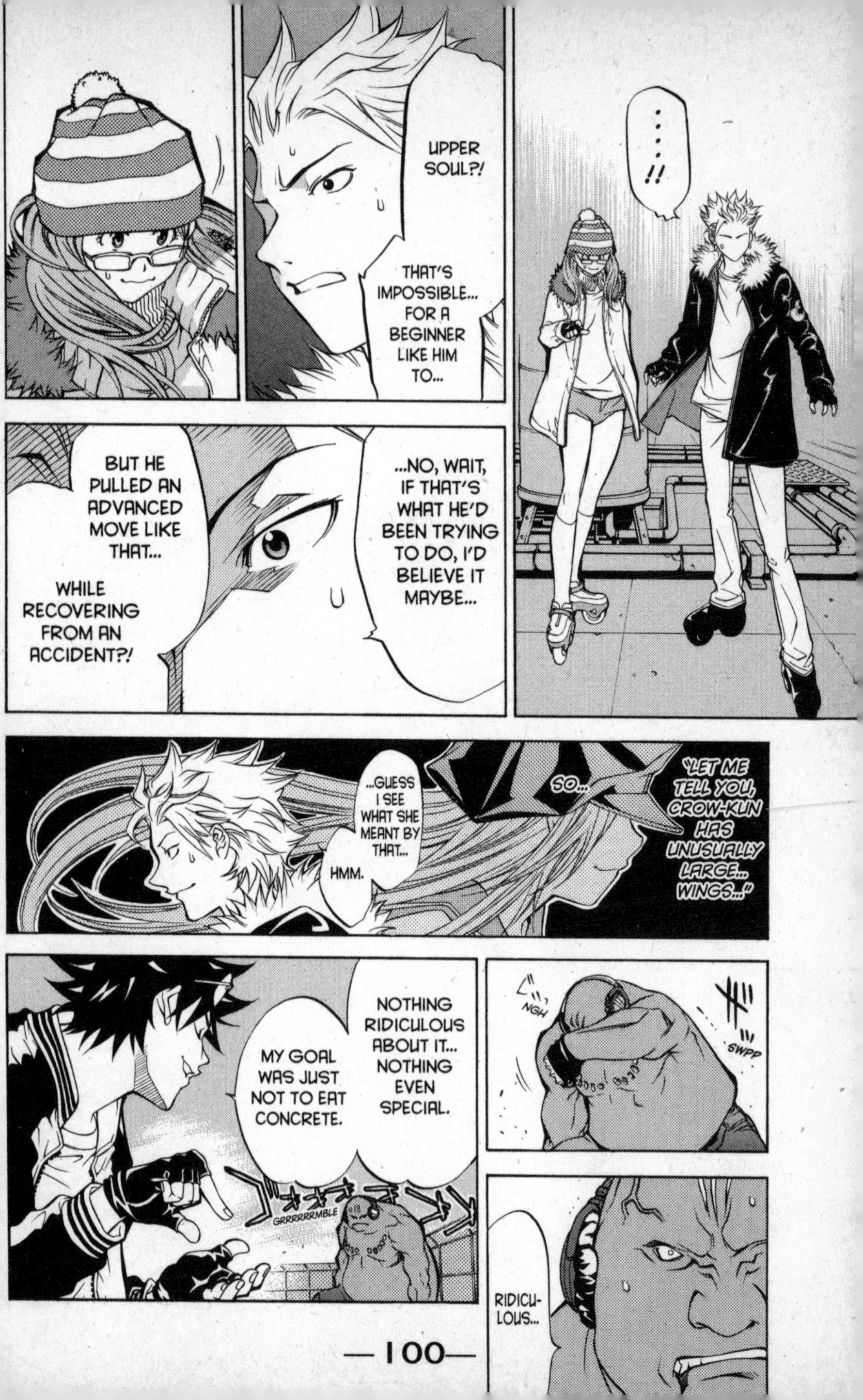

.....!!
UPPER SOUL?!
THAT'S IMPOSSIBLE... FOR A BEGINNER LIKE HIM TO...
...NO, WAIT, IF THAT'S WHAT HE'D BEEN TRYING TO DO, I'D BELIEVE IT MAYBE...
BUT HE PULLED AN ADVANCED MOVE LIKE THAT...
WHILE RECOVERING FROM AN ACCIDENT?!
"LET ME TELL YOU, CROW-KUN HAS UNUSUALLY LARGE... WINGS..."
SO...
HMM.
...GUESS I SEE WHAT SHE MEANT BY THAT...
NGH
SWPP
RIDICU-LOUS...
NOTHING RIDICULOUS ABOUT IT... NOTHING EVEN SPECIAL.
MY GOAL WAS JUST NOT TO EAT CONCRETE.
GRRRRRRMBLE

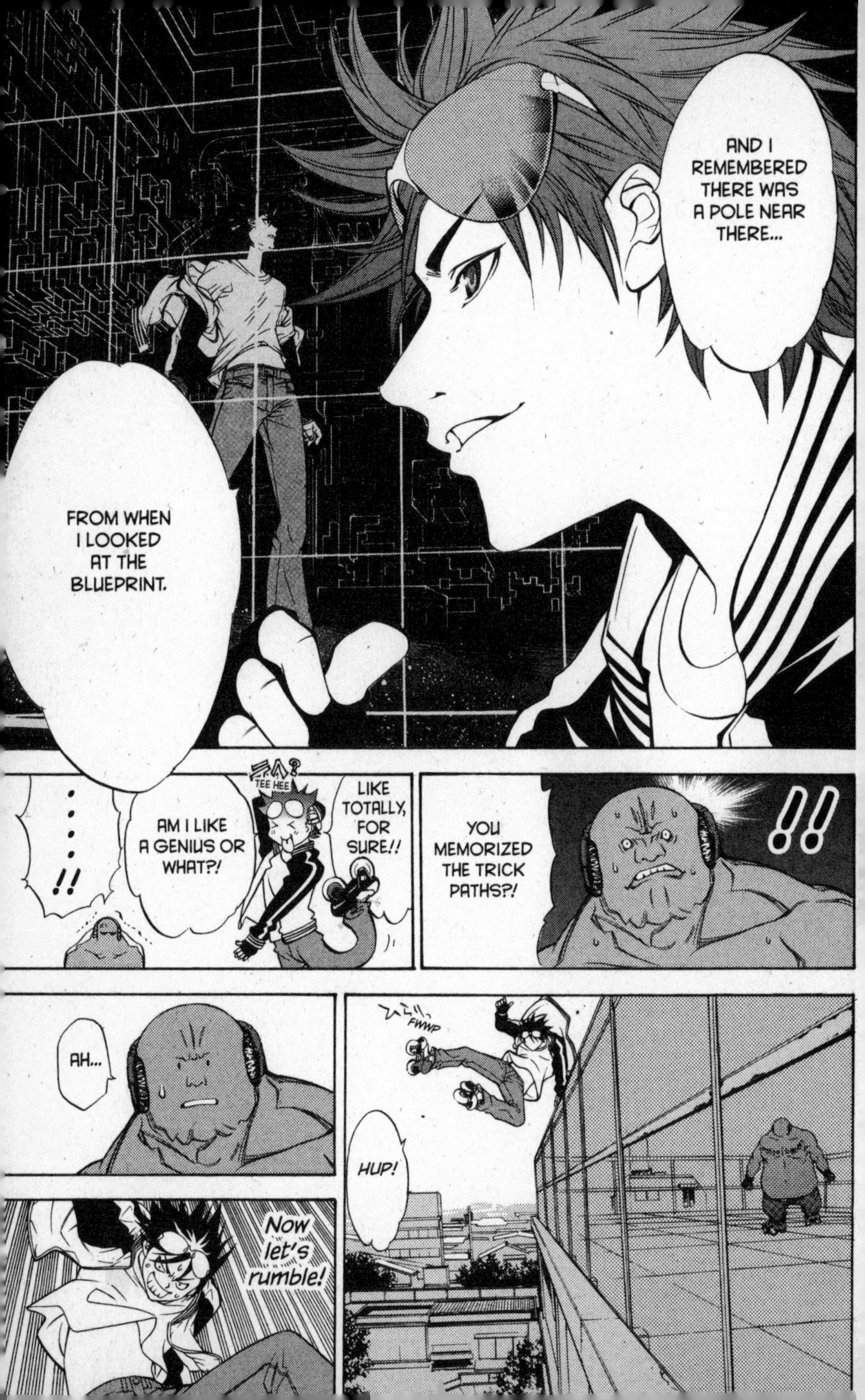
AND I REMEMBERED THERE WAS A POLE NEAR THERE...
FROM WHEN I LOOKED AT THE BLUEPRINT.
YOU MEMORIZED THE TRICK PATHS?!
!!
LIKE TOTALLY, FOR SURE!!
TEE HEE
AM I LIKE A GENIUS OR WHAT?!
....!!
FWWP
HUP!
AH...
Now let's rumble!

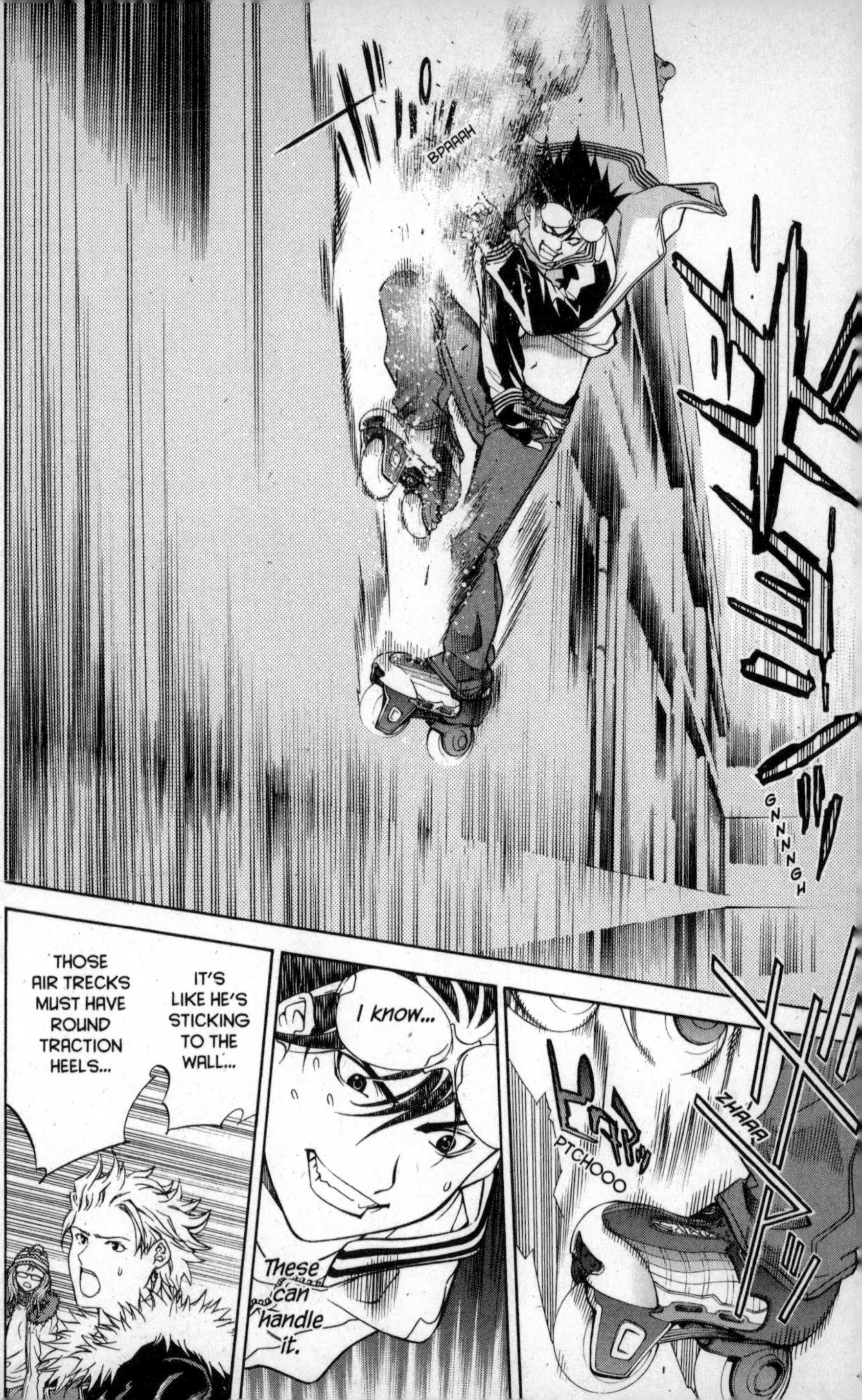
BPAAAH
GNNNNGH
ZHAAAA
PTCHOOO
I know...
These can handle it.
IT'S LIKE HE'S STICKING TO THE WALL...
THOSE AIR TRECKS MUST HAVE ROUND TRACTION HEELS...

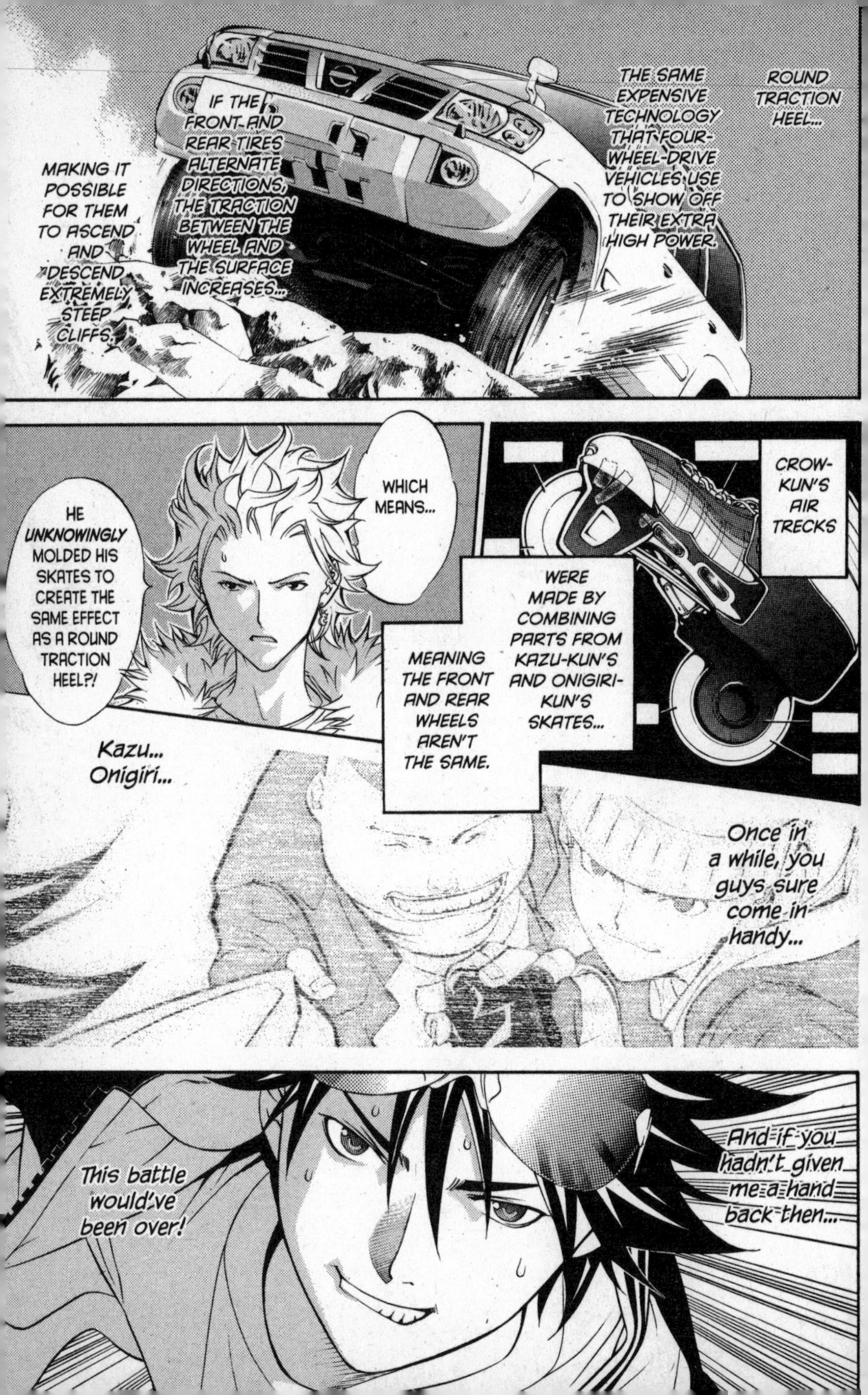

ROUND TRACTION HEEL...
THE SAME EXPENSIVE TECHNOLOGY THAT FOUR-WHEEL-DRIVE VEHICLES USE TO SHOW OFF THEIR EXTRA HIGH POWER.
IF THE FRONT AND REAR TIRES ALTERNATE DIRECTIONS, THE TRACTION BETWEEN THE WHEEL AND THE SURFACE INCREASES...
MAKING IT POSSIBLE FOR THEM TO ASCEND AND DESCEND EXTREMELY STEEP CLIFFS.
CROW-KUN'S AIR TRECKS
WERE MADE BY COMBINING PARTS FROM KAZU-KUN'S AND ONIGIRI-KUN'S SKATES...
MEANING THE FRONT AND REAR WHEELS AREN'T THE SAME.
WHICH MEANS...
HE *UNKNOWINGLY* MOLDED HIS SKATES TO CREATE THE SAME EFFECT AS A ROUND TRACTION HEEL?!
Kazu... Onigiri...
Once in a while, you guys sure come in handy...
And if you hadn't given me a hand back then...
This battle would've been over!

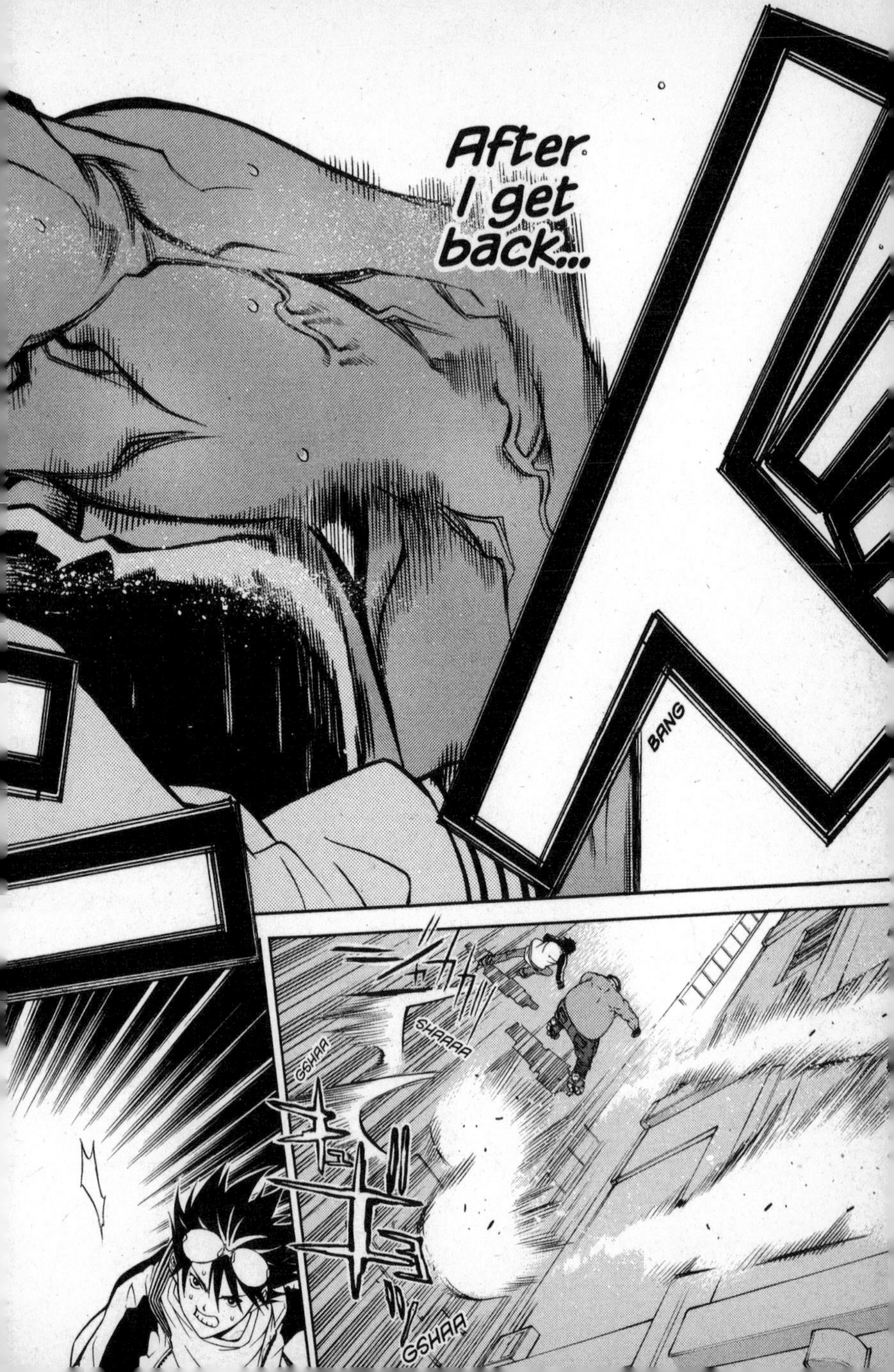
After I get back...
BANG
SHAAAA
GSHAA
GSHAA

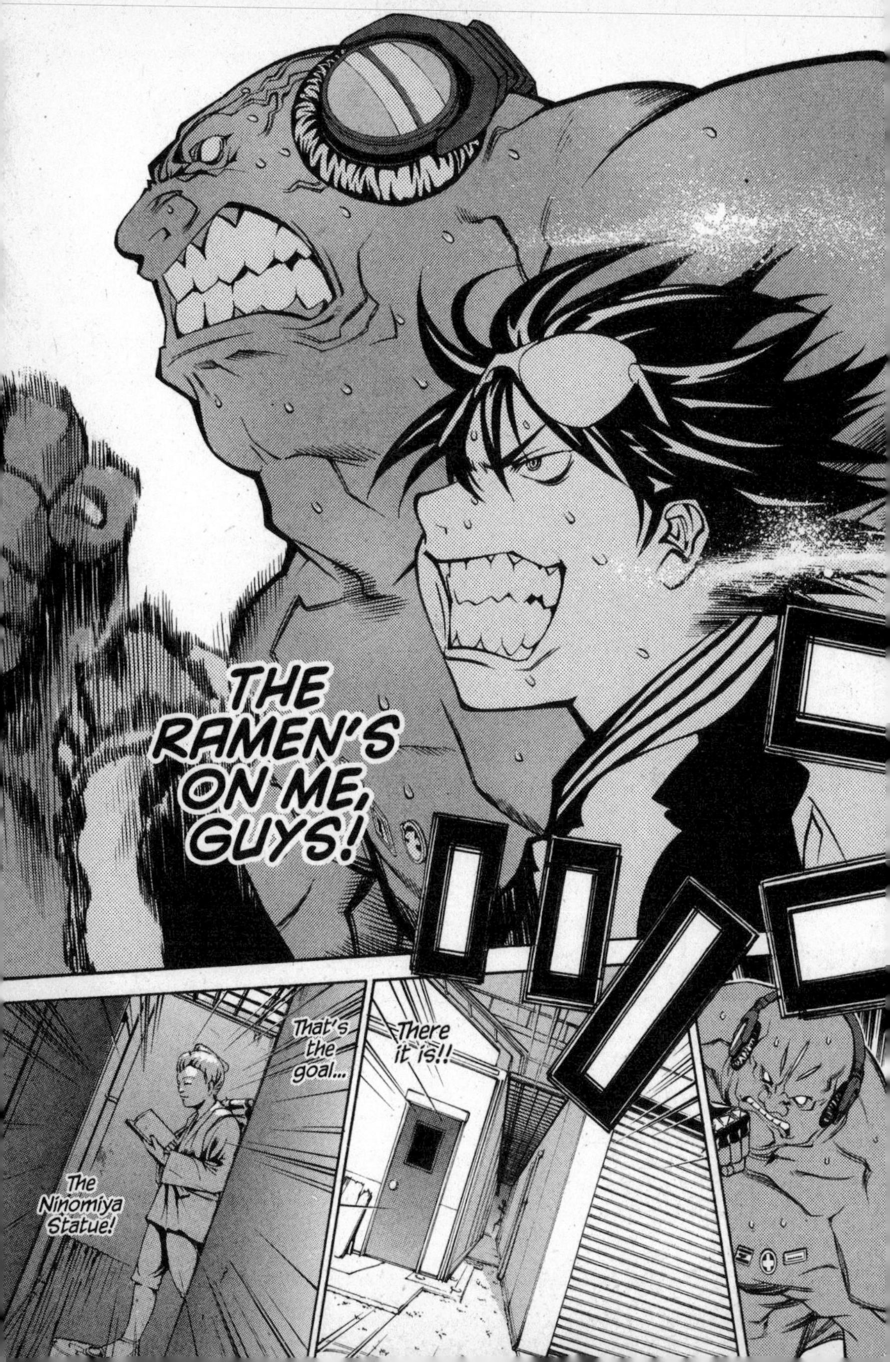
THE RAMEN'S ON ME, GUYS!
There it is!!
That's the goal...
The Ninomiya Statue!

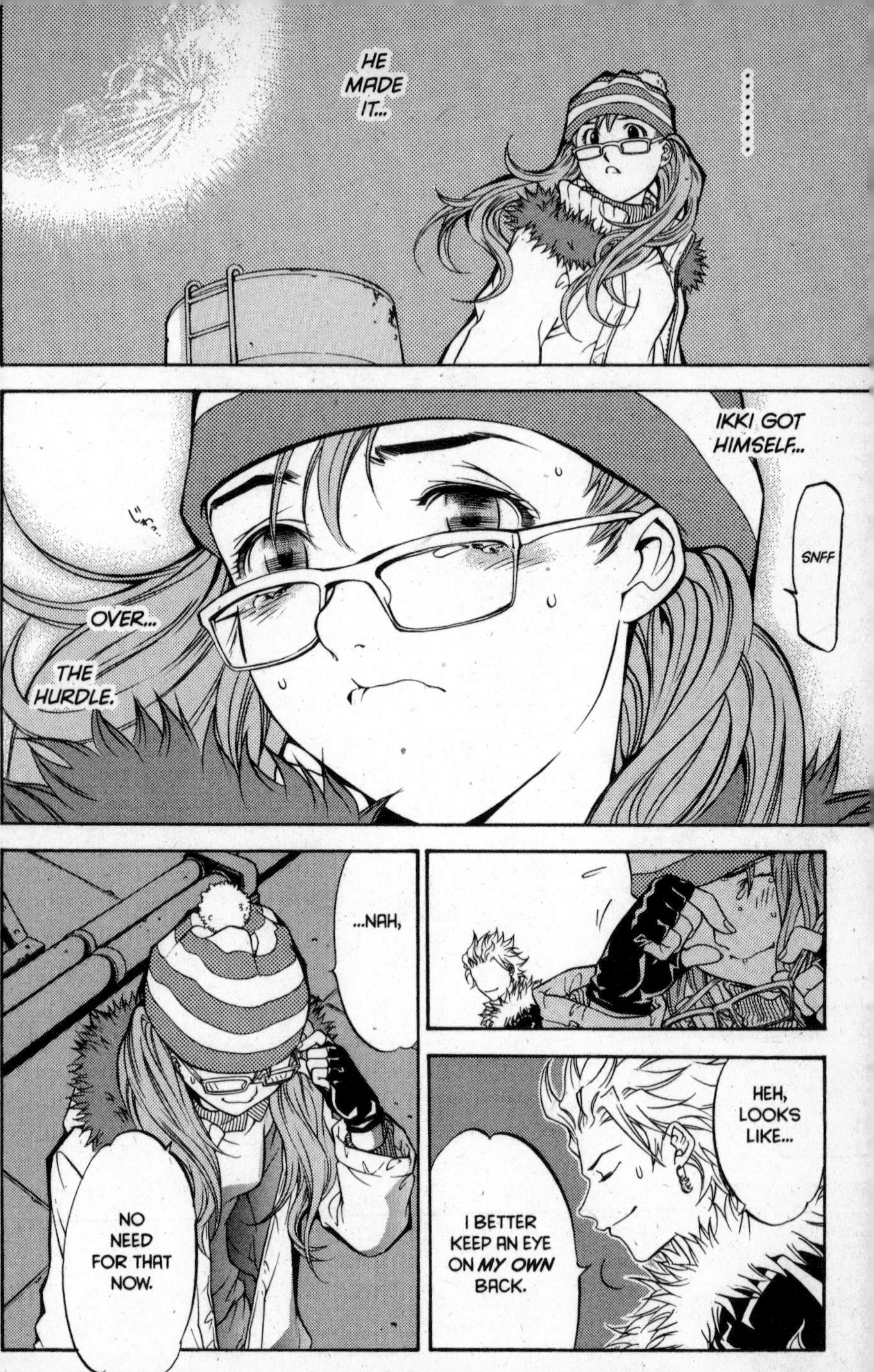
......
HE MADE IT...
IKKI GOT HIMSELF...
SNFF
OVER...
THE HURDLE.
HEH, LOOKS LIKE...
I BETTER KEEP AN EYE ON *MY OWN* BACK.
...NAH,
NO NEED FOR THAT NOW.

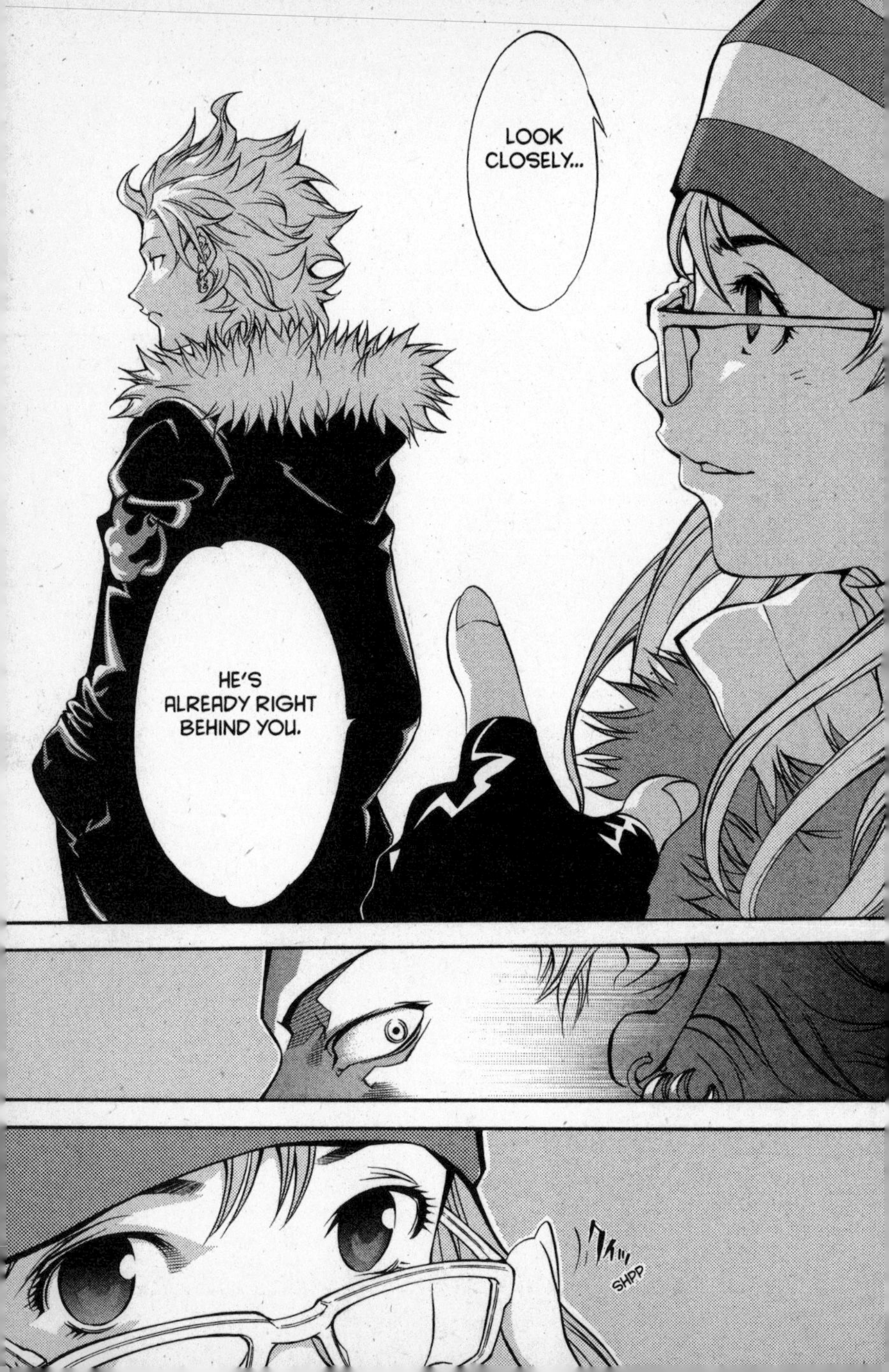
LOOK CLOSELY...
HE'S ALREADY RIGHT BEHIND YOU.
SHPP

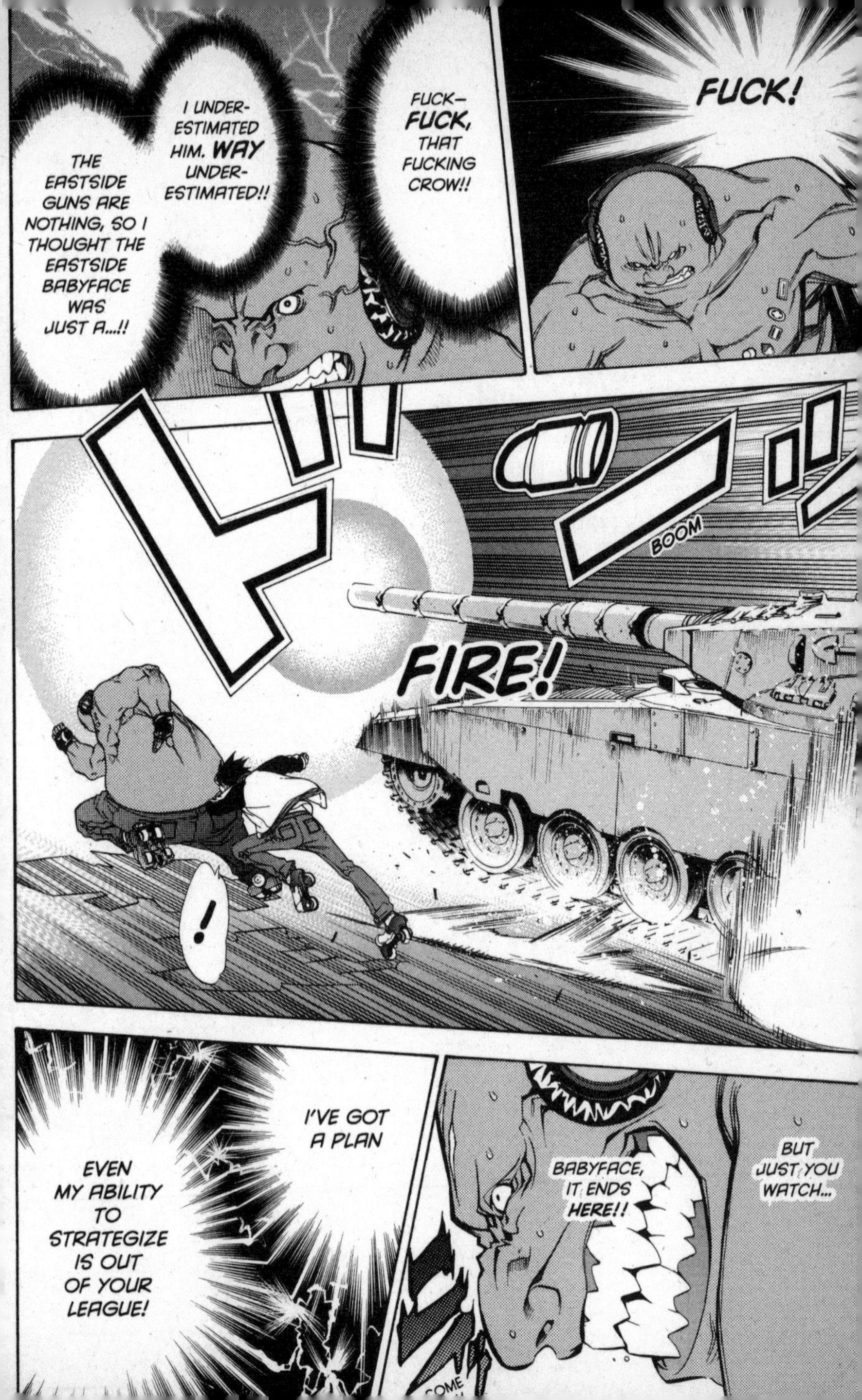
FUCK!
FUCK— FUCK, THAT FUCKING CROW!!
I UNDER-ESTIMATED HIM. WAY UNDER-ESTIMATED!!
THE EASTSIDE GUNS ARE NOTHING, SO I THOUGHT THE EASTSIDE BABYFACE WAS JUST A...!!
BOOM
FIRE!
!
BUT JUST YOU WATCH...
BABYFACE, IT ENDS HERE!!
I'VE GOT A PLAN
EVEN MY ABILITY TO STRATEGIZE IS OUT OF YOUR LEAGUE!
COME

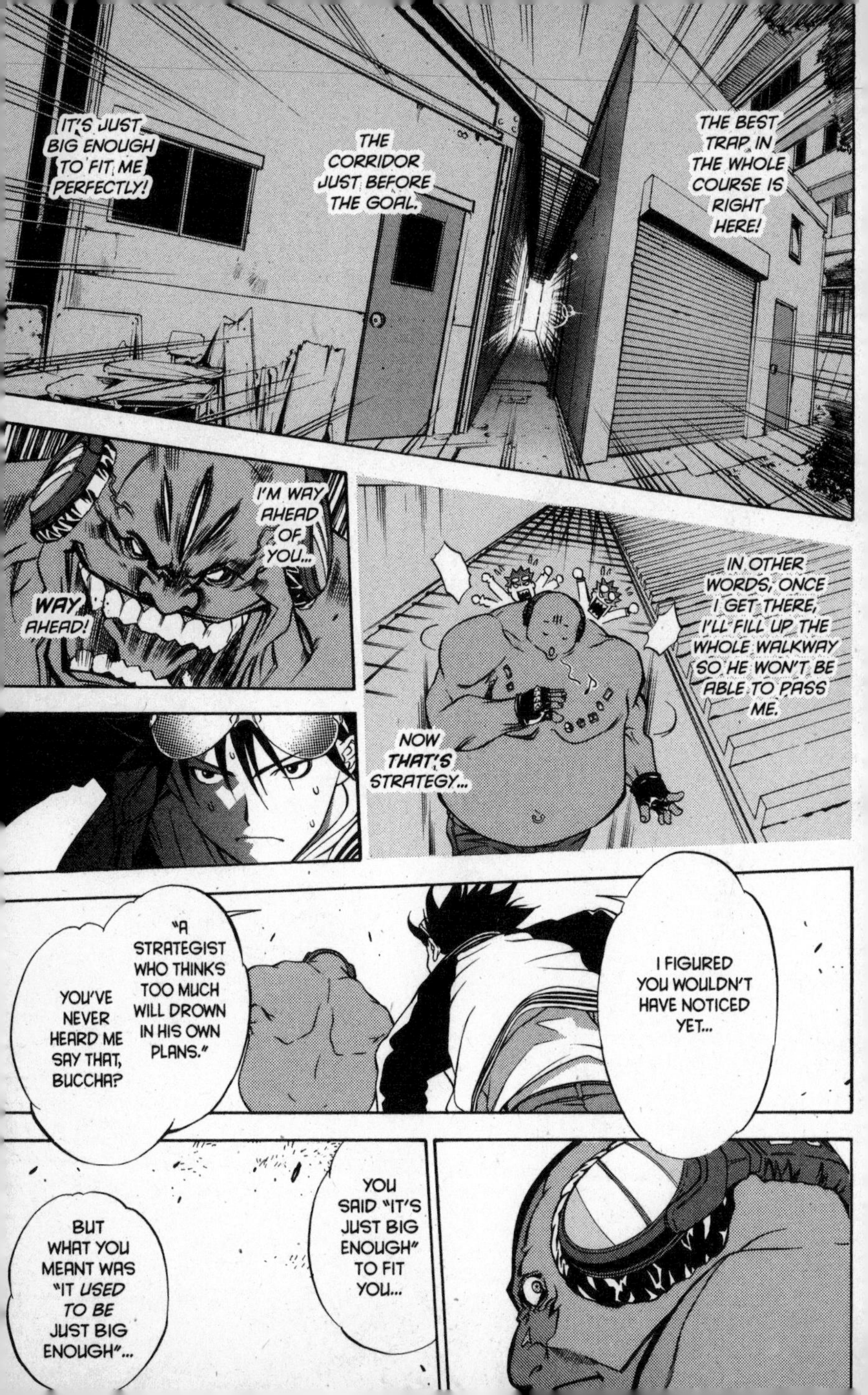
THE BEST TRAP IN THE WHOLE COURSE IS RIGHT HERE!
THE CORRIDOR JUST BEFORE THE GOAL.
IT'S JUST BIG ENOUGH TO FIT ME PERFECTLY!
IN OTHER WORDS, ONCE I GET THERE, I'LL FILL UP THE WHOLE WALKWAY SO HE WON'T BE ABLE TO PASS ME.
NOW THAT'S STRATEGY...
I'M WAY AHEAD OF YOU...
WAY AHEAD!
I FIGURED YOU WOULDN'T HAVE NOTICED YET...
"A STRATEGIST WHO THINKS TOO MUCH WILL DROWN IN HIS OWN PLANS."
YOU'VE NEVER HEARD ME SAY THAT, BUCCHA?
YOU SAID "IT'S JUST BIG ENOUGH" TO FIT YOU...
BUT WHAT YOU MEANT WAS "IT *USED TO BE* JUST BIG ENOUGH"...

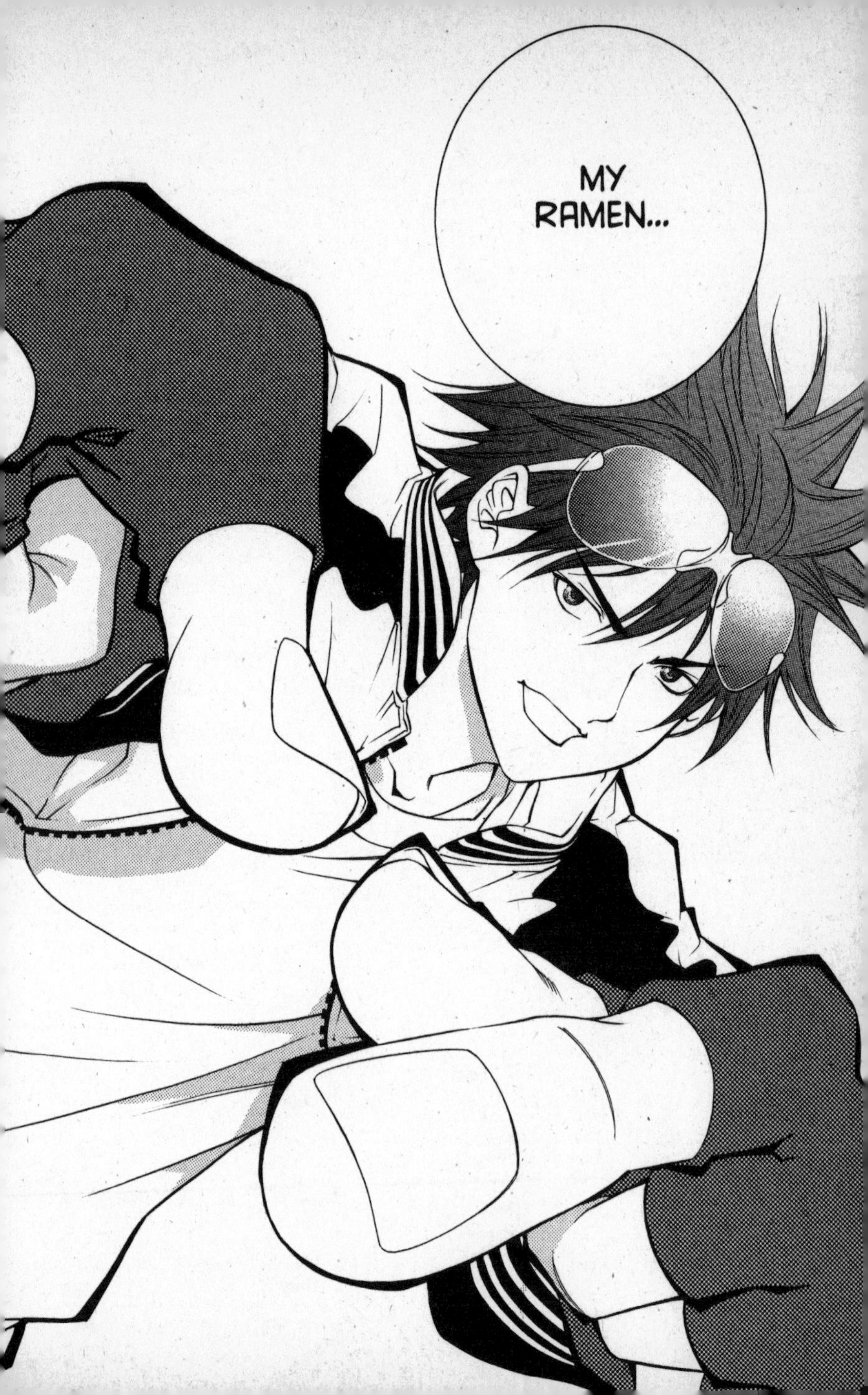
MY RAMEN...

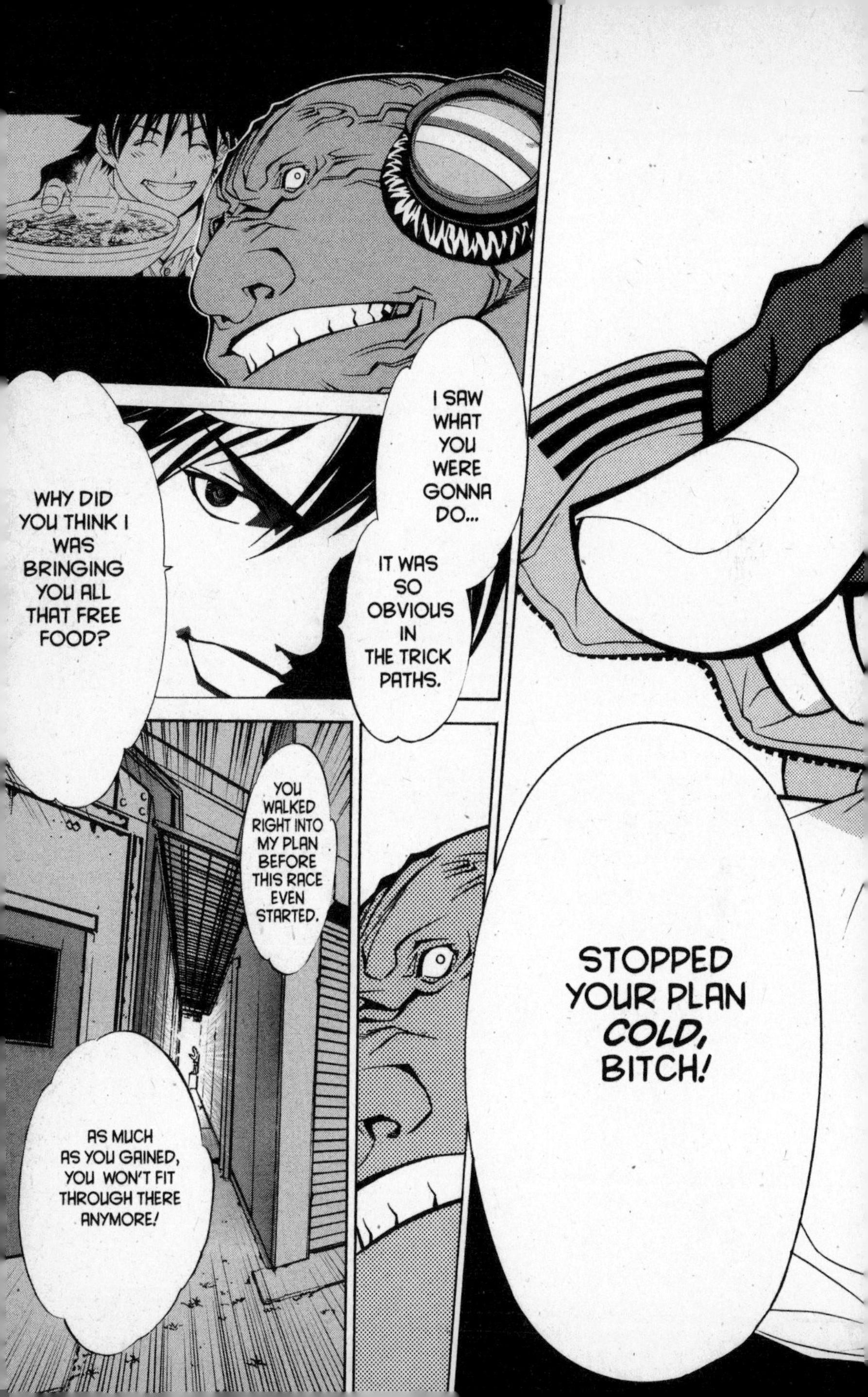
I SAW WHAT YOU WERE GONNA DO...
IT WAS SO OBVIOUS IN THE TRICK PATHS.
WHY DID YOU THINK I WAS BRINGING YOU ALL THAT FREE FOOD?
YOU WALKED RIGHT INTO MY PLAN BEFORE THIS RACE EVEN STARTED.
AS MUCH AS YOU GAINED, YOU WON'T FIT THROUGH THERE ANYMORE!
STOPPED YOUR PLAN *COLD,* BITCH!

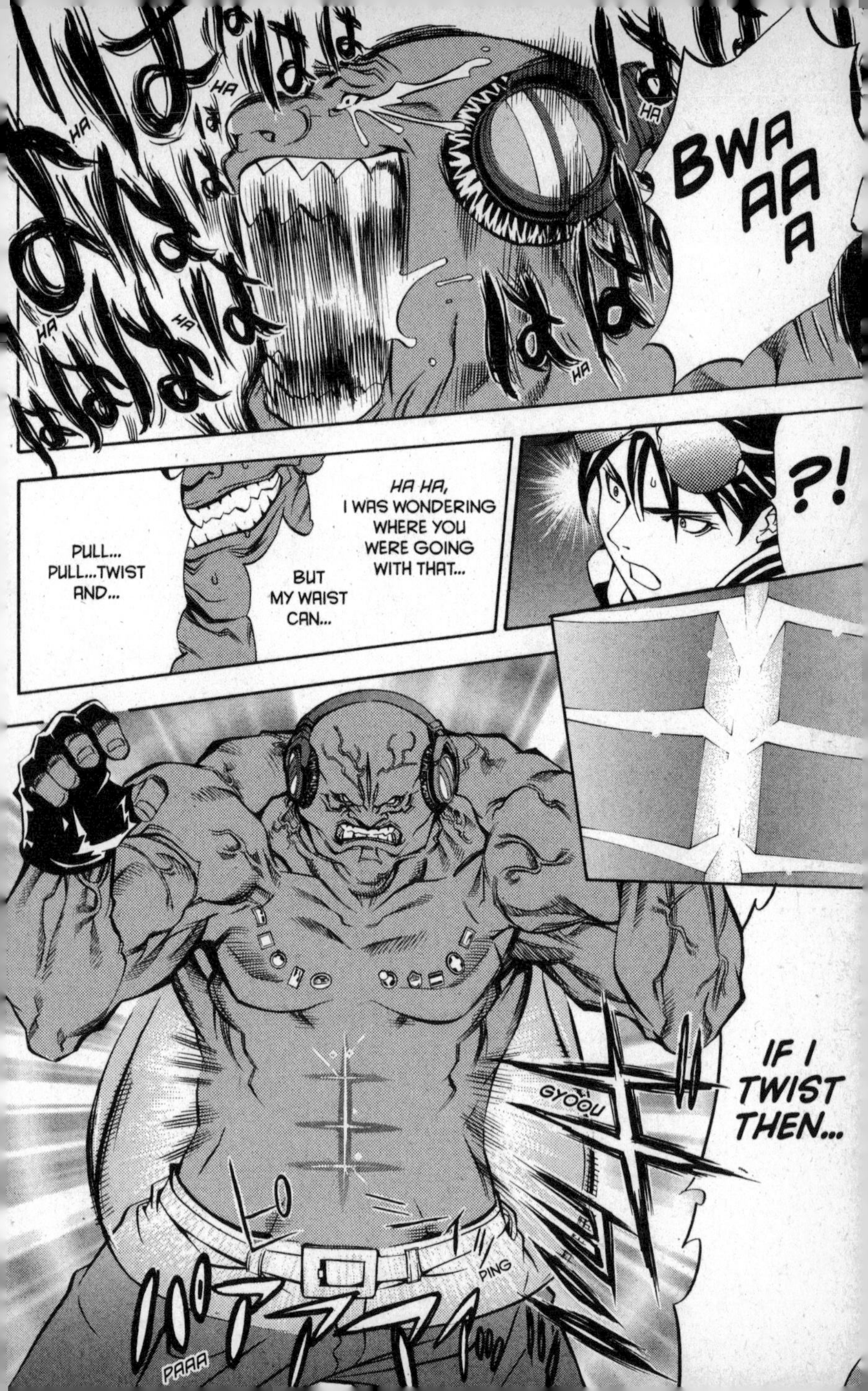
BWAAAAA
HA
HA
HA
HA
HA
?!
HA HA, I WAS WONDERING WHERE YOU WERE GOING WITH THAT...
BUT MY WAIST CAN...
PULL... PULL...TWIST AND...
IF I TWIST THEN...
GYOOU
PING
PAAA

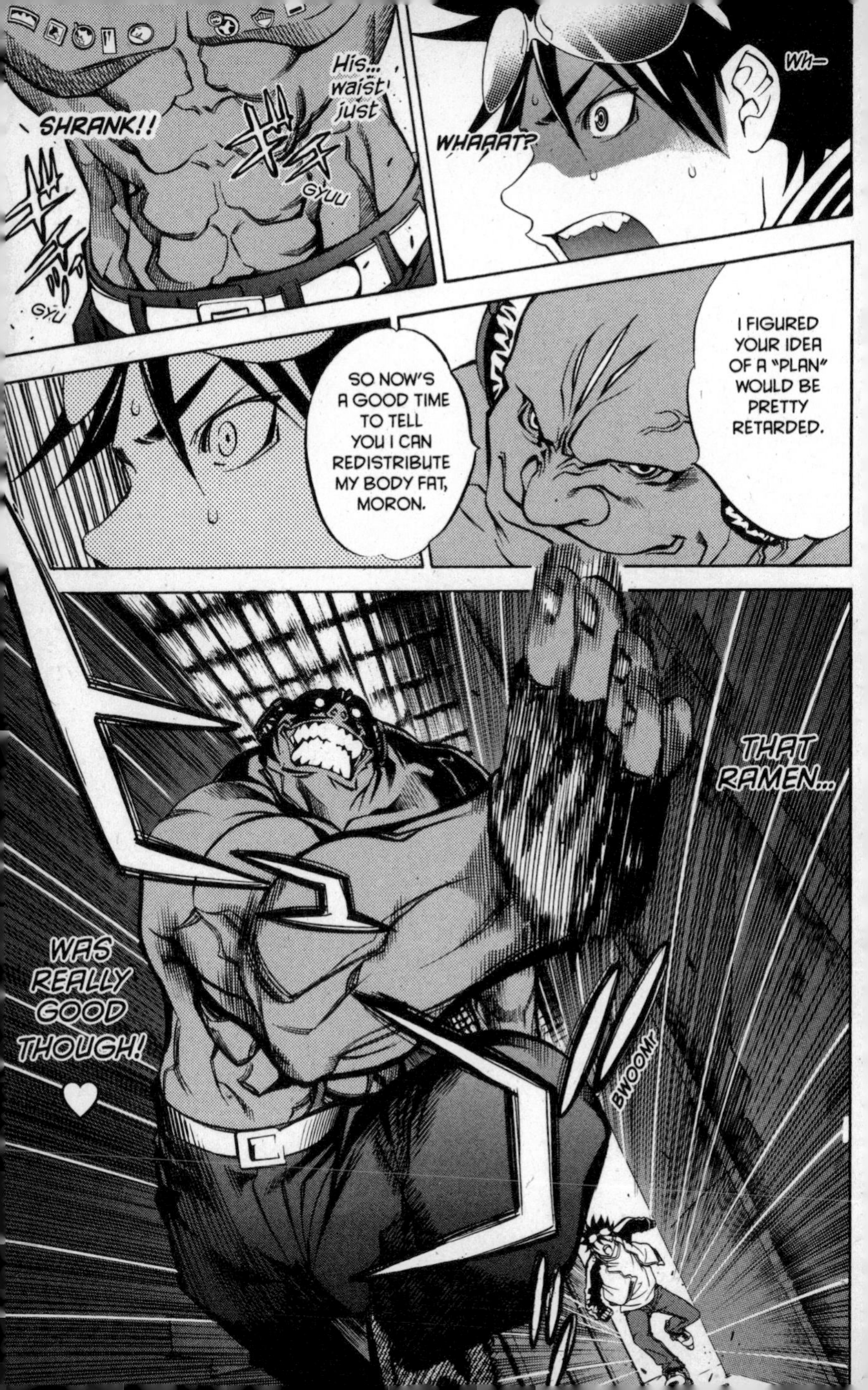
Wh–
WHAAAT?
SHRANK!!
His... waist just
GYUU
GYU
I FIGURED YOUR IDEA OF A "PLAN" WOULD BE PRETTY RETARDED.
SO NOW'S A GOOD TIME TO TELL YOU I CAN REDISTRIBUTE MY BODY FAT, MORON.
THAT RAMEN...
WAS REALLY GOOD THOUGH! ♥
BWOOM!

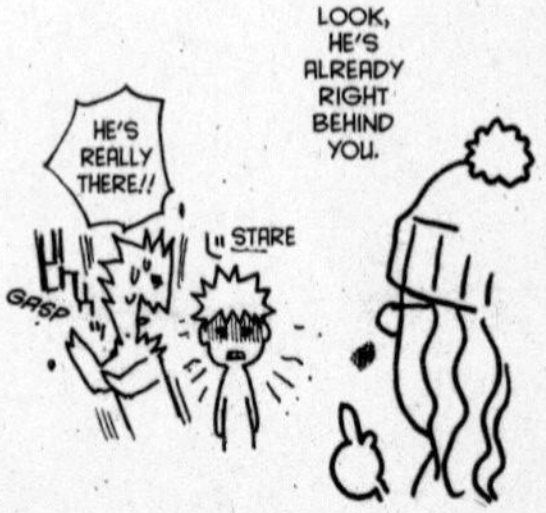
LOOK, HE'S ALREADY RIGHT BEHIND YOU.
HE'S REALLY THERE!!
STARE
GASP

Air Gear

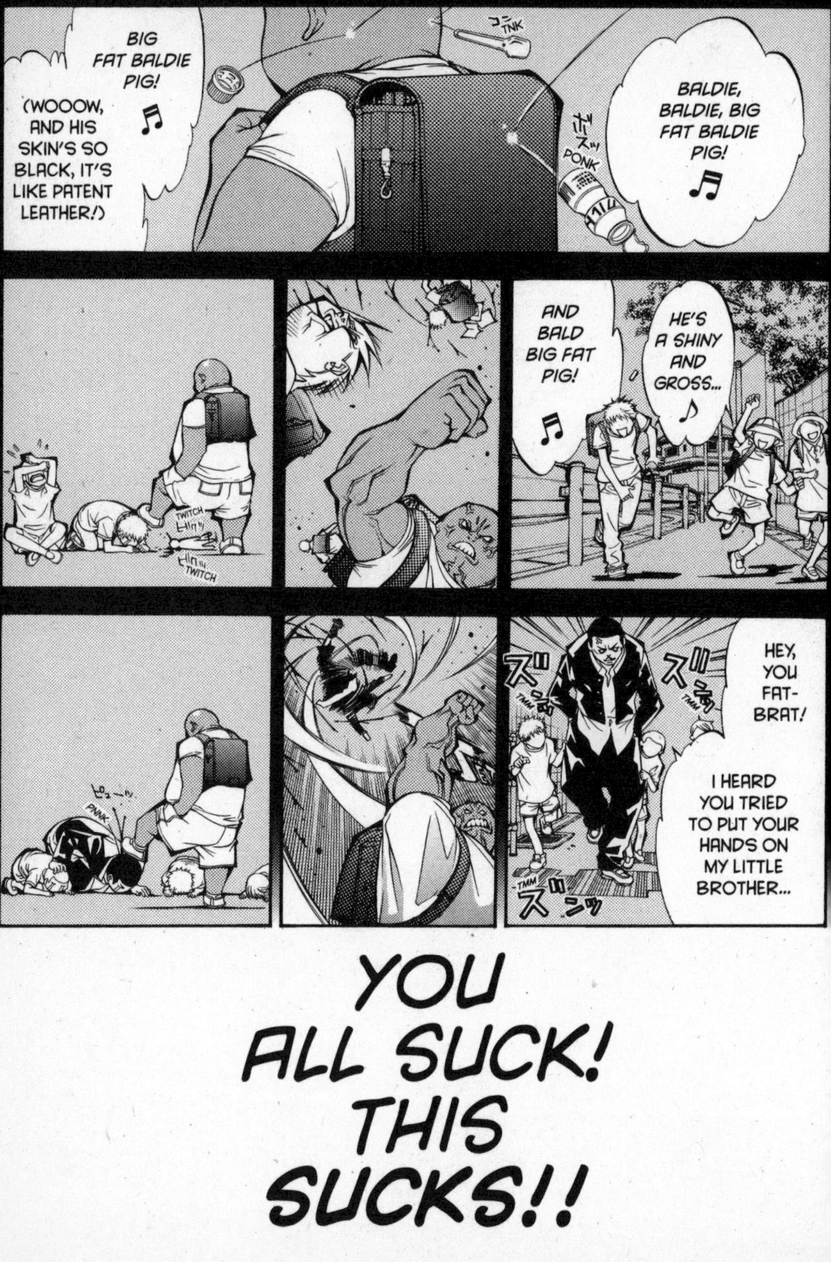
BALDIE, BALDIE, BIG FAT BALDIE PIG! ♫
PONK
TNK
BIG FAT BALDIE PIG! ♫
(WOOOW, AND HIS SKIN'S SO BLACK, IT'S LIKE PATENT LEATHER!)
HE'S A SHINY AND GROSS... ♪
AND BALD BIG FAT PIG! ♫
TWITCH
TWITCH
HEY, YOU FAT-BRAT!
I HEARD YOU TRIED TO PUT YOUR HANDS ON MY LITTLE BROTHER...
TMM
TMM
TMM
PNNK
YOU ALL SUCK! THIS SUCKS!!

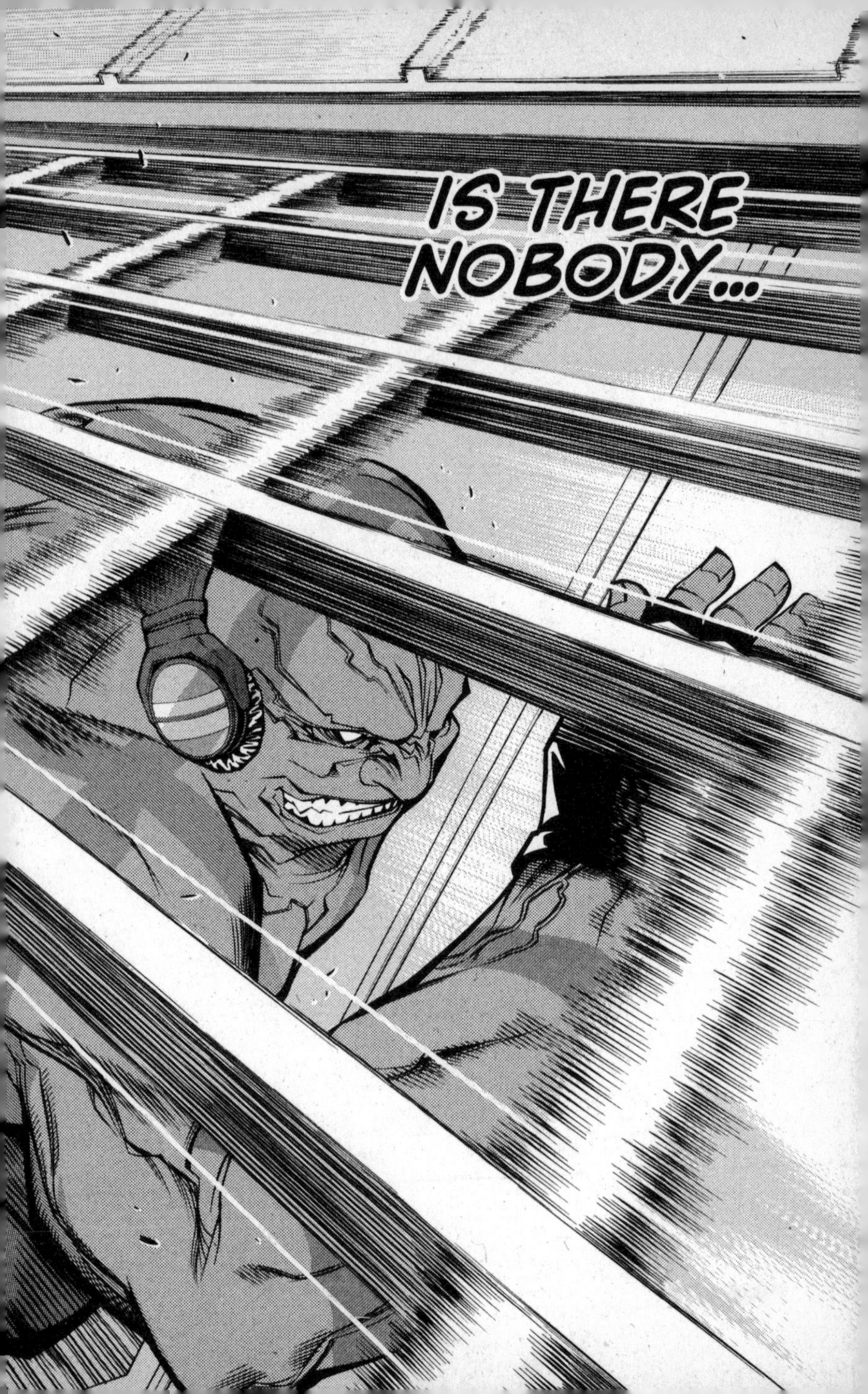
IS THERE NOBODY...

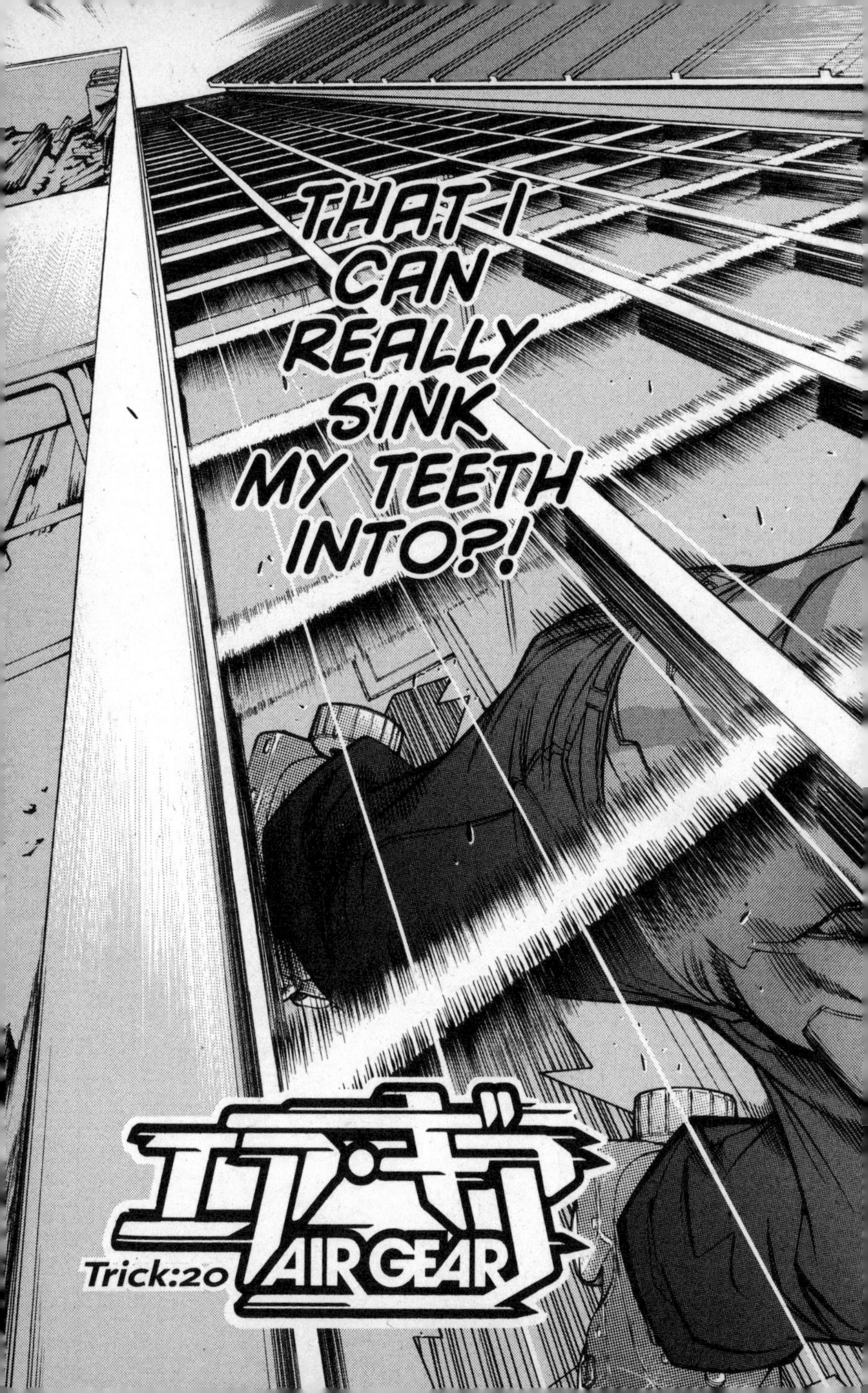
THAT I CAN REALLY SINK MY TEETH INTO?!
AIR GEAR
Trick:20

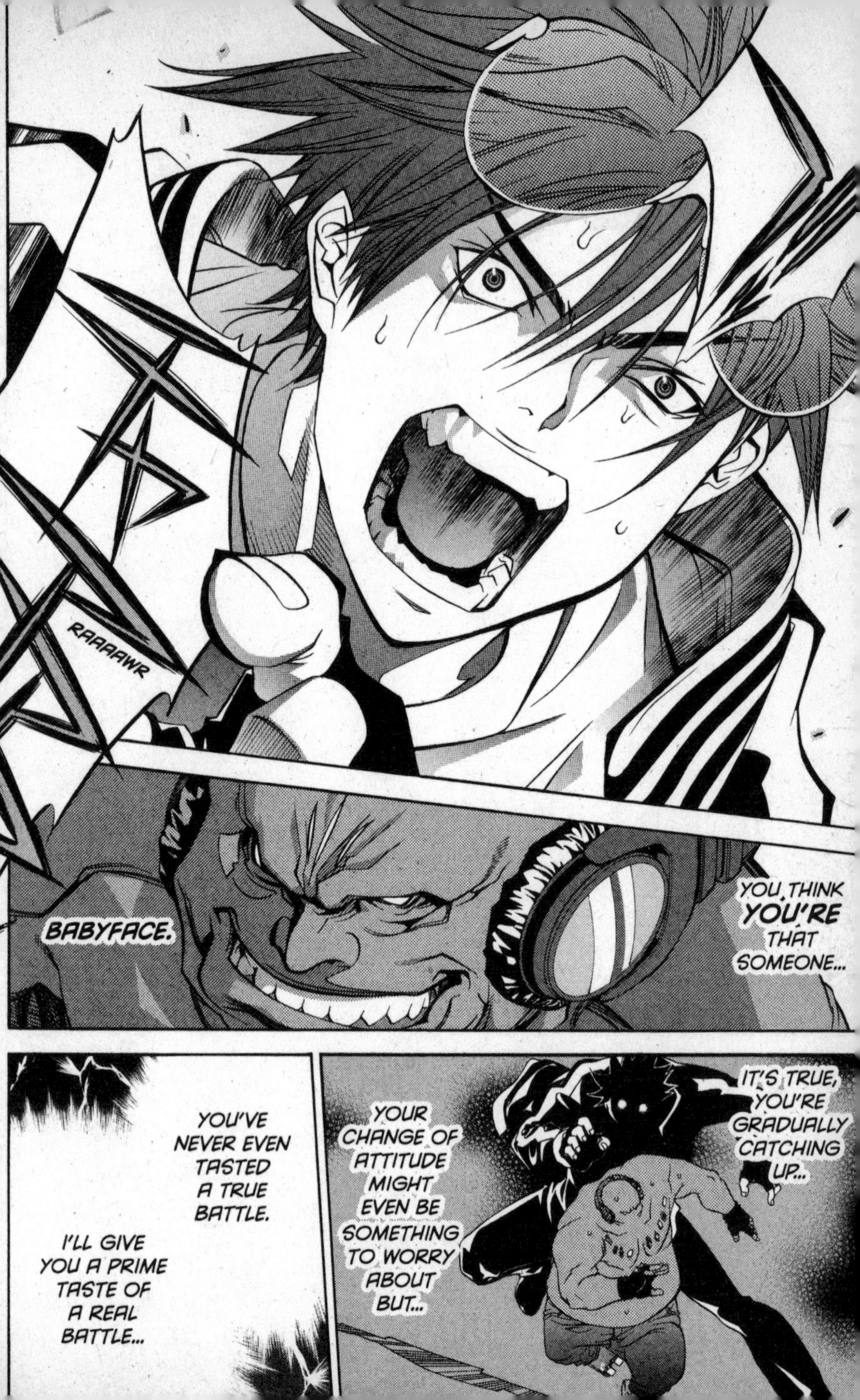
RAAAAWR
YOU THINK YOU'RE THAT SOMEONE...
BABYFACE.
IT'S TRUE, YOU'RE GRADUALLY CATCHING UP...
YOUR CHANGE OF ATTITUDE MIGHT EVEN BE SOMETHING TO WORRY ABOUT BUT...
YOU'VE NEVER EVEN TASTED A TRUE BATTLE.
I'LL GIVE YOU A PRIME TASTE OF A REAL BATTLE...

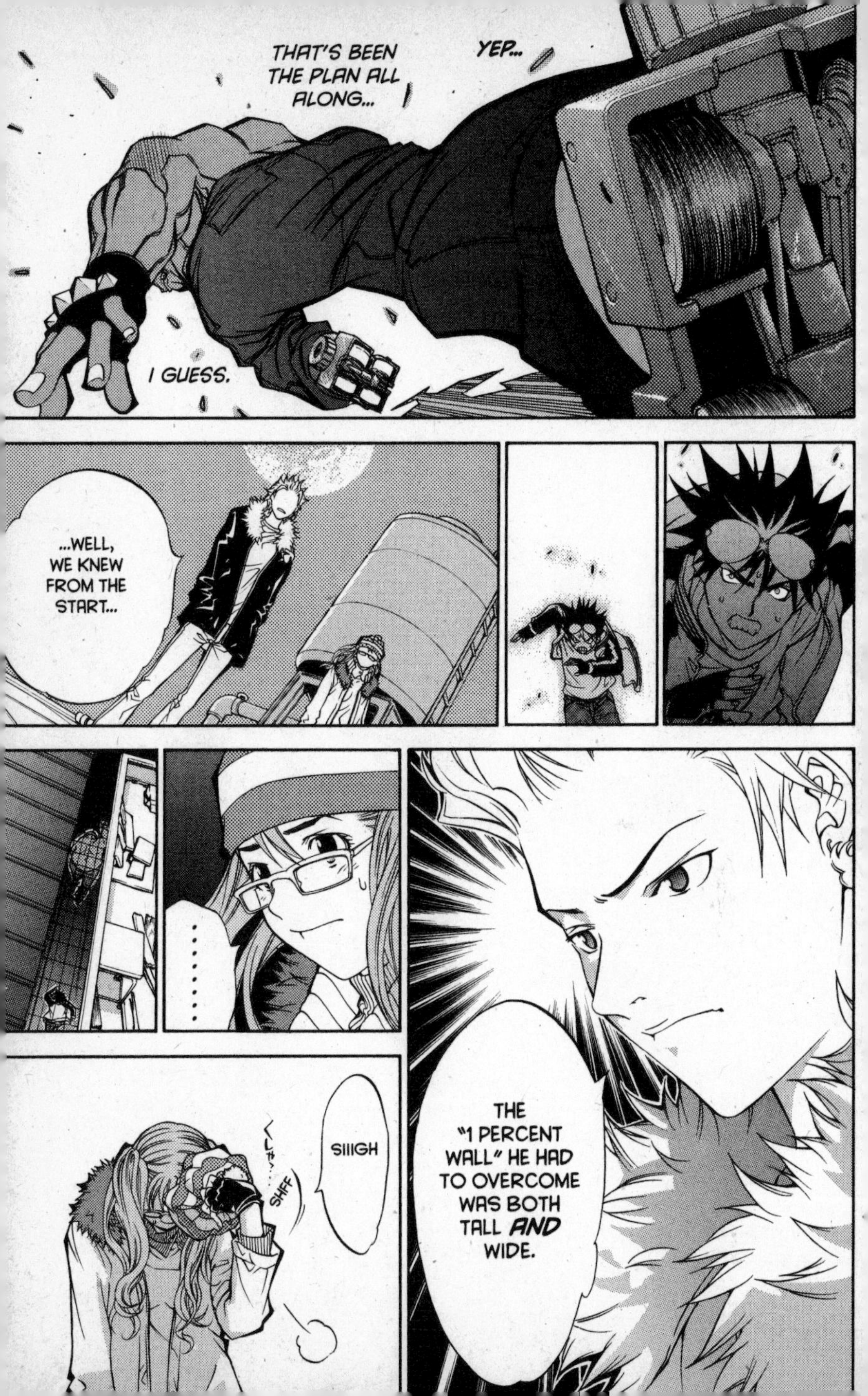

YEP...
THAT'S BEEN THE PLAN ALL ALONG...
I GUESS.
...WELL, WE KNEW FROM THE START...
THE "1 PERCENT WALL" HE HAD TO OVERCOME WAS BOTH TALL *AND* WIDE.
......
SIIIGH
SHFF

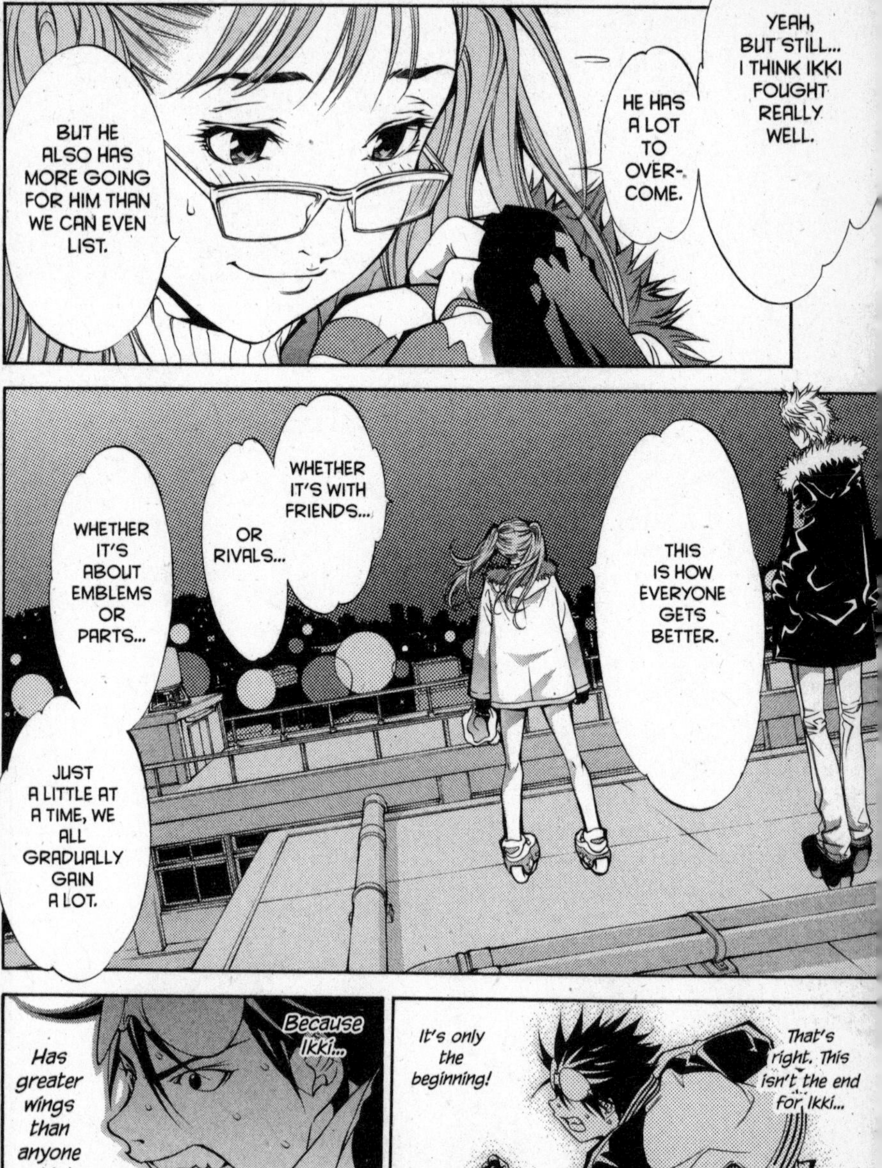
YEAH, BUT STILL... I THINK IKKI FOUGHT REALLY WELL.
HE HAS A LOT TO OVER-COME.
BUT HE ALSO HAS MORE GOING FOR HIM THAN WE CAN EVEN LIST.
THIS IS HOW EVERYONE GETS BETTER.
WHETHER IT'S WITH FRIENDS...
OR RIVALS...
WHETHER IT'S ABOUT EMBLEMS OR PARTS...
JUST A LITTLE AT A TIME, WE ALL GRADUALLY GAIN A LOT.
That's right. This isn't the end for Ikki...
It's only the beginning!
Because Ikki...
Has greater wings than anyone else!

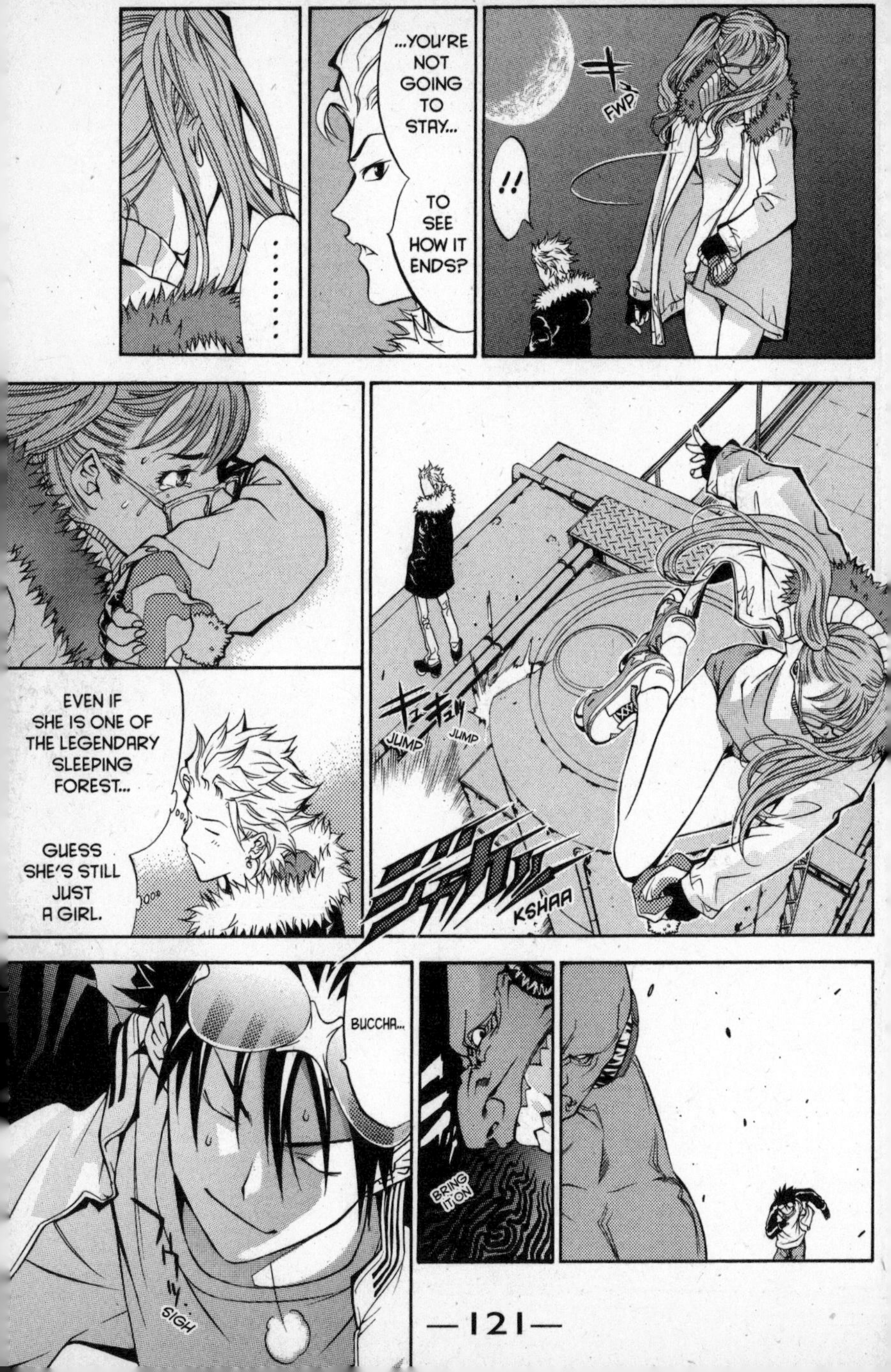
FWP
!!
...YOU'RE NOT GOING TO STAY...
TO SEE HOW IT ENDS?
......
JUMP
JUMP
KSHAA
EVEN IF SHE IS ONE OF THE LEGENDARY SLEEPING FOREST...
GUESS SHE'S STILL JUST A GIRL.
BRING IT ON
BUCCHA...
SIGH

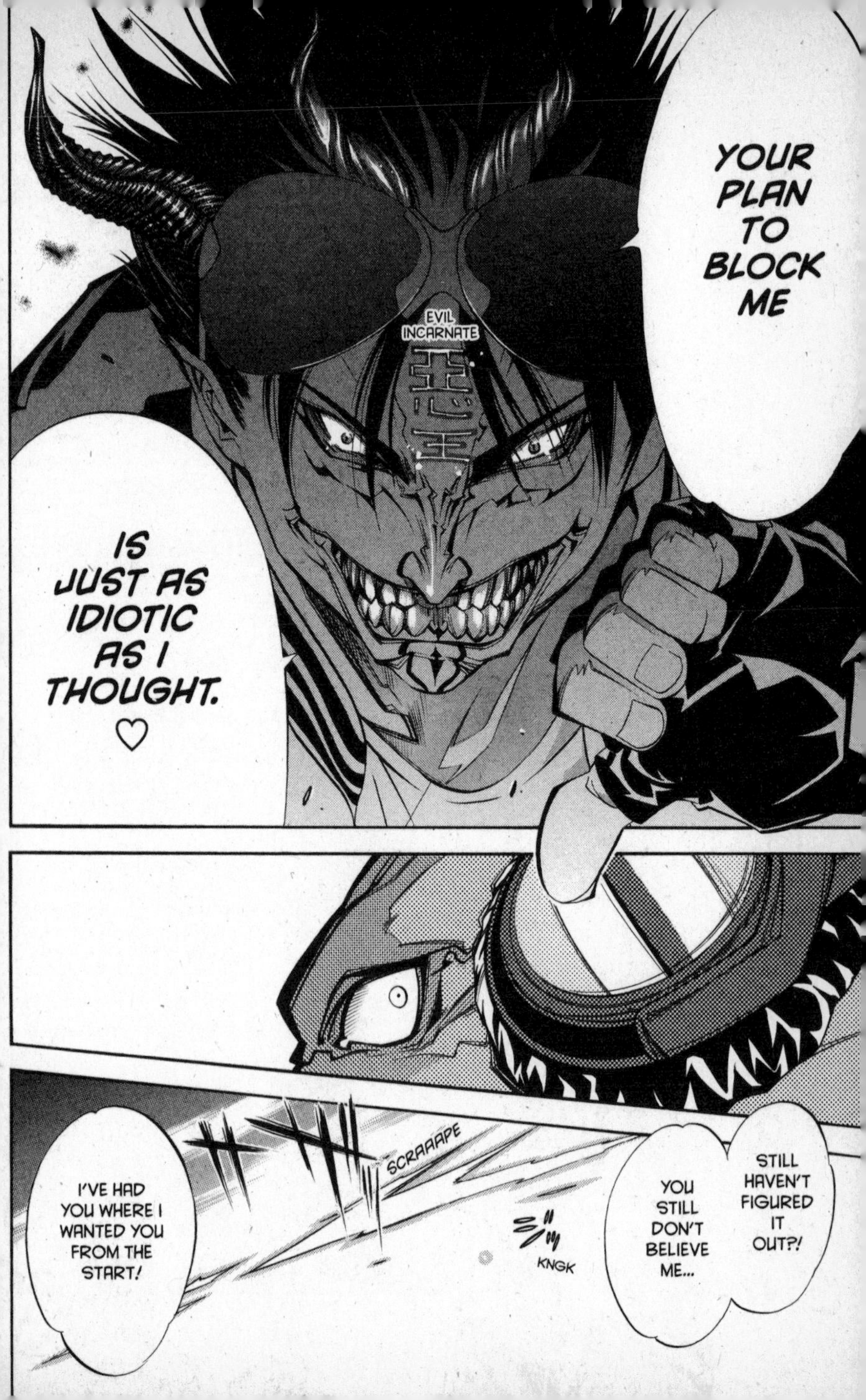
YOUR PLAN TO BLOCK ME
EVIL INCARNATE
IS JUST AS IDIOTIC AS I THOUGHT. ♡
STILL HAVEN'T FIGURED IT OUT?!
YOU STILL DON'T BELIEVE ME...
KNGK
SCRAAAPE
I'VE HAD YOU WHERE I WANTED YOU FROM THE START!

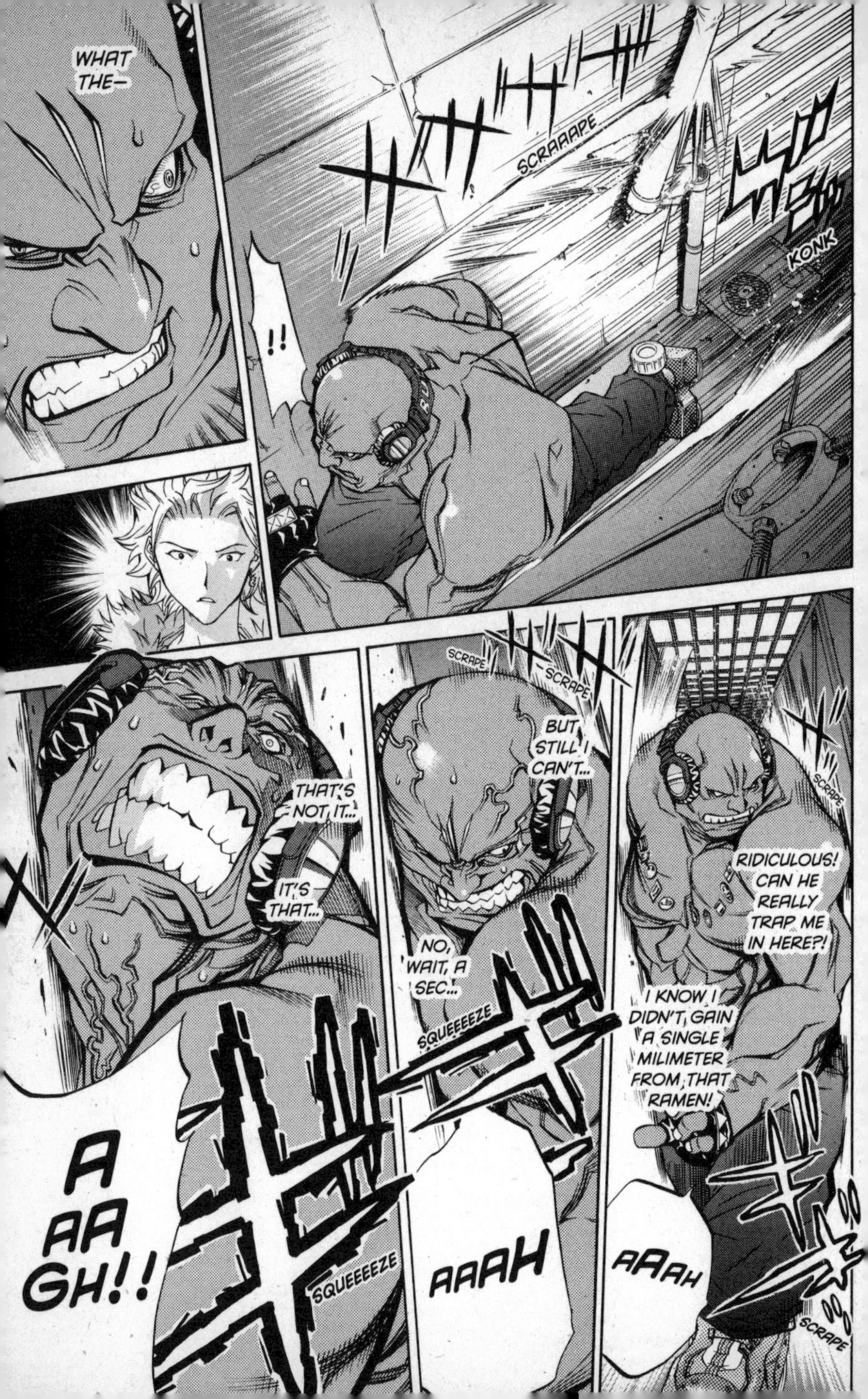
SCRAAAPE
KONK
!!
WHAT THE—
SCRAPE
RIDICULOUS! CAN HE REALLY TRAP ME IN HERE?!
I KNOW I DIDN'T GAIN A SINGLE MILIMETER FROM THAT RAMEN!
AAAH
SCRAPE
SCRAPE
SCRAPE
BUT, STILL I CAN'T...
NO, WAIT, A SEC...
SQUEEEEZE
AAAH
THAT'S NOT IT...
IT'S THAT...
SQUEEEEZE
A AAGH!!

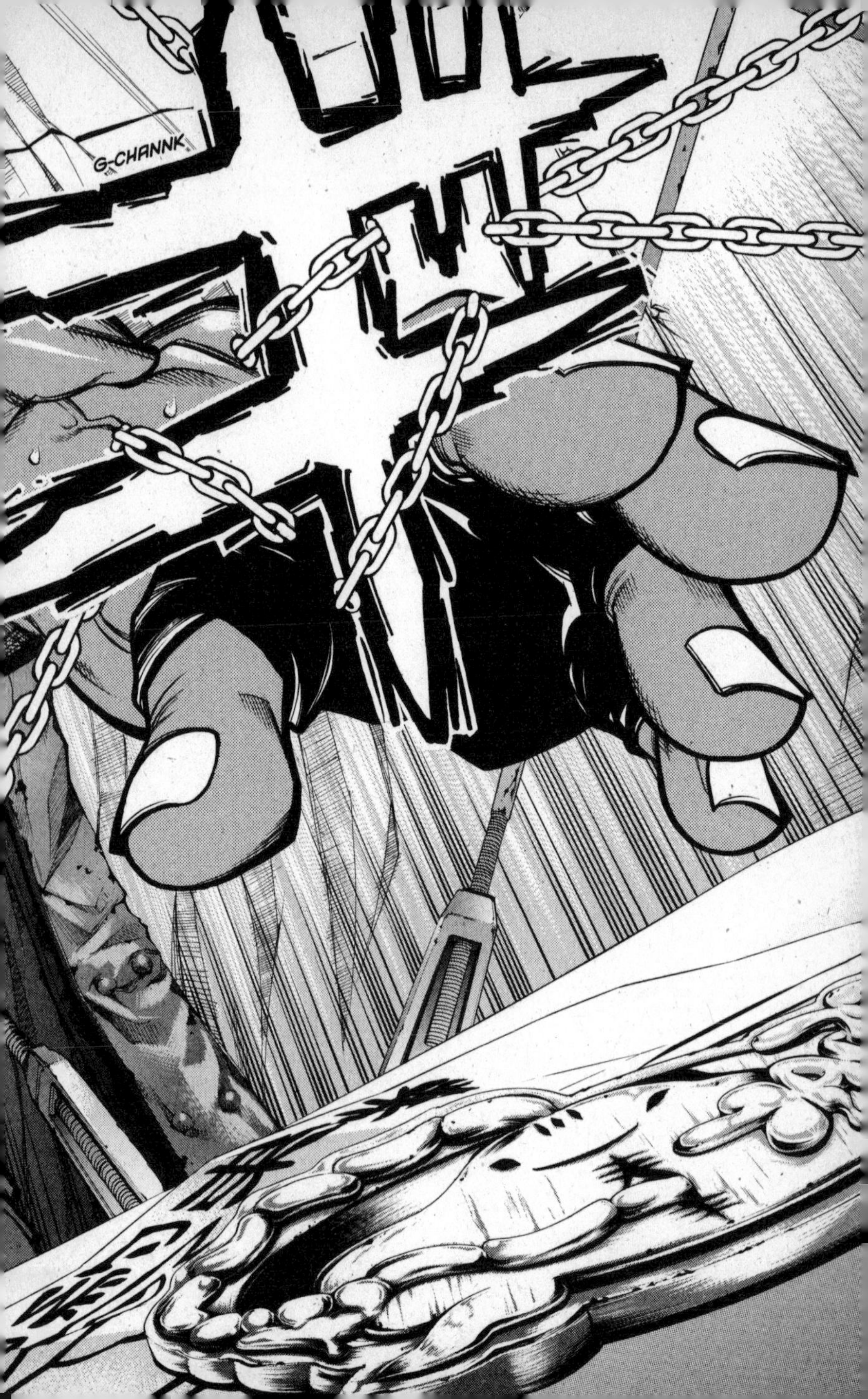
G-CHANNK

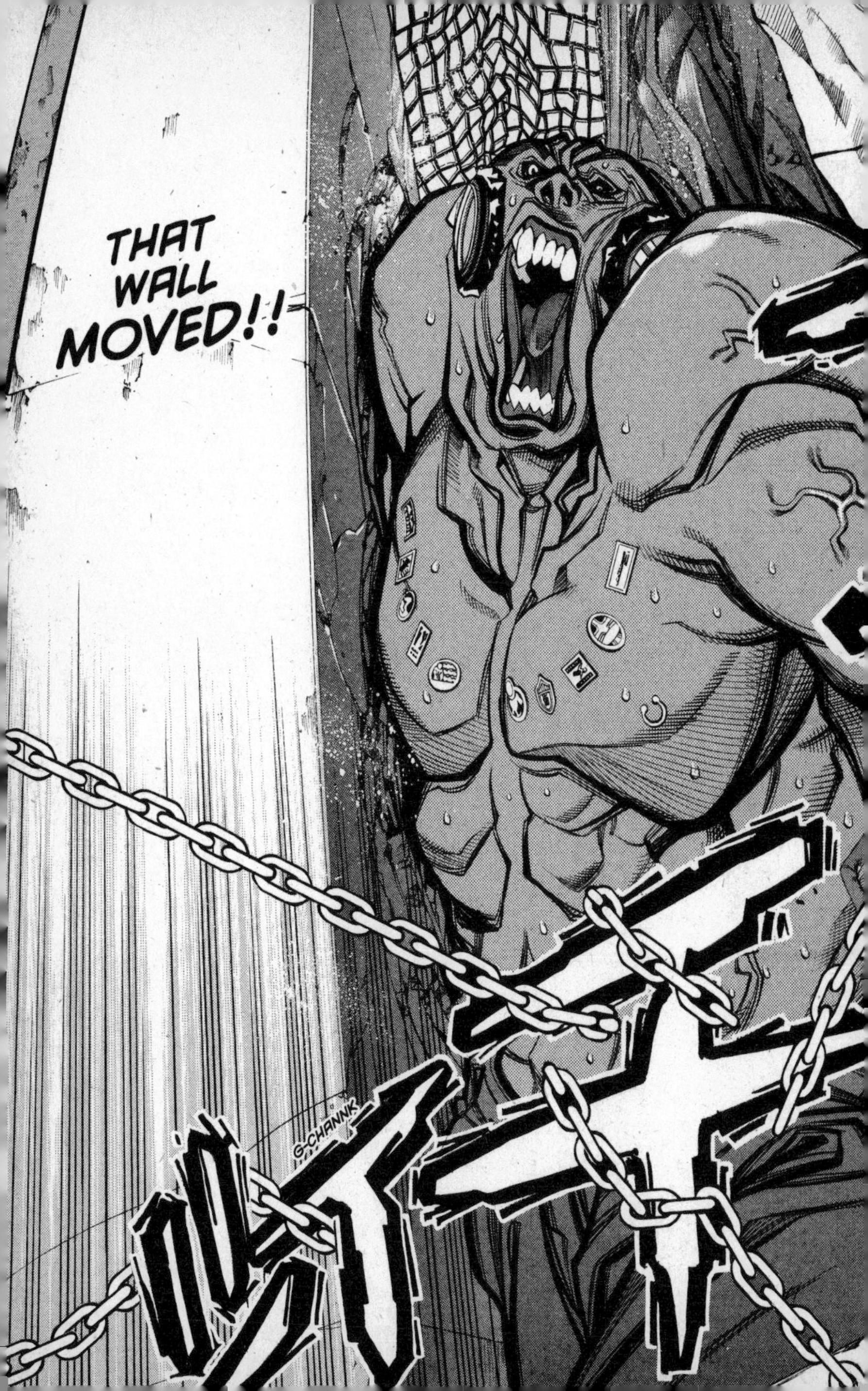
THAT WALL MOVED!!
G-CHANNK

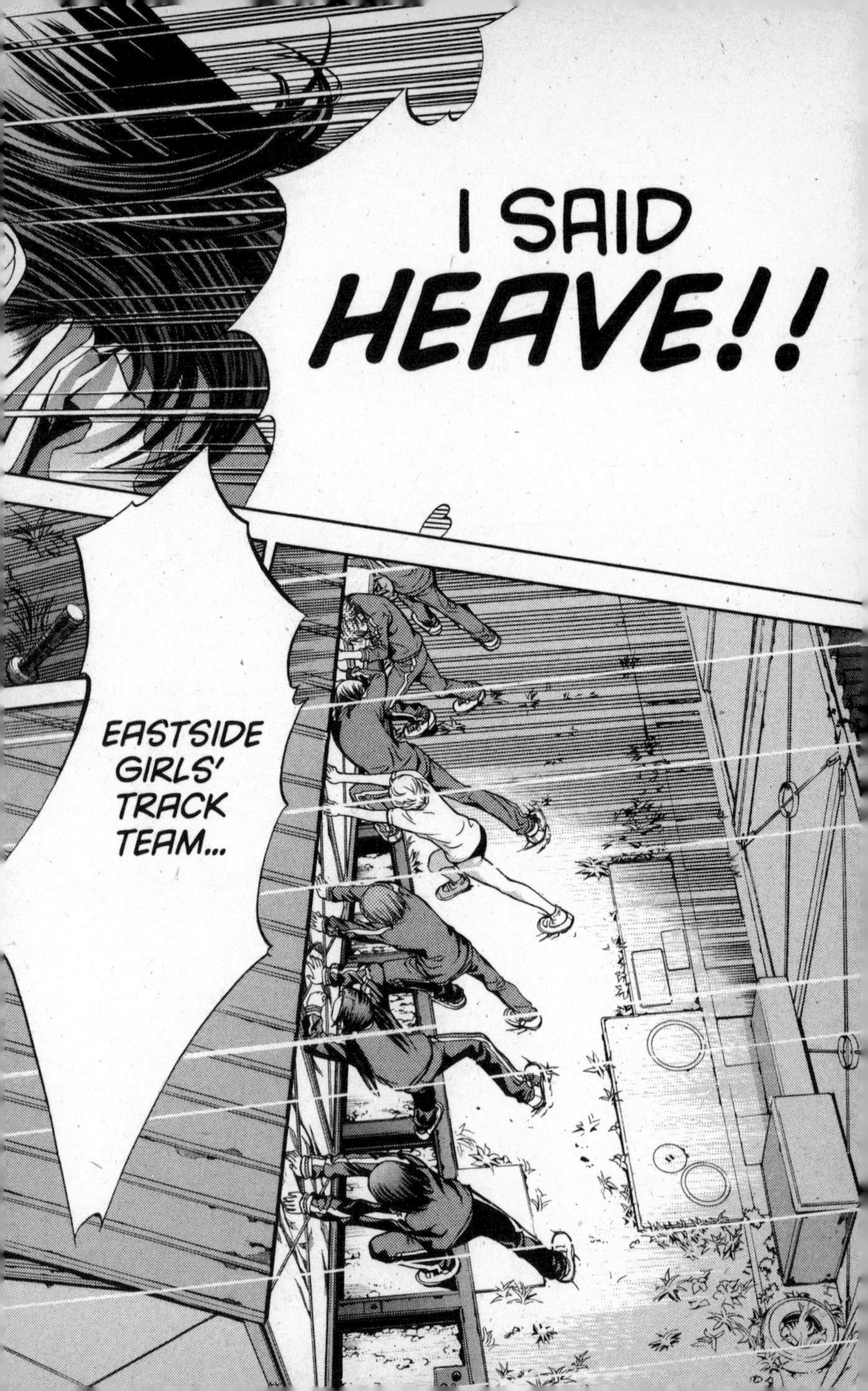
I SAID HEAVE!!
EASTSIDE GIRLS' TRACK TEAM...

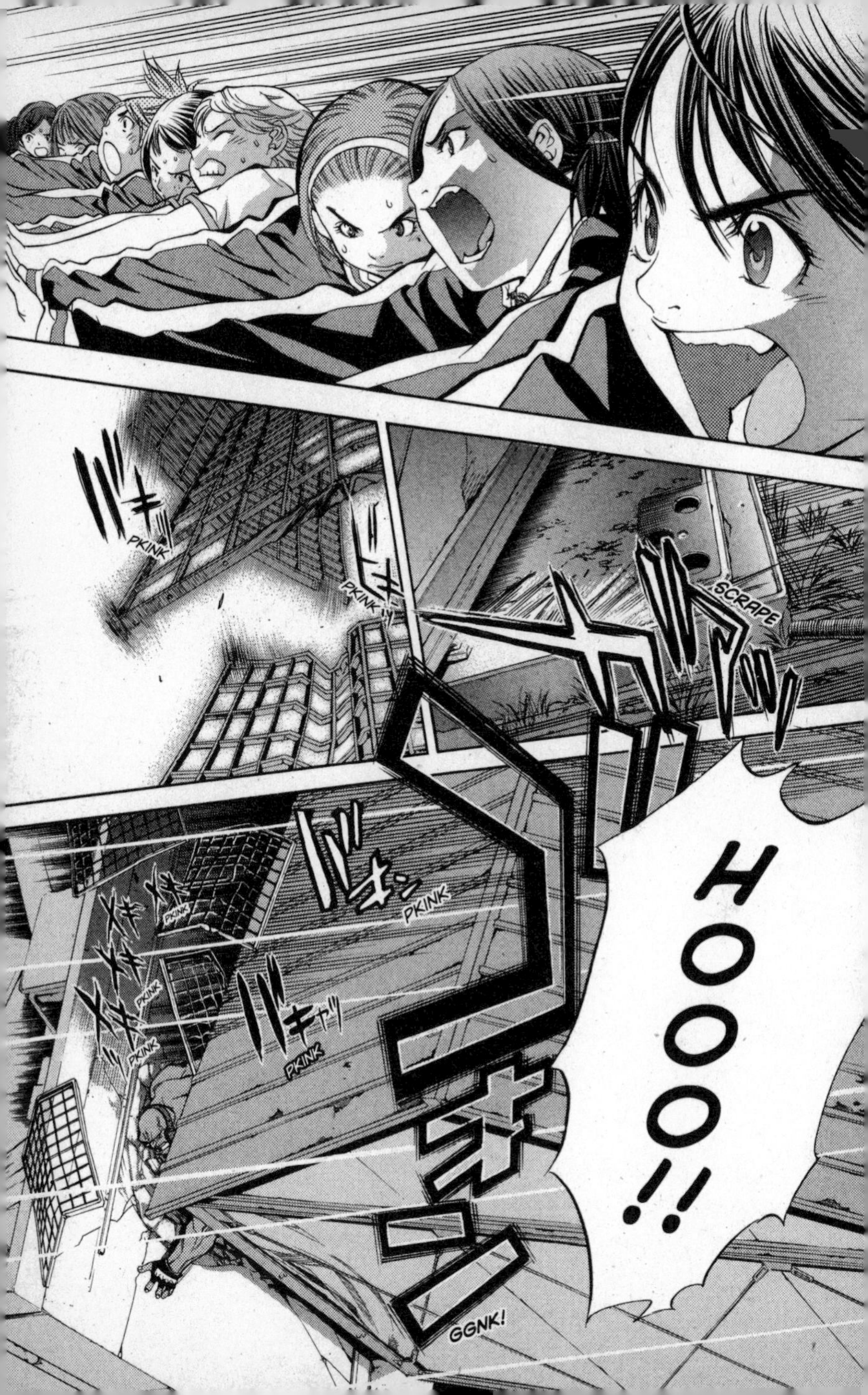
SCRAPE
PKINK
PKINK
HOOOO!!
PKINK
PKINK
PKINK
PKINK
PKINK
GGNK!

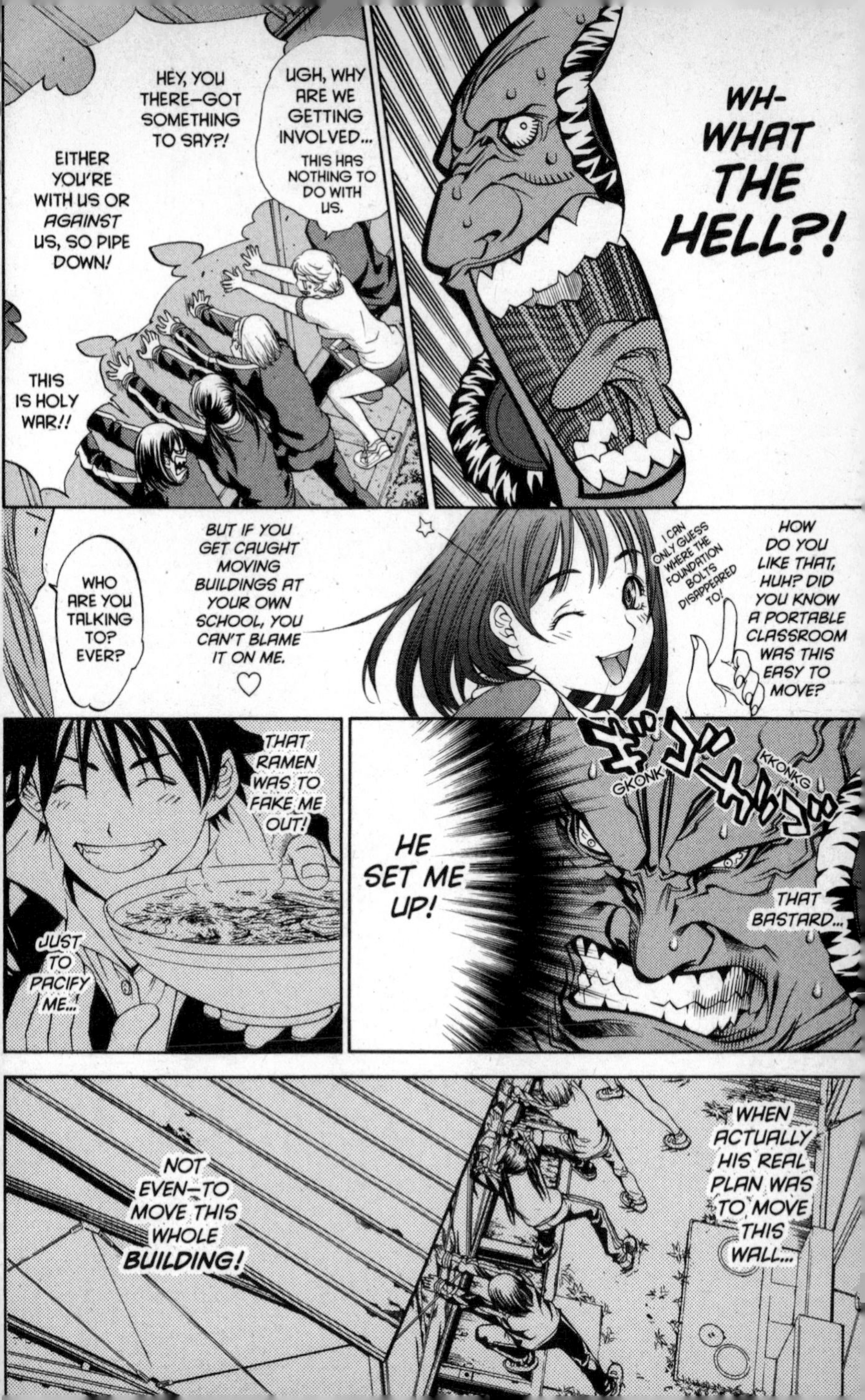
WH- WHAT THE HELL?!
UGH, WHY ARE WE GETTING INVOLVED...
THIS HAS NOTHING TO DO WITH US.
HEY, YOU THERE—GOT SOMETHING TO SAY?!
EITHER YOU'RE WITH US OR *AGAINST* US, SO PIPE DOWN!
THIS IS HOLY WAR!!
HOW DO YOU LIKE THAT, HUH? DID YOU KNOW A PORTABLE CLASSROOM WAS THIS EASY TO MOVE?
I CAN ONLY GUESS WHERE THE FOUNDATION BOLTS DISAPPEARED TO!
BUT IF YOU GET CAUGHT MOVING BUILDINGS AT YOUR OWN SCHOOL, YOU CAN'T BLAME IT ON ME. ♡
WHO ARE YOU TALKING TO? EVER?
KKONKG
GKONK
THAT BASTARD...
HE SET ME UP!
THAT RAMEN WAS TO FAKE ME OUT!
JUST TO PACIFY ME...
WHEN ACTUALLY HIS REAL PLAN WAS TO MOVE THIS WALL...
NOT EVEN—TO MOVE THIS WHOLE **BUILDING!**

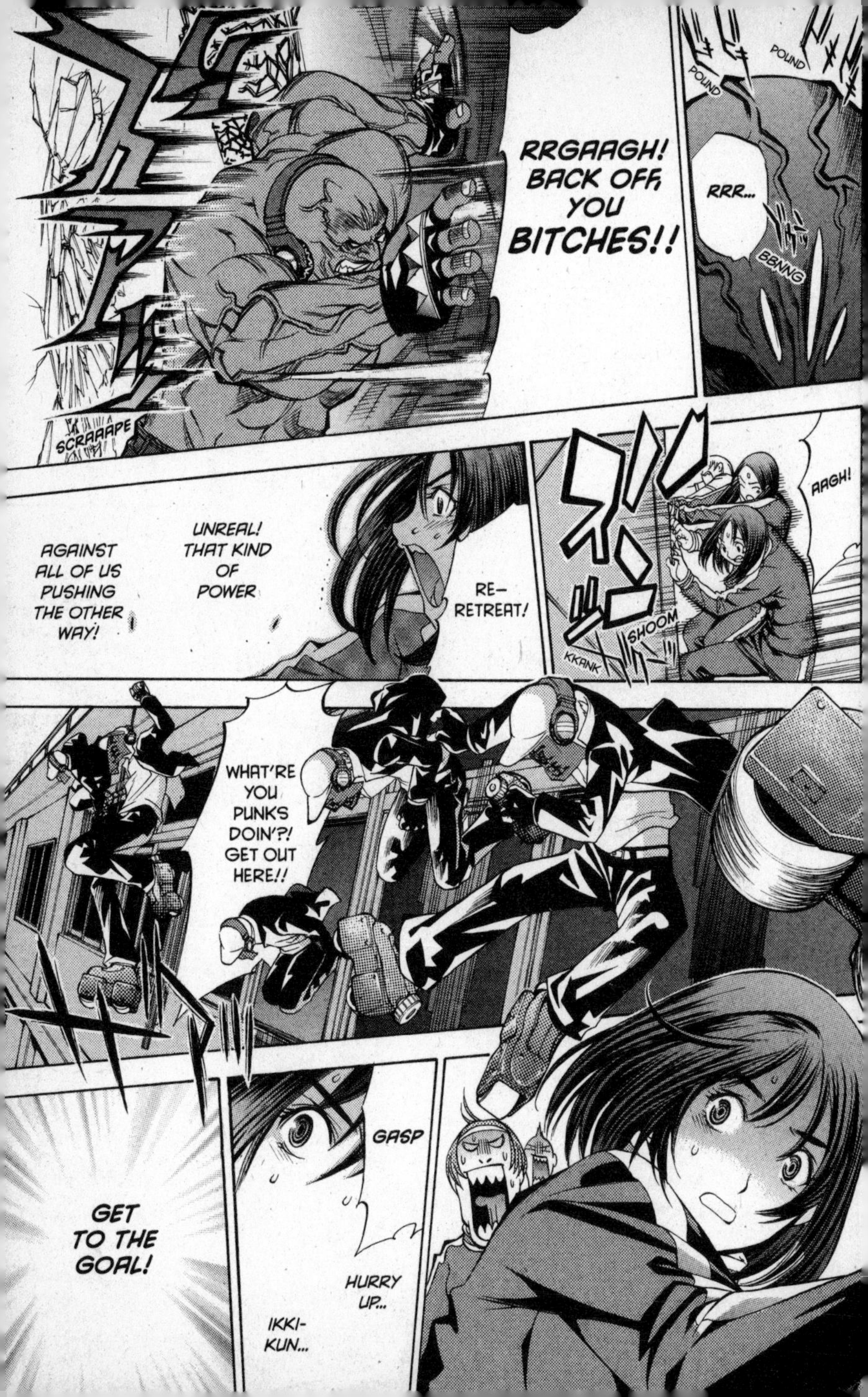
POUND
POUND
RRR...
BBNNG
RRGAAGH! BACK OFF, YOU BITCHES!!
SCRAAAPE
AAGH!
SHOOM
KKANK
RE-RETREAT!
UNREAL! THAT KIND OF POWER
AGAINST ALL OF US PUSHING THE OTHER WAY!
WHAT'RE YOU PUNKS DOIN'?! GET OUT HERE!!
HURRY UP...
IKKI-KUN...
GASP
GET TO THE GOAL!

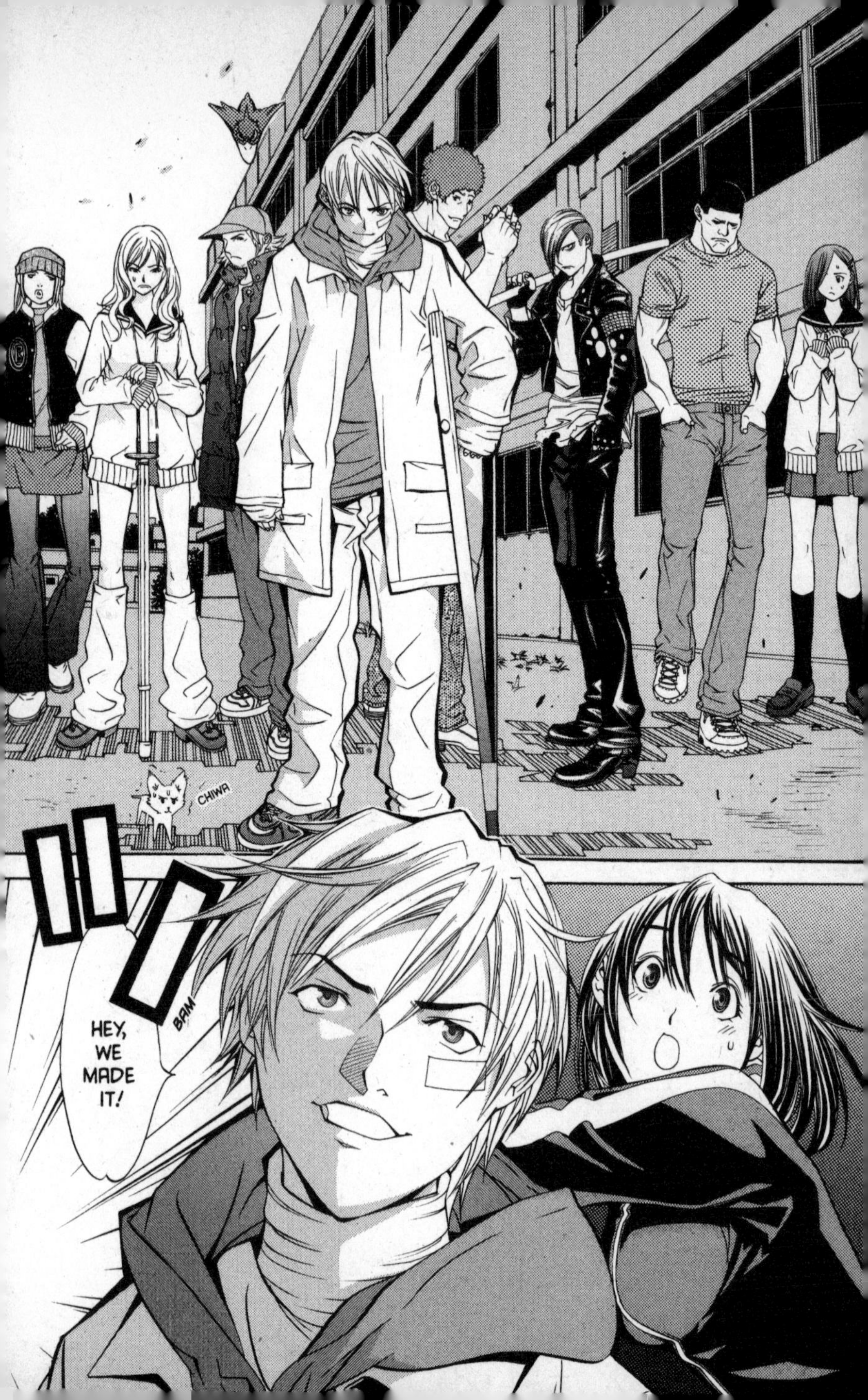
CHIWA
BAM
HEY, WE MADE IT!

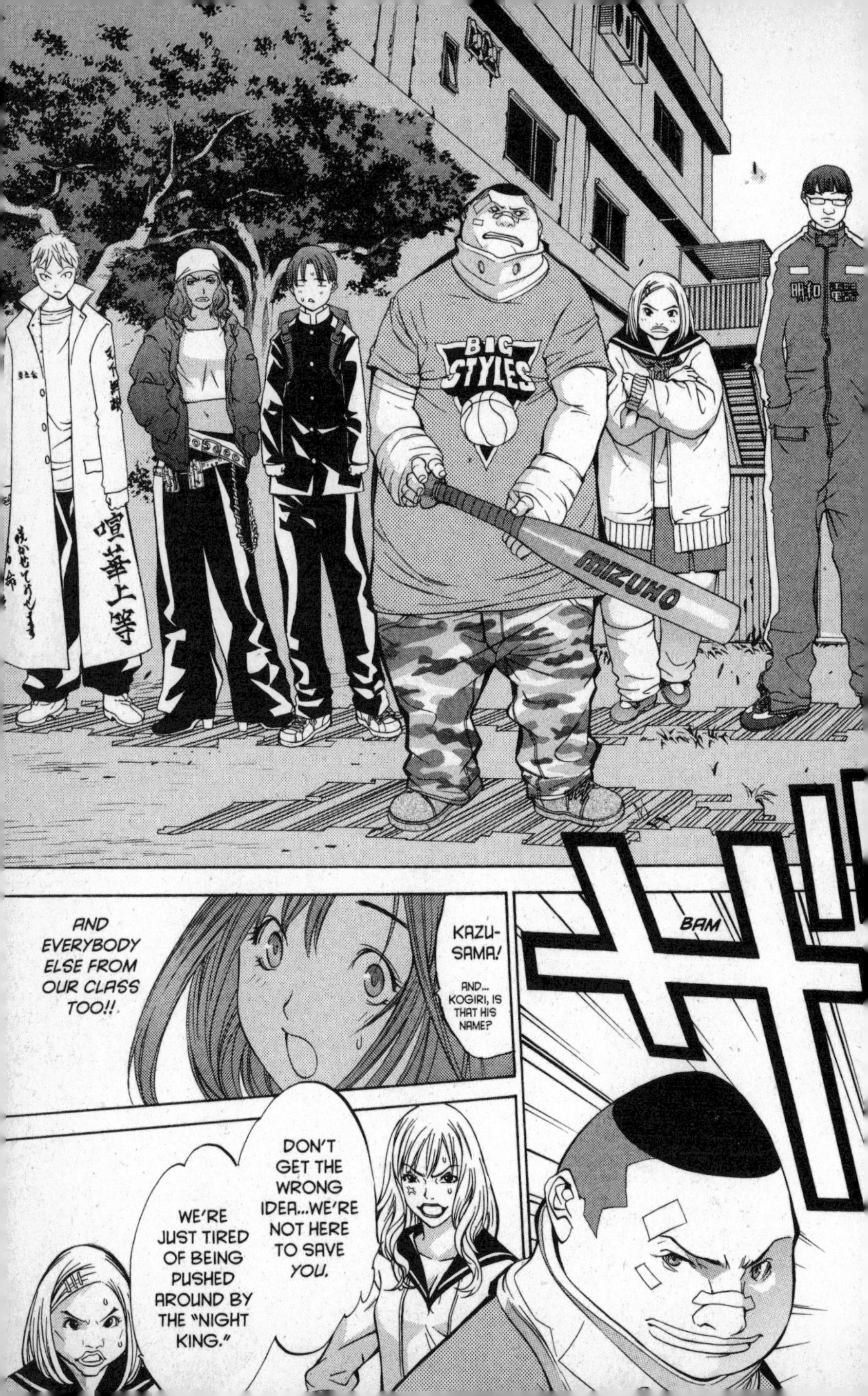

喧華上等
BIG STYLES
MIZUHO
BAM
KAZU-SAMA!
AND... KOGIRI, IS THAT HIS NAME?
AND EVERYBODY ELSE FROM OUR CLASS TOO!!
DON'T GET THE WRONG IDEA...WE'RE NOT HERE TO SAVE YOU.
WE'RE JUST TIRED OF BEING PUSHED AROUND BY THE "NIGHT KING."

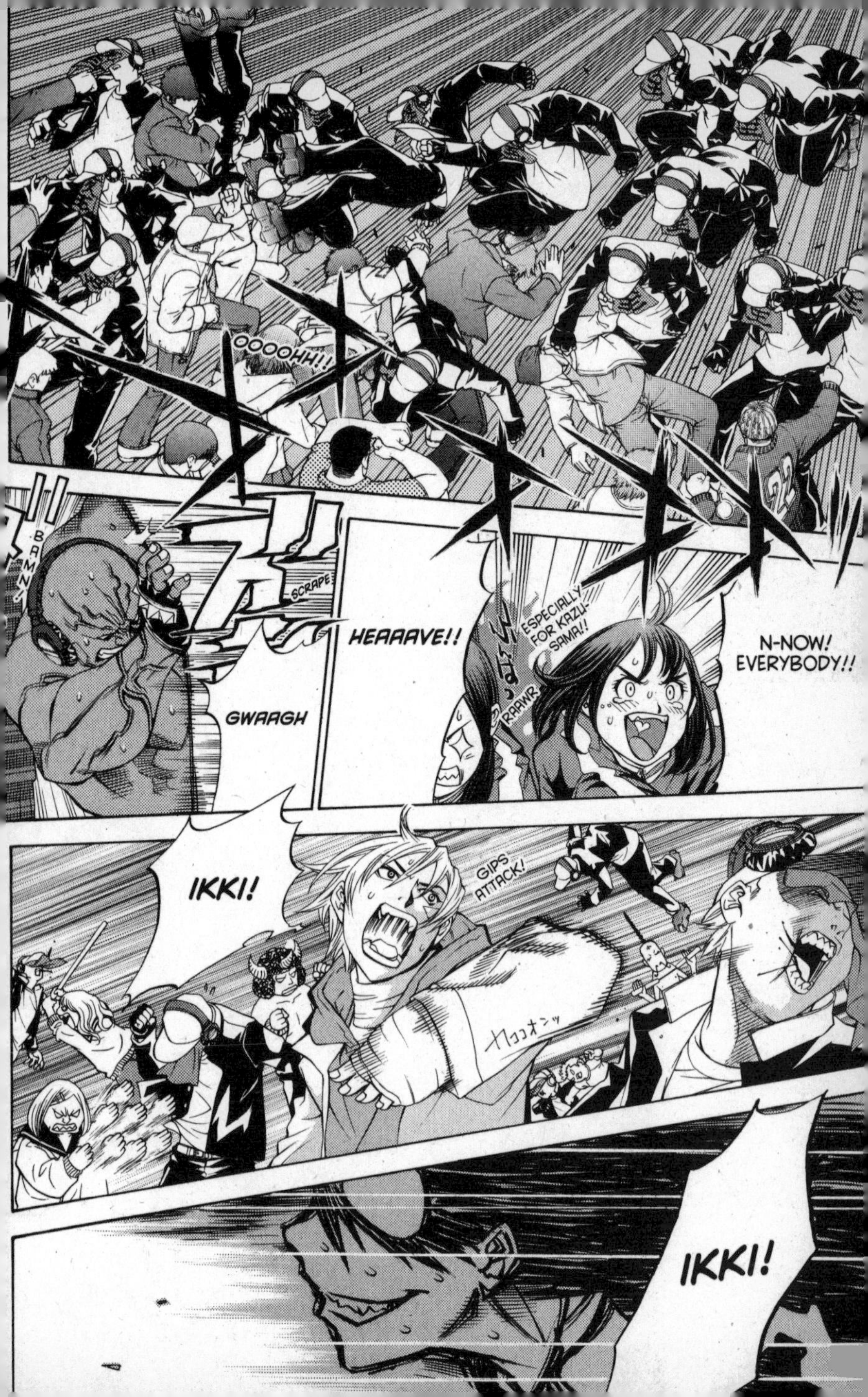
OOOOHH!!
N-NOW! EVERYBODY!!
ESPECIALLY FOR KAZU-SAMA!!
RAAWR
HEAAAVE!!
BAMN
SCRAPE
GWAAGH
IKKI!
GIPS ATTACK!
IKKI!

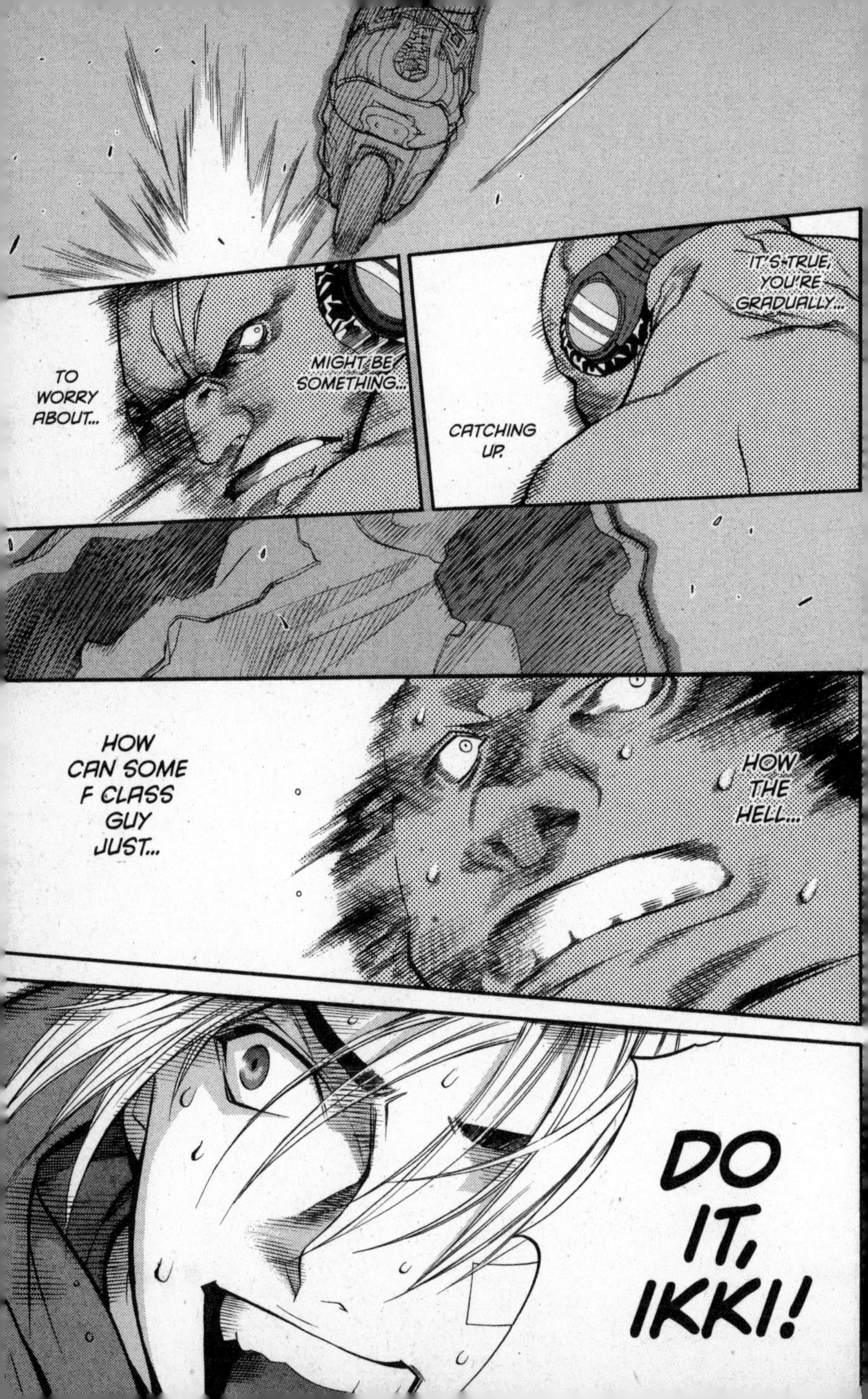
IT'S TRUE, YOU'RE GRADUALLY...
CATCHING UP.
MIGHT BE SOMETHING...
TO WORRY ABOUT...
HOW THE HELL...
HOW CAN SOME F CLASS GUY JUST...
DO IT, IKKI!

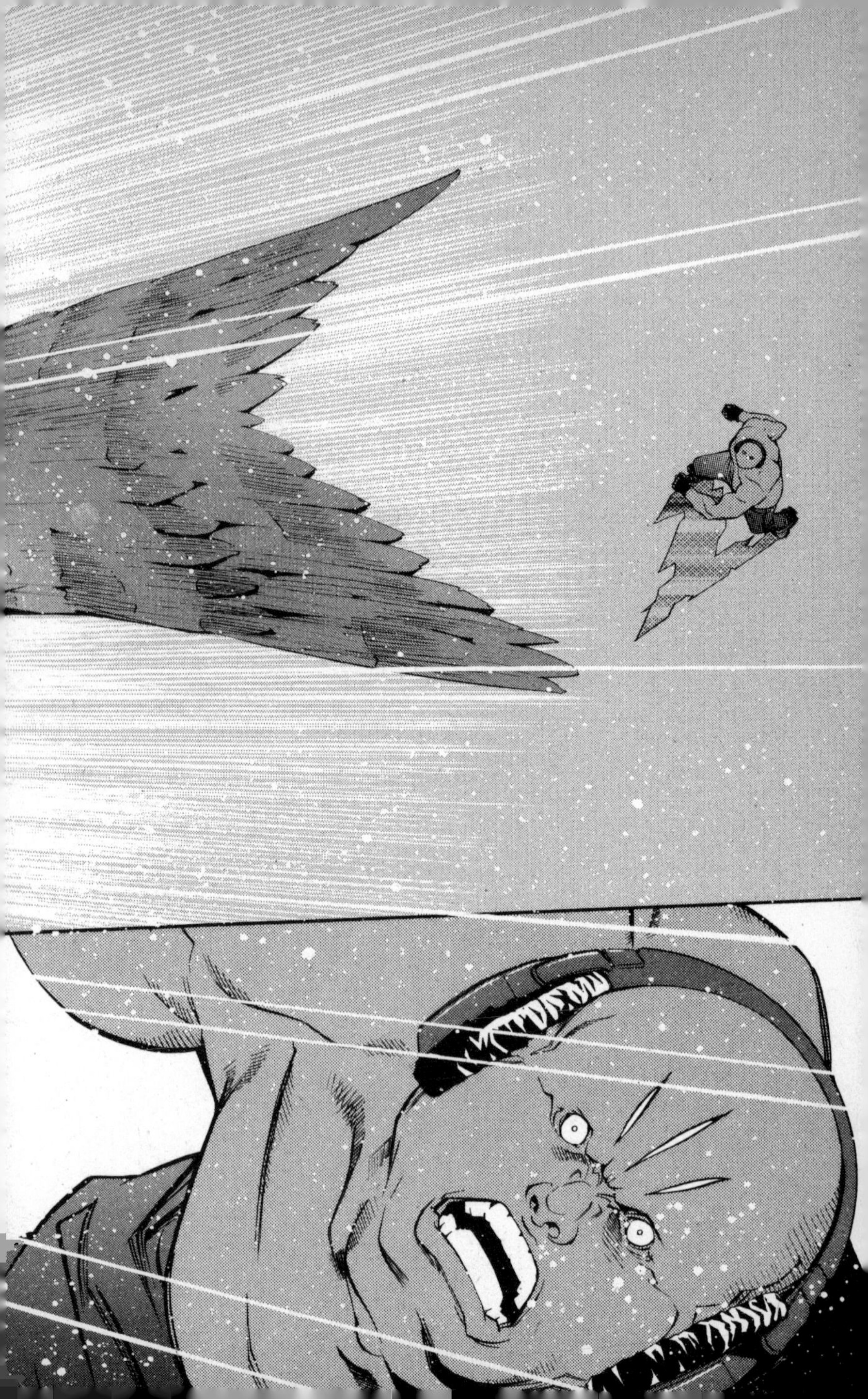

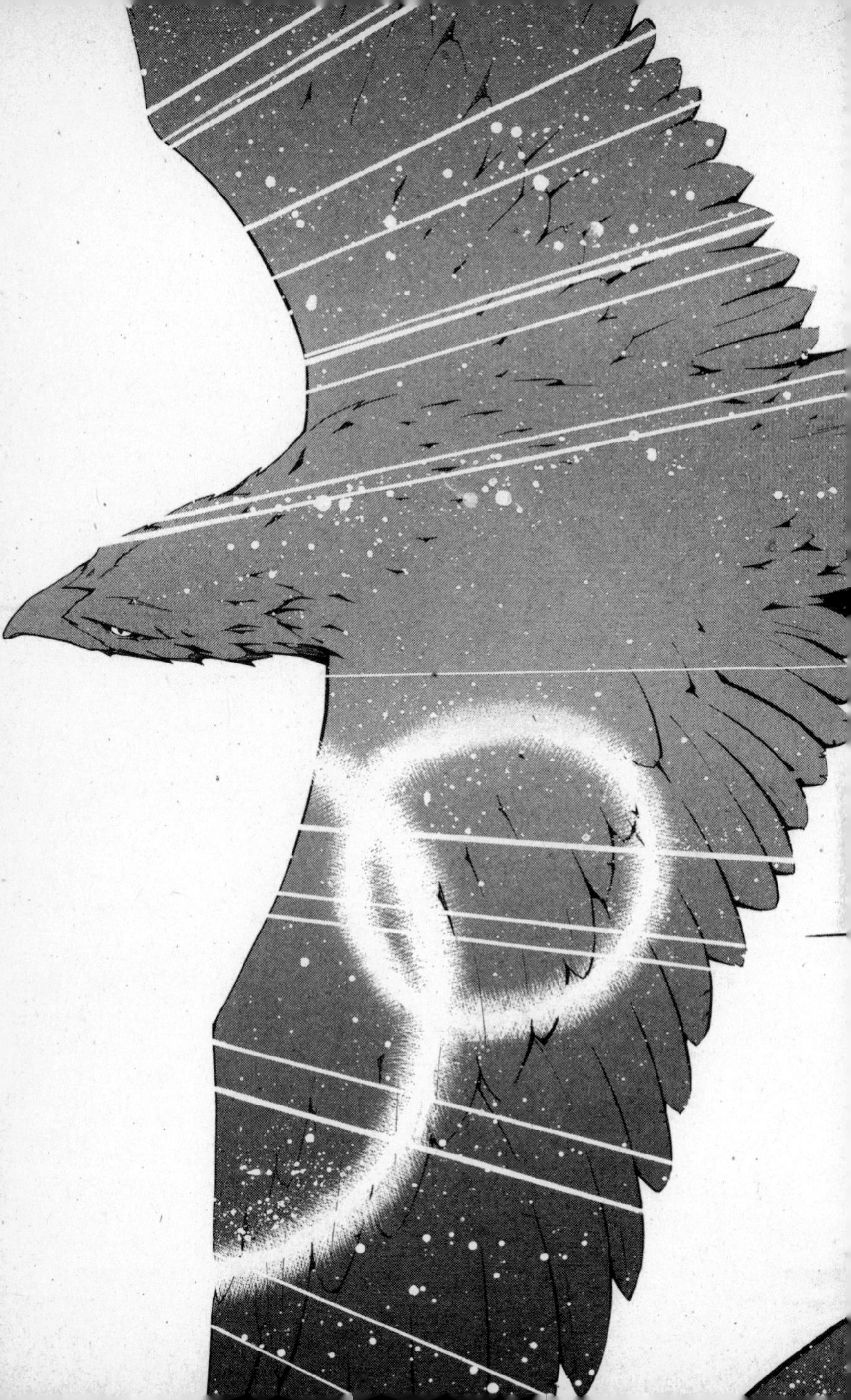

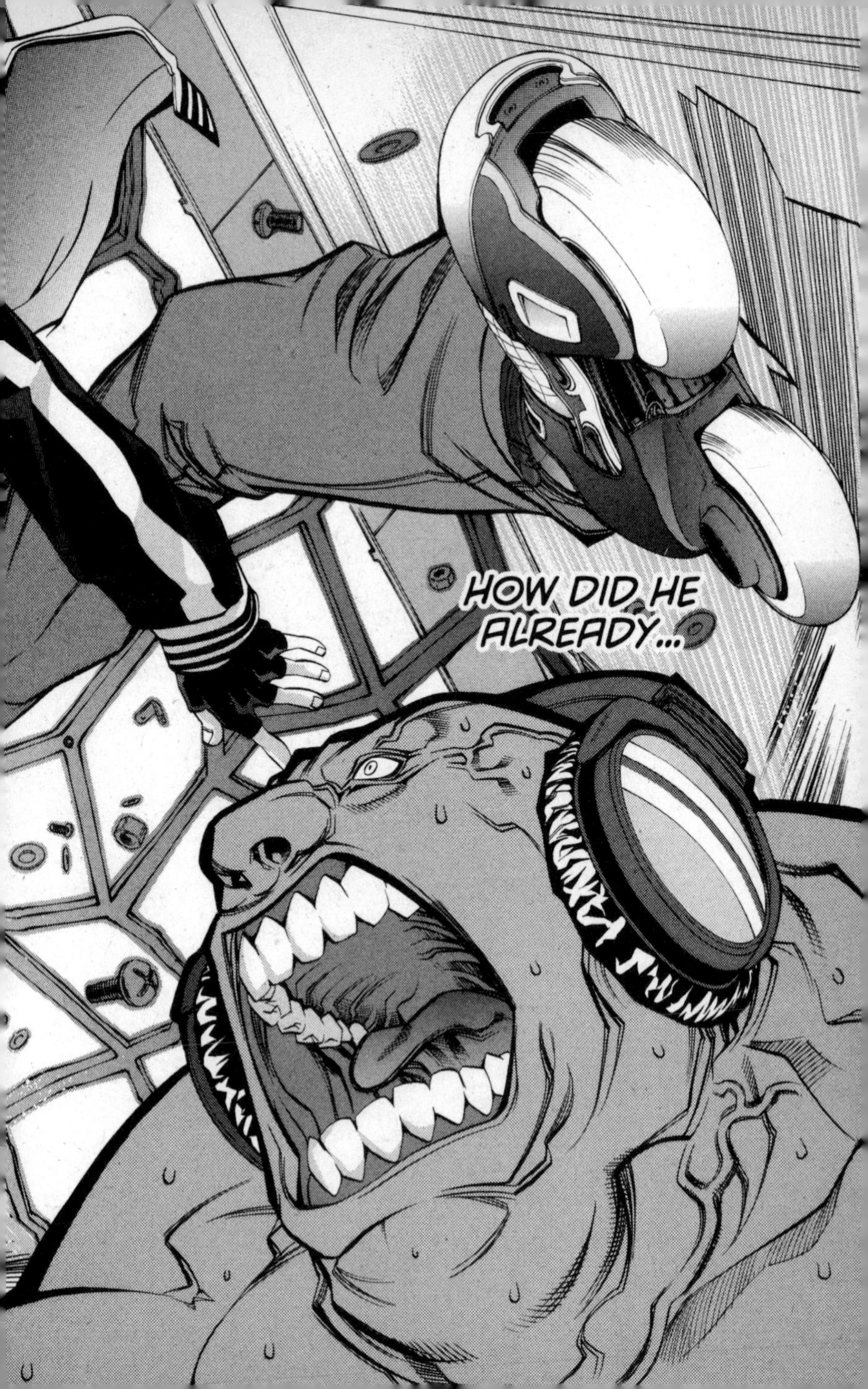
HOW DID HE ALREADY...

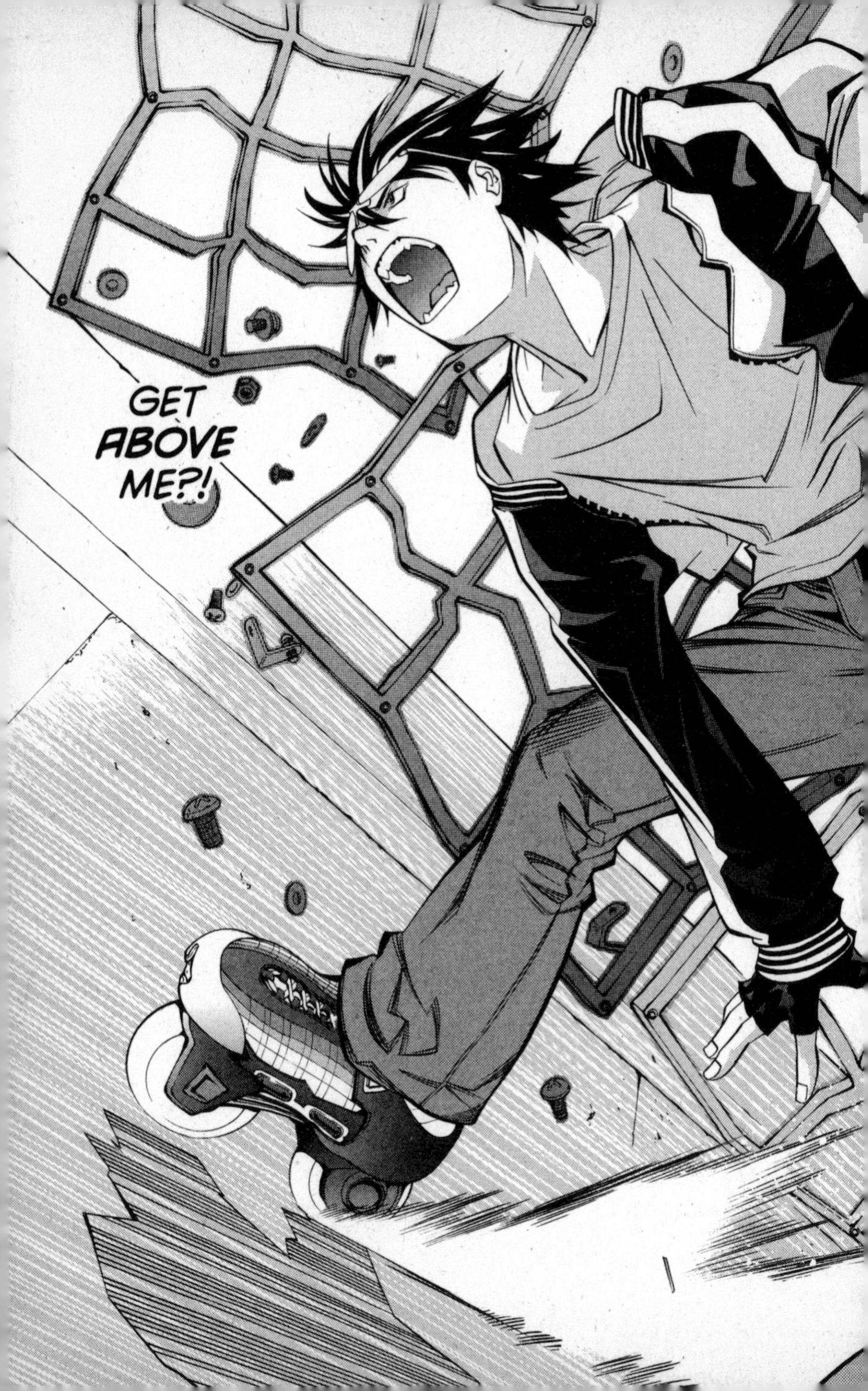
GET ABOVE ME?!

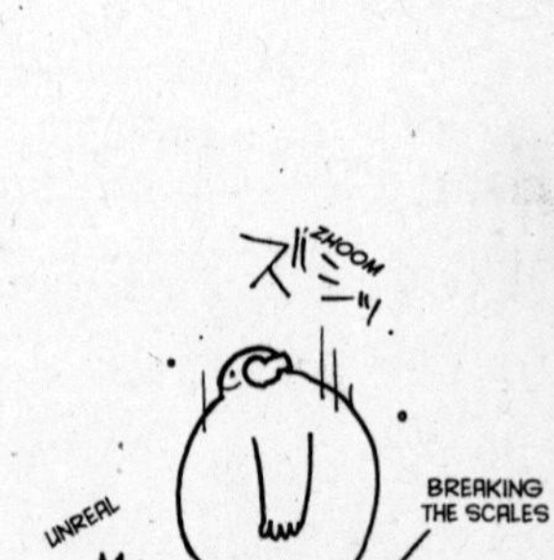
ズバーッ
ZHOOM
UNREAL
BREAKING
THE SCALES
グシャッ
GNK

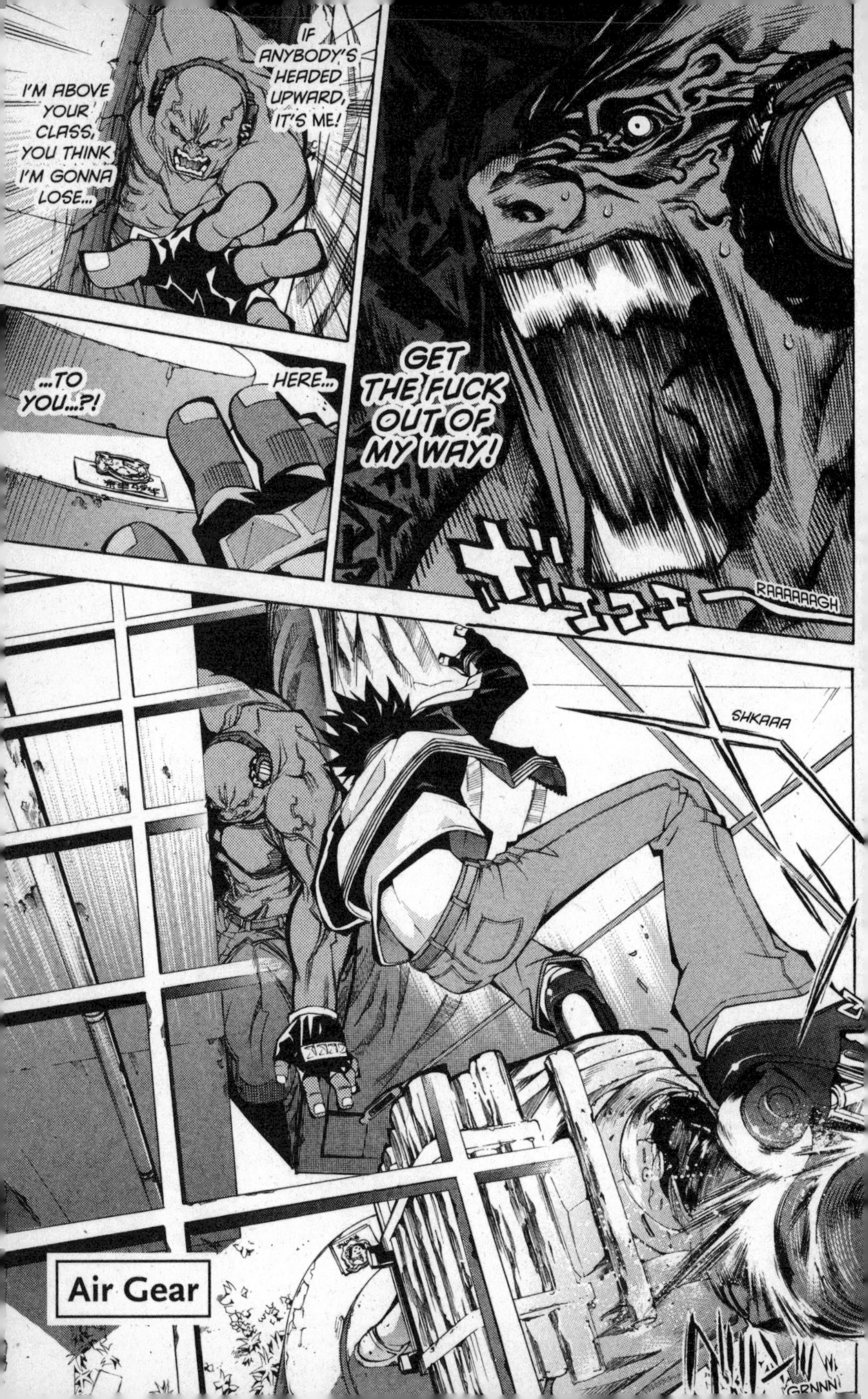
GET THE FUCK OUT OF MY WAY!
RAAAAAAGH
IF ANYBODY'S HEADED UPWARD, IT'S ME!
I'M ABOVE YOUR CLASS, YOU THINK I'M GONNA LOSE...
HERE...
...TO YOU...?!
SHKAAA
GRNNN
Air Gear

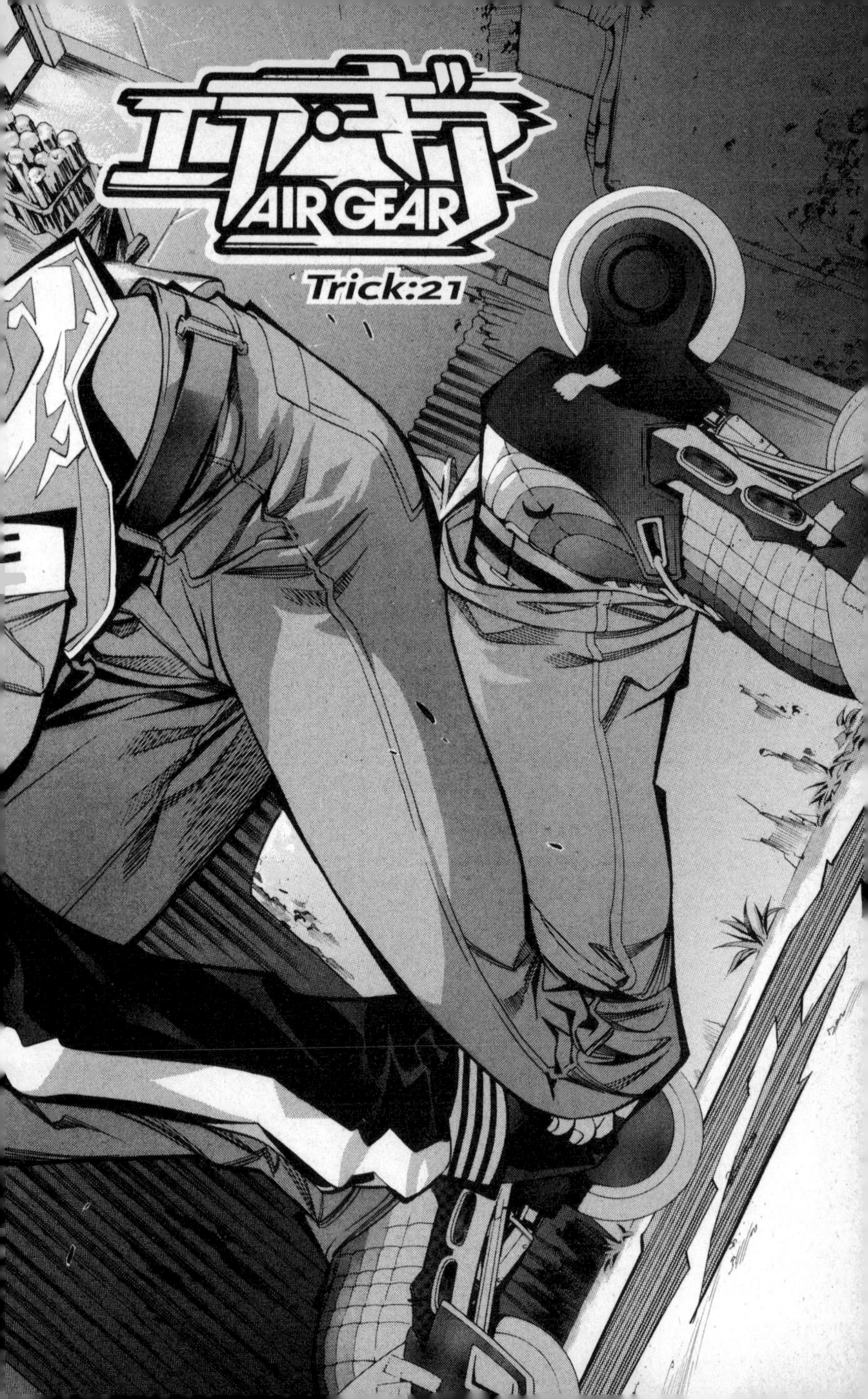
エア・ギア
AIR GEAR
Trick:21

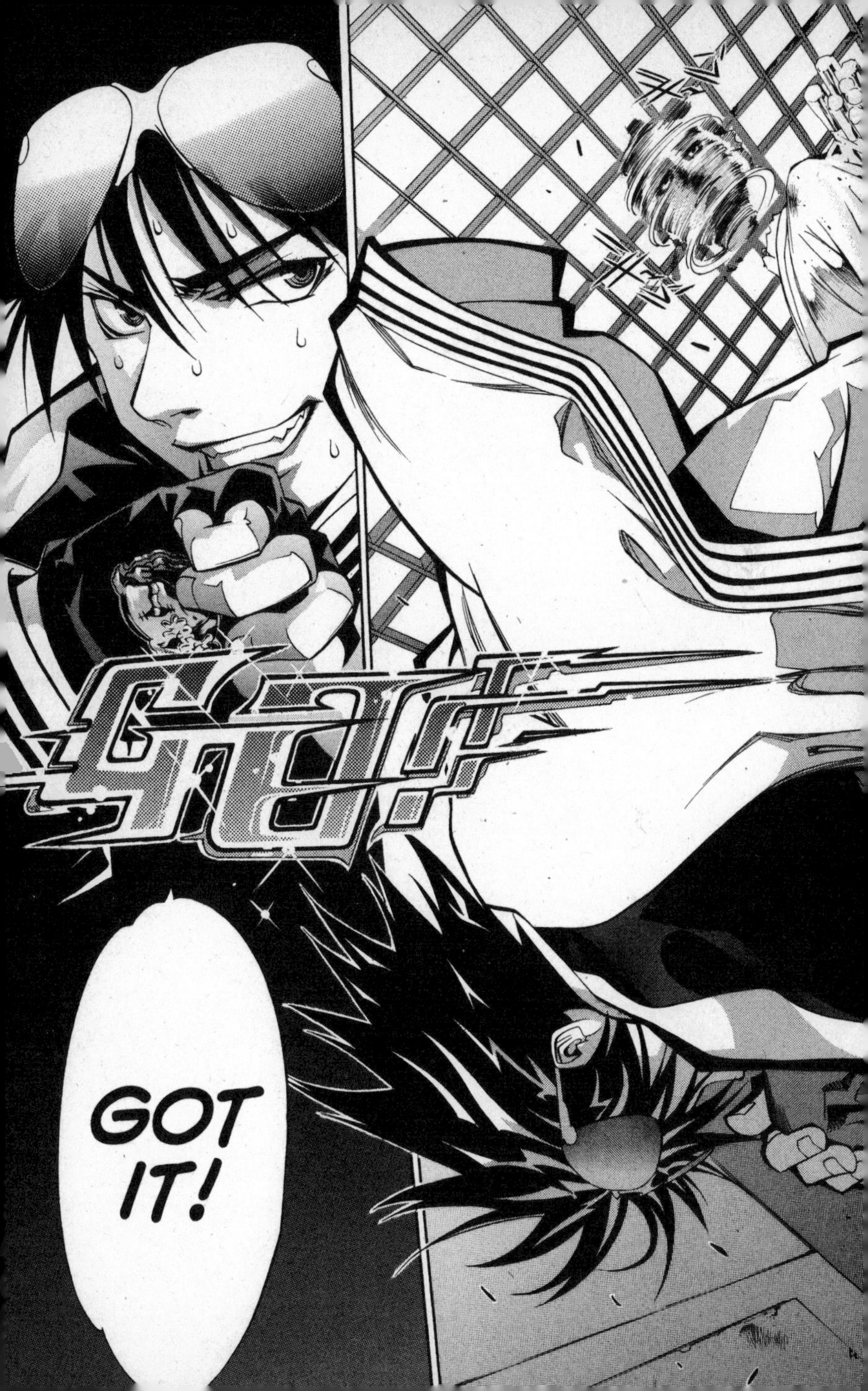
GOT IT!

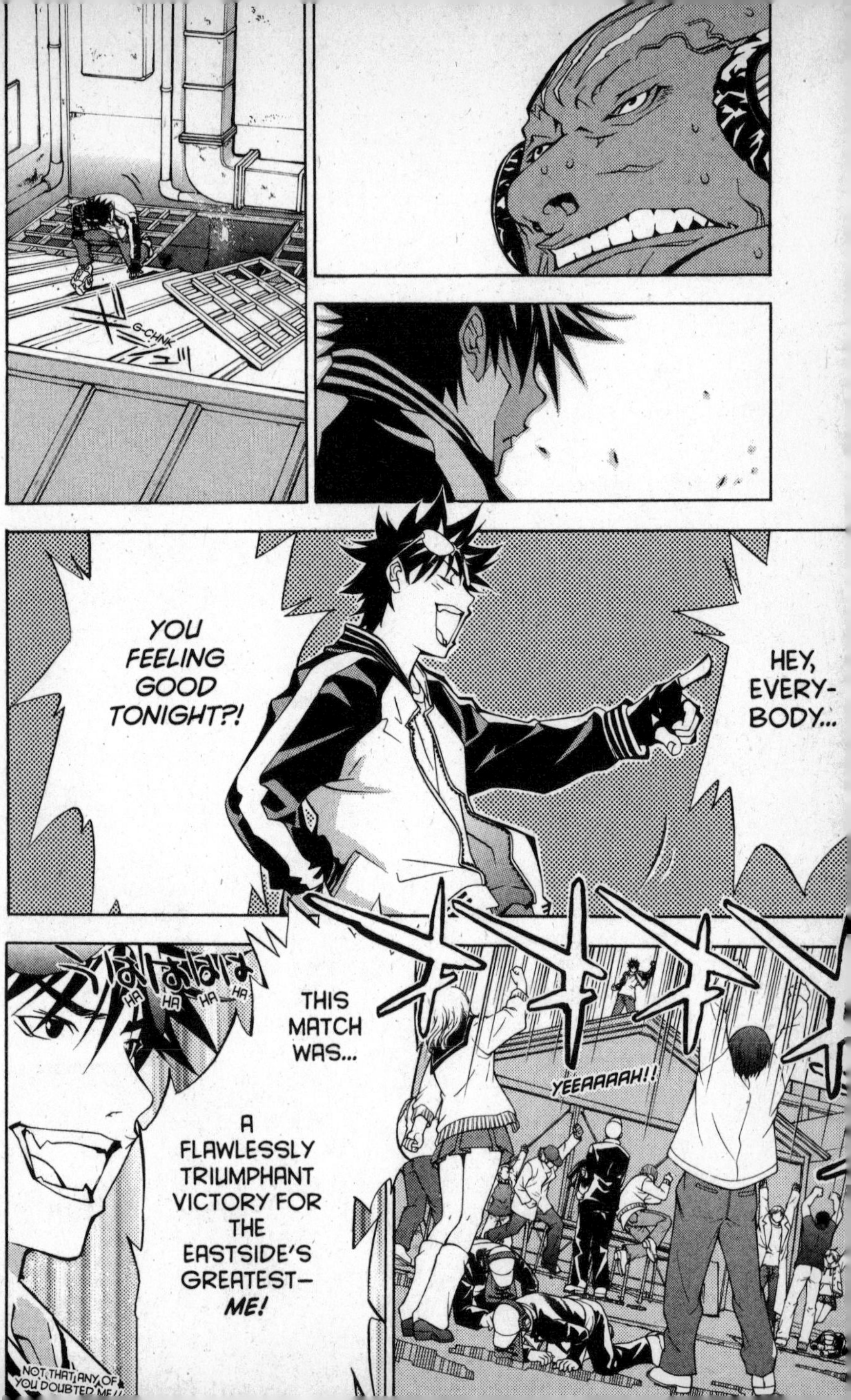
G-CHNK
HEY, EVERY-BODY...
YOU FEELING GOOD TONIGHT?!
YEEAAAAH!!
HA HA HA HA
THIS MATCH WAS...
A FLAWLESSLY TRIUMPHANT VICTORY FOR THE EASTSIDE'S GREATEST— ME!
NOT THAT ANY OF YOU DOUBTED ME!!

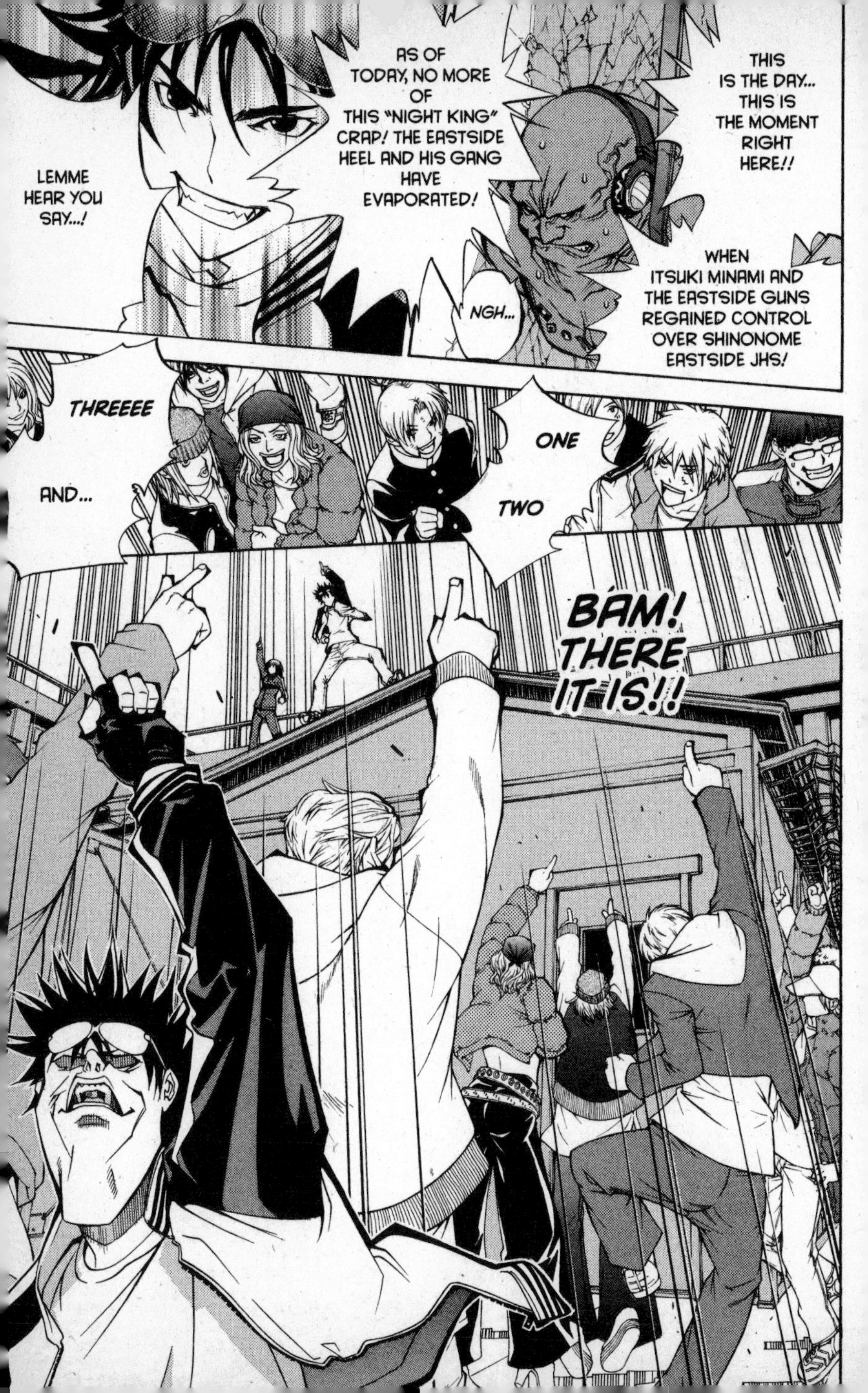
THIS IS THE DAY... THIS IS THE MOMENT RIGHT HERE!!
WHEN ITSUKI MINAMI AND THE EASTSIDE GUNS REGAINED CONTROL OVER SHINONOME EASTSIDE JHS!
AS OF TODAY, NO MORE OF THIS "NIGHT KING" CRAP! THE EASTSIDE HEEL AND HIS GANG HAVE EVAPORATED!
NGH...
LEMME HEAR YOU SAY...!
ONE
TWO
THREEEE
AND...
BAM! THERE IT IS!!

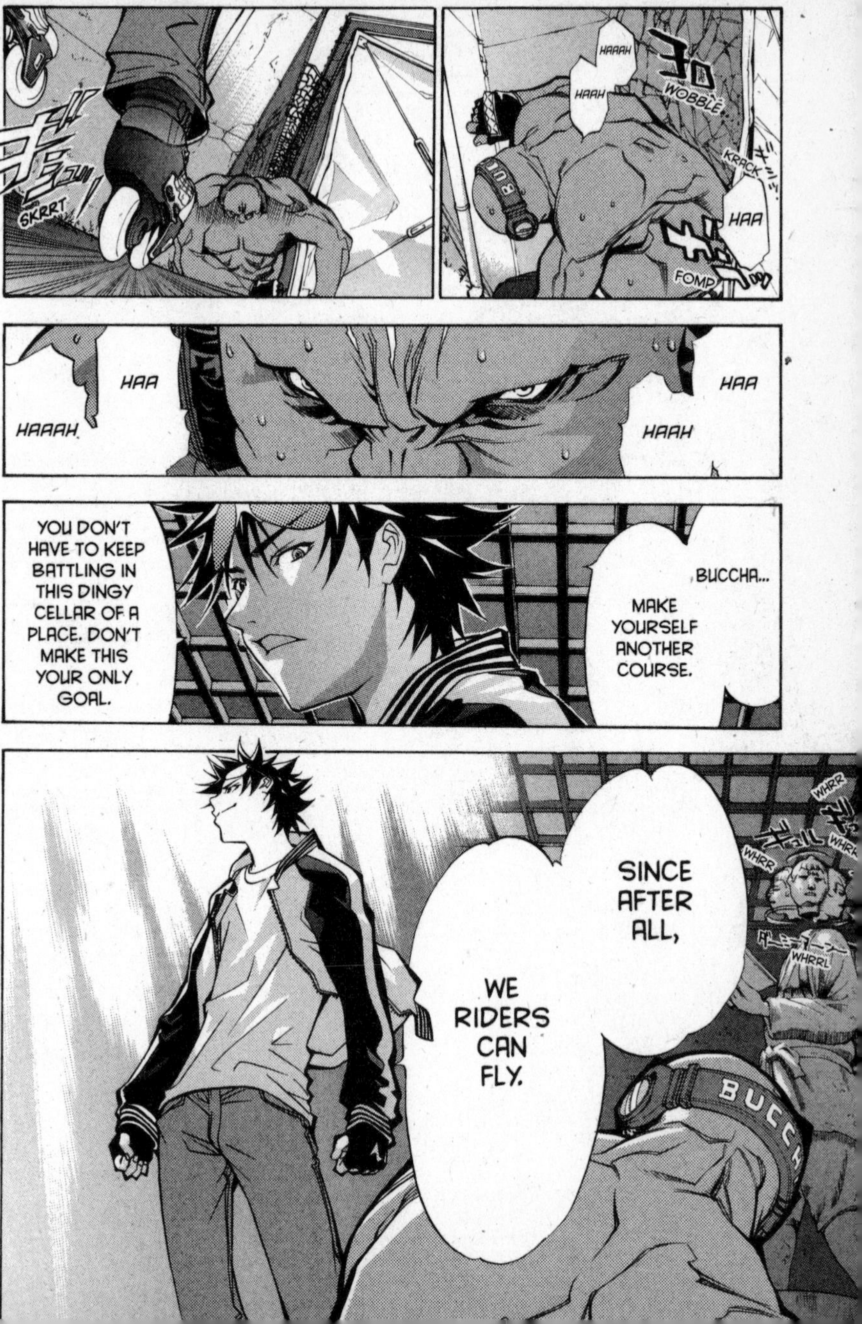
HAAAH
HAAH
WOBBLE
KRACK
HAA
FOMP
SKRRT
HAA
HAAH
HAA
HAAAH
BUCCHA... MAKE YOURSELF ANOTHER COURSE.
YOU DON'T HAVE TO KEEP BATTLING IN THIS DINGY CELLAR OF A PLACE. DON'T MAKE THIS YOUR ONLY GOAL.
WHRR
WHRR
WHRR
WHRRL
SINCE AFTER ALL,
WE RIDERS CAN FLY.

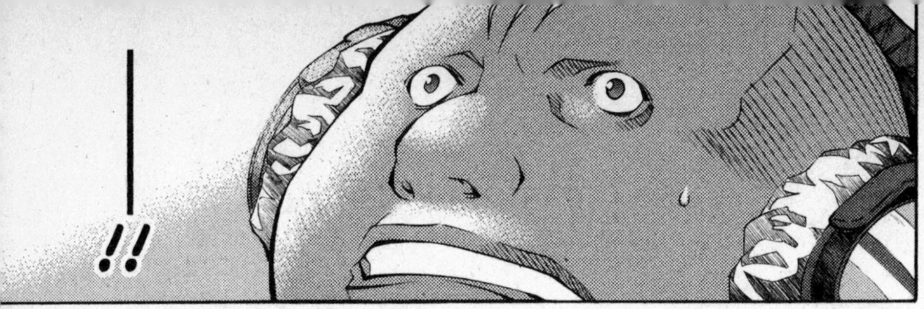
—!!
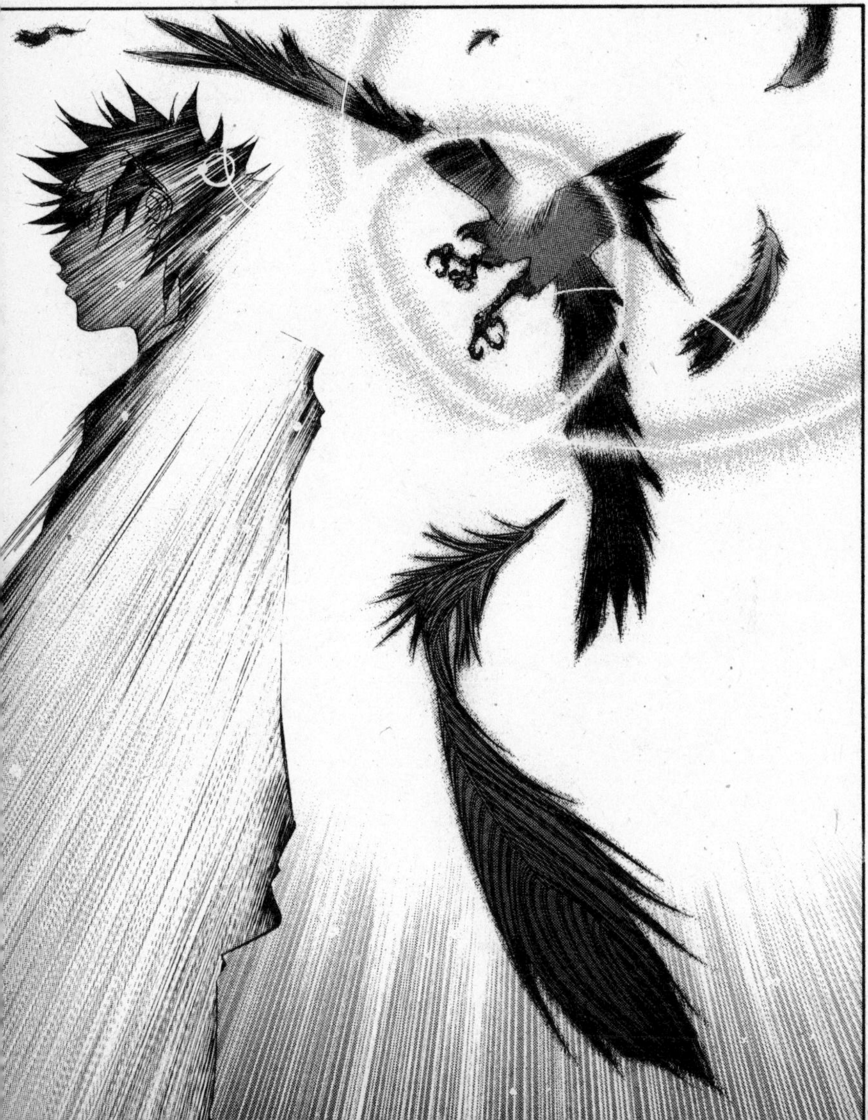

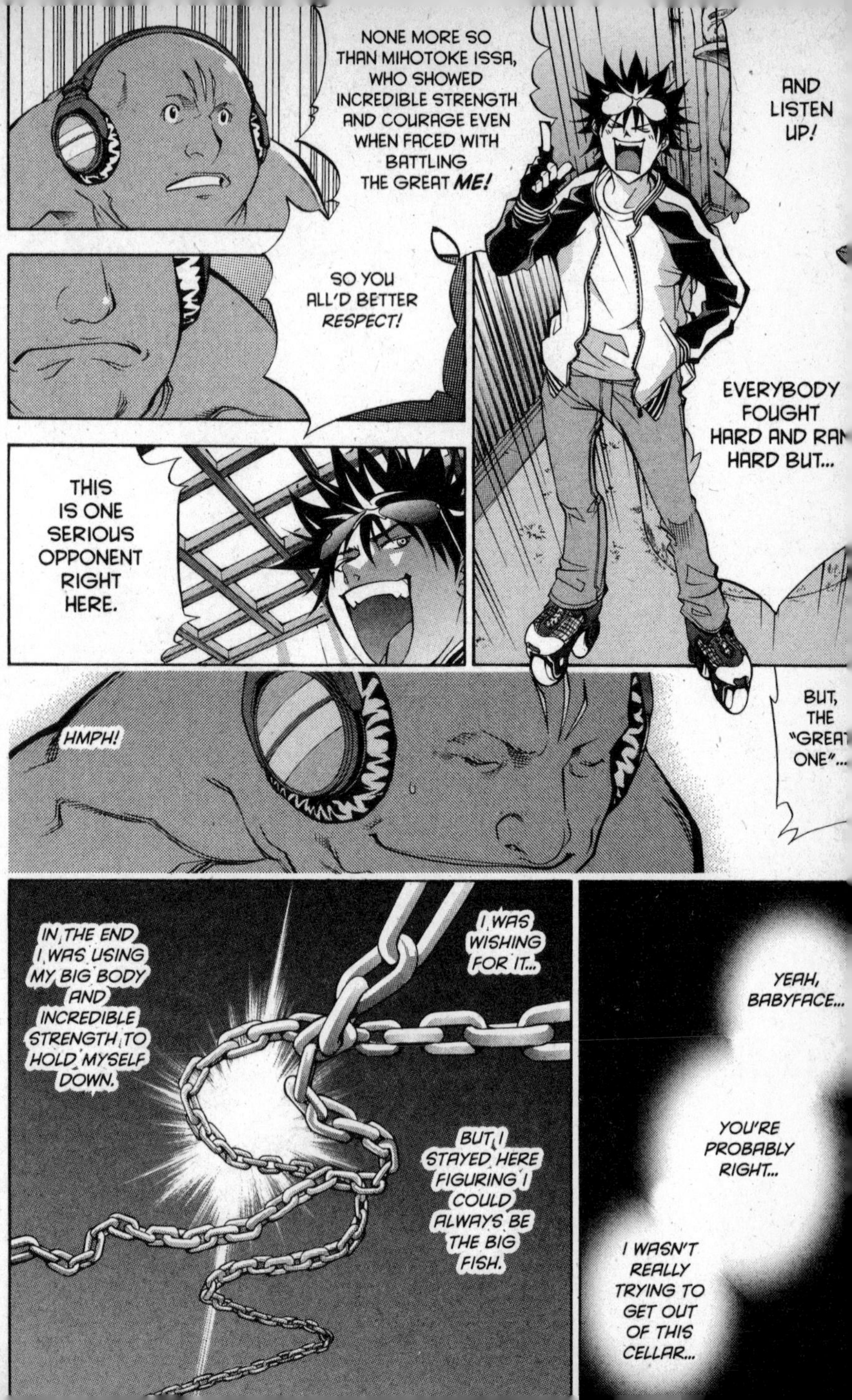
AND LISTEN UP!
EVERYBODY FOUGHT HARD AND RAN HARD BUT...
NONE MORE SO THAN MIHOTOKE ISSA, WHO SHOWED INCREDIBLE STRENGTH AND COURAGE EVEN WHEN FACED WITH BATTLING THE GREAT *ME!*
SO YOU ALL'D BETTER *RESPECT!*
THIS IS ONE SERIOUS OPPONENT RIGHT HERE.
BUT, THE "GREAT ONE"...
HMPH!
YEAH, BABYFACE...
YOU'RE PROBABLY RIGHT...
I WASN'T REALLY TRYING TO GET OUT OF THIS CELLAR...
I WAS WISHING FOR IT...
IN THE END I WAS USING MY BIG BODY AND INCREDIBLE STRENGTH TO HOLD MYSELF DOWN.
BUT I STAYED HERE FIGURING I COULD ALWAYS BE THE BIG FISH.

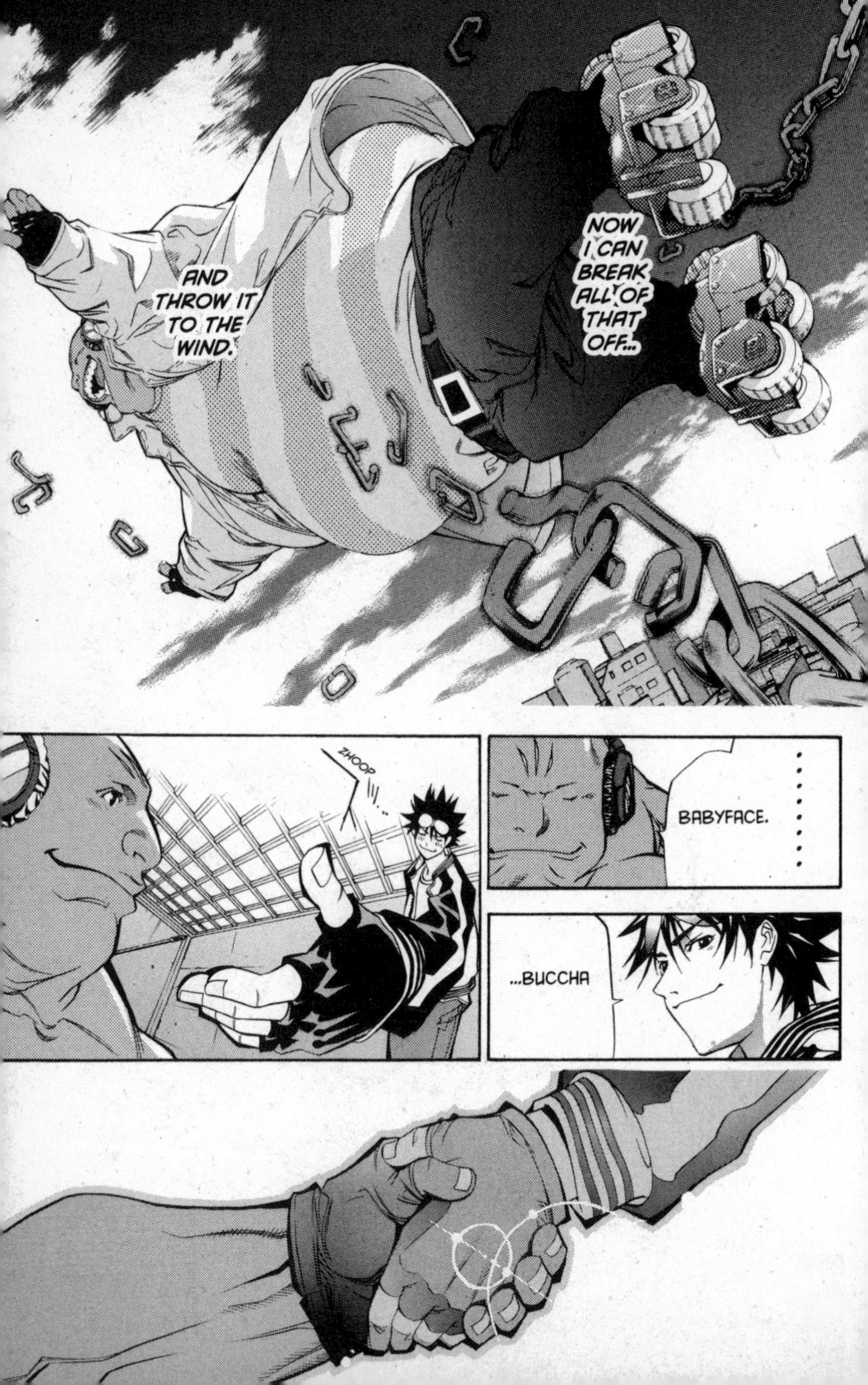
NOW I CAN BREAK ALL OF THAT OFF...
AND THROW IT TO THE WIND.
BABYFACE.
...BUCCHA
ZHOOP

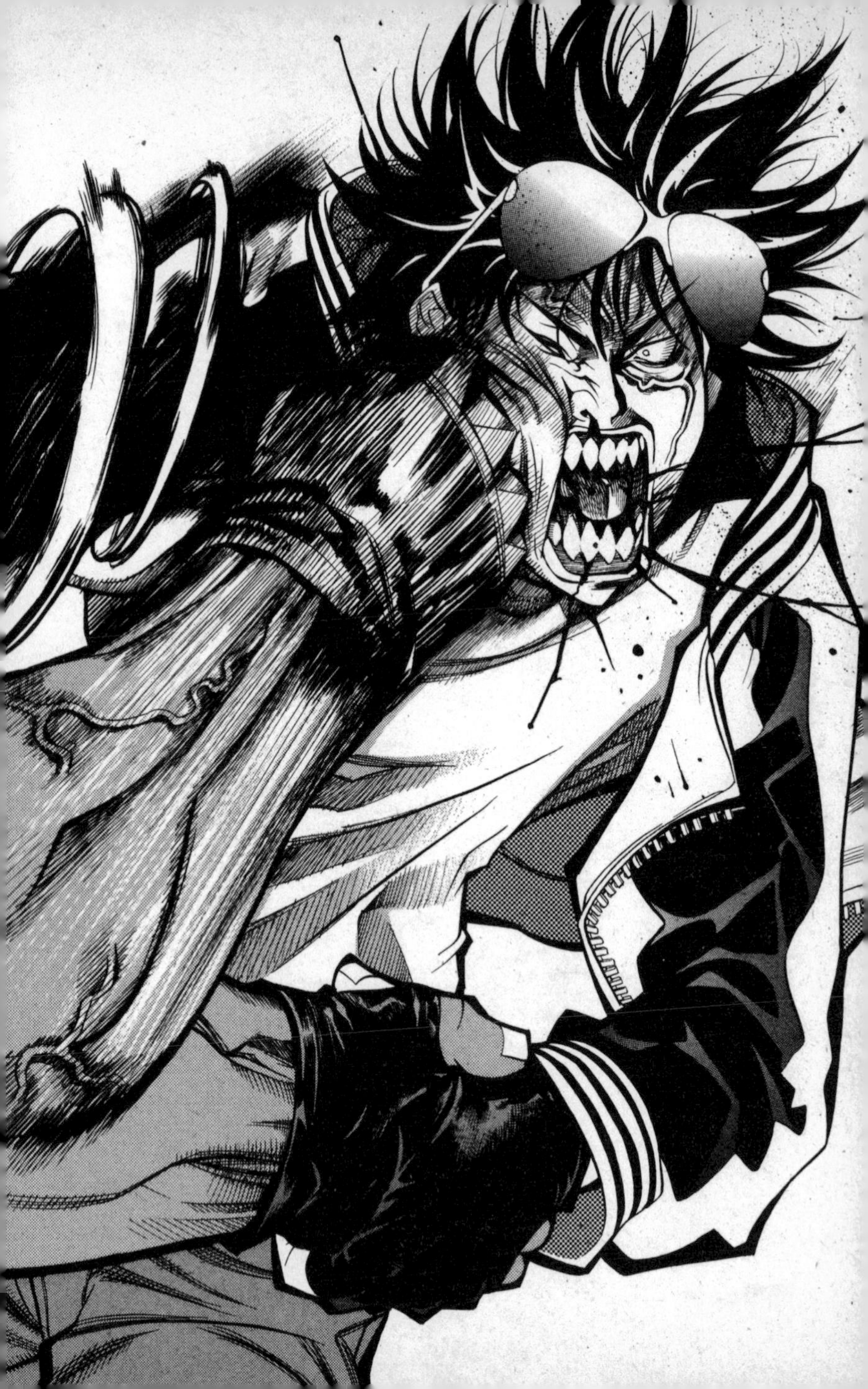

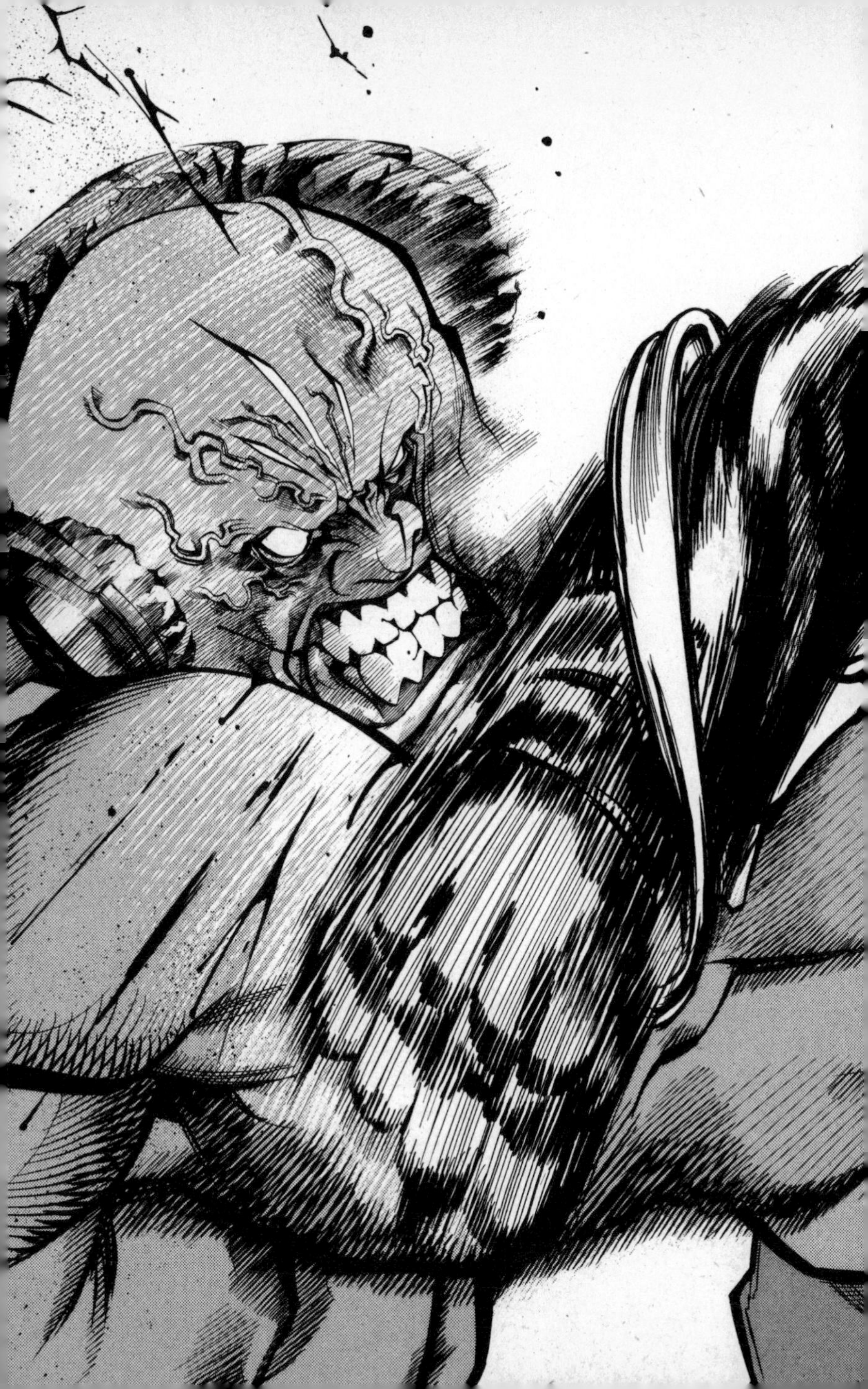

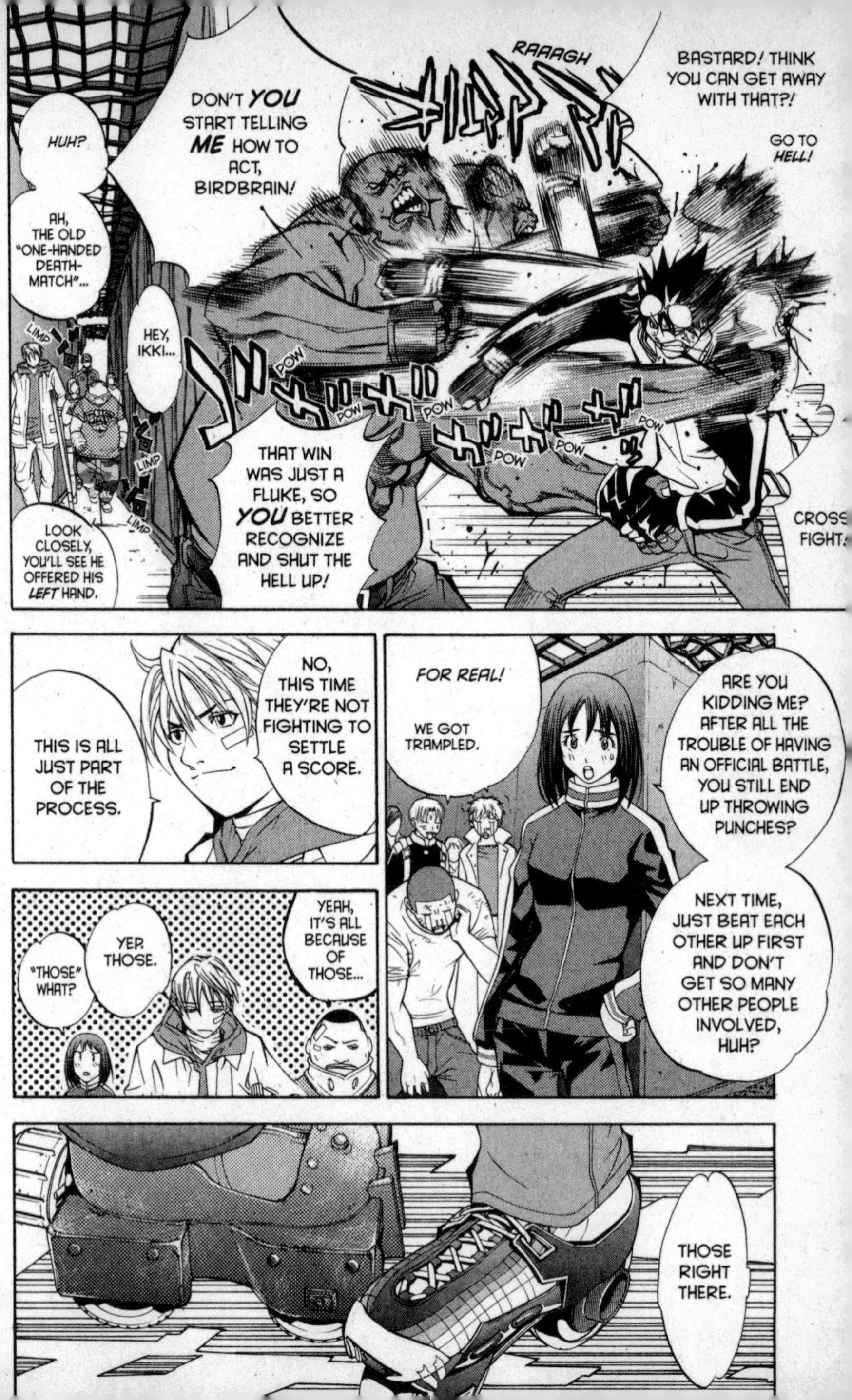
BASTARD! THINK YOU CAN GET AWAY WITH THAT?!
GO TO HELL!
RAAAGH
DON'T YOU START TELLING ME HOW TO ACT, BIRDBRAIN!
HUH?
AH, THE OLD "ONE-HANDED DEATH-MATCH"...
HEY, IKKI...
LIMP
LIMP
LIMP
POW
POW
POW
POW
POW
POW
THAT WIN WAS JUST A FLUKE, SO YOU BETTER RECOGNIZE AND SHUT THE HELL UP!
CROSS FIGHT
LOOK CLOSELY, YOU'LL SEE HE OFFERED HIS LEFT HAND.
ARE YOU KIDDING ME? AFTER ALL THE TROUBLE OF HAVING AN OFFICIAL BATTLE, YOU STILL END UP THROWING PUNCHES?
FOR REAL!
WE GOT TRAMPLED.
NEXT TIME, JUST BEAT EACH OTHER UP FIRST AND DON'T GET SO MANY OTHER PEOPLE INVOLVED, HUH?
NO, THIS TIME THEY'RE NOT FIGHTING TO SETTLE A SCORE.
THIS IS ALL JUST PART OF THE PROCESS.
YEAH, IT'S ALL BECAUSE OF THOSE...
YEP. THOSE.
"THOSE" WHAT?
THOSE RIGHT THERE.

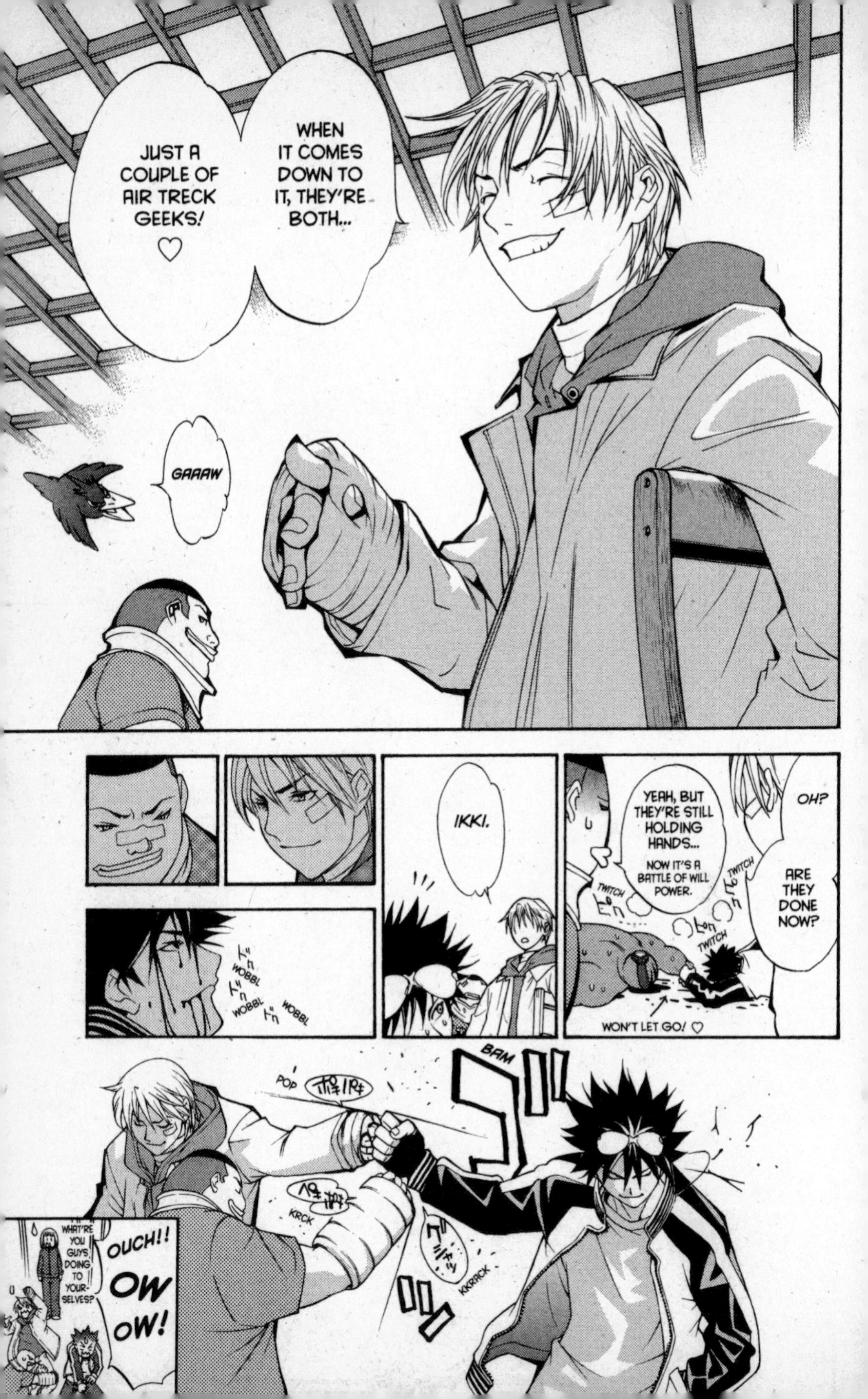
WHEN IT COMES DOWN TO IT, THEY'RE BOTH...
JUST A COUPLE OF AIR TRECK GEEKS! ♡
GAAAW
OH?
ARE THEY DONE NOW?
YEAH, BUT THEY'RE STILL HOLDING HANDS...
NOW IT'S A BATTLE OF WILL POWER.
TWITCH
TWITCH
TWITCH
WON'T LET GO! ♡
IKKI.
WOBBL
WOBBL
WOBBL
BAM
POP
KRCK
KKRACK
OUCH!!
OW OW!
WHAT'RE YOU GUYS DOING TO YOUR-SELVES?

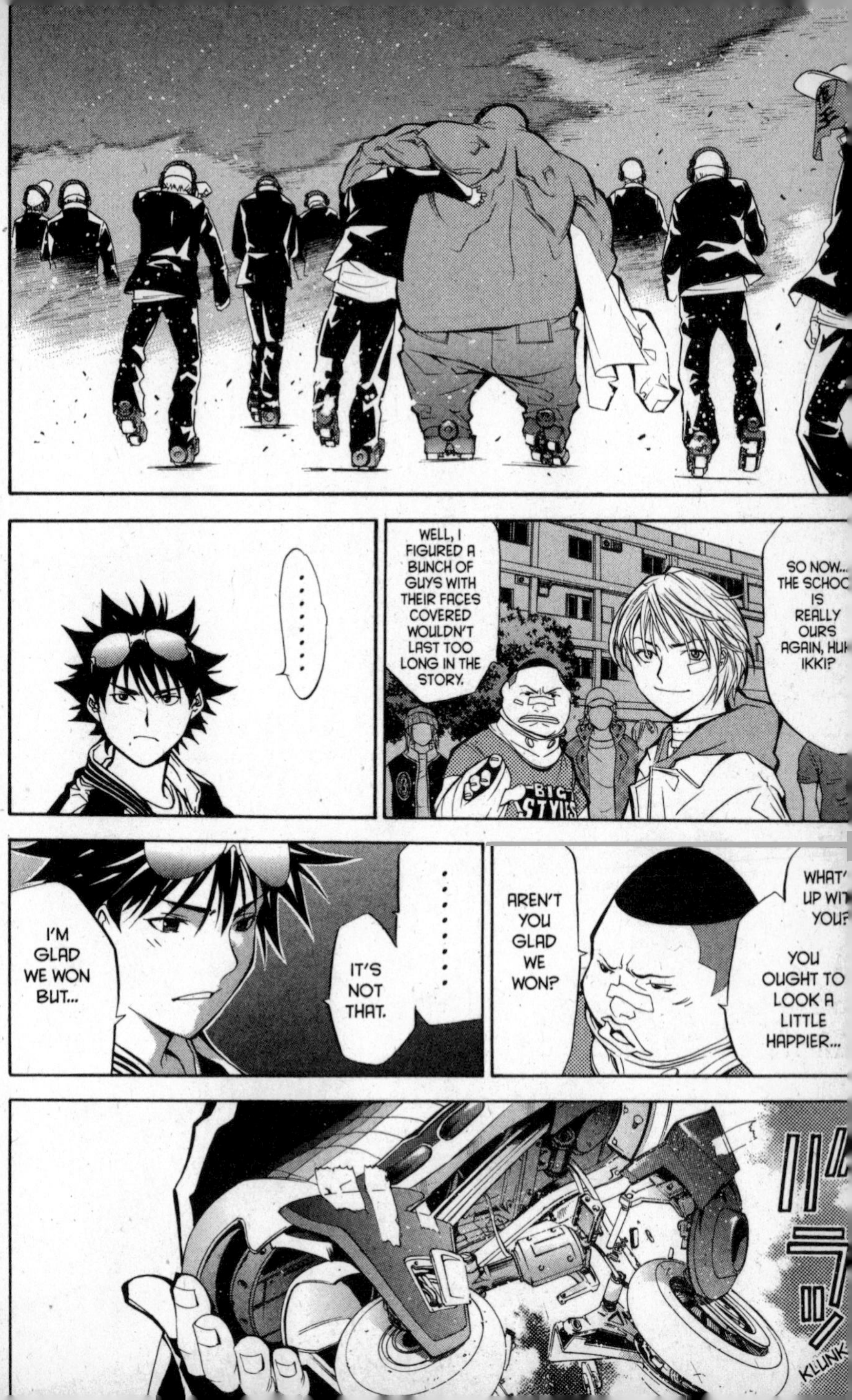
SO NOW... THE SCHOO IS REALLY OURS AGAIN, HU IKKI?
WELL, I FIGURED A BUNCH OF GUYS WITH THEIR FACES COVERED WOULDN'T LAST TOO LONG IN THE STORY.
......
WHAT' UP WI YOU?
YOU OUGHT TO LOOK A LITTLE HAPPIER...
AREN'T YOU GLAD WE WON?
......
IT'S NOT THAT.
I'M GLAD WE WON BUT...
KLUNK

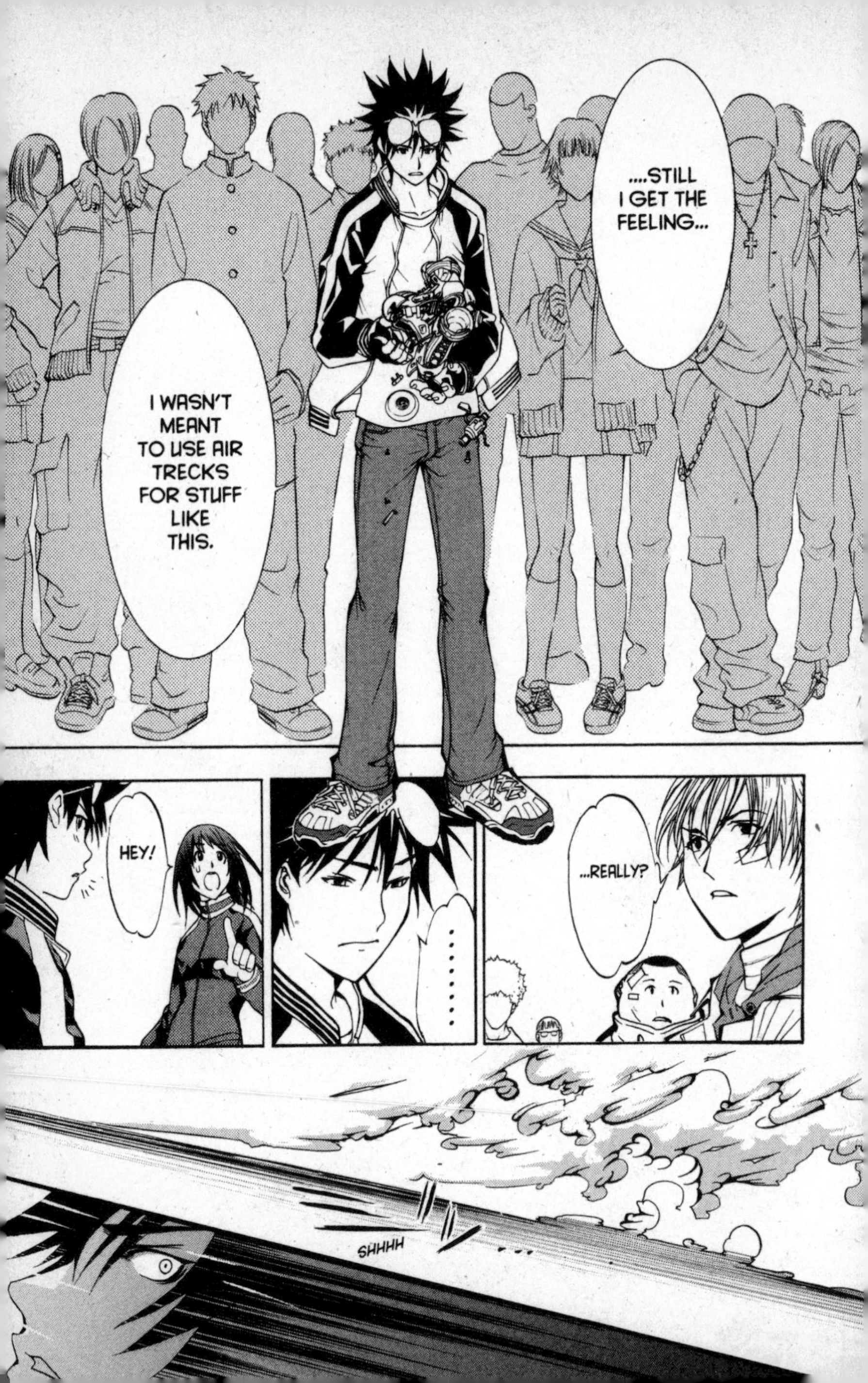
....STILL I GET THE FEELING...
I WASN'T MEANT TO USE AIR TRECKS FOR STUFF LIKE THIS.
...REALLY?
......
HEY!
SHHHH

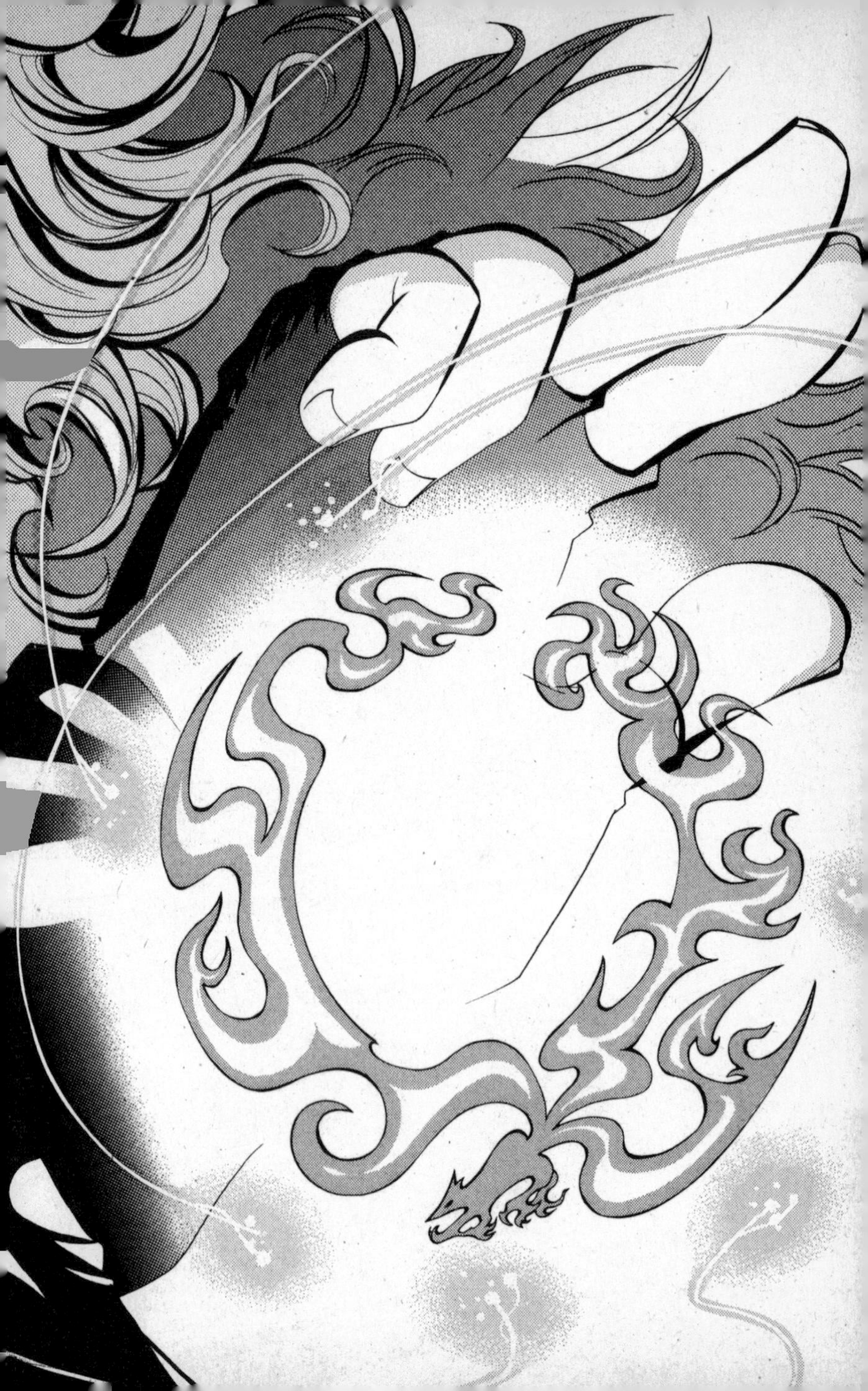

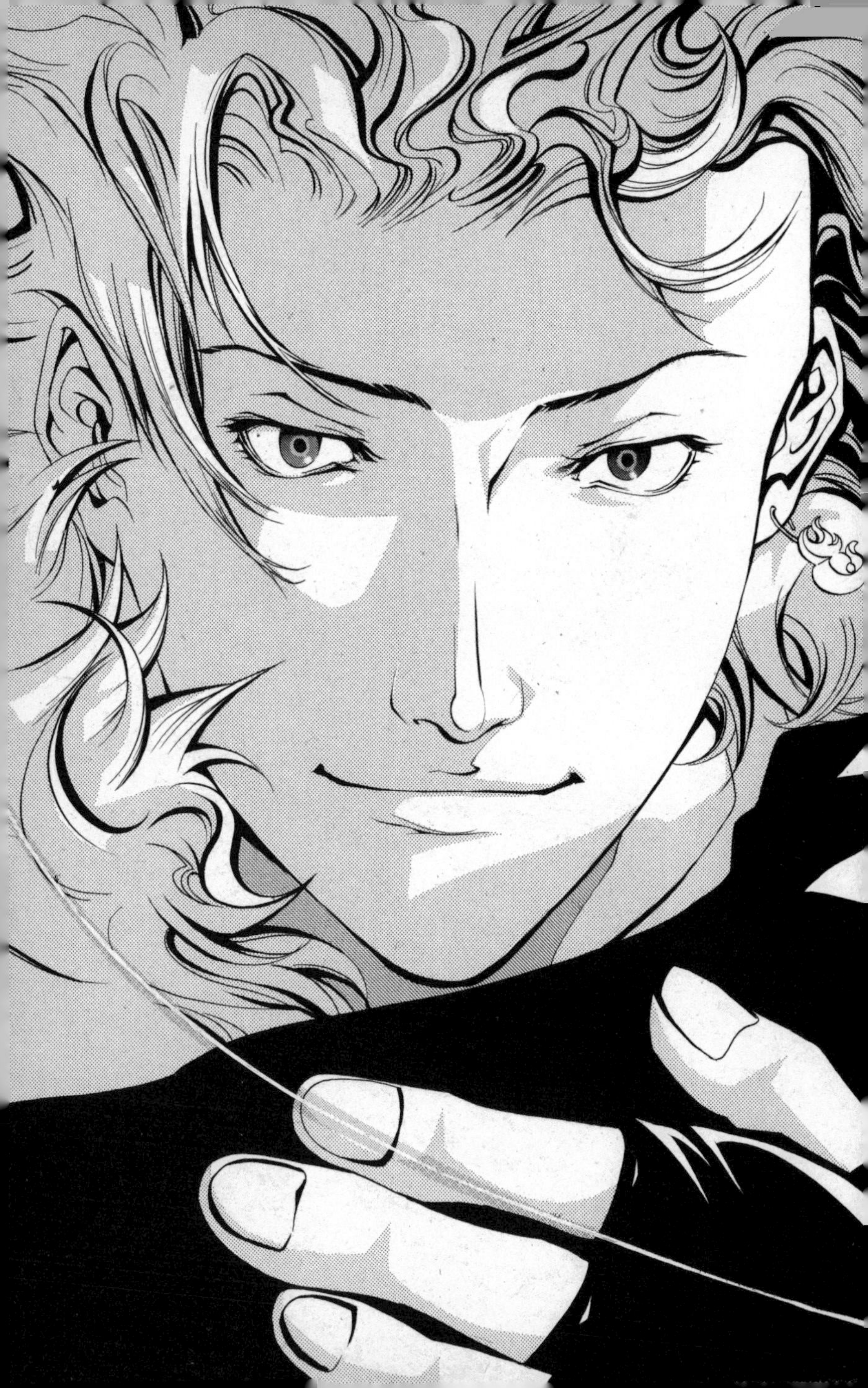

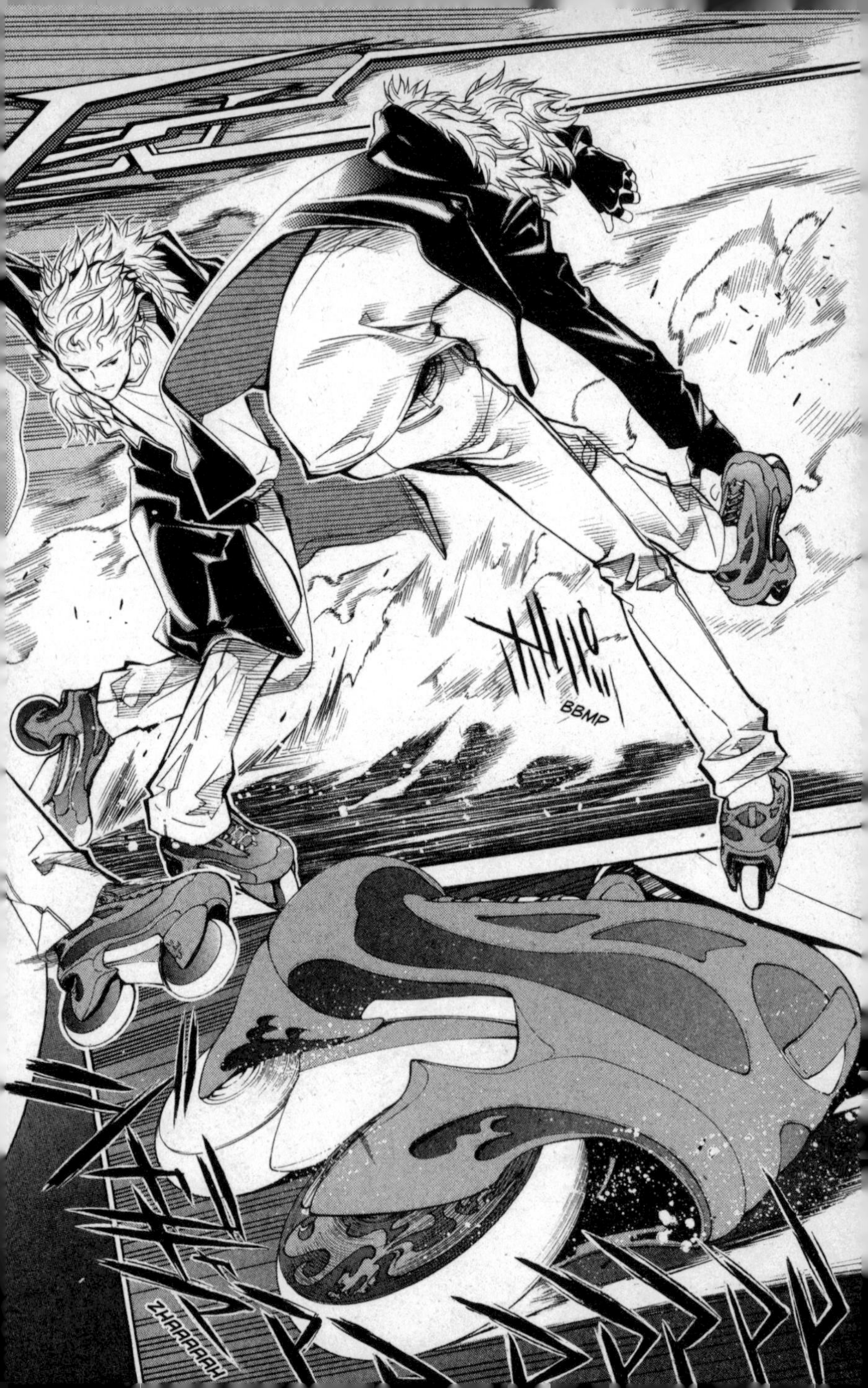
BBMP
ZHAAAAAH

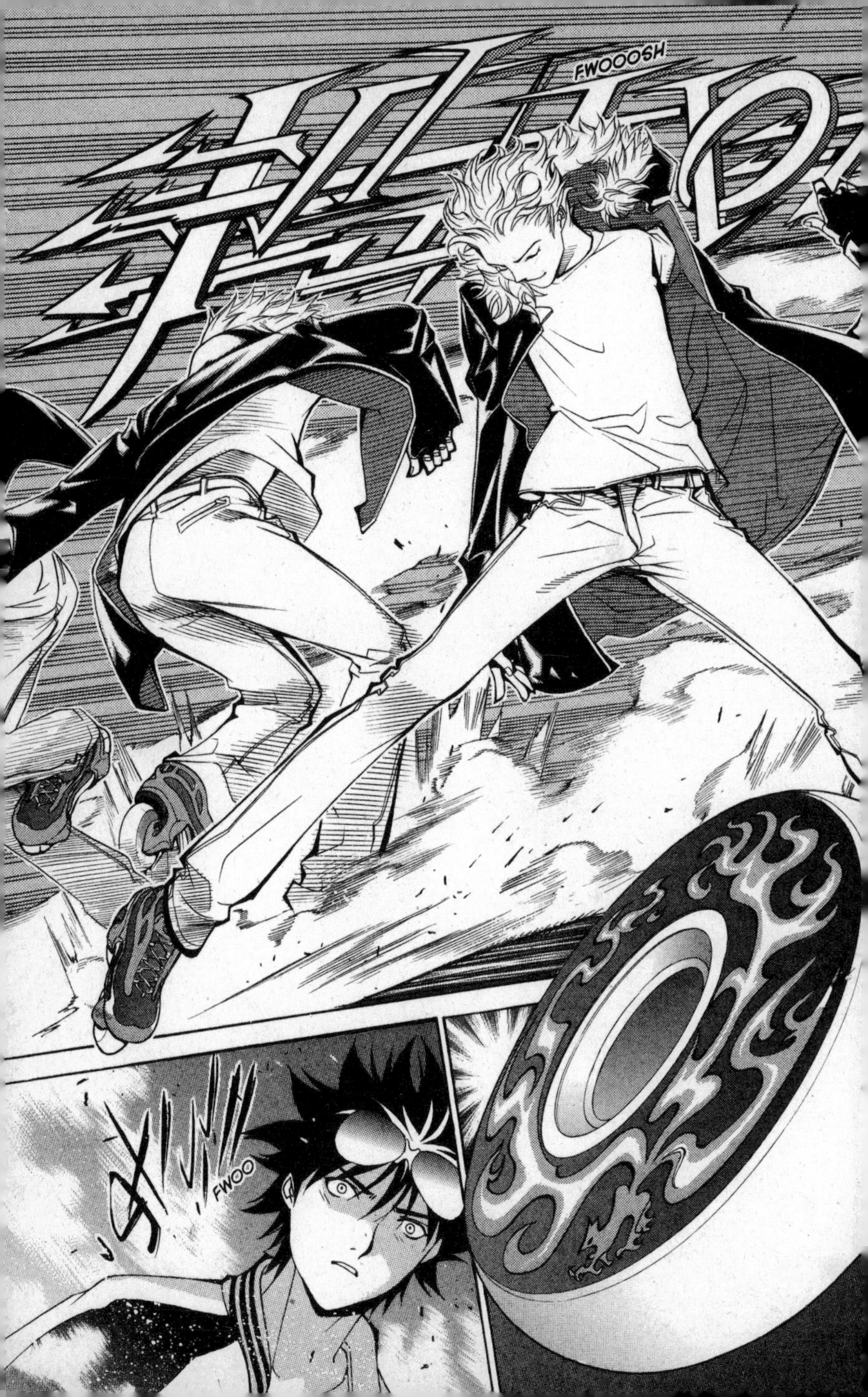
FWOOOSH
FWOO

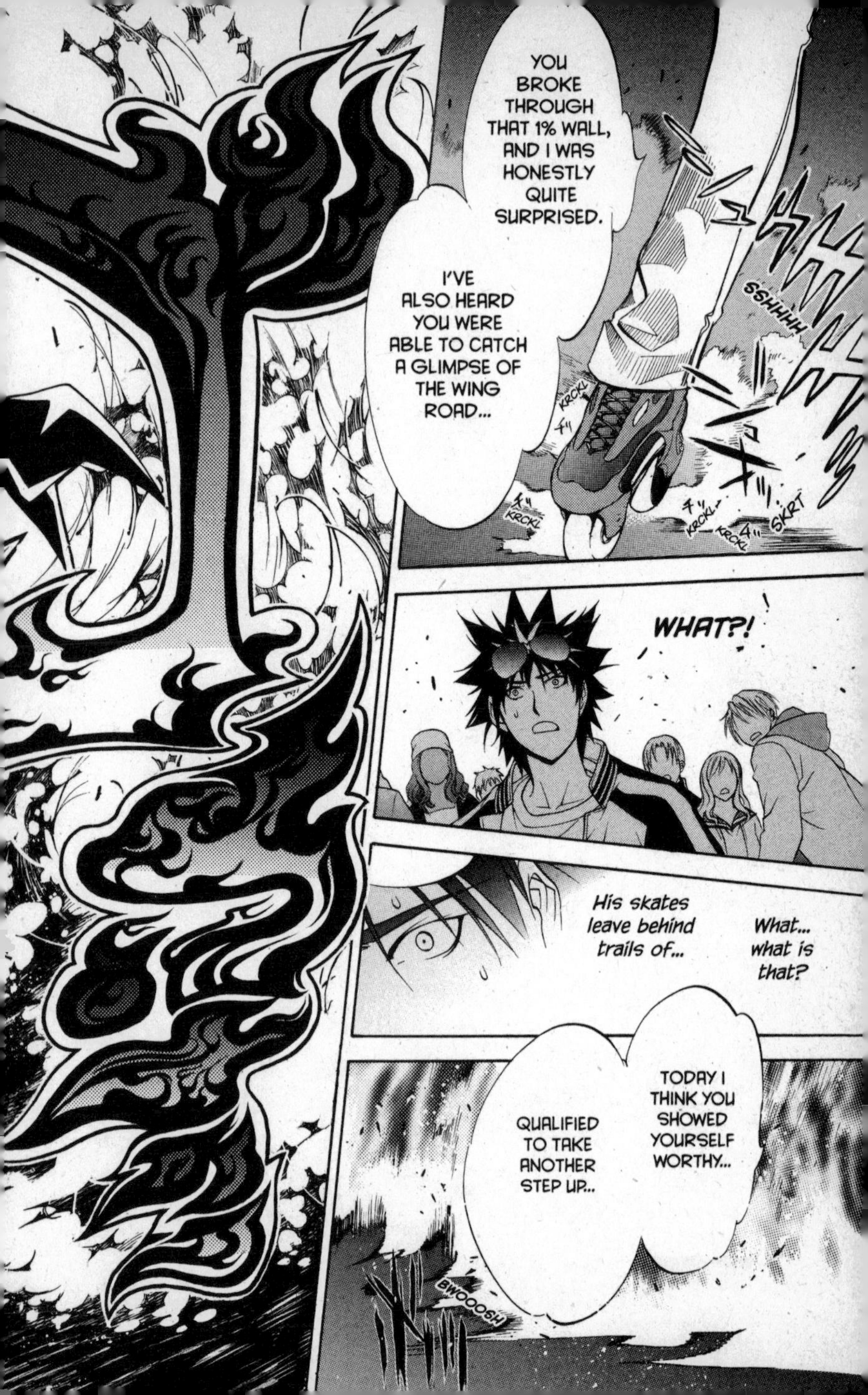
YOU BROKE THROUGH THAT 1% WALL, AND I WAS HONESTLY QUITE SURPRISED.
I'VE ALSO HEARD YOU WERE ABLE TO CATCH A GLIMPSE OF THE WING ROAD...
SSHHHH
KRCKL
KRCKL
KRCKL
KRCKL
SKRT
WHAT?!
What... what is that?
His skates leave behind trails of...
TODAY I THINK YOU SHOWED YOURSELF WORTHY...
QUALIFIED TO TAKE ANOTHER STEP UP...
BWOOOSH

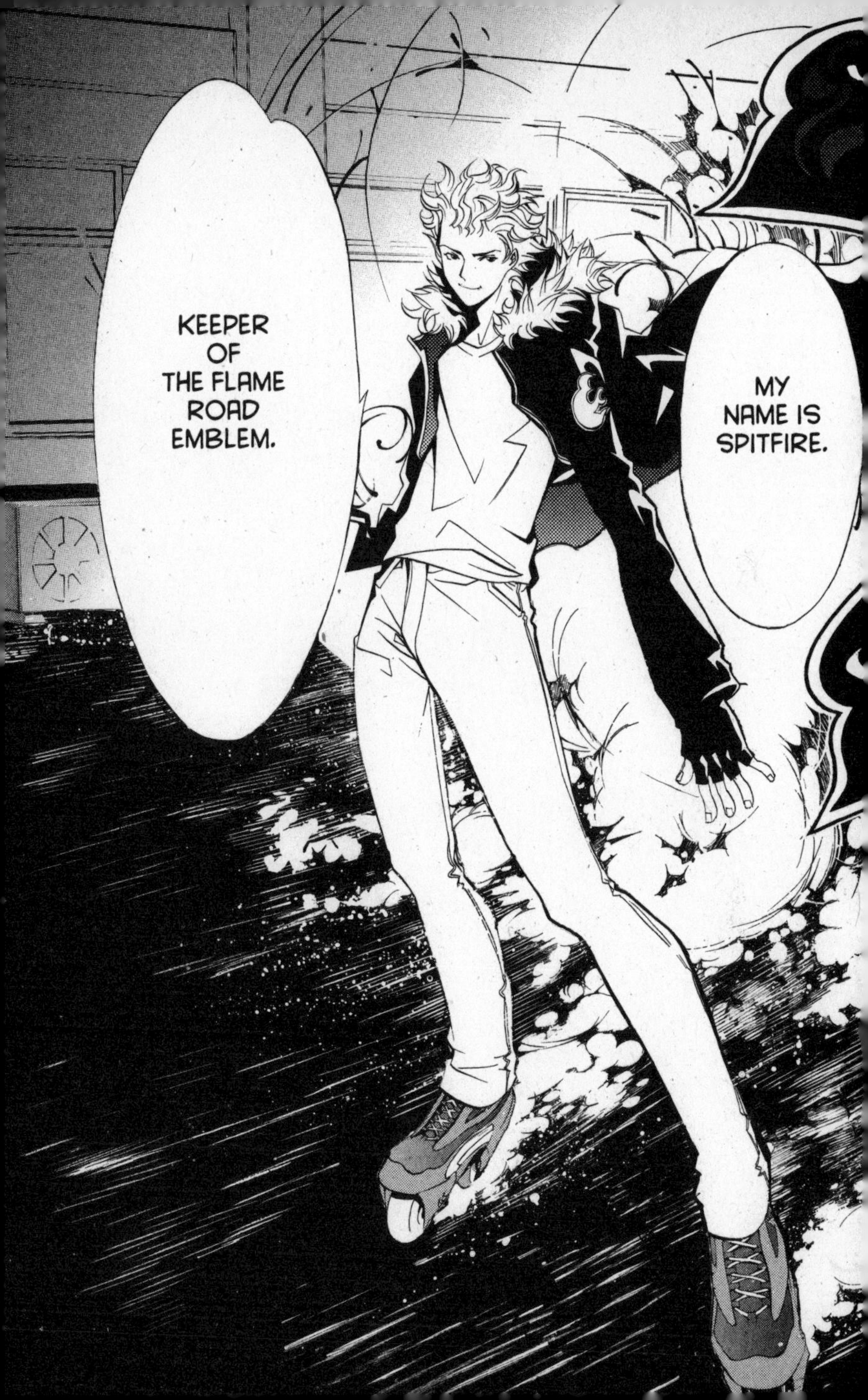
MY NAME IS SPITFIRE.
KEEPER OF THE FLAME ROAD EMBLEM.

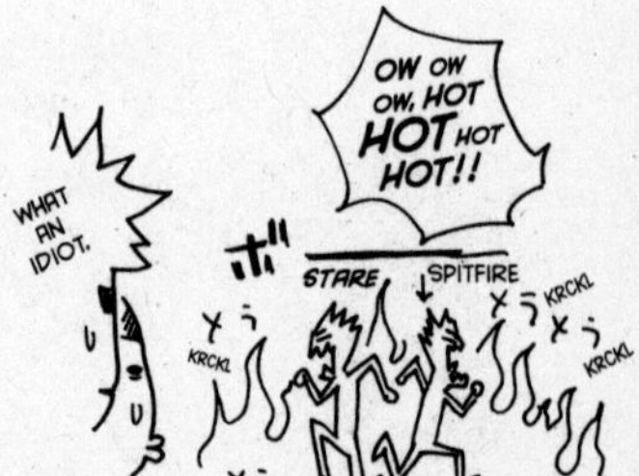
OW OW OW, HOT HOT HOT HOT!!
WHAT AN IDIOT.
ボ
STARE
SPITFIRE
メラ KRCKL
メラ KRCKL
メラ KRCKL
メラ KRCKL
AAAHH!

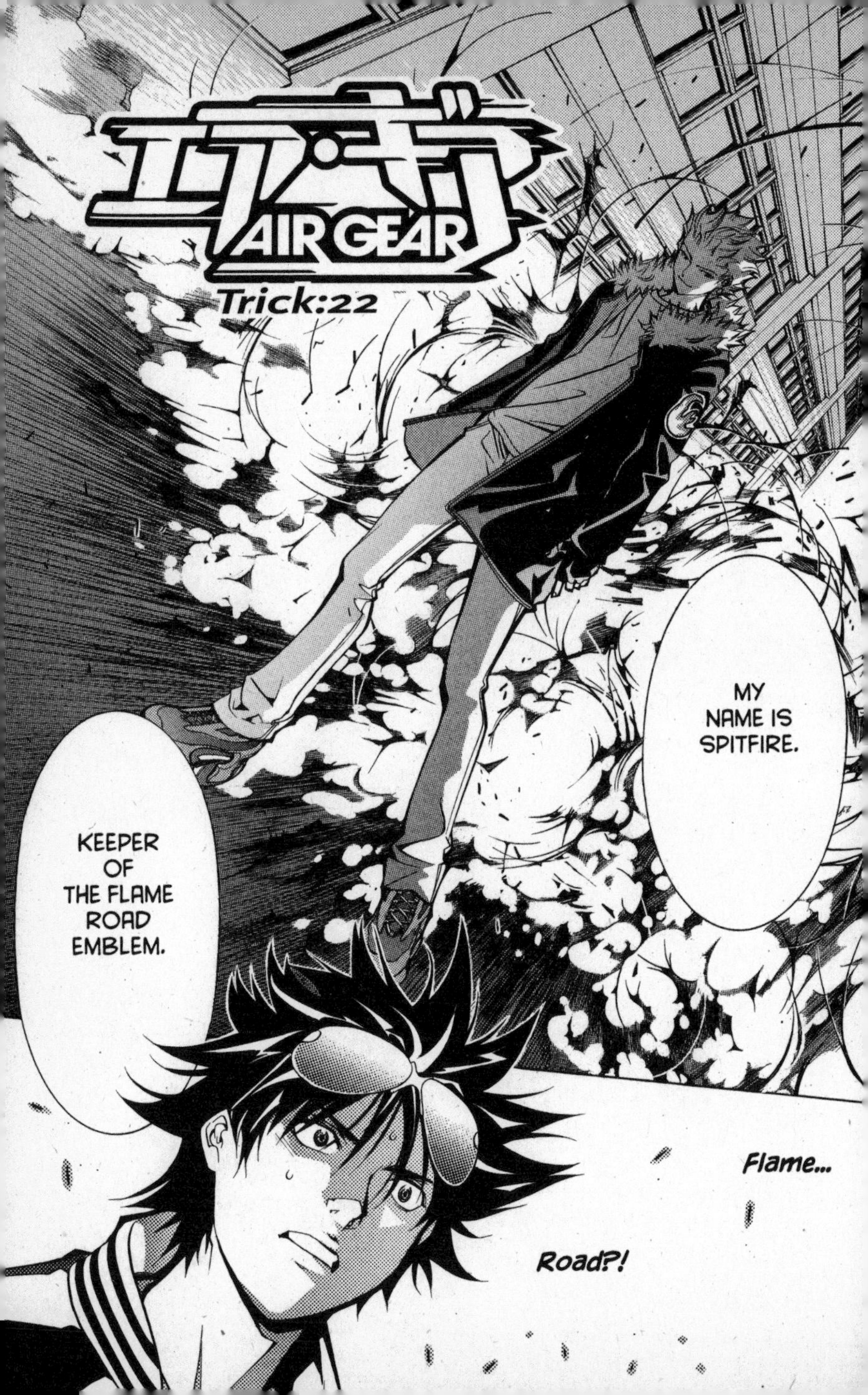
エア・ギア
AIR GEAR
Trick:22
MY NAME IS SPITFIRE.
KEEPER OF THE FLAME ROAD EMBLEM.
Flame...
Road?!

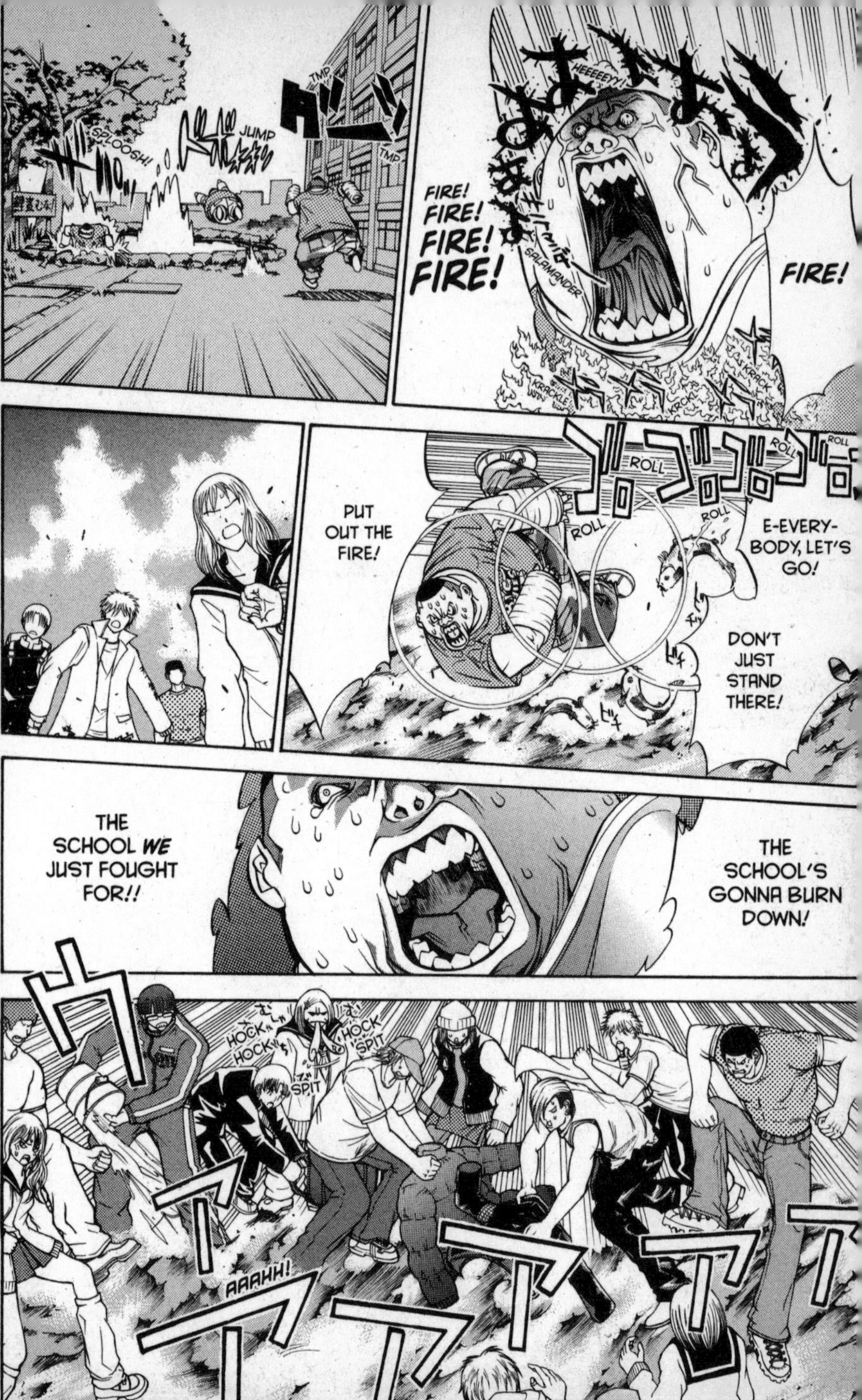
HEEEEEYY!
SALAMANDER
FIRE!
FIRE!
FIRE!
FIRE!
FIRE!
KRACK
KRACKLE
KRAK
TMP
TMP
JUMP
SPLOOSH!
ROLL
ROLL
ROLL
ROLL
ROLL
E-EVERY-BODY, LET'S GO!
DON'T JUST STAND THERE!
PUT OUT THE FIRE!
THE SCHOOL'S GONNA BURN DOWN!
THE SCHOOL WE JUST FOUGHT FOR!!
HOCK SPIT
HOCK HOCK
SPIT
AAAHH!

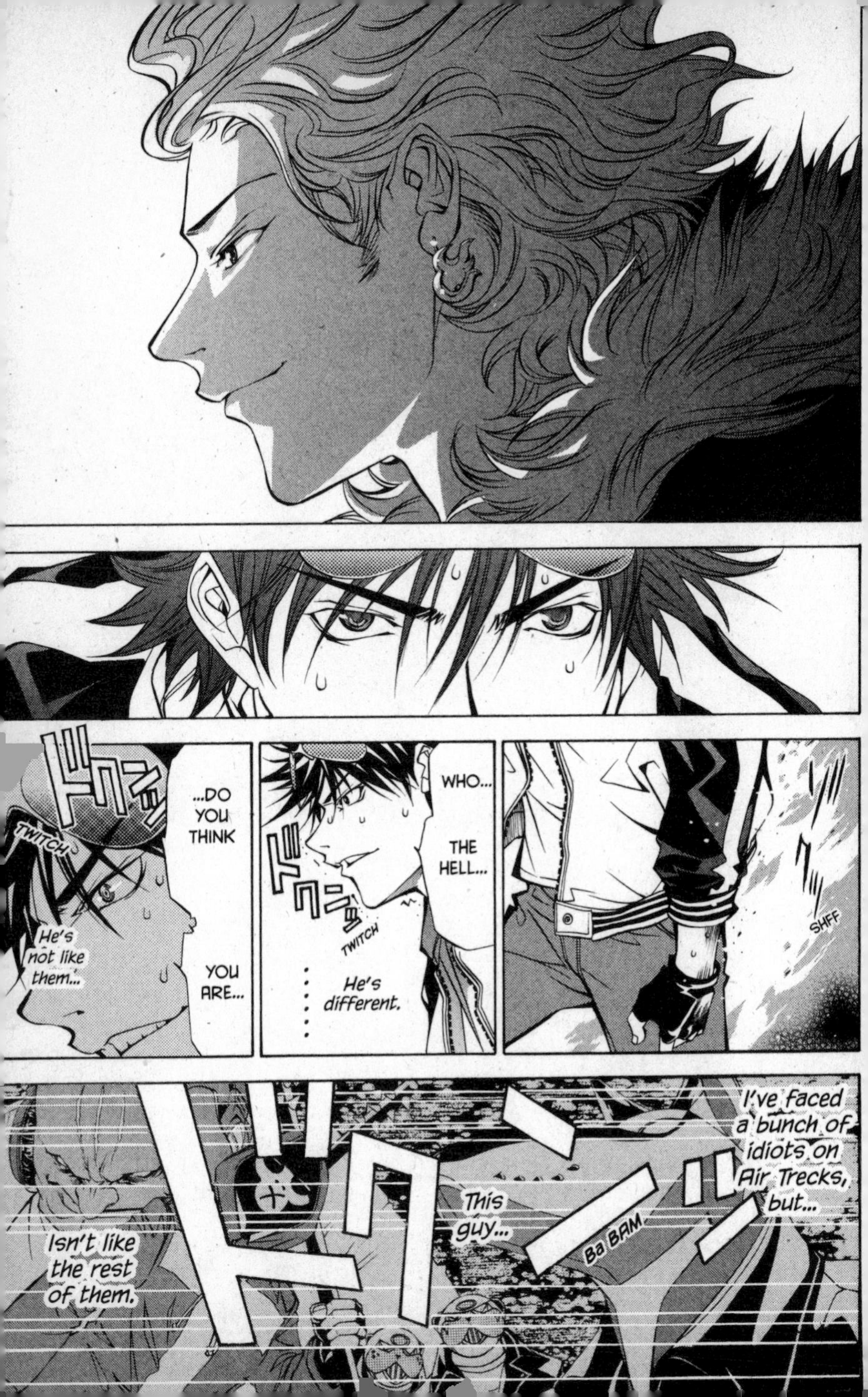
SHFF
WHO...
THE HELL...
TWITCH
He's different.
...DO YOU THINK
YOU ARE...
TWITCH
He's not like them...
I've faced a bunch of idiots on Air Trecks, but...
Ba BAM
This guy...
Isn't like the rest of them.

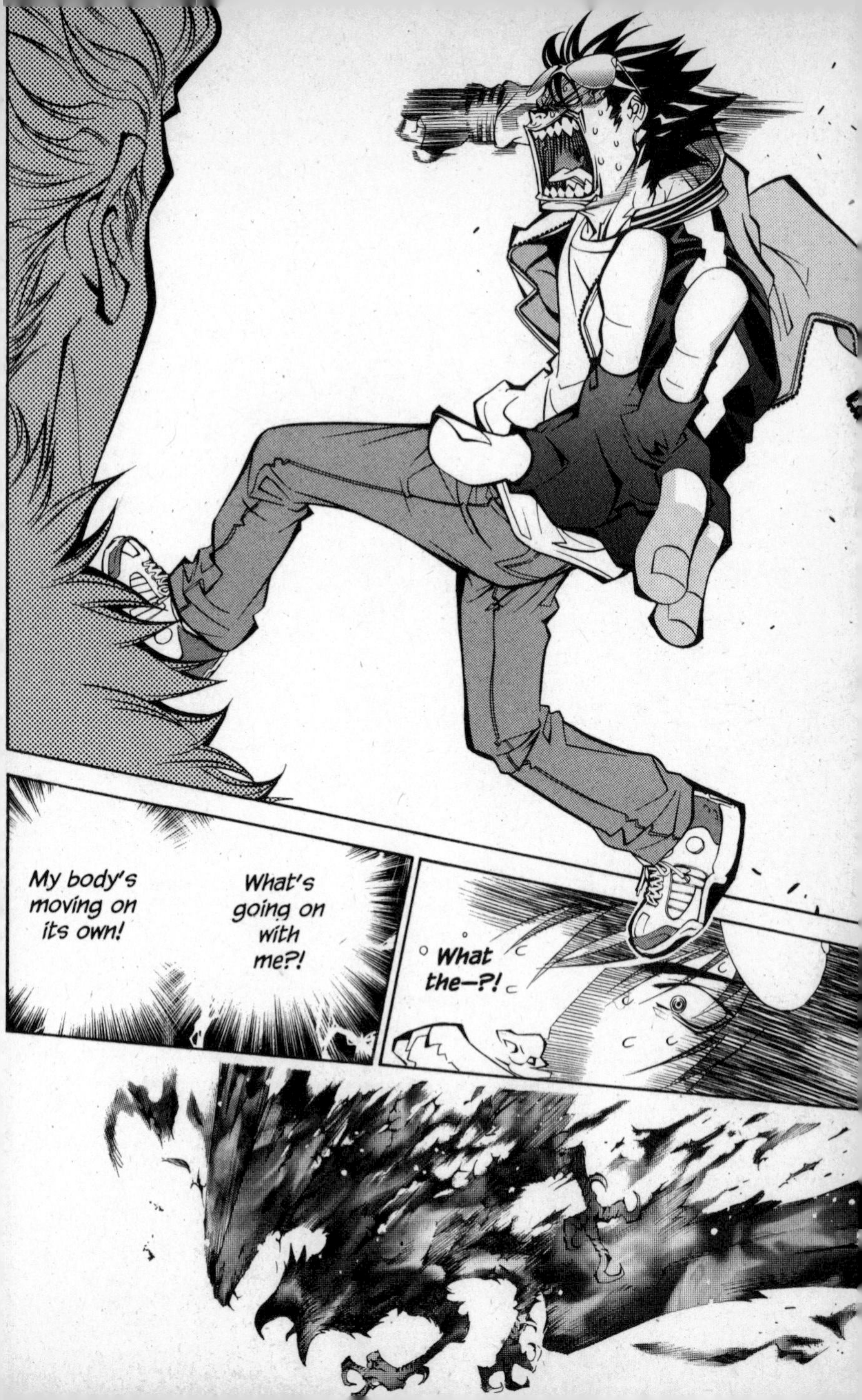
What the—?!
What's going on with me?!
My body's moving on its own!

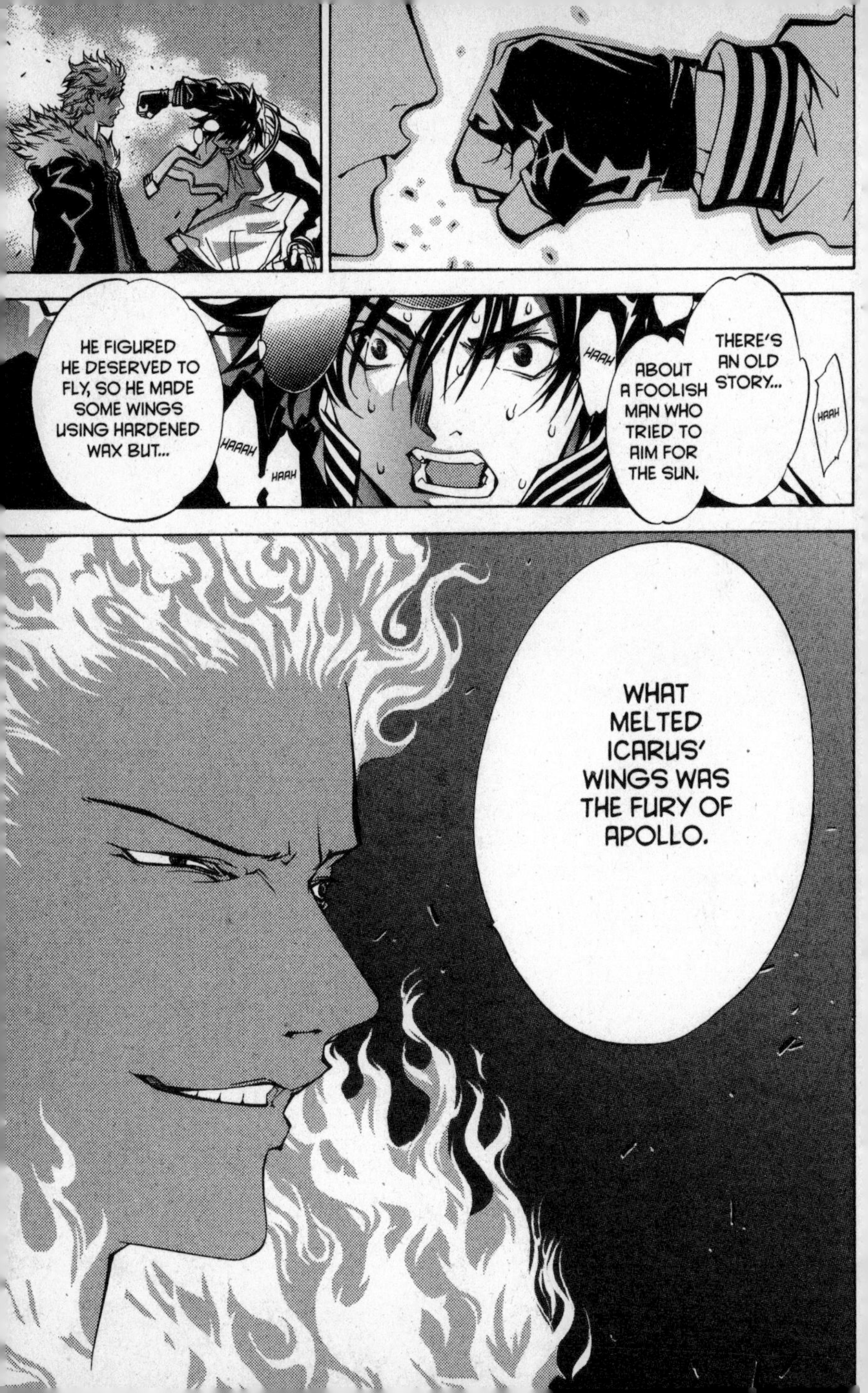
THERE'S AN OLD STORY...
HAAH
ABOUT A FOOLISH MAN WHO TRIED TO AIM FOR THE SUN.
HAAH
HE FIGURED HE DESERVED TO FLY, SO HE MADE SOME WINGS USING HARDENED WAX BUT...
HAAAH
HAAH
WHAT MELTED ICARUS' WINGS WAS THE FURY OF APOLLO.

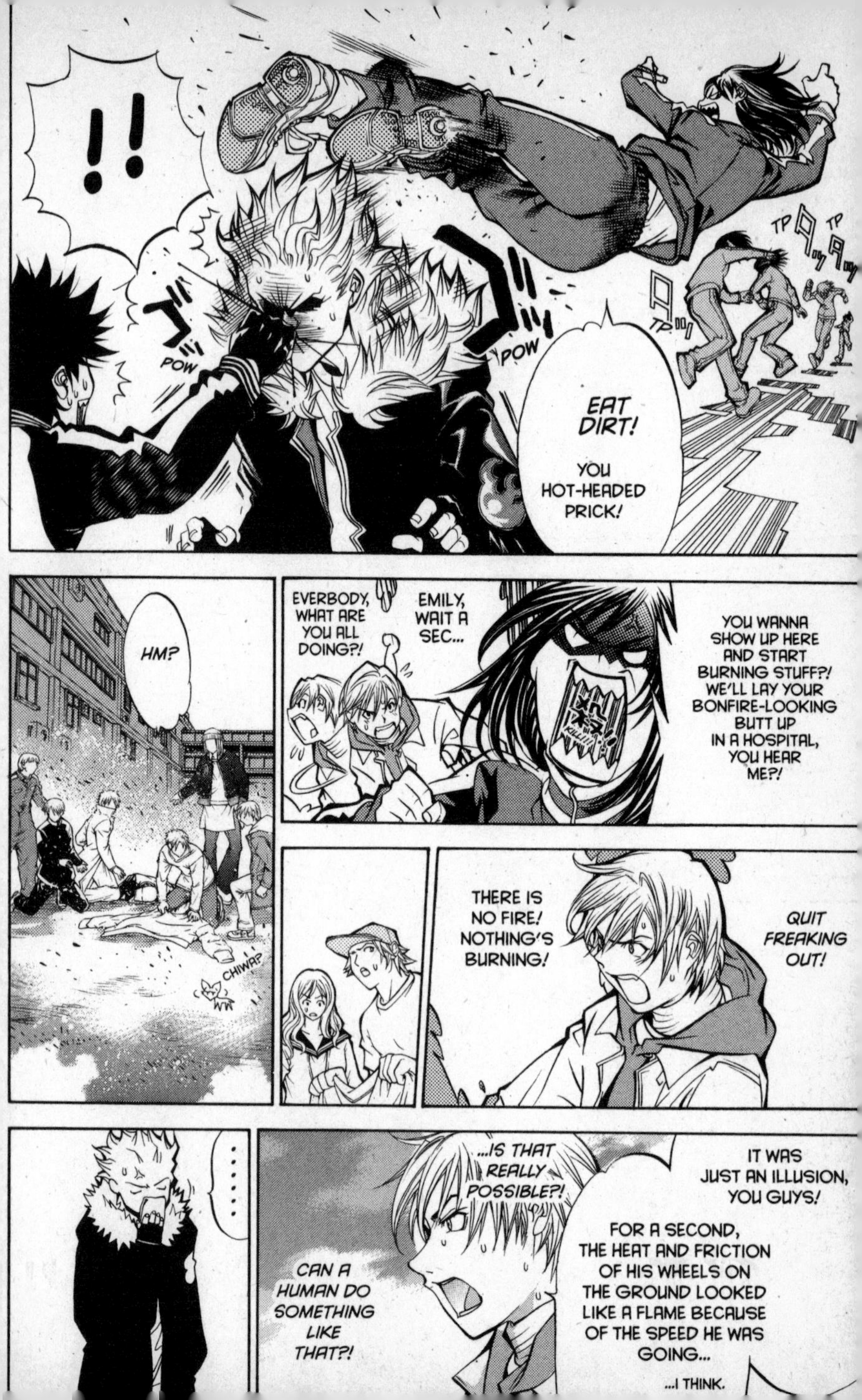
TP
TP
TP
EAT DIRT!
YOU HOT-HEADED PRICK!
POW
POW
!!
YOU WANNA SHOW UP HERE AND START BURNING STUFF?! WE'LL LAY YOUR BONFIRE-LOOKING BUTT UP IN A HOSPITAL, YOU HEAR ME?!
EMILY, WAIT A SEC...
EVERBODY, WHAT ARE YOU ALL DOING?!
QUIT FREAKING OUT!
THERE IS NO FIRE! NOTHING'S BURNING!
HM?
CHIWA?
IT WAS JUST AN ILLUSION, YOU GUYS!
...IS THAT REALLY POSSIBLE?!
FOR A SECOND, THE HEAT AND FRICTION OF HIS WHEELS ON THE GROUND LOOKED LIKE A FLAME BECAUSE OF THE SPEED HE WAS GOING...
CAN A HUMAN DO SOMETHING LIKE THAT?!
...I THINK.
......

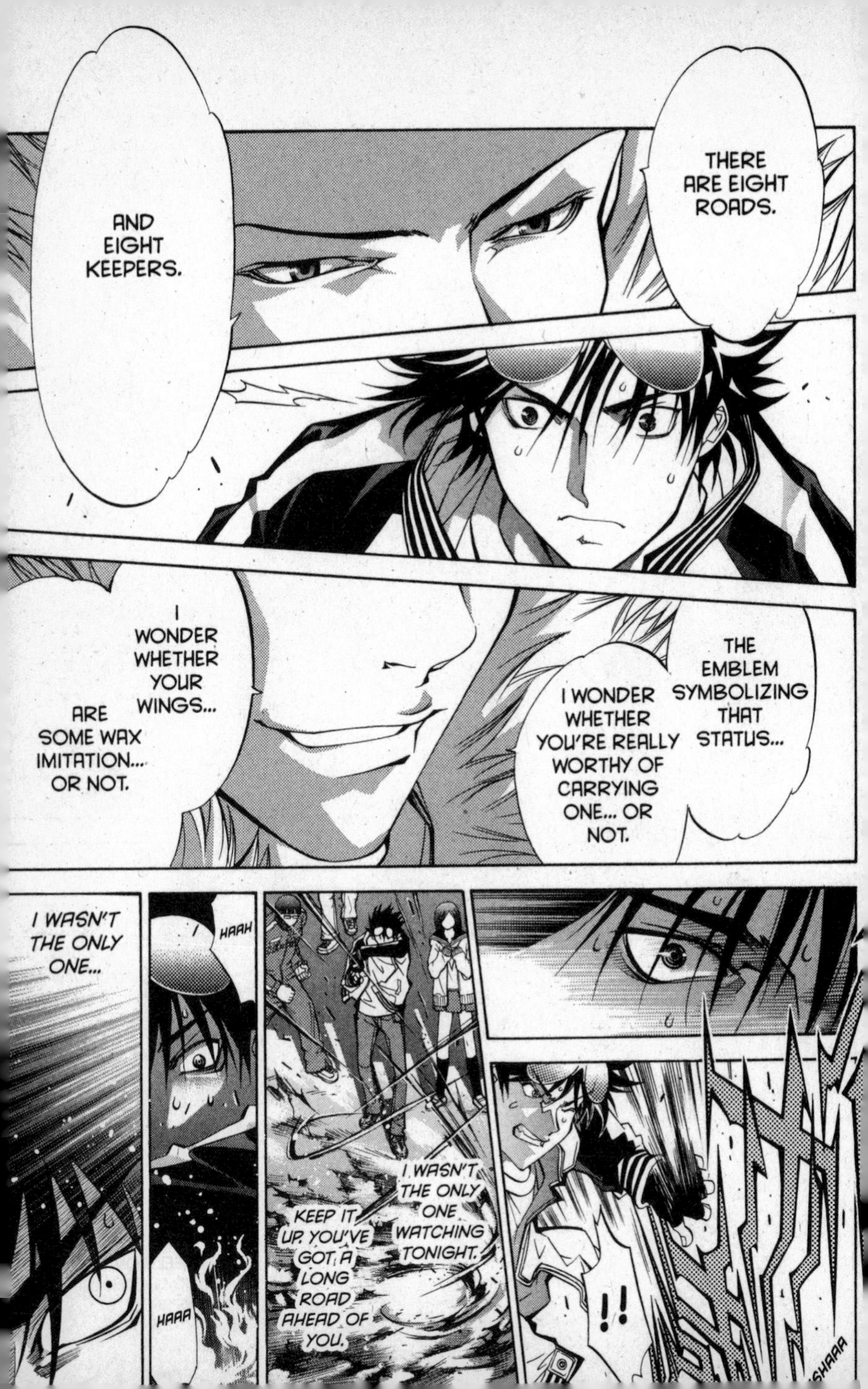
THERE ARE EIGHT ROADS.
AND EIGHT KEEPERS.
THE EMBLEM SYMBOLIZING THAT STATUS...
I WONDER WHETHER YOU'RE REALLY WORTHY OF CARRYING ONE... OR NOT.
I WONDER WHETHER YOUR WINGS...
ARE SOME WAX IMITATION... OR NOT.
!!
SHAAA
I WASN'T THE ONLY ONE WATCHING TONIGHT.
KEEP IT UP. YOU'VE GOT A LONG ROAD AHEAD OF YOU.
HAAH
HAAA
I WASN'T THE ONLY ONE...

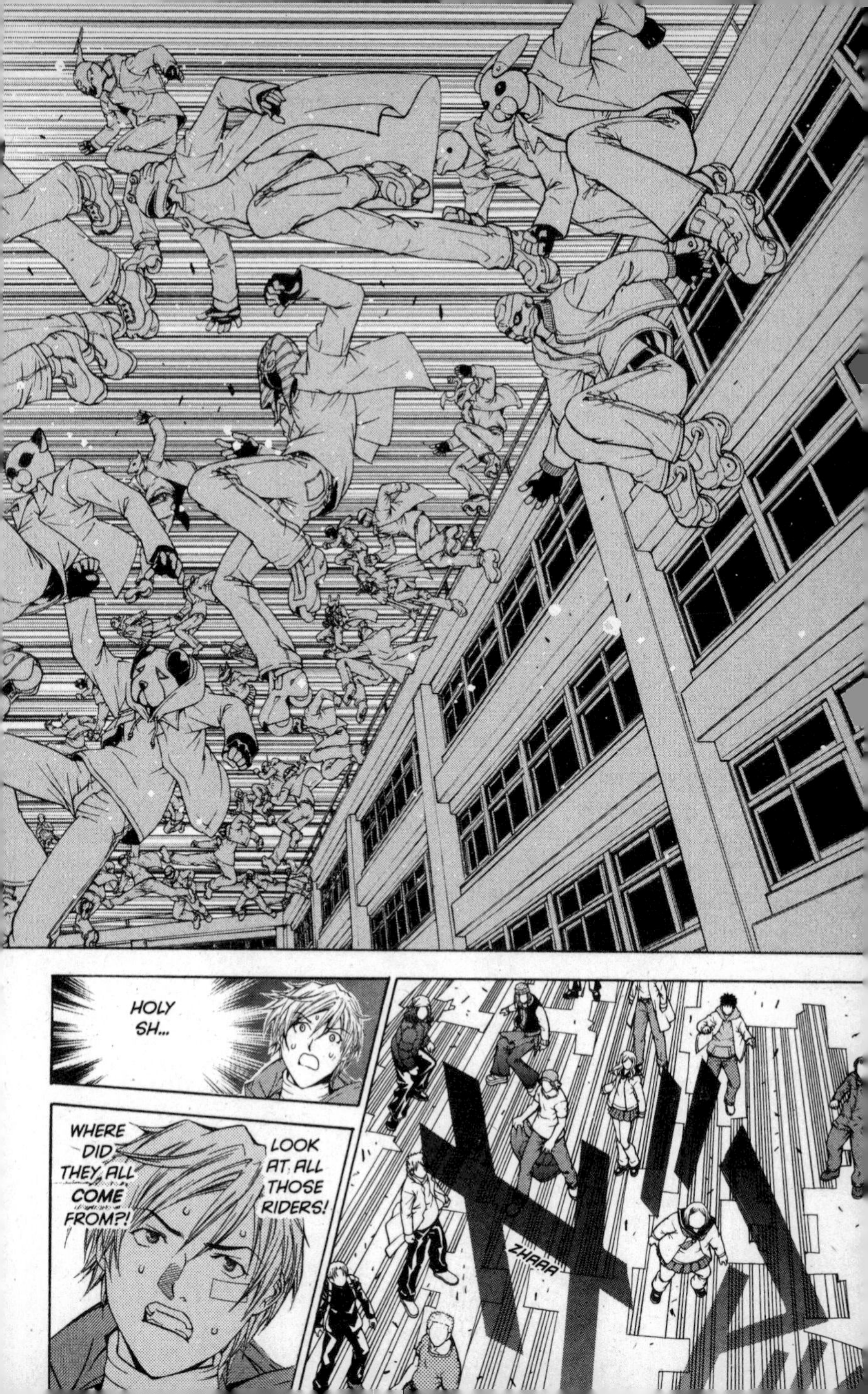
ZHAAA
HOLY SH...
LOOK AT ALL THOSE RIDERS!
WHERE DID THEY ALL COME FROM?!

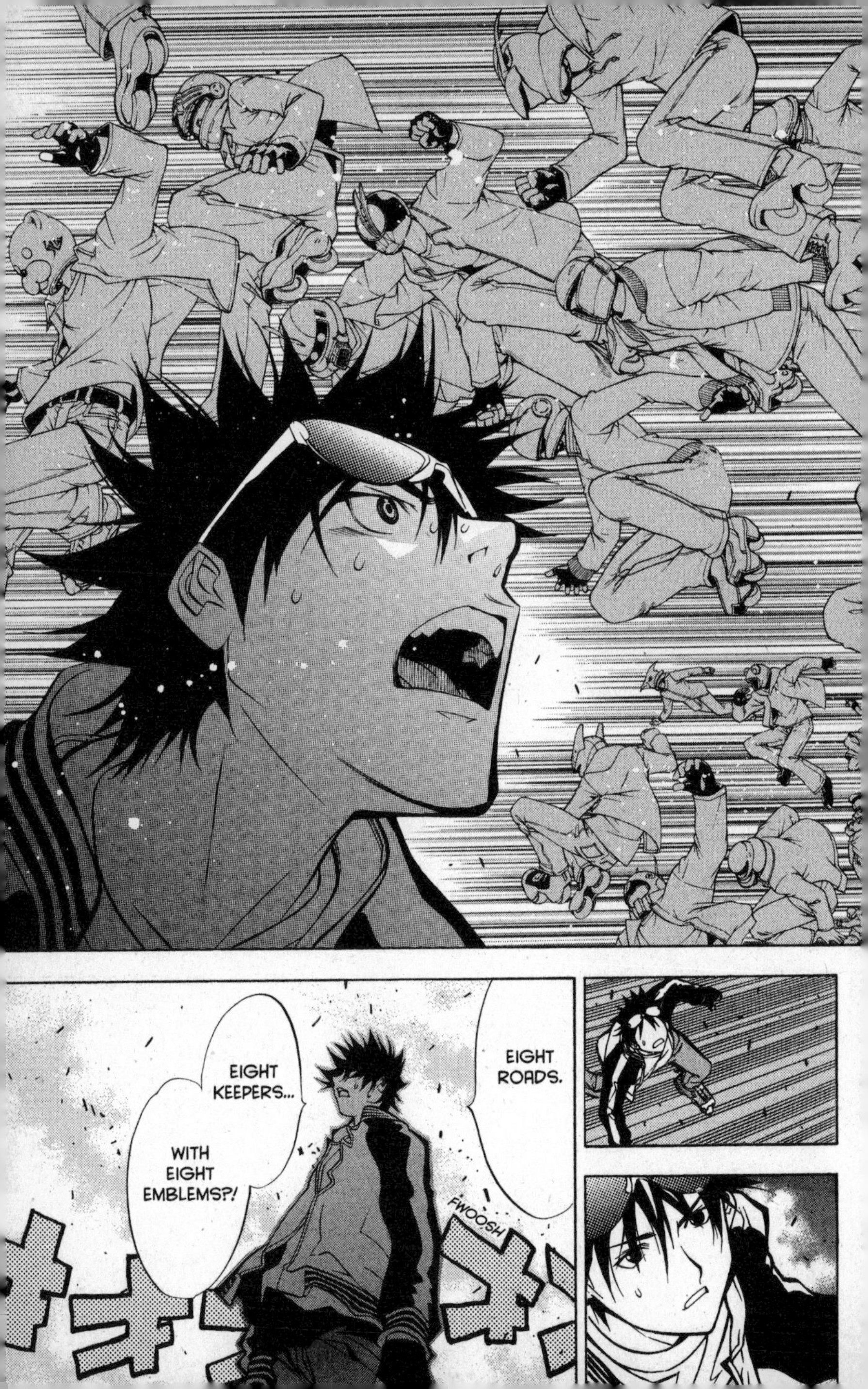
EIGHT ROADS.
FWOOSH
EIGHT KEEPERS...
WITH EIGHT EMBLEMS?!

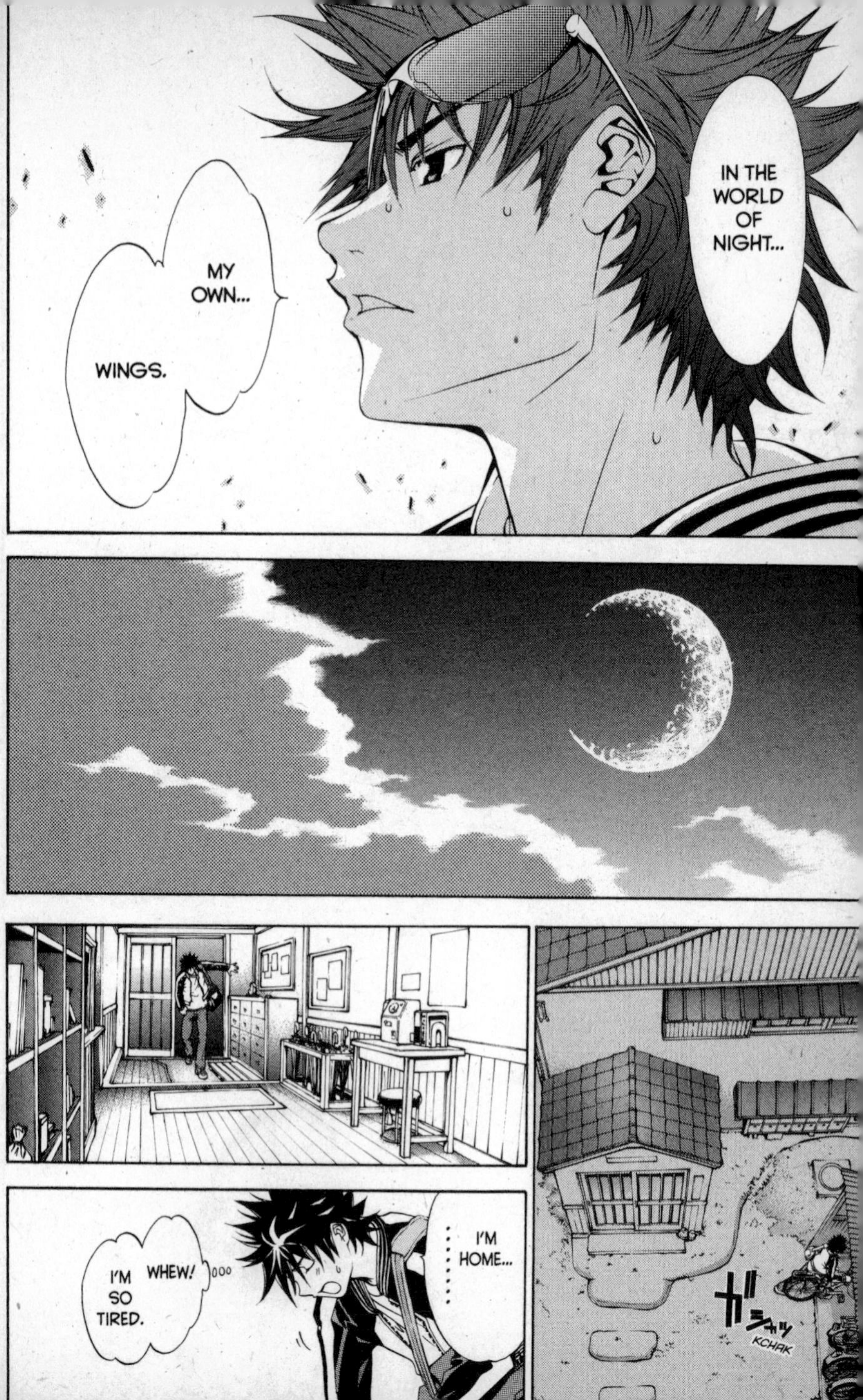
IN THE WORLD OF NIGHT...
MY OWN... WINGS.
ガシャッ
KCHAK
...... I'M HOME...
WHEW!
I'M SO TIRED.

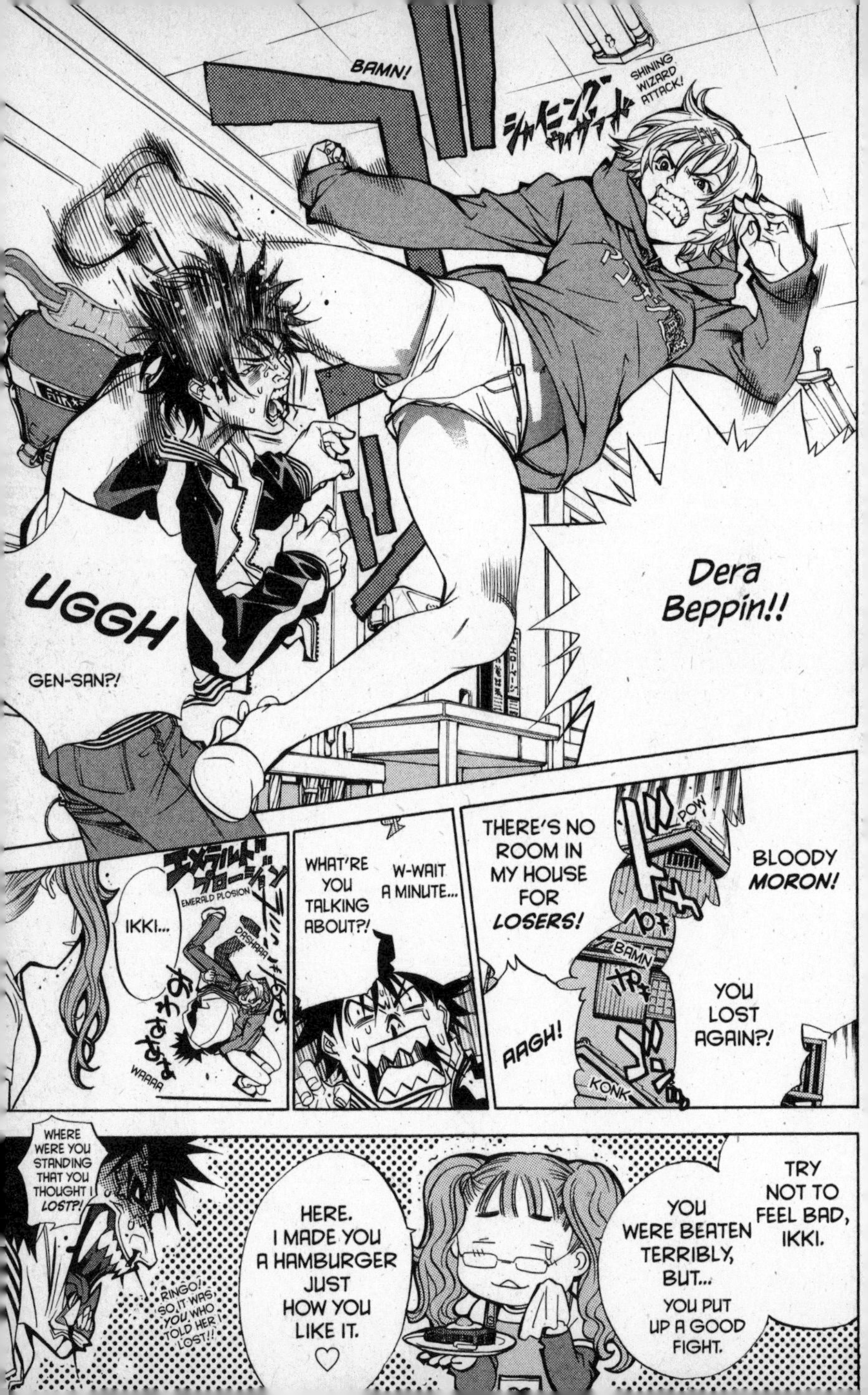
SHINING WIZARD ATTACK!
BAMN!
Dera Beppin!!
UGGH
GEN-SAN?!
BLOODY MORON!
POW
YOU LOST AGAIN?!
BAMN
KONK
AAGH!
THERE'S NO ROOM IN MY HOUSE FOR LOSERS!
W-WAIT A MINUTE...
WHAT'RE YOU TALKING ABOUT?!
EMERALD PLOSION
DASHAAA
IKKI...
WAAAA
TRY NOT TO FEEL BAD, IKKI.
YOU WERE BEATEN TERRIBLY, BUT...
YOU PUT UP A GOOD FIGHT.
HERE. I MADE YOU A HAMBURGER JUST HOW YOU LIKE IT.
WHERE WERE YOU STANDING THAT YOU THOUGHT I LOST?!
RINGO! SO IT WAS YOU WHO TOLD HER I LOST!!

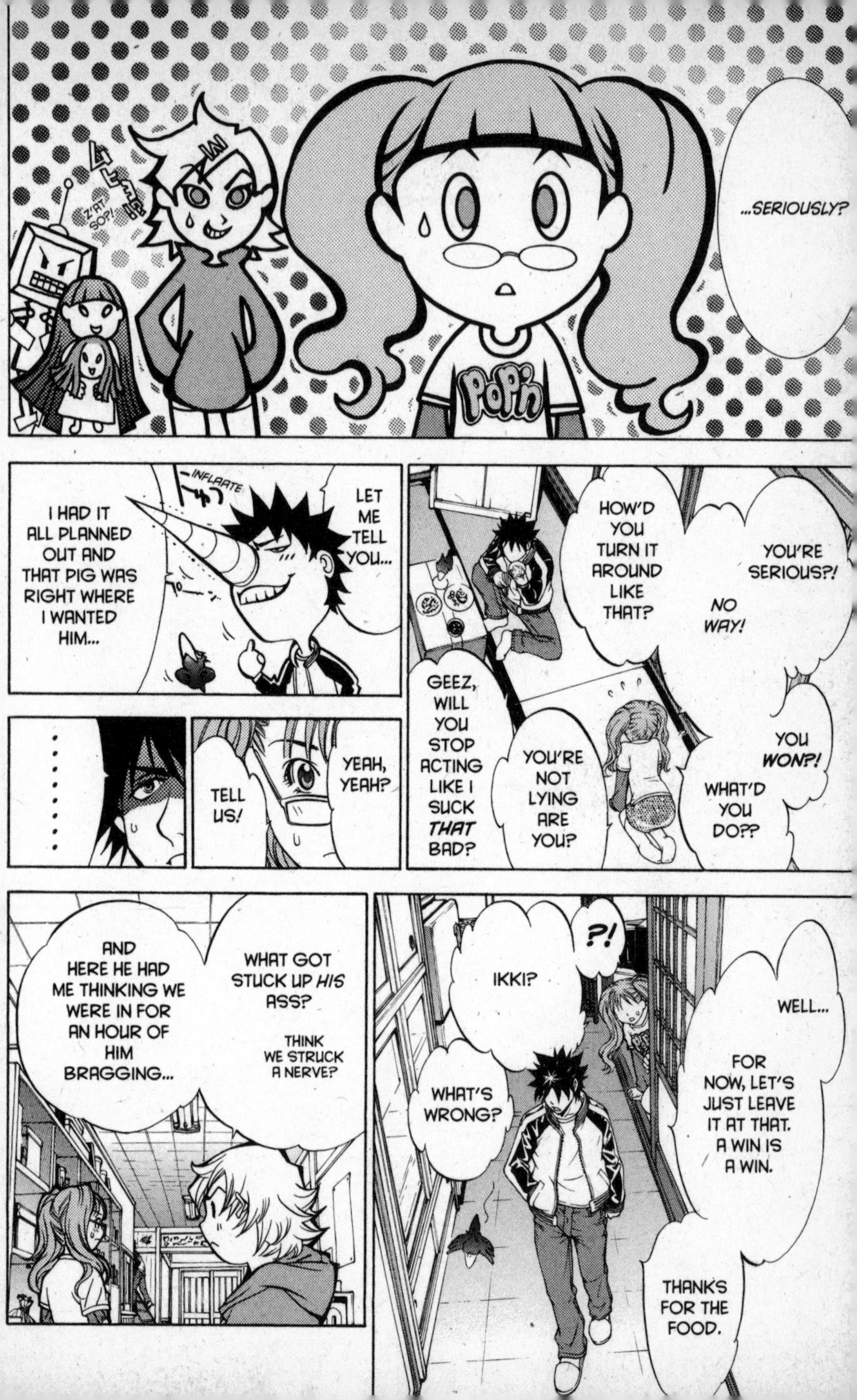
...SERIOUSLY?
Z'AT SO?!
YOU'RE SERIOUS?!
NO WAY!
HOW'D YOU TURN IT AROUND LIKE THAT?
YOU WON?!
WHAT'D YOU DO??
YOU'RE NOT LYING ARE YOU?
GEEZ, WILL YOU STOP ACTING LIKE I SUCK *THAT* BAD?
LET ME TELL YOU...
INFLAATE
I HAD IT ALL PLANNED OUT AND THAT PIG WAS RIGHT WHERE I WANTED HIM...
YEAH, YEAH?
TELL US!
....
?!
WELL...
IKKI?
FOR NOW, LET'S JUST LEAVE IT AT THAT. A WIN IS A WIN.
WHAT'S WRONG?
THANKS FOR THE FOOD.
WHAT GOT STUCK UP *HIS* ASS?
AND HERE HE HAD ME THINKING WE WERE IN FOR AN HOUR OF HIM BRAGGING...
THINK WE STRUCK A NERVE?

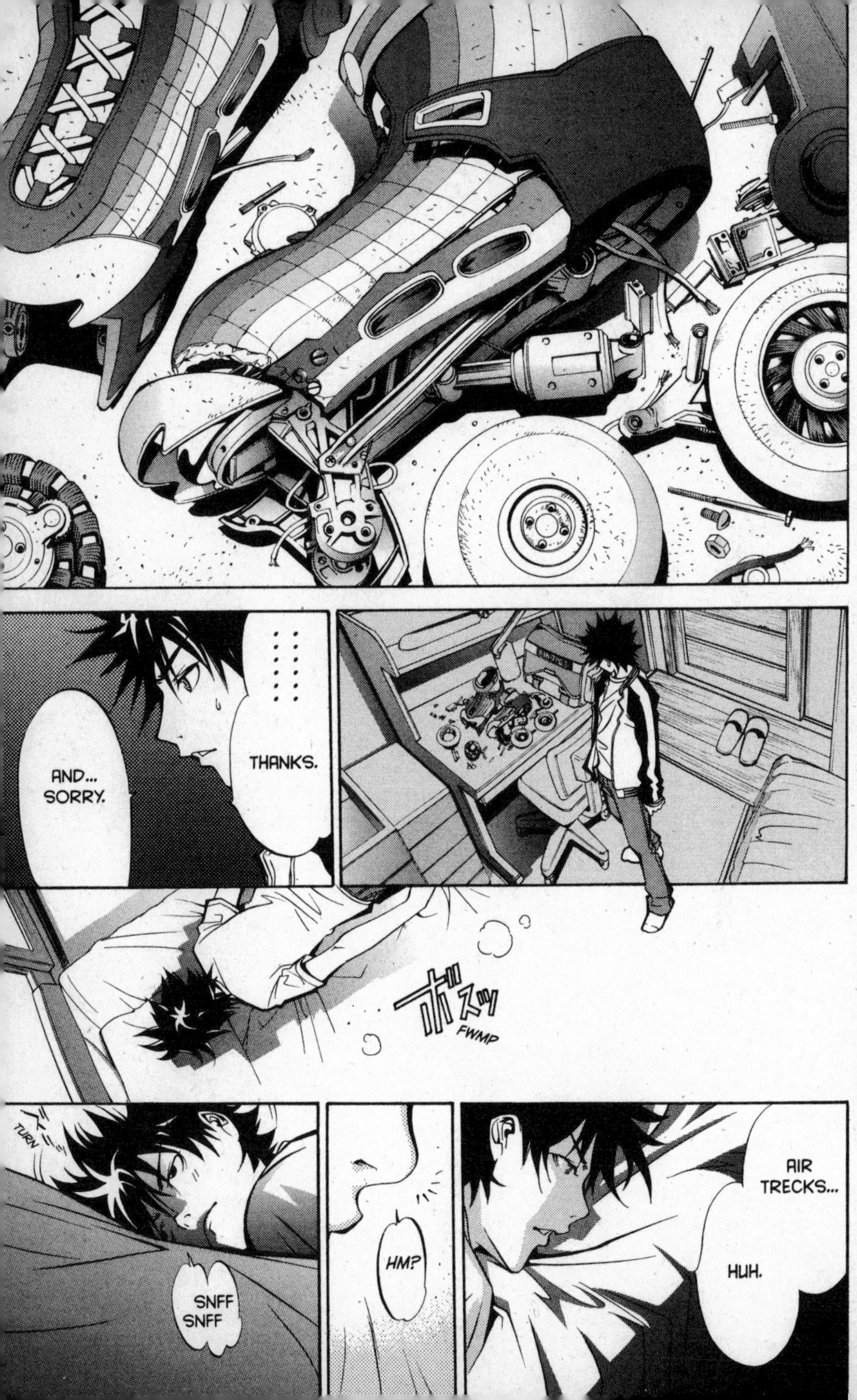
......
THANKS.
AND... SORRY.
ボスッ
FWMP
AIR TRECKS...
HUH.
HM?
TURN
SNFF SNFF

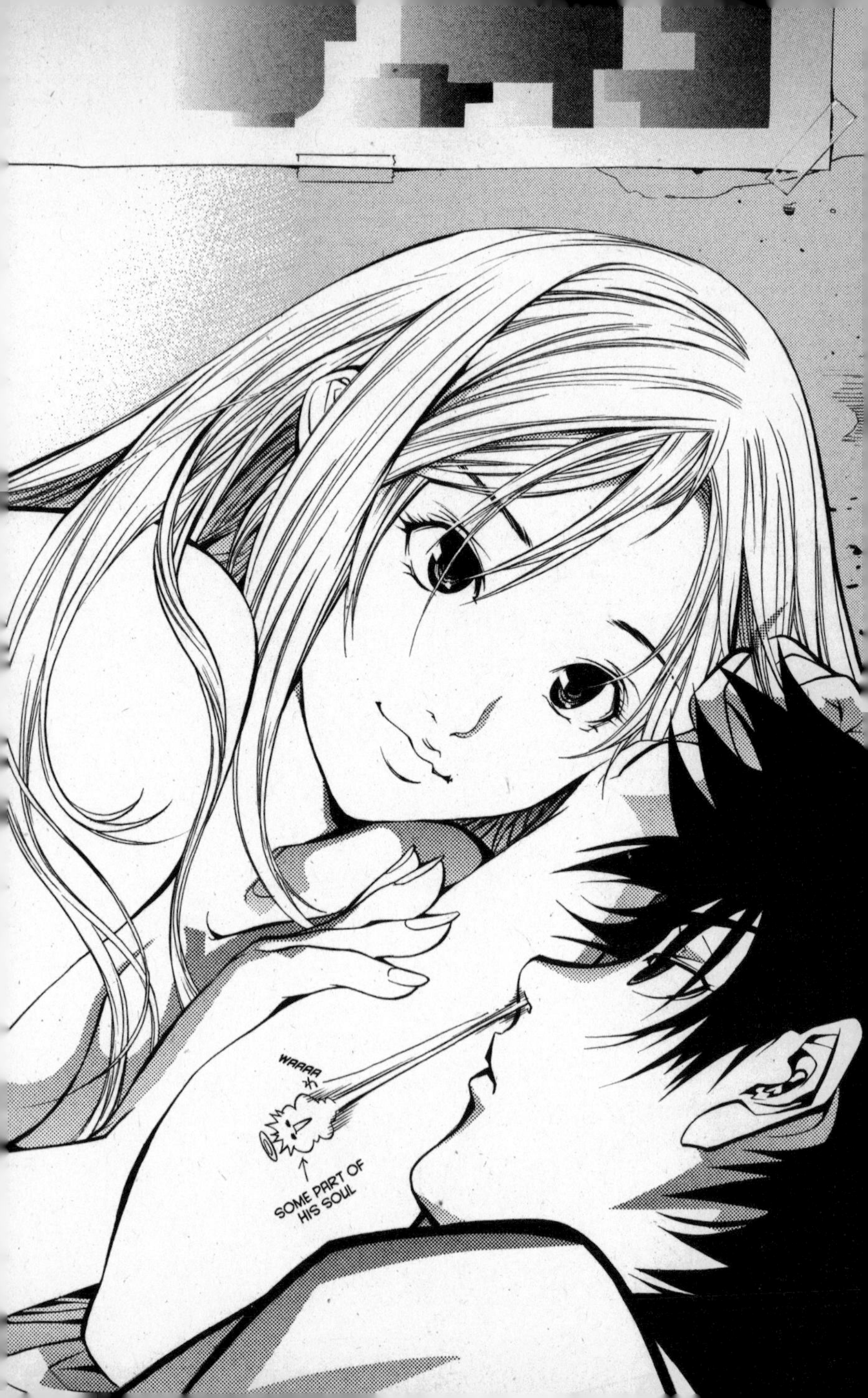
WAAAA
SOME PART OF HIS SOUL

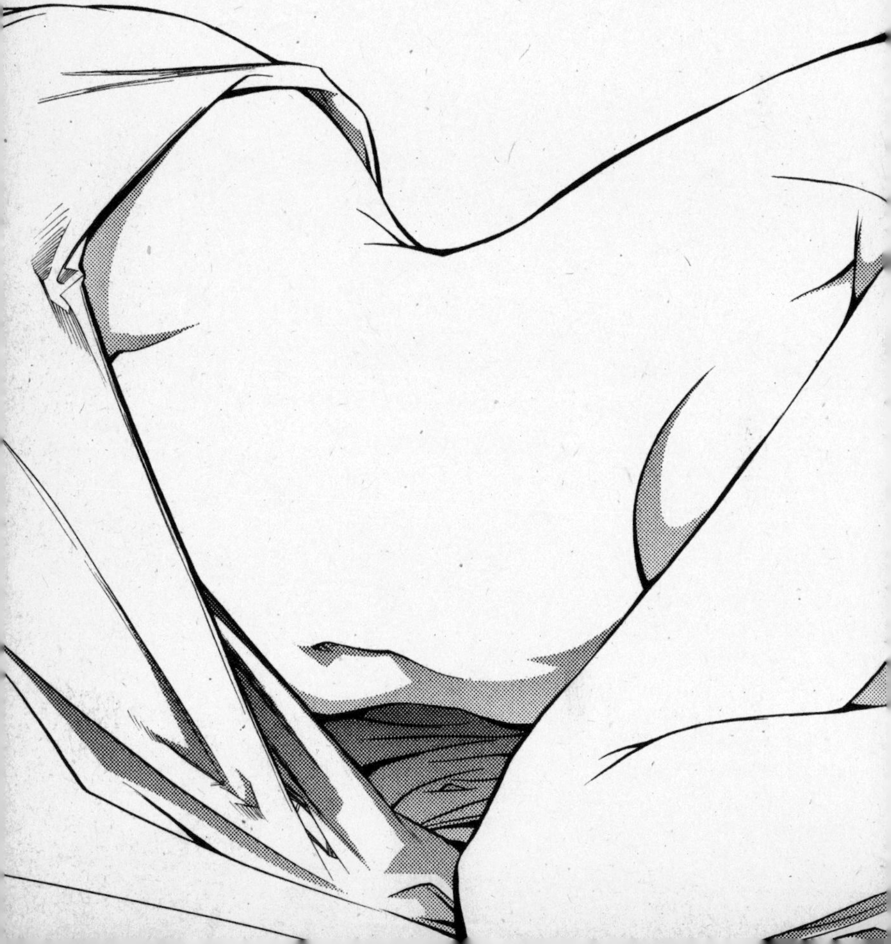

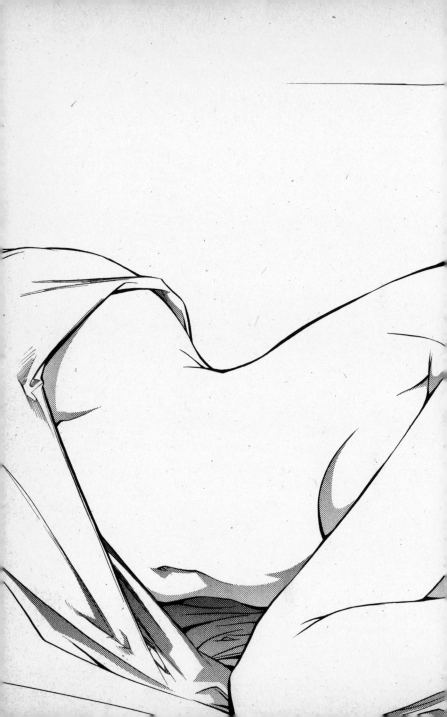

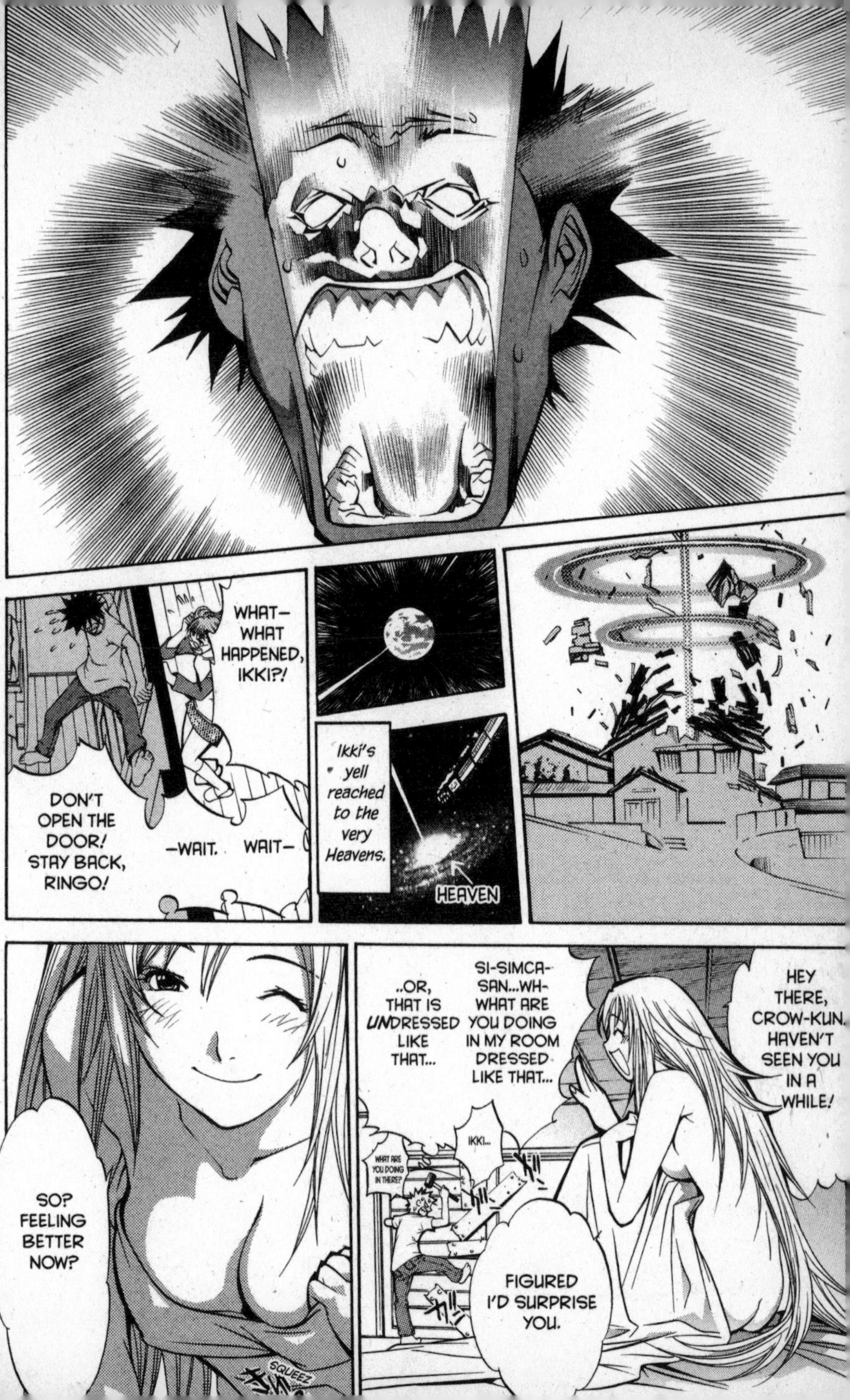
Ikki's yell reached to the very Heavens.
HEAVEN
WHAT—WHAT HAPPENED, IKKI?!
—WAIT. WAIT—
DON'T OPEN THE DOOR! STAY BACK, RINGO!
HEY THERE, CROW-KUN. HAVEN'T SEEN YOU IN A WHILE!
SI-SIMCA-SAN...WH-WHAT ARE YOU DOING IN MY ROOM DRESSED LIKE THAT...
..OR, THAT IS UNDRESSED LIKE THAT...
IKKI...
WHAT ARE YOU DOING IN THERE?
FIGURED I'D SURPRISE YOU.
SO? FEELING BETTER NOW?
SQUEEZ

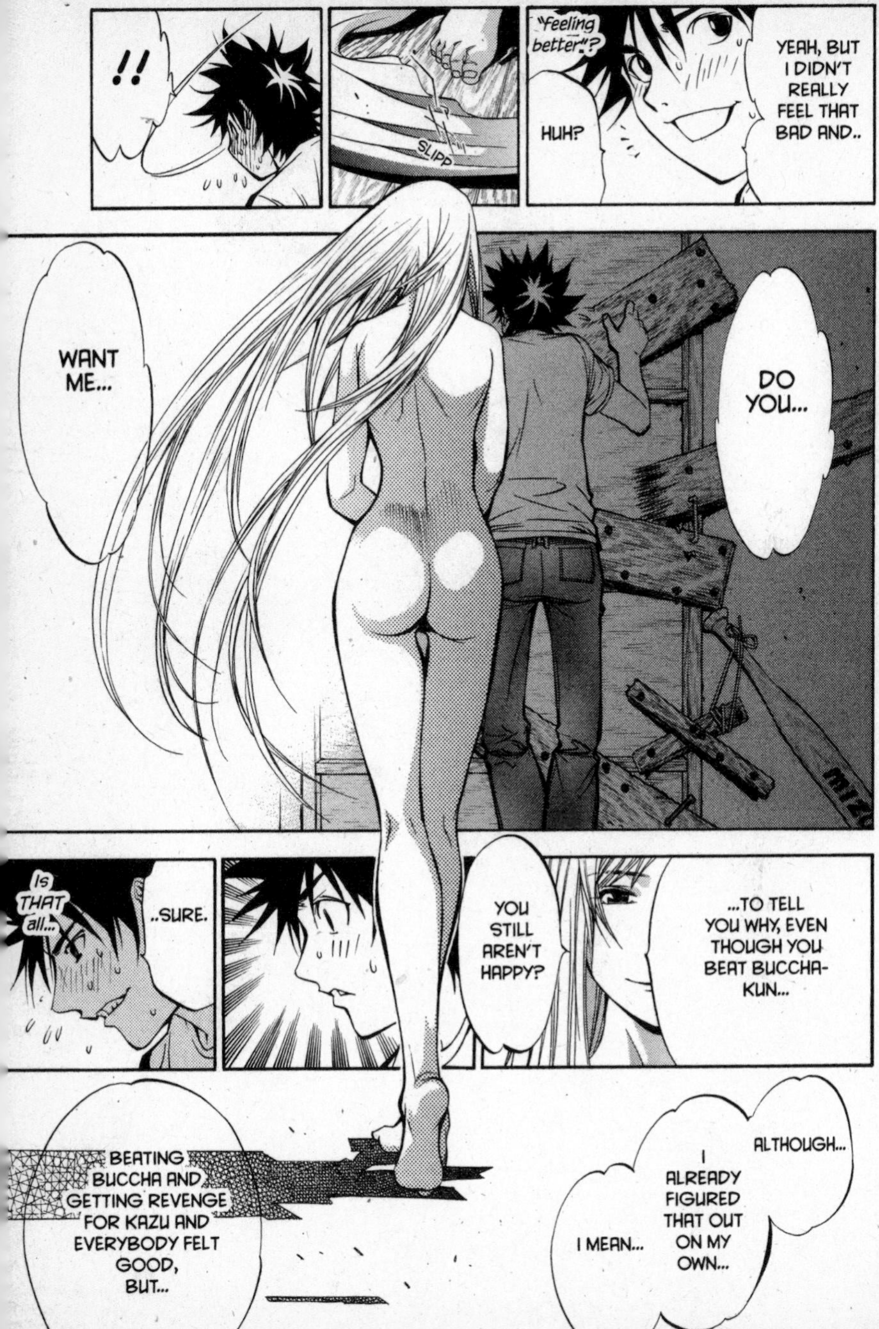
YEAH, BUT I DIDN'T REALLY FEEL THAT BAD AND..
"feeling better"?
HUH?
SLIPP
!!
DO YOU...
WANT ME...
...TO TELL YOU WHY, EVEN THOUGH YOU BEAT BUCCHA-KUN...
YOU STILL AREN'T HAPPY?
..SURE.
Is THAT all...
ALTHOUGH...
I ALREADY FIGURED THAT OUT ON MY OWN...
I MEAN...
BEATING BUCCHA AND GETTING REVENGE FOR KAZU AND EVERYBODY FELT GOOD, BUT...

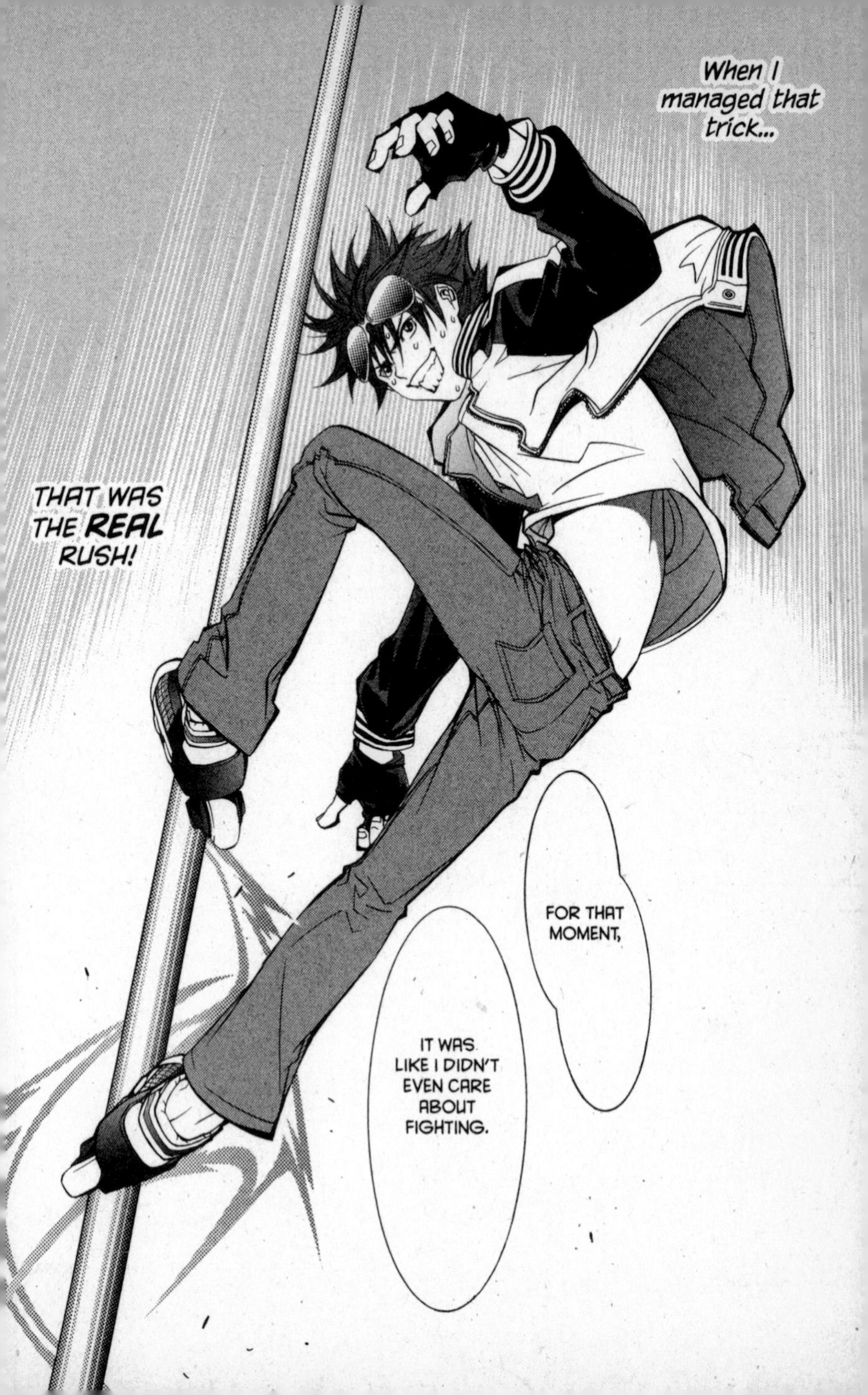
When I managed that trick...
THAT WAS THE REAL RUSH!
FOR THAT MOMENT,
IT WAS LIKE I DIDN'T EVEN CARE ABOUT FIGHTING.

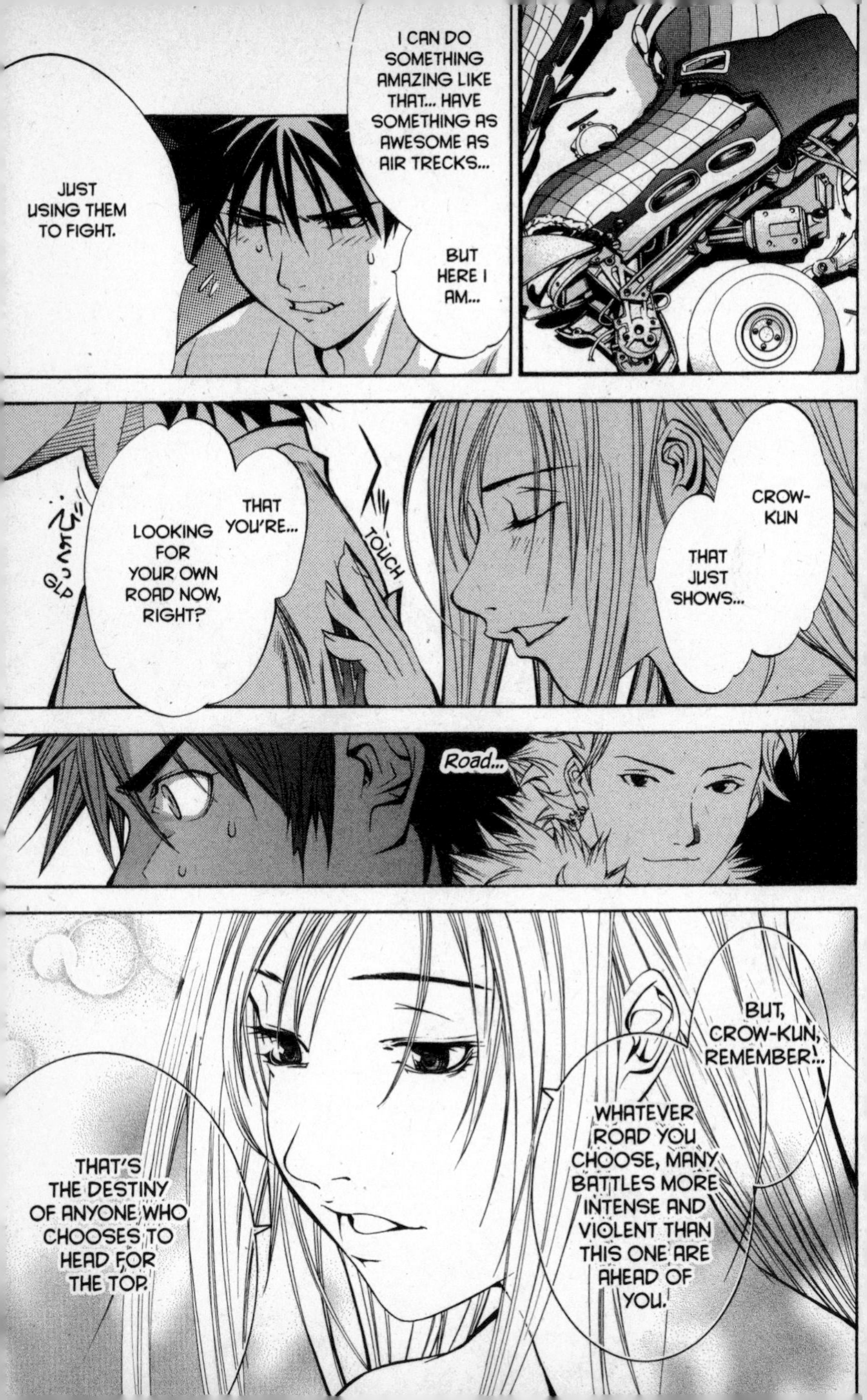
I CAN DO SOMETHING AMAZING LIKE THAT... HAVE SOMETHING AS AWESOME AS AIR TRECKS...
BUT HERE I AM...
JUST USING THEM TO FIGHT.
CROW-KUN
THAT JUST SHOWS...
TOUCH
THAT YOU'RE...
LOOKING FOR YOUR OWN ROAD NOW, RIGHT?
GLP
Road...
BUT, CROW-KUN, REMEMBER!...
WHATEVER ROAD YOU CHOOSE, MANY BATTLES MORE INTENSE AND VIOLENT THAN THIS ONE ARE AHEAD OF YOU.
THAT'S THE DESTINY OF ANYONE WHO CHOOSES TO HEAD FOR THE TOP.

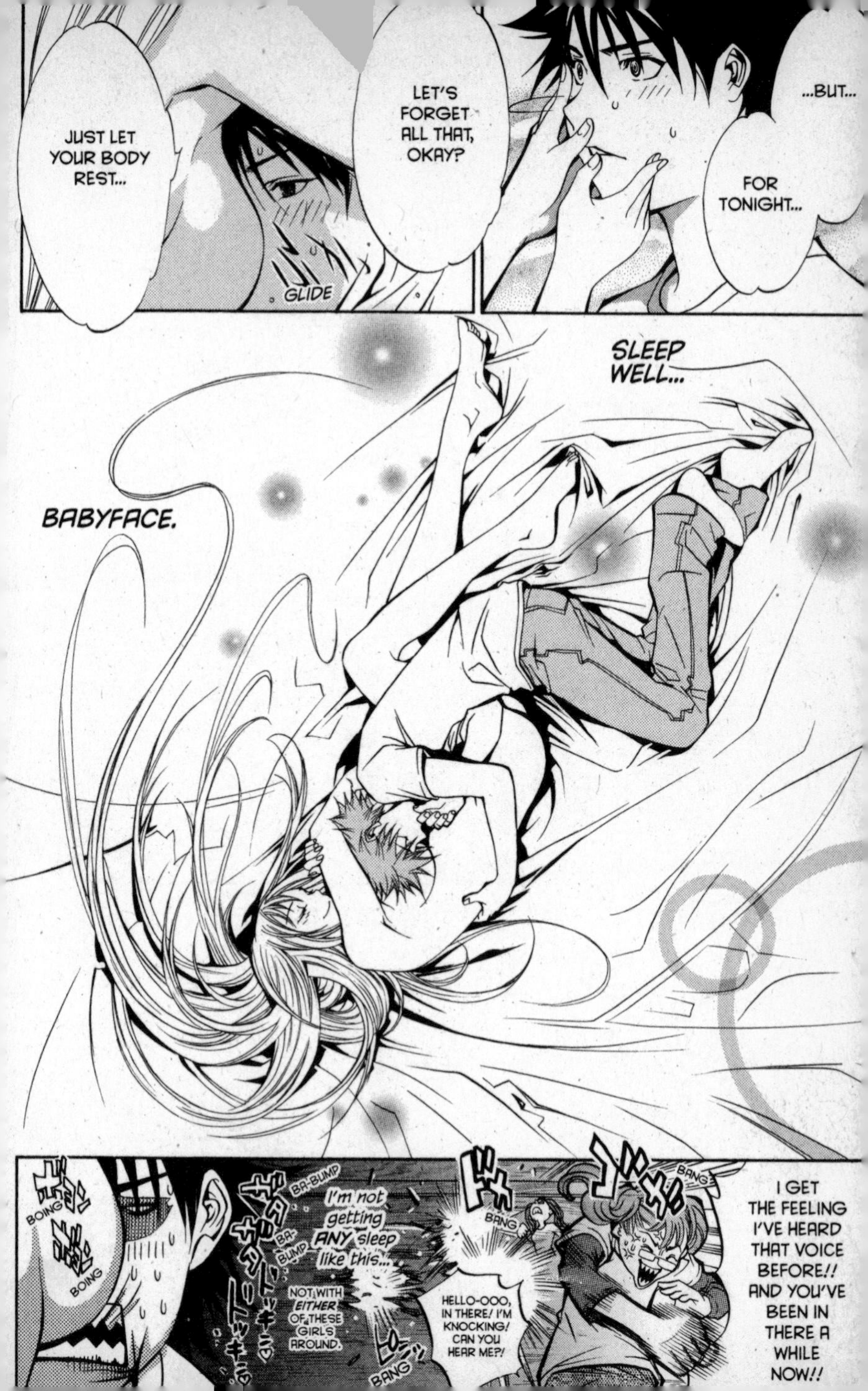
...BUT...
FOR TONIGHT...
LET'S FORGET ALL THAT, OKAY?
JUST LET YOUR BODY REST...
GLIDE
SLEEP WELL...
BABYFACE.
I GET THE FEELING I'VE HEARD THAT VOICE BEFORE!! AND YOU'VE BEEN IN THERE A WHILE NOW!!
BANG
BANG
HELLO-OOO, IN THERE! I'M KNOCKING! CAN YOU HEAR ME?!
BANG
I'm not getting ANY sleep like this...
NOT WITH EITHER OF THESE GIRLS AROUND.
BA-BUMP
BA-BUMP
BOING
BOING

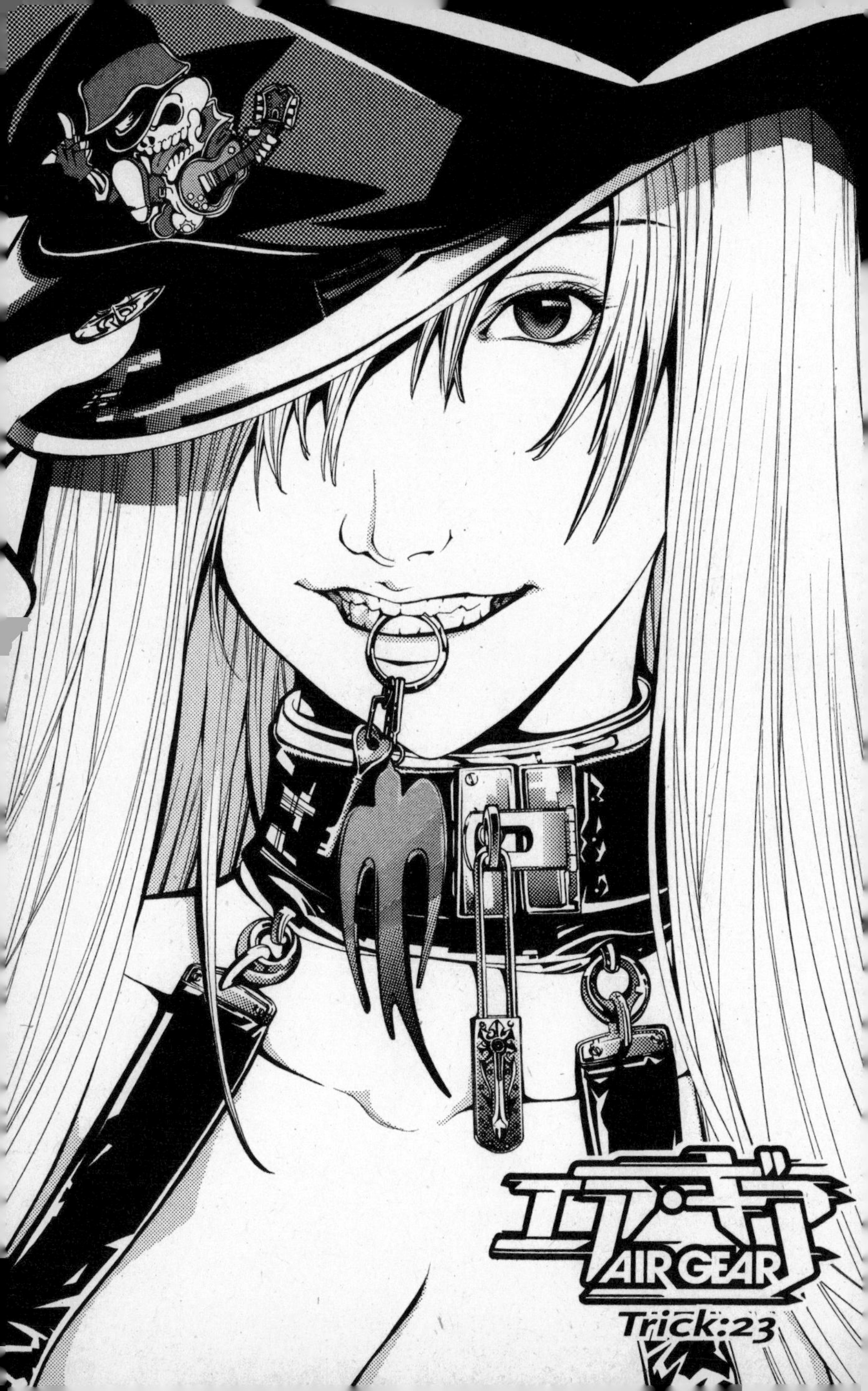
エア・ギア
AIR GEAR
Trick:23

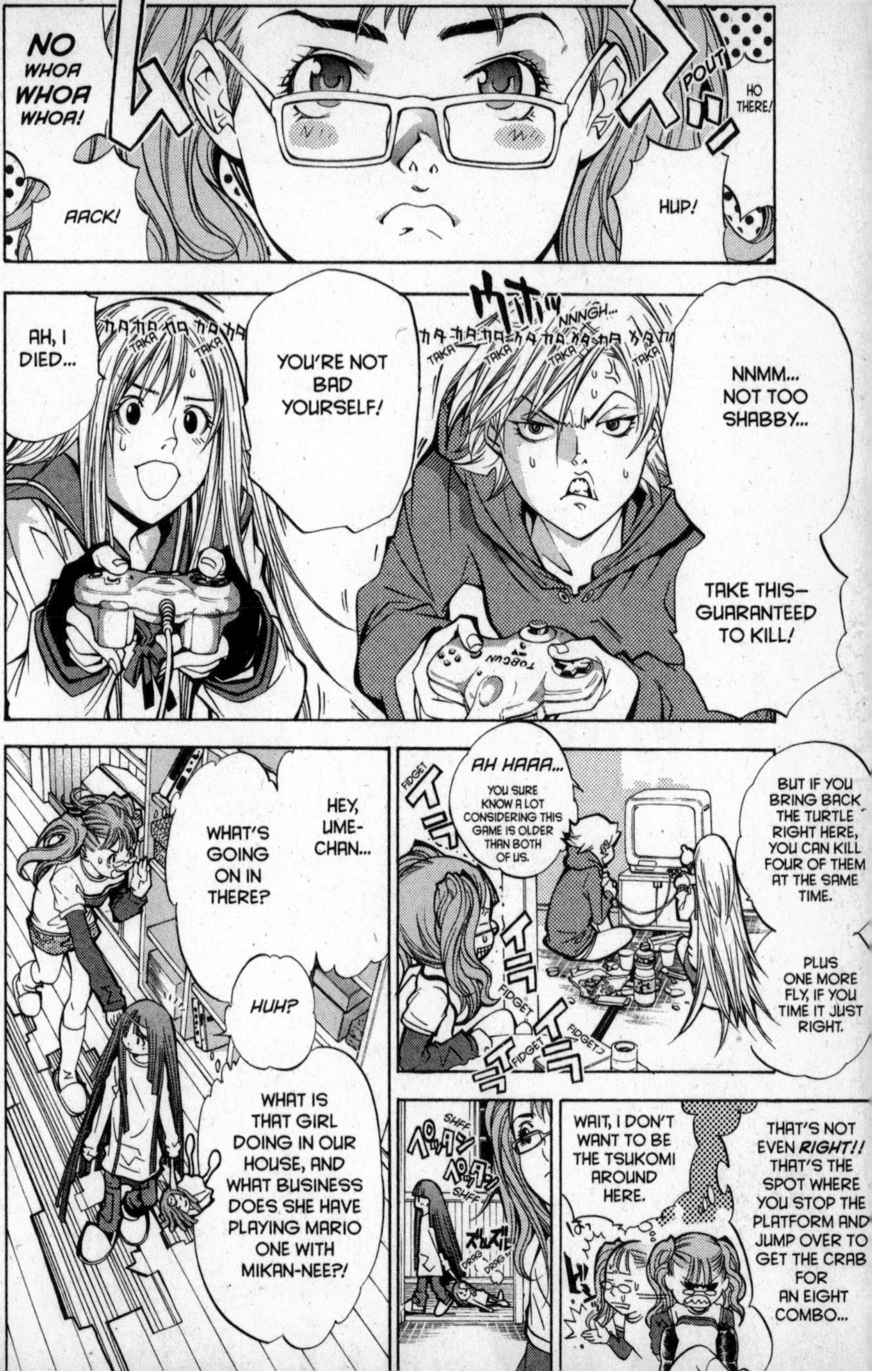
POUT
HO THERE!
HUP!
NO WHOA WHOA WHOA!
AACK!
NNMM... NOT TOO SHABBY...
NNNGH...
TAKA
TAKE THIS— GUARANTEED TO KILL!
YOU'RE NOT BAD YOURSELF!
AH, I DIED...
BUT IF YOU BRING BACK THE TURTLE RIGHT HERE, YOU CAN KILL FOUR OF THEM AT THE SAME TIME.
AH HAAA...
YOU SURE KNOW A LOT CONSIDERING THIS GAME IS OLDER THAN BOTH OF US.
FIDGET
PLUS ONE MORE FLY, IF YOU TIME IT JUST RIGHT.
FIDGET
FIDGET
FIDGET
THAT'S NOT EVEN *RIGHT!!* THAT'S THE SPOT WHERE YOU STOP THE PLATFORM AND JUMP OVER TO GET THE CRAB FOR AN EIGHT COMBO...
WAIT, I DON'T WANT TO BE THE TSUKOMI AROUND HERE.
SHFF
SHFF
DRAG
DRAG
HEY, UME-CHAN...
WHAT'S GOING ON IN THERE?
HUH?
WHAT IS THAT GIRL DOING IN OUR HOUSE, AND WHAT BUSINESS DOES SHE HAVE PLAYING MARIO ONE WITH MIKAN-NEE?!

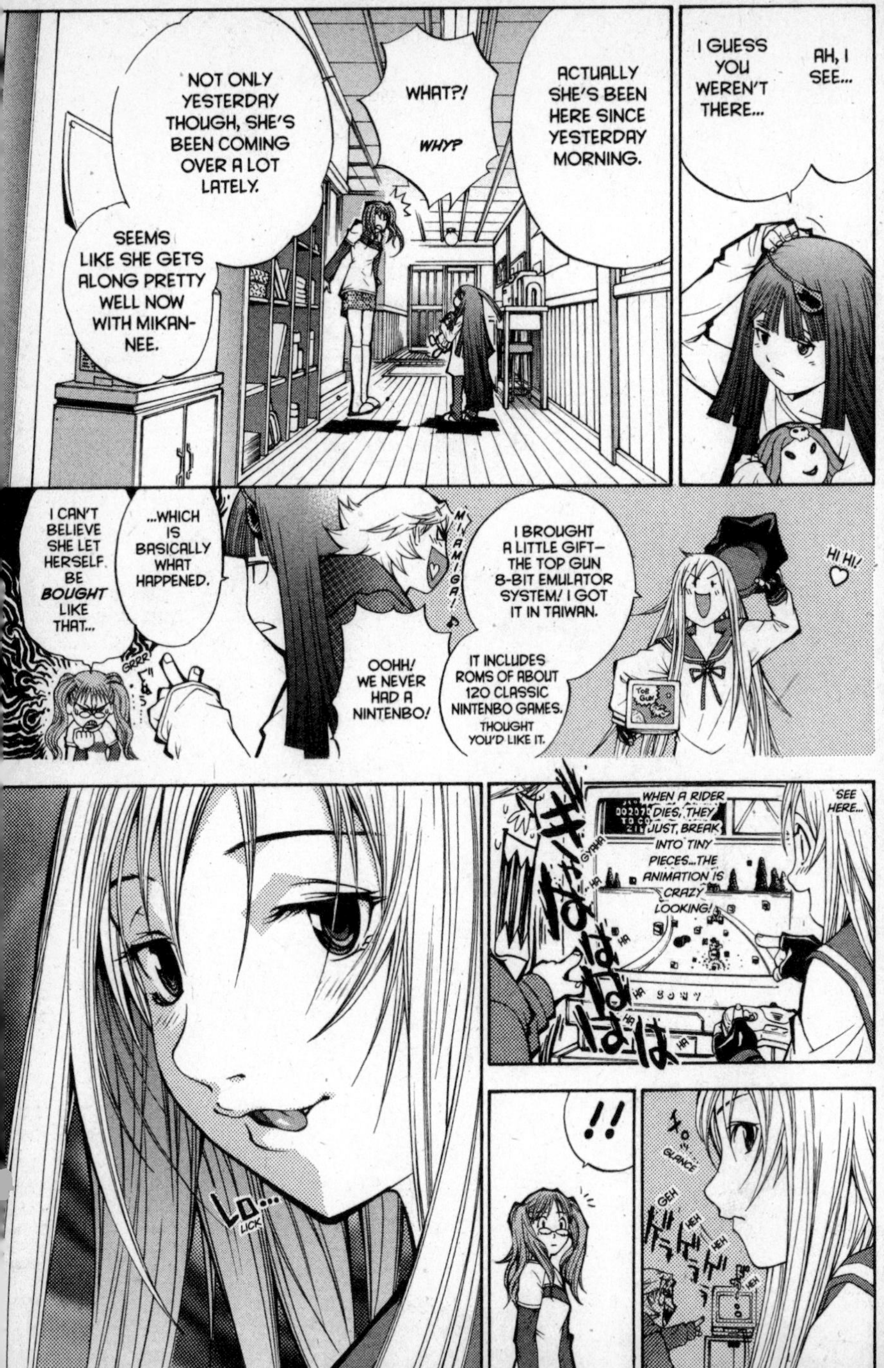

AH, I SEE...
I GUESS YOU WEREN'T THERE...
ACTUALLY SHE'S BEEN HERE SINCE YESTERDAY MORNING.
WHAT?!
WHY?
NOT ONLY YESTERDAY THOUGH, SHE'S BEEN COMING OVER A LOT LATELY.
SEEMS LIKE SHE GETS ALONG PRETTY WELL NOW WITH MIKAN-NEE.
HI HI!
I BROUGHT A LITTLE GIFT— THE TOP GUN 8-BIT EMULATOR SYSTEM! I GOT IT IN TAIWAN.
IT INCLUDES ROMS OF ABOUT 120 CLASSIC NINTENBO GAMES.
THOUGHT YOU'D LIKE IT.
TOP GUN
MI AMIGA!
OOHH! WE NEVER HAD A NINTENBO!
...WHICH IS BASICALLY WHAT HAPPENED.
I CAN'T BELIEVE SHE LET HERSELF BE *BOUGHT* LIKE THAT...
GRRR
SEE HERE...
WHEN A RIDER DIES, THEY JUST, BREAK INTO TINY PIECES...THE ANIMATION IS CRAZY LOOKING!
ぎゃははははは
GYAHA HA HA HA HA HA
SONY
GLANCE
GEH HEH HEH HEH
!!
LICK

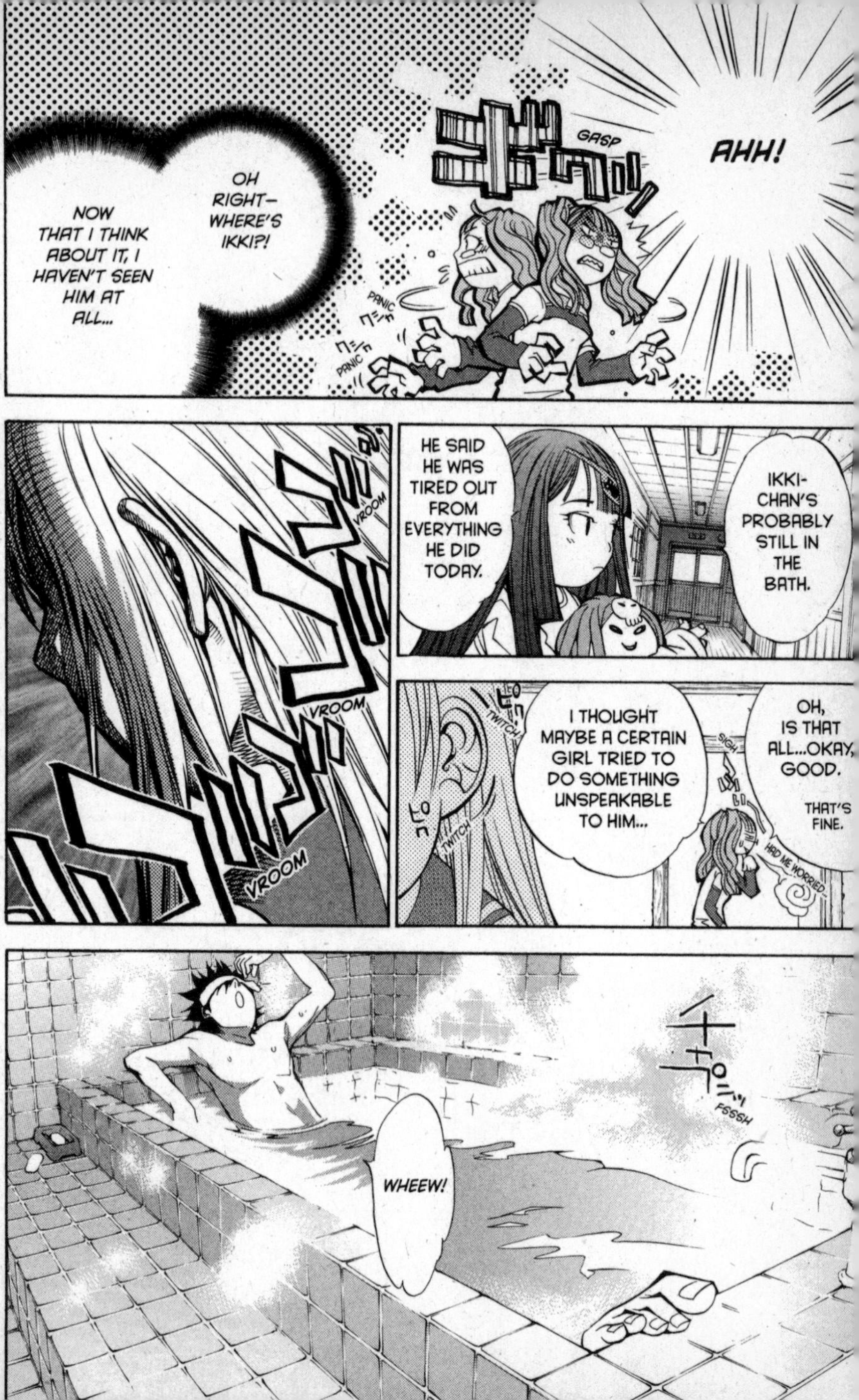
AHH!
GASP
OH RIGHT— WHERE'S IKKI?!
NOW THAT I THINK ABOUT IT, I HAVEN'T SEEN HIM AT ALL...
PANIC
PANIC
IKKI-CHAN'S PROBABLY STILL IN THE BATH.
HE SAID HE WAS TIRED OUT FROM EVERYTHING HE DID TODAY.
OH, IS THAT ALL...OKAY, GOOD.
THAT'S FINE.
SIGH
HAD ME WORRIED...
I THOUGHT MAYBE A CERTAIN GIRL TRIED TO DO SOMETHING UNSPEAKABLE TO HIM...
TWITCH
TWITCH
VROOM
VROOM
VROOM
FSSSH
WHEEW!

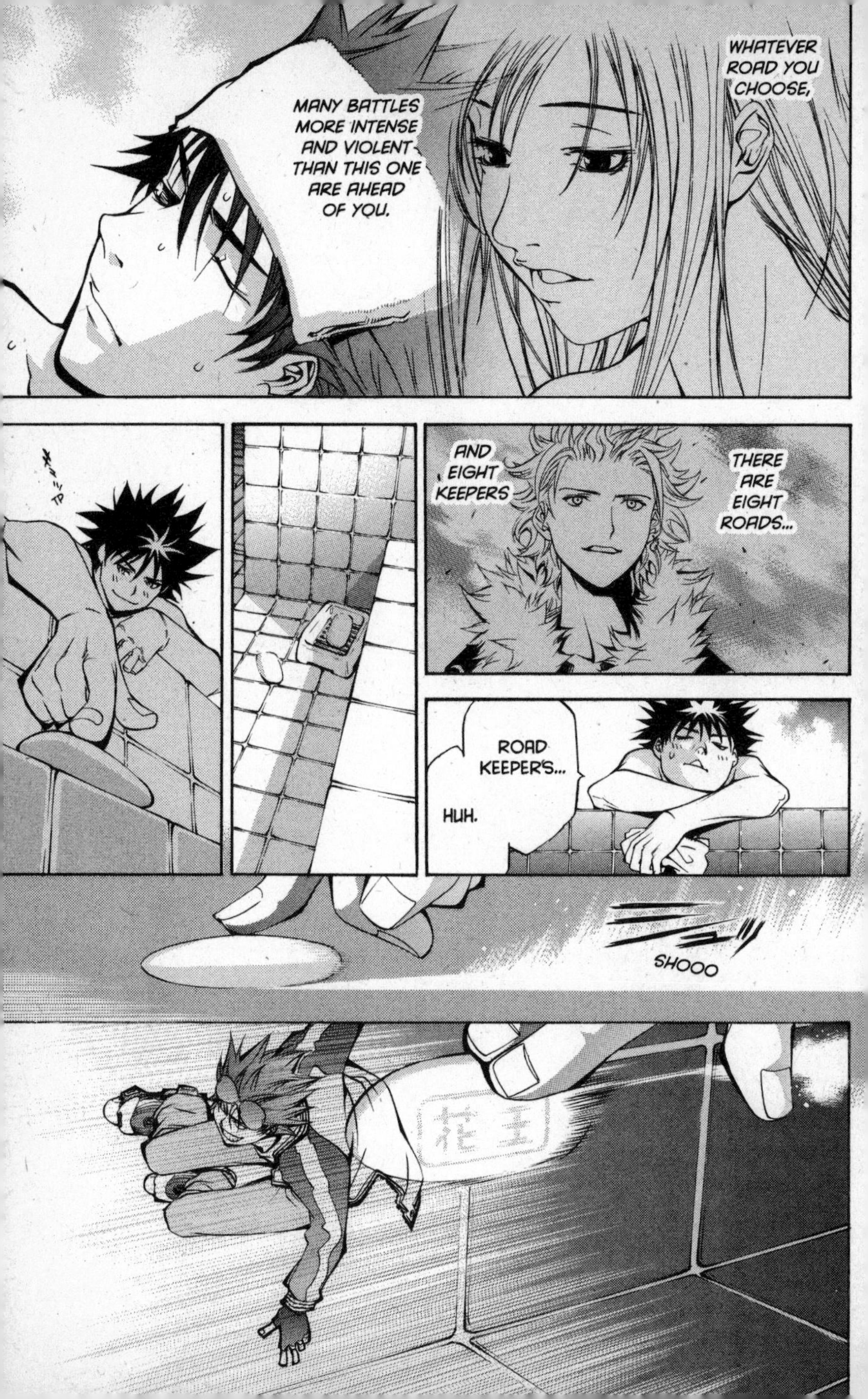
WHATEVER ROAD YOU CHOOSE,
MANY BATTLES MORE INTENSE AND VIOLENT THAN THIS ONE ARE AHEAD OF YOU.
THERE ARE EIGHT ROADS...
AND EIGHT KEEPERS
ROAD KEEPER'S...
HUH.
SHOOO

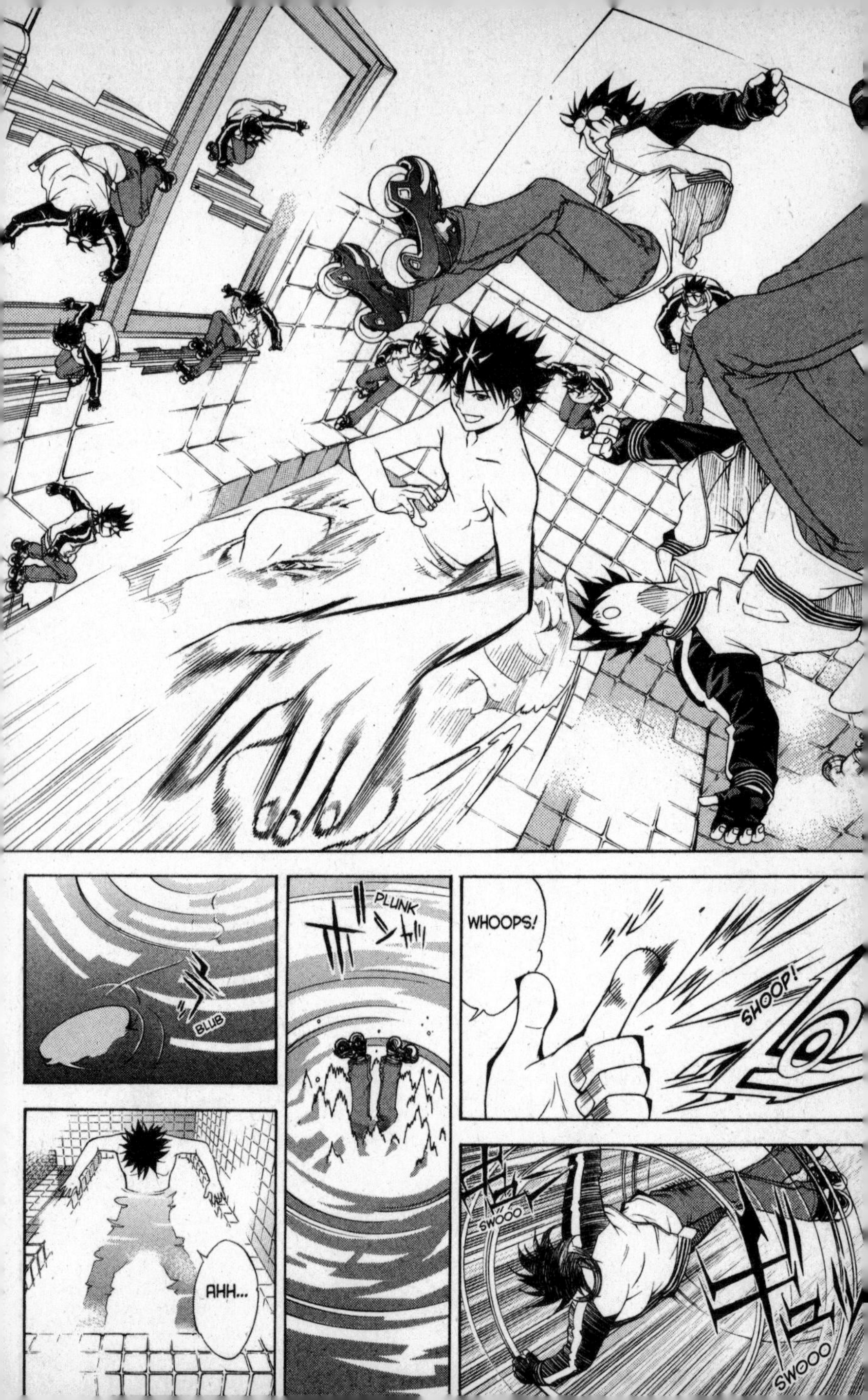
WHOOPS!
SHOOP!
SWOOO
SWOOO
PLUNK
BLUB
AHH...

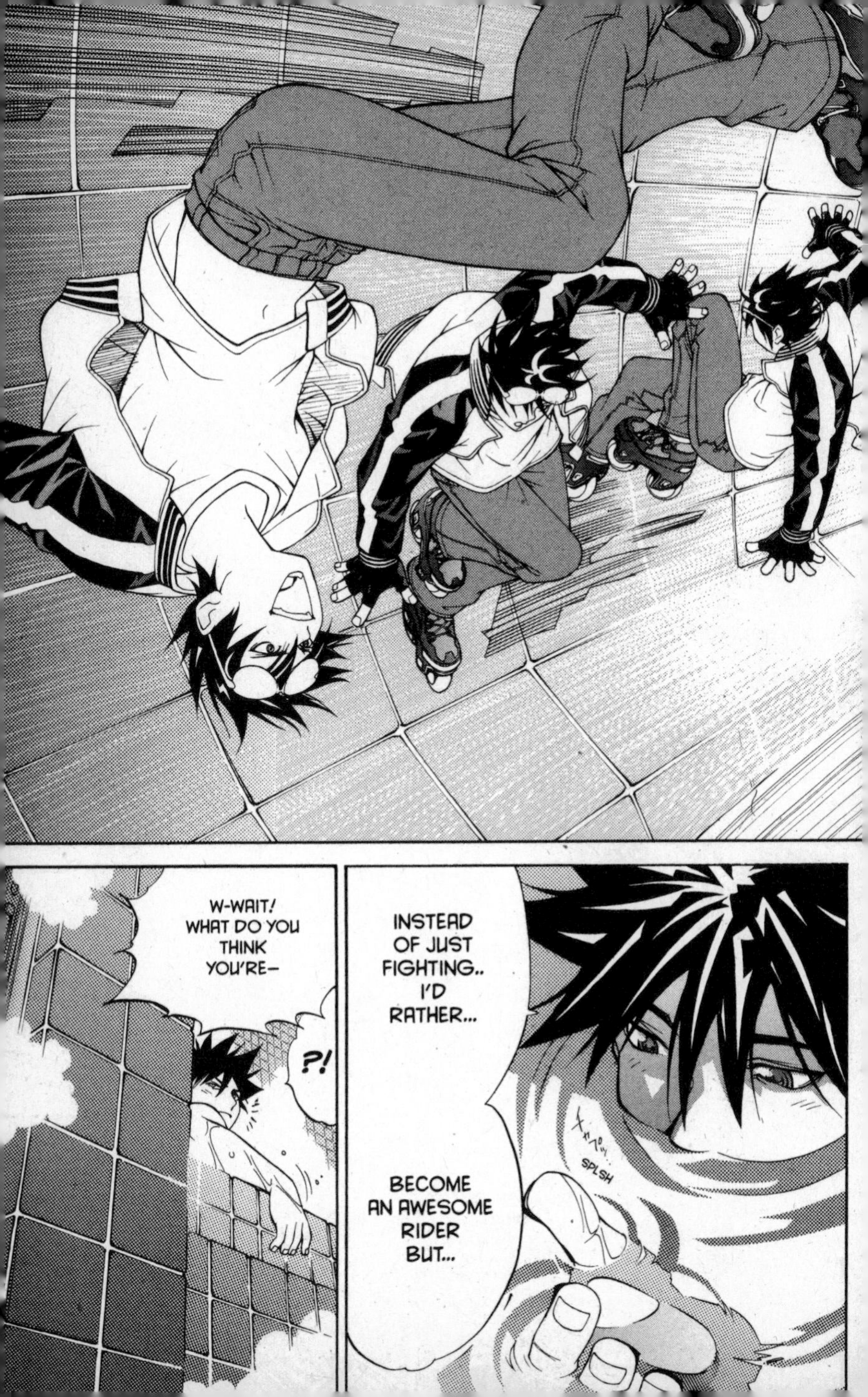
INSTEAD OF JUST FIGHTING.. I'D RATHER...
BECOME AN AWESOME RIDER BUT...
SPLSH
W-WAIT! WHAT DO YOU THINK YOU'RE–
?!

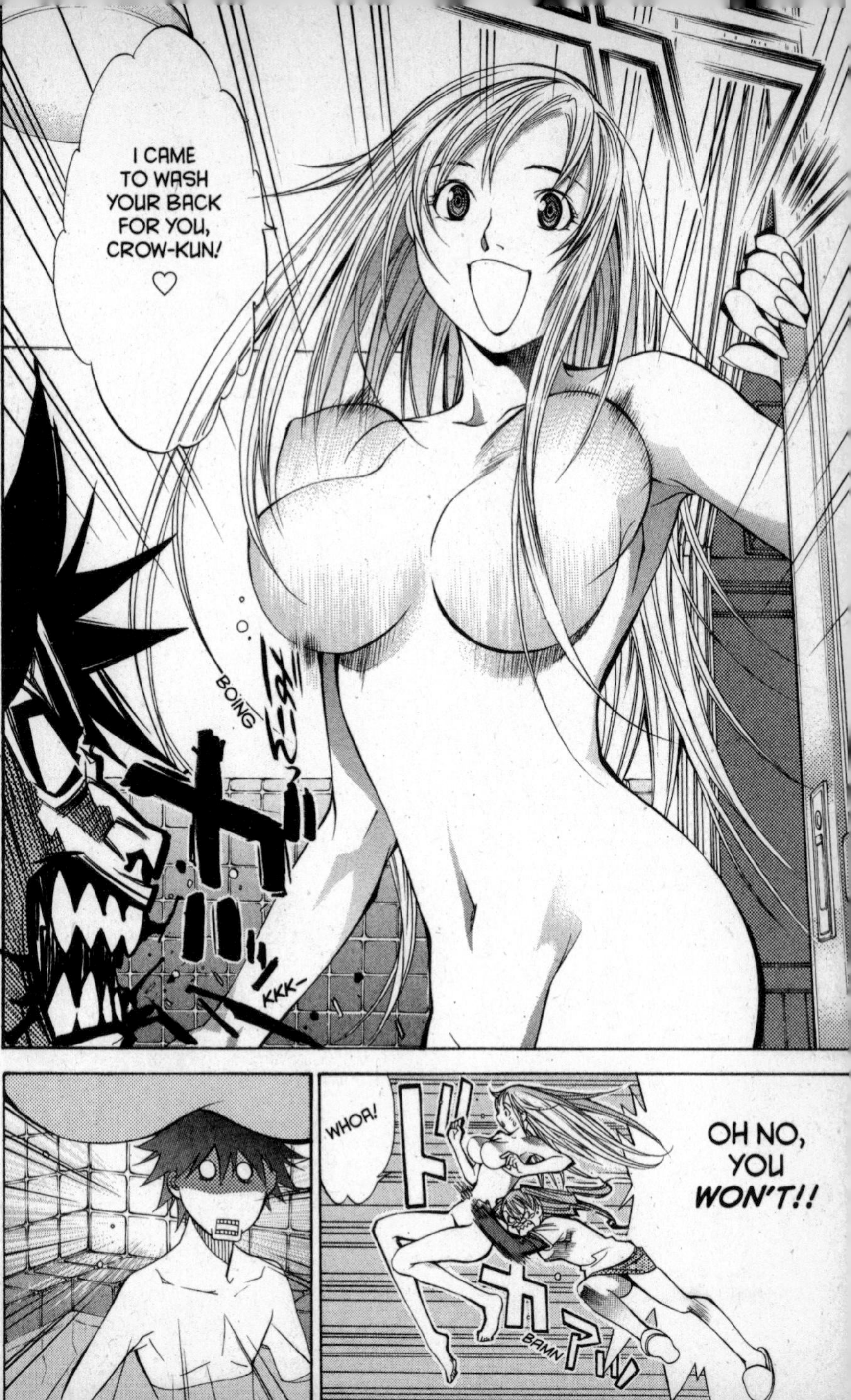
I CAME TO WASH YOUR BACK FOR YOU, CROW-KUN! ♡
BOING
KKK-
OH NO, YOU *WON'T!!*
WHOA!
BAMN

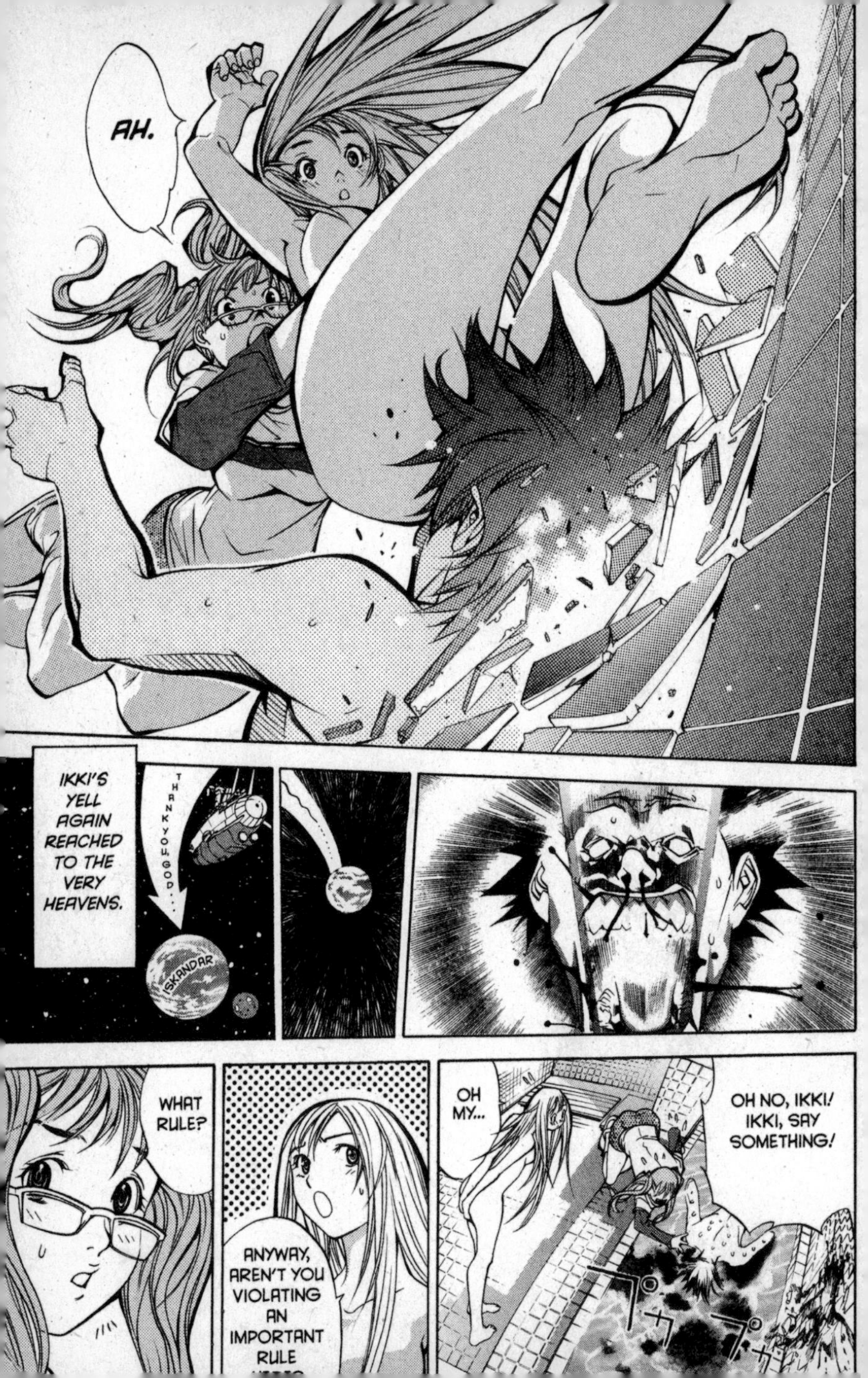
AH.
THANK YOU, GOD...
IKKI'S YELL AGAIN REACHED TO THE VERY HEAVENS.
ISKANDAR
OH NO, IKKI! IKKI, SAY SOMETHING!
OH MY...
ANYWAY, AREN'T YOU VIOLATING AN IMPORTANT RULE
WHAT RULE?

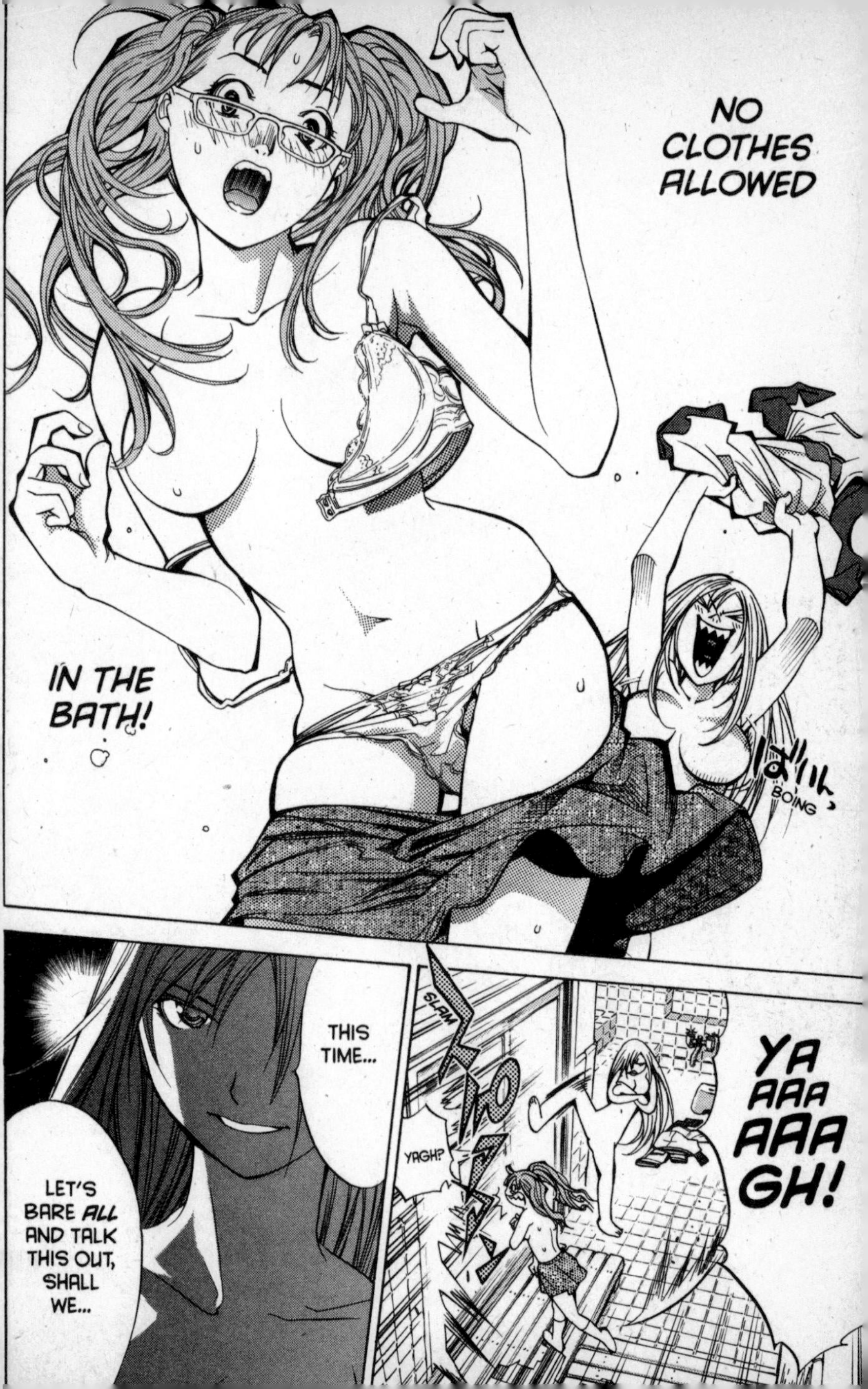
NO CLOTHES ALLOWED
IN THE BATH!
BOING
YAAAAAAAGH!
SLAM
YAGH?
THIS TIME...
LET'S BARE ALL AND TALK THIS OUT, SHALL WE...

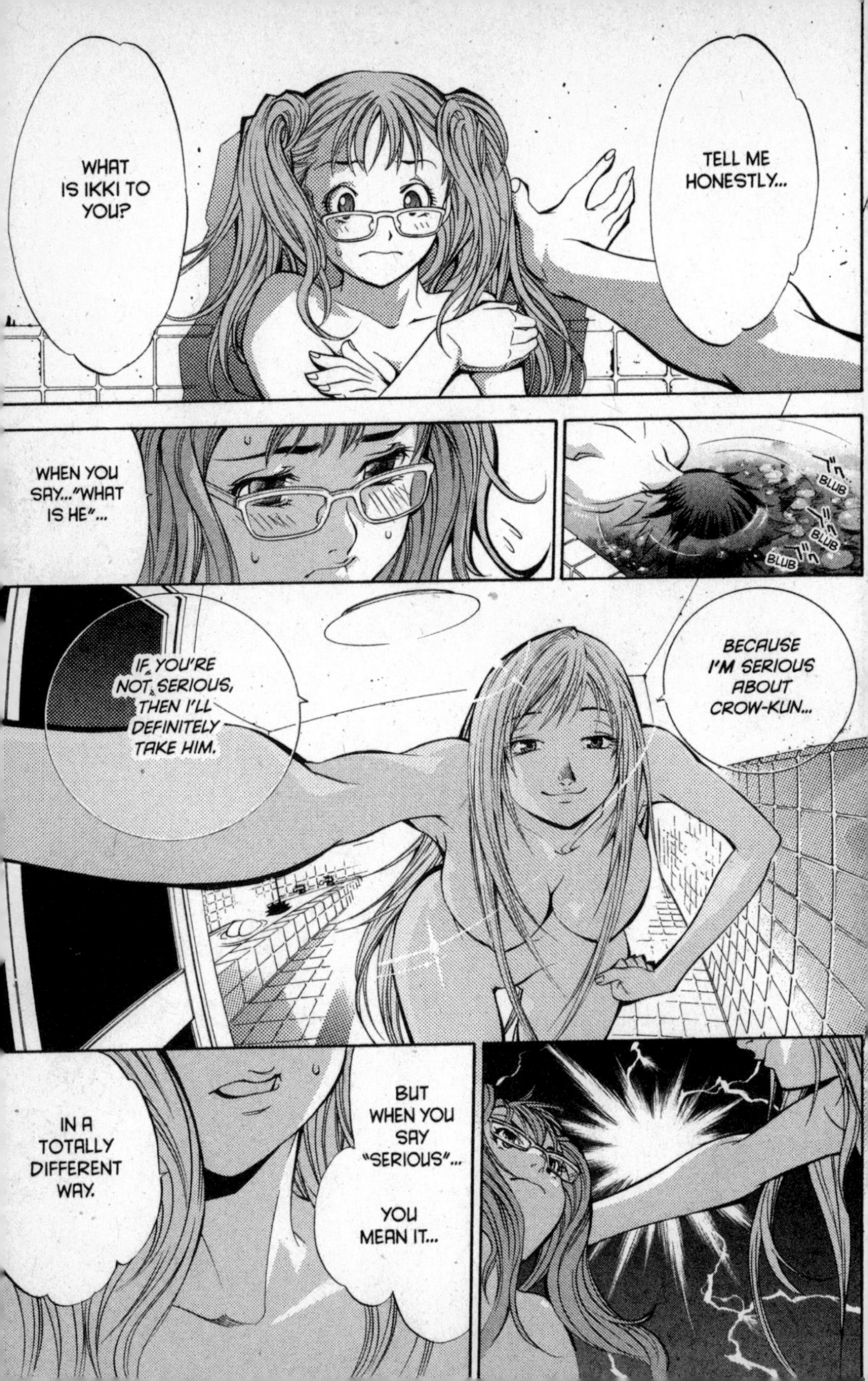
TELL ME HONESTLY...
WHAT IS IKKI TO YOU?
BLUB
BLUB
BLUB
WHEN YOU SAY..."WHAT IS HE"...
BECAUSE I'M SERIOUS ABOUT CROW-KUN...
IF YOU'RE NOT SERIOUS, THEN I'LL DEFINITELY TAKE HIM.
BUT WHEN YOU SAY "SERIOUS"...
YOU MEAN IT...
IN A TOTALLY DIFFERENT WAY.

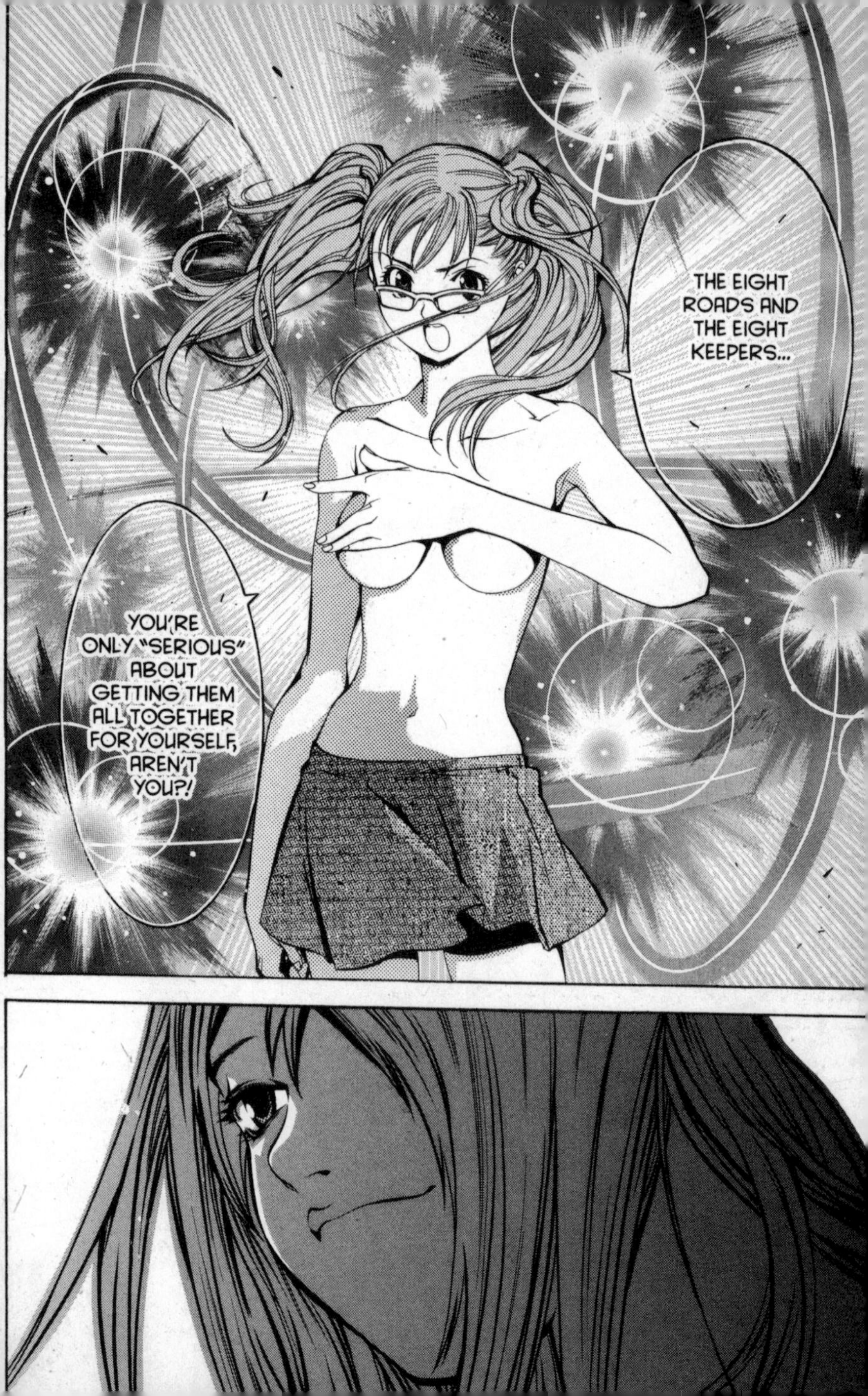
THE EIGHT ROADS AND THE EIGHT KEEPERS...
YOU'RE ONLY "SERIOUS" ABOUT GETTING THEM ALL TOGETHER FOR YOURSELF, AREN'T YOU?!

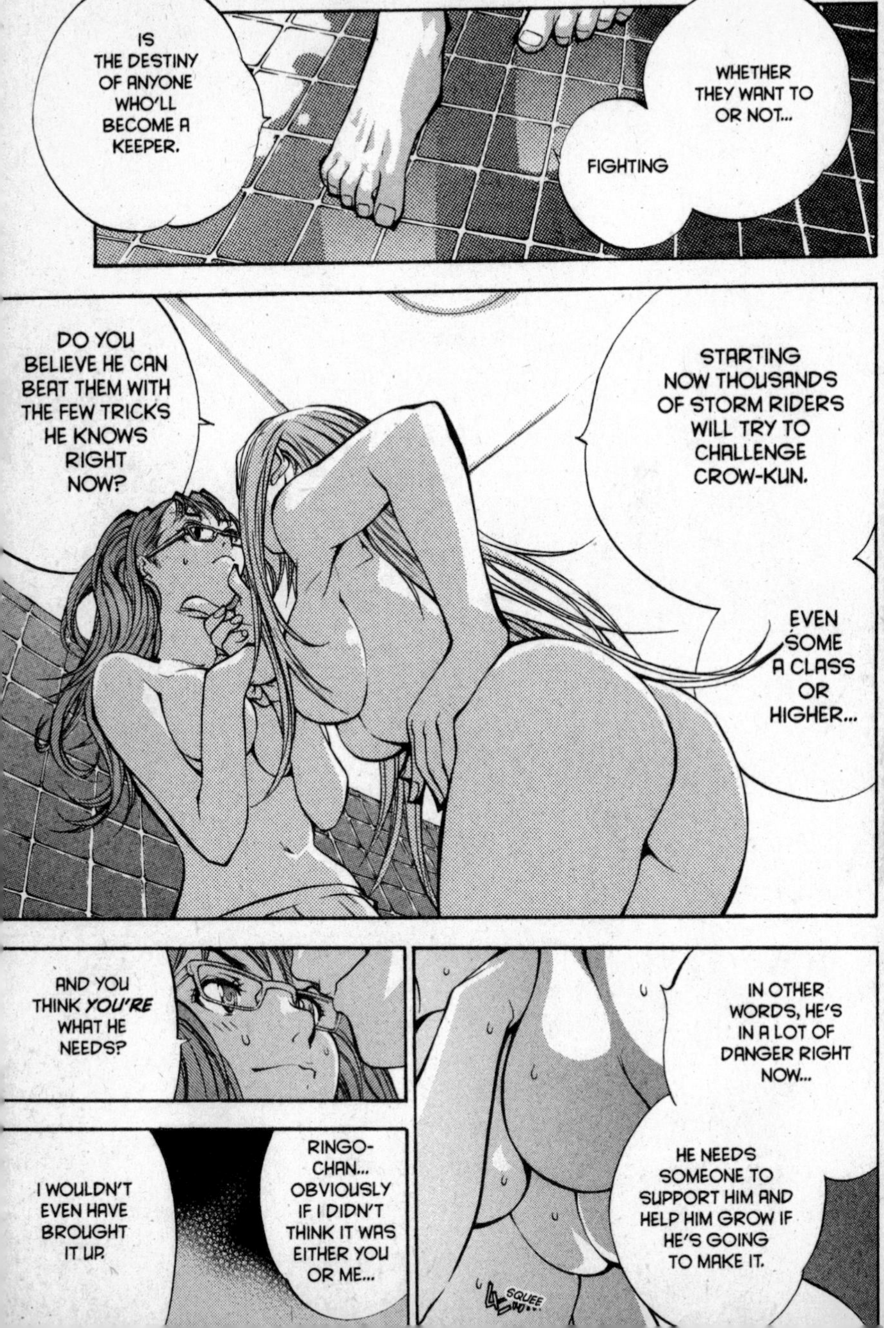
WHETHER THEY WANT TO OR NOT...
FIGHTING
IS THE DESTINY OF ANYONE WHO'LL BECOME A KEEPER.
STARTING NOW THOUSANDS OF STORM RIDERS WILL TRY TO CHALLENGE CROW-KUN.
EVEN SOME A CLASS OR HIGHER...
DO YOU BELIEVE HE CAN BEAT THEM WITH THE FEW TRICKS HE KNOWS RIGHT NOW?
IN OTHER WORDS, HE'S IN A LOT OF DANGER RIGHT NOW...
HE NEEDS SOMEONE TO SUPPORT HIM AND HELP HIM GROW IF HE'S GOING TO MAKE IT.
SQUEE
AND YOU THINK *YOU'RE* WHAT HE NEEDS?
RINGO-CHAN... OBVIOUSLY IF I DIDN'T THINK IT WAS EITHER YOU OR ME...
I WOULDN'T EVEN HAVE BROUGHT IT UP.

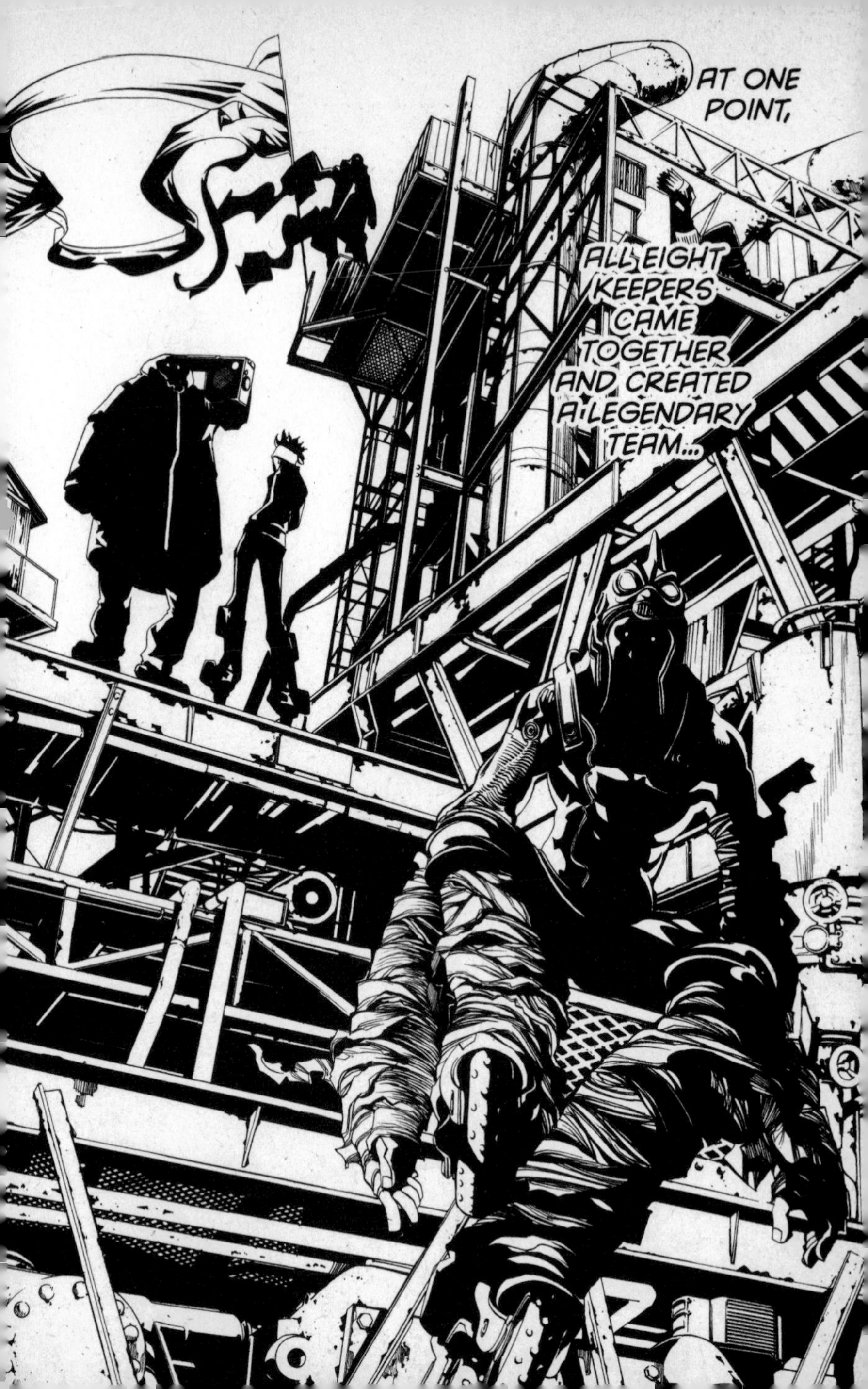
AT ONE POINT,
ALL EIGHT KEEPERS CAME TOGETHER AND CREATED A LEGENDARY TEAM...

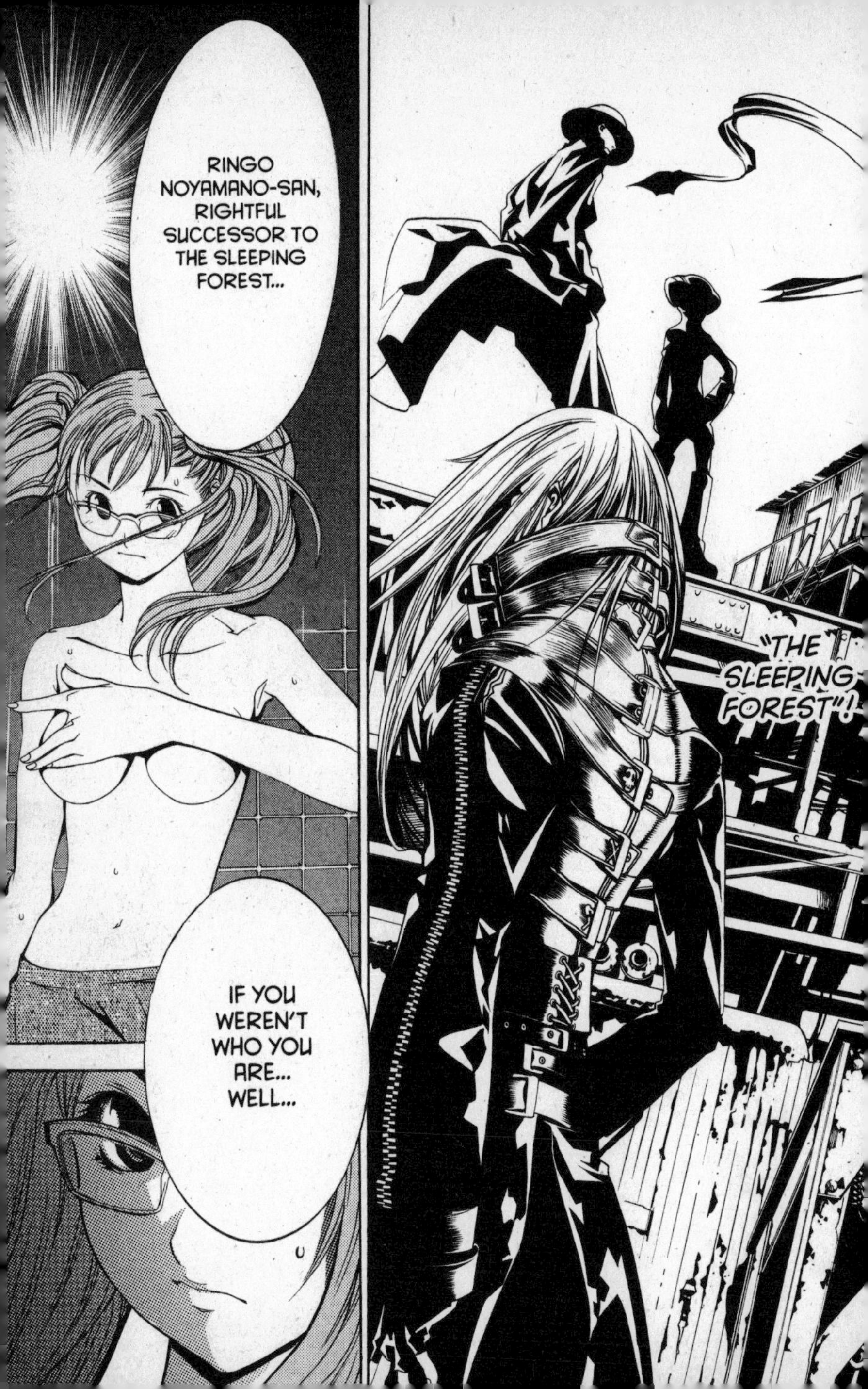
"THE SLEEPING FOREST"!
RINGO NOYAMANO-SAN, RIGHTFUL SUCCESSOR TO THE SLEEPING FOREST...
IF YOU WEREN'T WHO YOU ARE... WELL...

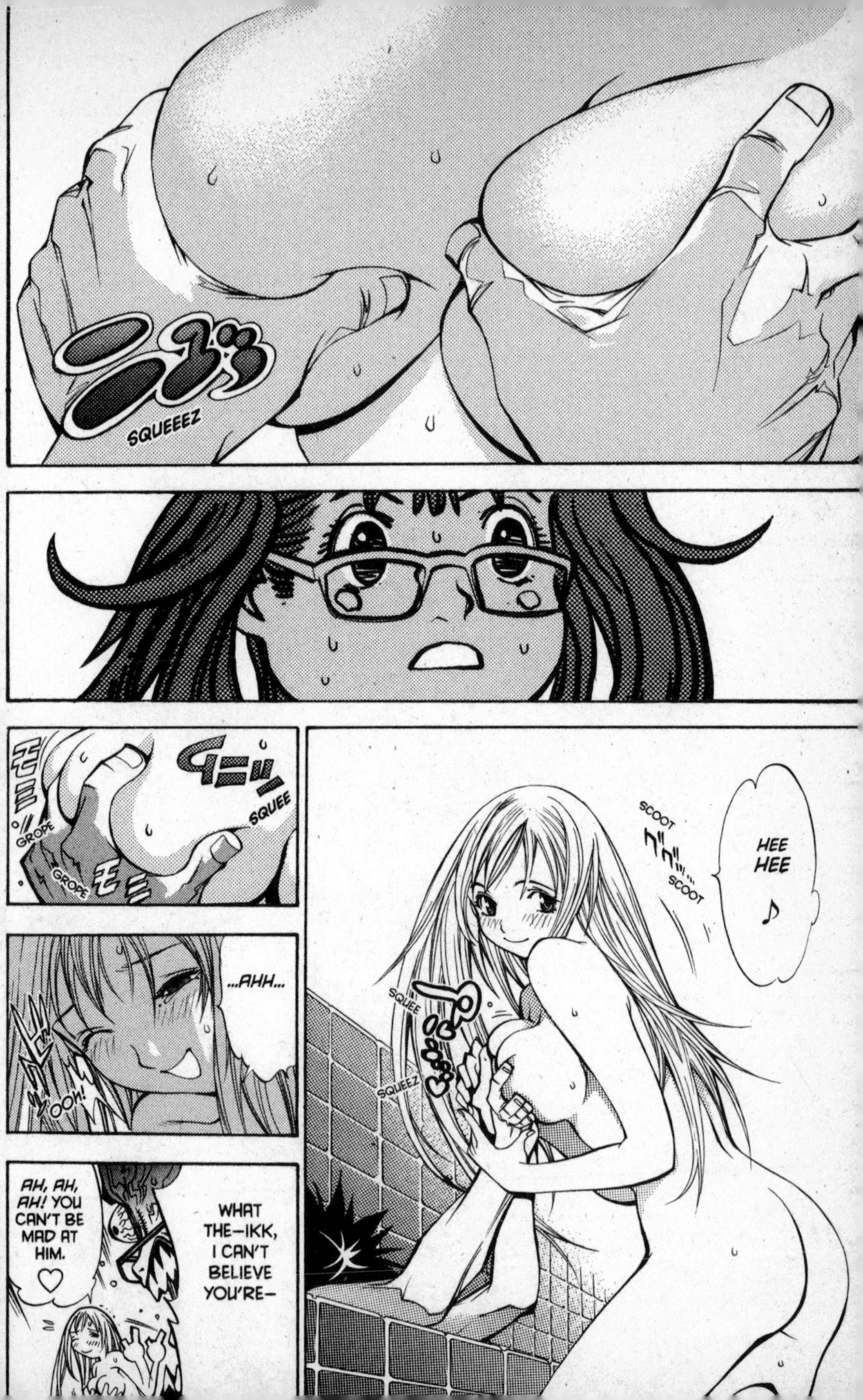
SQUEEEZ
HEE HEE ♪
SCOOT
SCOOT
SQUEE
SQUEEZ
SQUEE
GROPE
GROPE
...AHH...
OOH!
WHAT THE—IKK, I CAN'T BELIEVE YOU'RE—
AH, AH, AH! YOU CAN'T BE MAD AT HIM. ♡

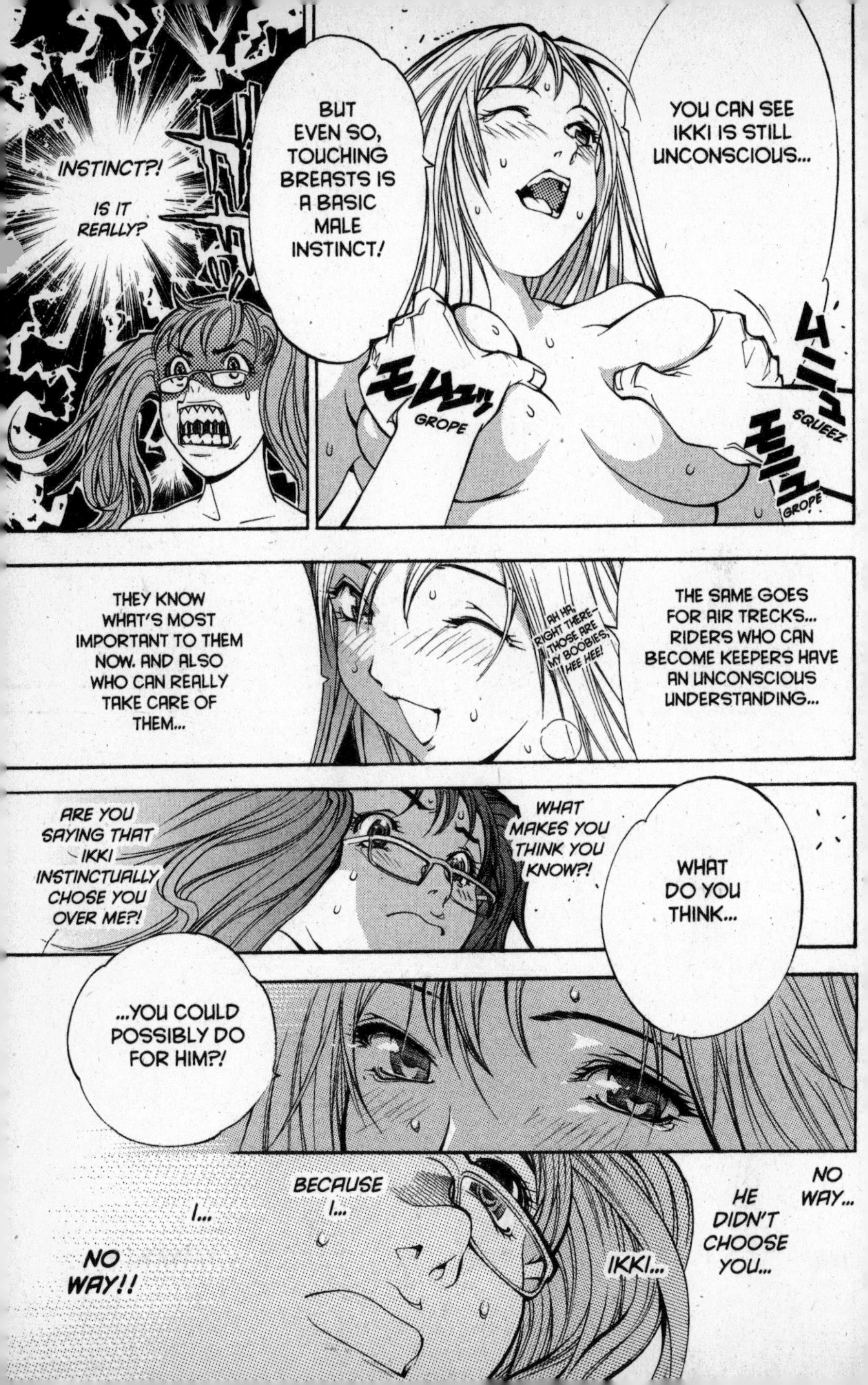

YOU CAN SEE IKKI IS STILL UNCONSCIOUS...
BUT EVEN SO, TOUCHING BREASTS IS A BASIC MALE INSTINCT!
SQUEEZ
GROPE
GROPE
INSTINCT?!
IS IT REALLY?
THE SAME GOES FOR AIR TRECKS... RIDERS WHO CAN BECOME KEEPERS HAVE AN UNCONSCIOUS UNDERSTANDING...
AH HA, RIGHT THERE— THOSE ARE MY BOOBIES, HEE HEE!
THEY KNOW WHAT'S MOST IMPORTANT TO THEM NOW. AND ALSO WHO CAN REALLY TAKE CARE OF THEM...
WHAT DO YOU THINK...
WHAT MAKES YOU THINK YOU KNOW?!
ARE YOU SAYING THAT IKKI INSTINCTUALLY CHOSE YOU OVER ME?!
...YOU COULD POSSIBLY DO FOR HIM?!
NO WAY...
HE DIDN'T CHOOSE YOU...
IKKI...
BECAUSE I...
I...
NO WAY!!

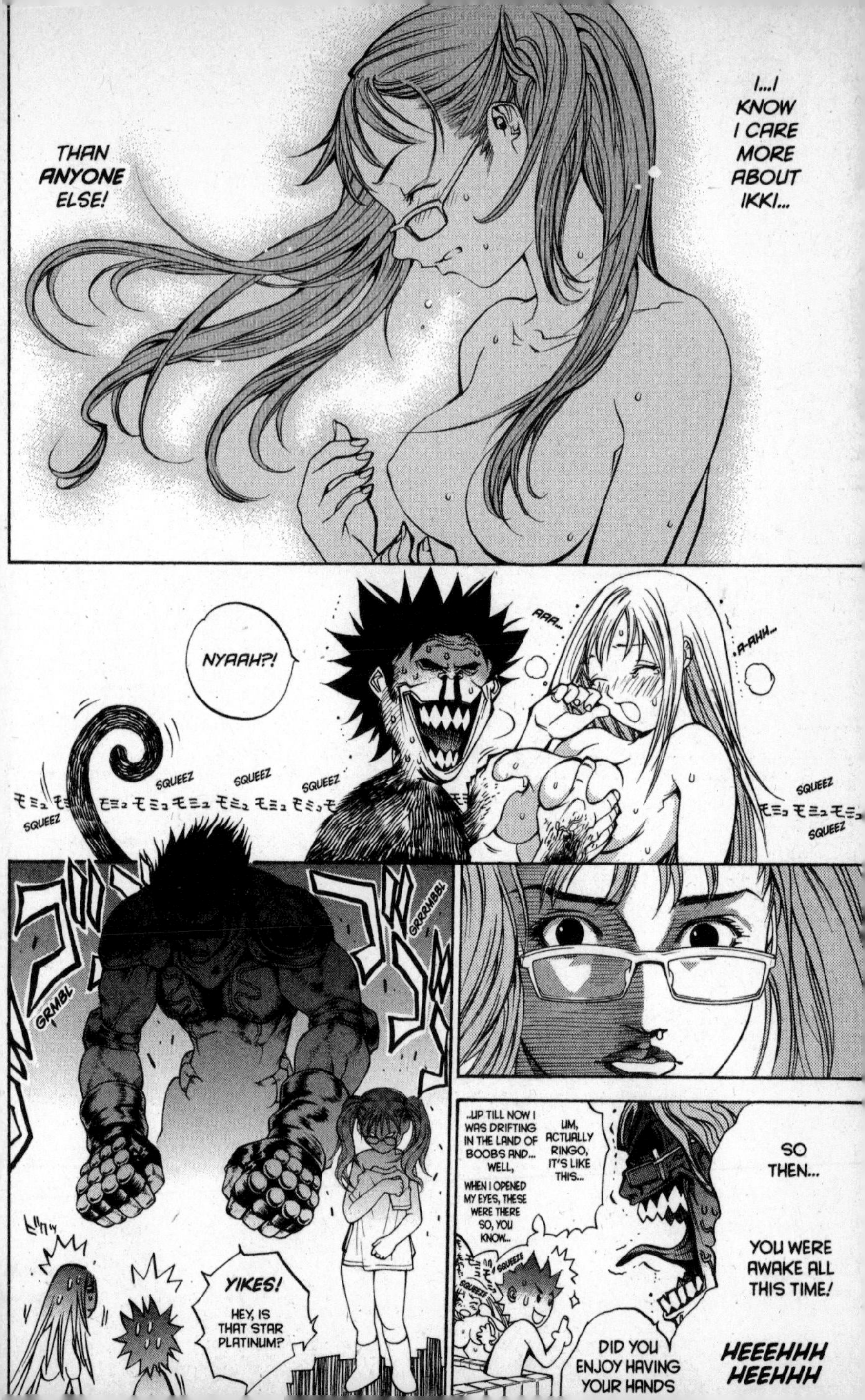
I...I KNOW I CARE MORE ABOUT IKKI...
THAN ANYONE ELSE!
A-AHH...
AAA...
NYAAH?!
SQUEEZ
SQUEEZ
SQUEEZ
SQUEEZ
SQUEEZ
SQUEEZ
SO THEN...
YOU WERE AWAKE ALL THIS TIME!
HEEEHHH HEEHHH
DID YOU ENJOY HAVING YOUR HANDS
UM, ACTUALLY RINGO, IT'S LIKE THIS...
...UP TILL NOW I WAS DRIFTING IN THE LAND OF BOOBS AND... WELL,
WHEN I OPENED MY EYES, THESE WERE THERE SO, YOU KNOW...
GRRRMBBL
GRMBL
YIKES!
HEY, IS THAT STAR PLATINUM?

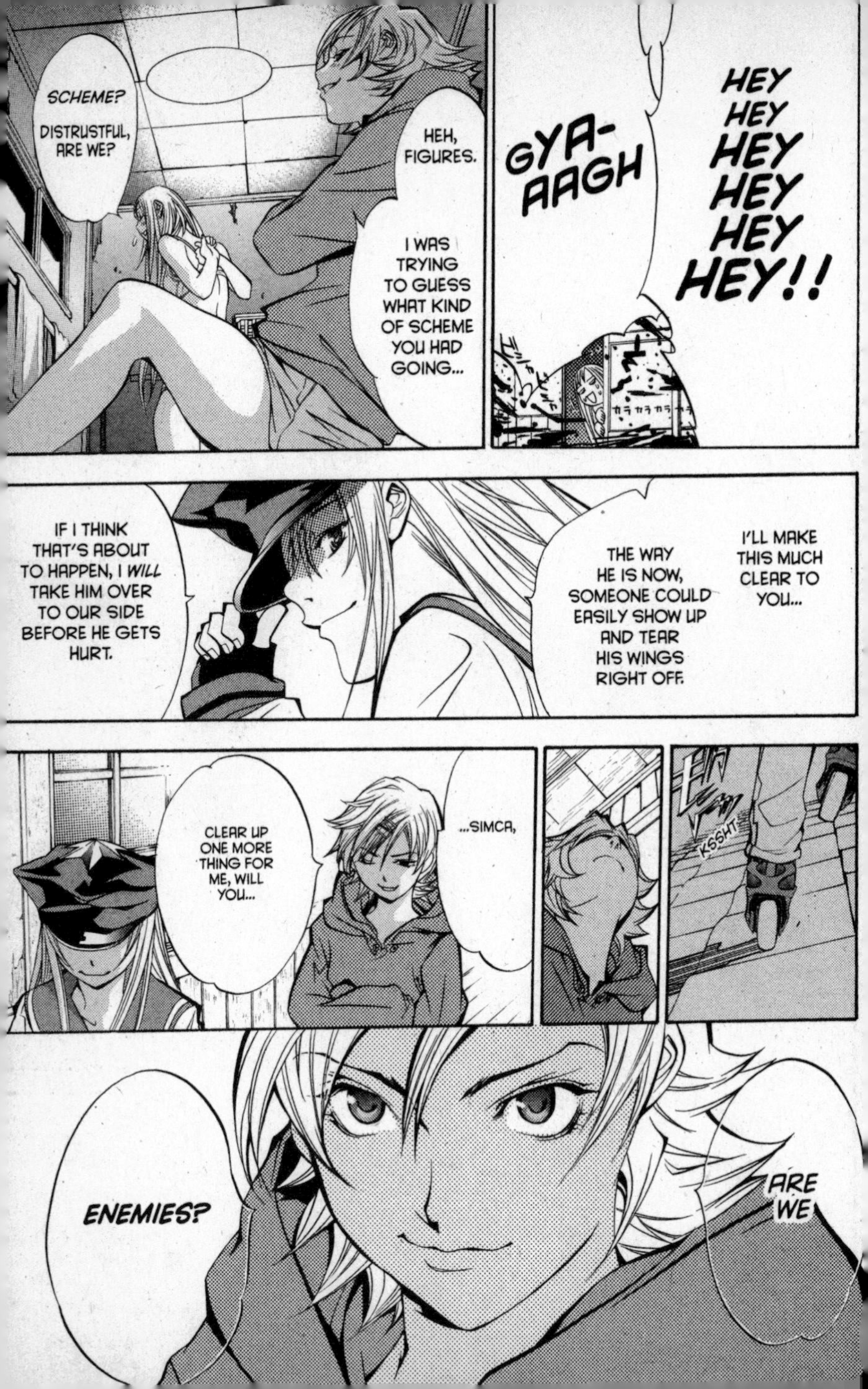
HEY HEY HEY HEY HEY HEY!!
GYA-AAGH
HEH, FIGURES.
I WAS TRYING TO GUESS WHAT KIND OF SCHEME YOU HAD GOING...
SCHEME?
DISTRUSTFUL, ARE WE?
I'LL MAKE THIS MUCH CLEAR TO YOU...
THE WAY HE IS NOW, SOMEONE COULD EASILY SHOW UP AND TEAR HIS WINGS RIGHT OFF.
IF I THINK THAT'S ABOUT TO HAPPEN, I *WILL* TAKE HIM OVER TO OUR SIDE BEFORE HE GETS HURT.
KSSHT
...SIMCA,
CLEAR UP ONE MORE THING FOR ME, WILL YOU...
ARE WE
ENEMIES?

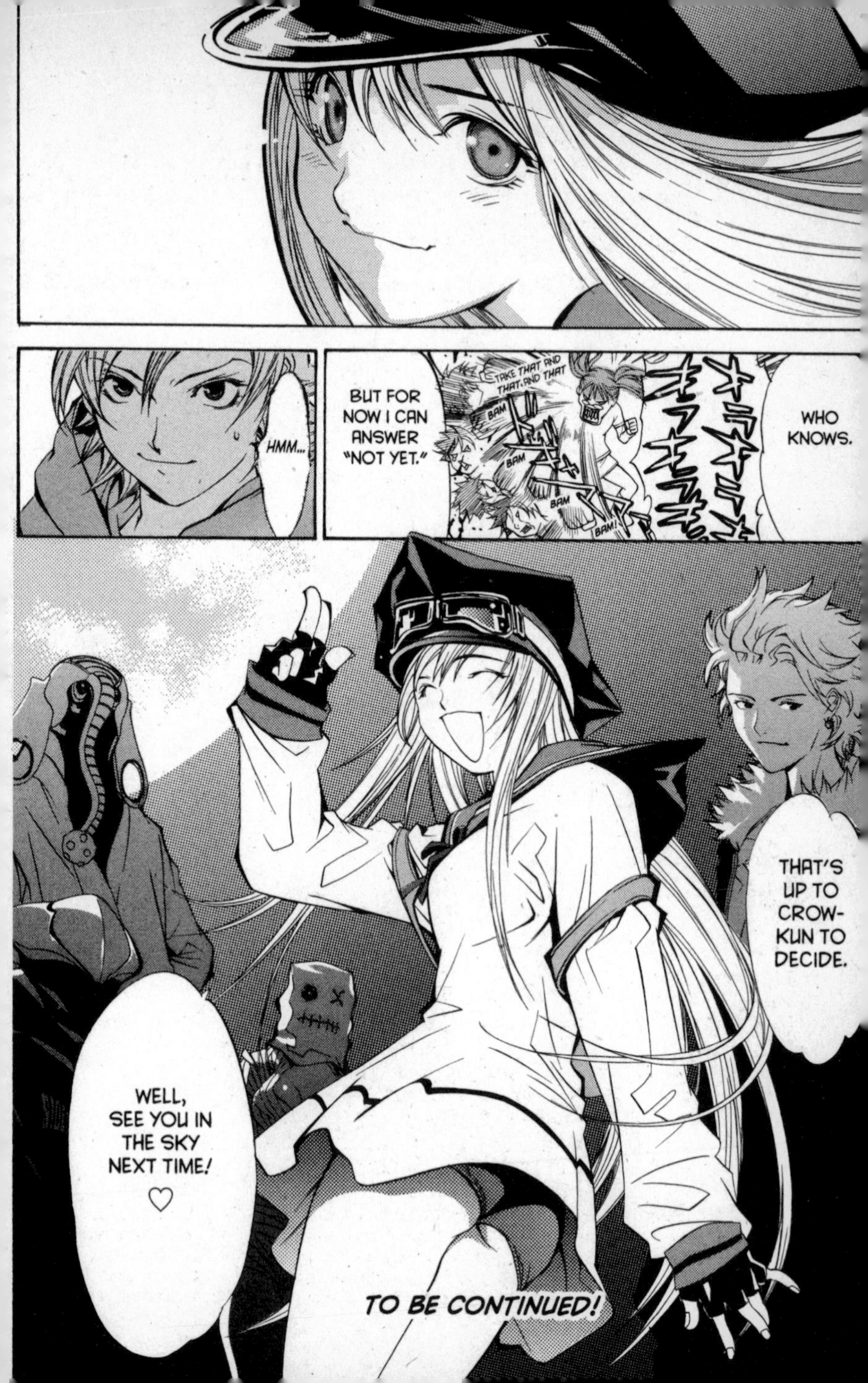
WHO KNOWS.
TAKE THAT AND THAT AND THAT
BAM
BAM
BAM
BAM!
BUT FOR NOW I CAN ANSWER "NOT YET."
HMM...
THAT'S UP TO CROW-KUN TO DECIDE.
WELL, SEE YOU IN THE SKY NEXT TIME! ♡
TO BE CONTINUED!

HYPER!EXTREME EXTRA!

AIR GEAR REFERENCE GUIDE

"HEY, HEY, WHAT'S A PARTS WAR?"
"WHAT'RE THEY DOING, HUH?"

GURE
SPECIAL INFO—
CHECK IT OUT!

WHAT IS PARTS WAR?

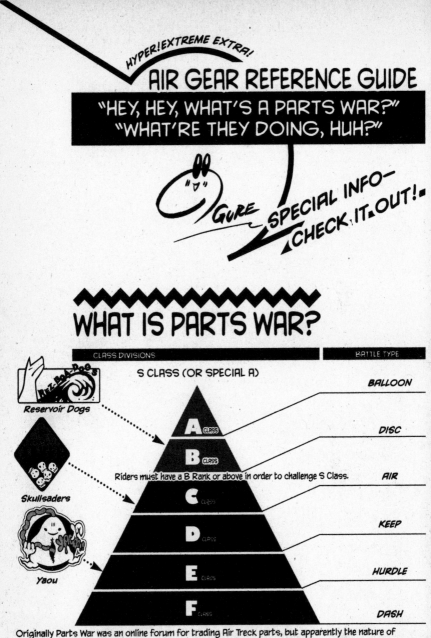

CLASS DIVISIONS
BATTLE TYPE
S CLASS (OR SPECIAL A)
Reservoir Dogs
Skullsaders
Yaou
A CLASS
B CLASS
Riders must have a B Rank or above in order to challenge S Class.
C CLASS
D CLASS
E CLASS
F CLASS
BALLOON
DISC
AIR
KEEP
HURDLE
DASH

Originally Parts War was an online forum for trading Air Treck parts, but apparently the nature of the board changed and it became a place to post parts and challenge others to get them.

A rider can bet just about anything, but the vast majority of Parts Wars are for spare or used Air Treck parts. Betting an emblem or your team's pride and existence on this kind of battle is acceptable but really unusual.

HERE'S HOW *YOU* CAN GET INTO PARTS WAR!!

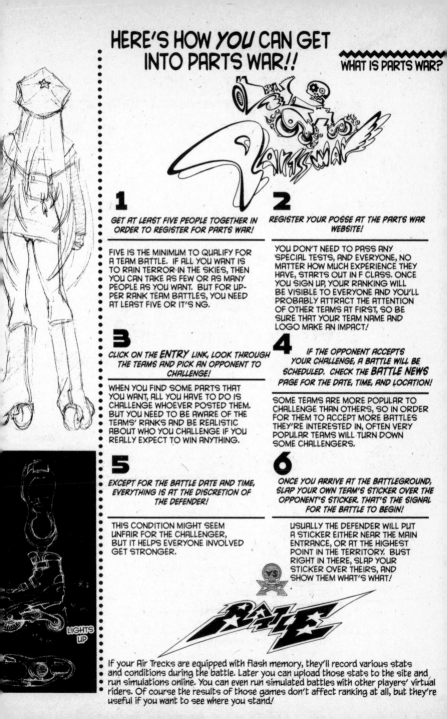

WHAT IS PARTS WAR?

1
GET AT LEAST FIVE PEOPLE TOGETHER IN ORDER TO REGISTER FOR PARTS WAR!

FIVE IS THE MINIMUM TO QUALIFY FOR A TEAM BATTLE. IF ALL YOU WANT IS TO RAIN TERROR IN THE SKIES, THEN YOU CAN TAKE AS FEW OR AS MANY PEOPLE AS YOU WANT. BUT FOR UP-PER RANK TEAM BATTLES, YOU NEED AT LEAST FIVE OR IT'S NG.

2
REGISTER YOUR POSSE AT THE PARTS WAR WEBSITE!

YOU DON'T NEED TO PASS ANY SPECIAL TESTS, AND EVERYONE, NO MATTER HOW MUCH EXPERIENCE THEY HAVE, STARTS OUT IN F CLASS. ONCE YOU SIGN UP, YOUR RANKING WILL BE VISIBLE TO EVERYONE AND YOU'LL PROBABLY ATTRACT THE ATTENTION OF OTHER TEAMS AT FIRST, SO BE SURE THAT YOUR TEAM NAME AND LOGO MAKE AN IMPACT!

3
CLICK ON THE ENTRY LINK, LOOK THROUGH THE TEAMS AND PICK AN OPPONENT TO CHALLENGE!

WHEN YOU FIND SOME PARTS THAT YOU WANT, ALL YOU HAVE TO DO IS CHALLENGE WHOEVER POSTED THEM. BUT YOU NEED TO BE AWARE OF THE TEAMS' RANKS AND BE REALISTIC ABOUT WHO YOU CHALLENGE IF YOU REALLY EXPECT TO WIN ANYTHING.

4
IF THE OPPONENT ACCEPTS YOUR CHALLENGE, A BATTLE WILL BE SCHEDULED. CHECK THE BATTLE NEWS PAGE FOR THE DATE, TIME, AND LOCATION!

SOME TEAMS ARE MORE POPULAR TO CHALLENGE THAN OTHERS, SO IN ORDER FOR THEM TO ACCEPT MORE BATTLES THEY'RE INTERESTED IN, OFTEN VERY POPULAR TEAMS WILL TURN DOWN SOME CHALLENGERS.

5
EXCEPT FOR THE BATTLE DATE AND TIME, EVERYTHING IS AT THE DISCRETION OF THE DEFENDER!

THIS CONDITION MIGHT SEEM UNFAIR FOR THE CHALLENGER, BUT IT HELPS EVERYONE INVOLVED GET STRONGER.

6
ONCE YOU ARRIVE AT THE BATTLEGROUND, SLAP YOUR OWN TEAM'S STICKER OVER THE OPPONENT'S STICKER. THAT'S THE SIGNAL FOR THE BATTLE TO BEGIN!

USUALLY THE DEFENDER WILL PUT A STICKER EITHER NEAR THE MAIN ENTRANCE, OR AT THE HIGHEST POINT IN THE TERRITORY. BUST RIGHT IN THERE, SLAP YOUR STICKER OVER THEIRS, AND SHOW THEM WHAT'S WHAT!

LIGHTS UP

If your Air Trecks are equipped with flash memory, they'll record various stats and conditions during the battle. Later you can upload those stats to the site and run simulations online. You can even run simulated battles with other players' virtual riders. Of course the results of those games don't affect ranking at all, but they're useful if you want to see where you stand!

WHEN SHE GETS REALLY UPSET HER EYES OPEN REALLY WIDE

- SIMCA: A mysterious girl with amazing breasts. She might be about 17 years old.

Height: 158 cm (5'3") Bust: 92 cm (36")
Waist: 59 cm (23") Hips: 88 cm (34")

It seems like she sees something special inside Ikki, and also like she might have her own agenda for it. On top of that, she's always showing off her naked body...?! Later in the story, Simca and her associates will definitely have a strong influence in some major events. At first glance, she seems like a selfish girl who uses men like toys and who makes every move with some secret goal in mind...that's the impression that I get.

SIMCA

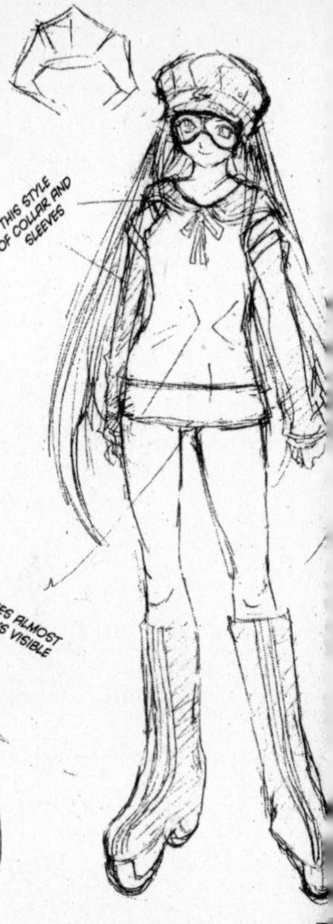

HAT CAN BE SHAPED LIKE THIS TOO?
THIS STYLE OF COLLAR AND SLEEVES

SNEAK PEEK!

SIMCA'S ORIGINAL DESIGN

MYSTERIOUS BEAUTY TSUBAME

Works at the shop where Itsuki goes for parts...
Whimsical, "my pace" kind of girl
Basically migrates just like birds
Built for speed

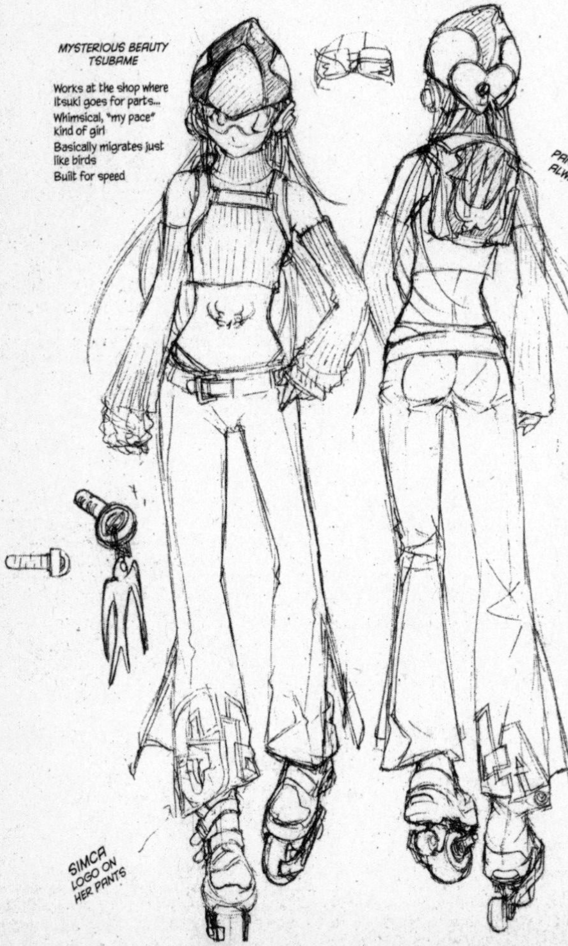

PANTIES ALMOST ALWAYS VISIBLE
SIMCA LOGO ON HER PANTS

Simca's Shoes

Simca wears Fashion Brand 109, part of the American Graffiti Series. Her skates are built for fashion, not for heavy use or special tricks. The standard issue specs of her Air Trecks are really low. If Ringo and Mikan wear skates like a McLaren F1, then Simca's skates are about like a Suzuki Alto, or [Scion XB]. Of course she's tuned them a bit, but given how well she skates with such weak equipment, other riders agree—if she equipped her Air Trecks to match her ability, she might be truly incredible.

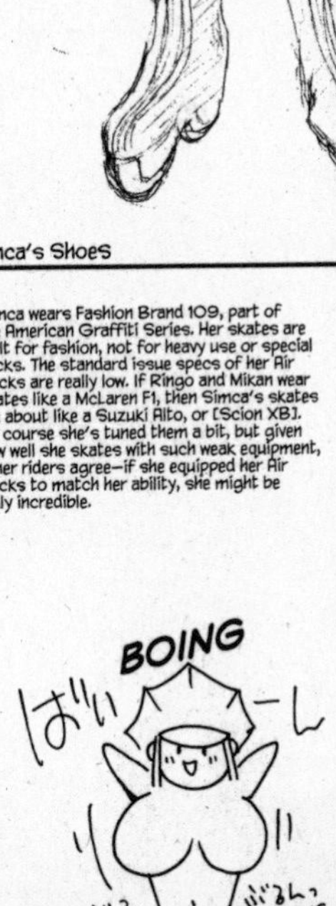

BOING
ばいーん
ぶるん
OIING
ぶるんっ
OI-OI-OING

● SPITFIRE: Keeper of the Flame Road. His Parts War rank is A, which makes him one of the best riders in town.

He'll have a strong effect on Ikki as time goes on. For now, all we know is that he seems to be planning something along with Simca and the other Keepers.

Spitfire's Shoe

The base for his skates are ETONES Sol23, brand created by the legendary champion, Paul Andre. But more important than the brand of his skates are those wheels! He leaves a trail of flames wherever he skates, and the motif on his wheels must have something to do with that. Those wheels will become a clue later on.

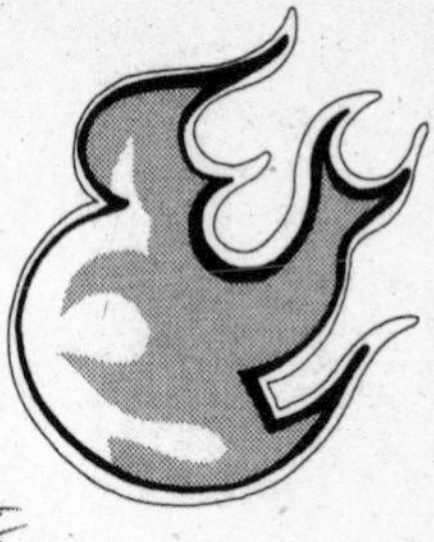

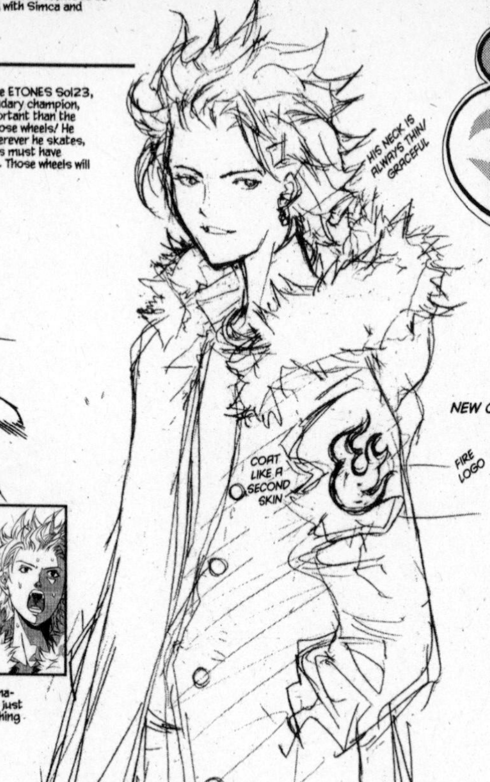
HIS NECK IS ALWAYS THIN/ GRACEFUL
NEW CHARACTER, UNNAMED
COAT LIKE A SECOND SKIN
FIRE LOGO
A FEW HIGHLIGHTS HERE TO INDICATE SHINE
THE REST, SOLID BLACK TONE
WHOLE BODY IS EXTRA SLIM
LIKE STICKS

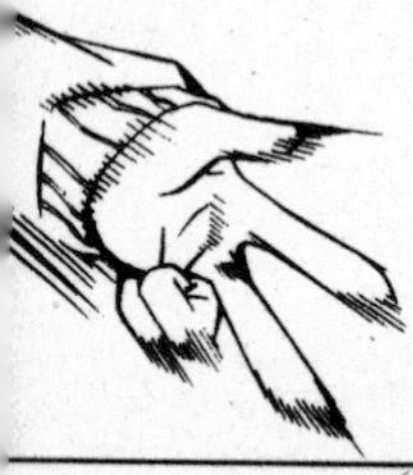

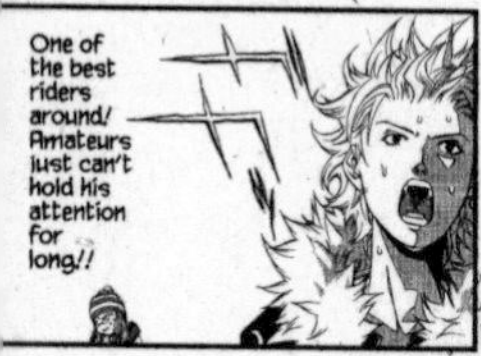
One of the best riders around! Amateurs just can't hold his attention for long!!

The messy kid "I-don't-wanna-brush-my-hair!" look?! It's just one of Spitfire's distinguishing traits.

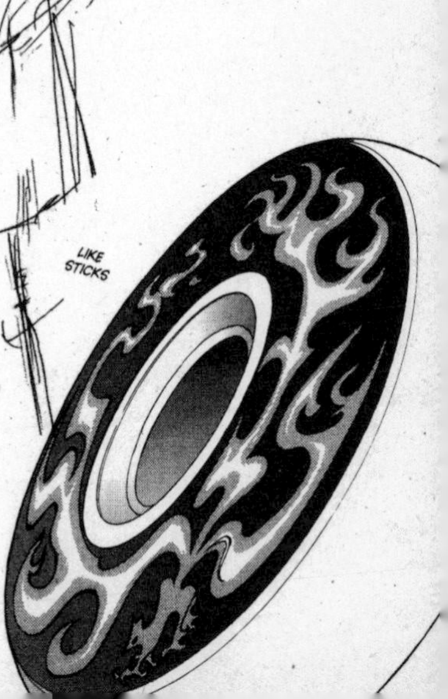

He was able to withstand Emily's Full Body Jump Kick to the head, barely even bending his neck! This is a testimony to the strength of his abs and back muscles!!

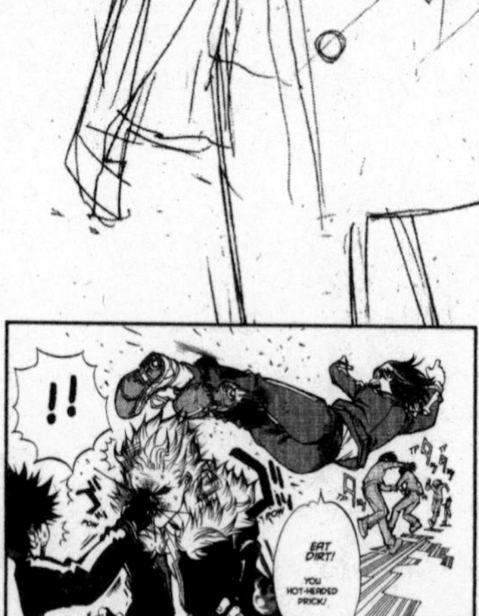
!!
EAT DIRT!
YOU HOT-HEADED PRICK!

TRACK TEAM DUO!

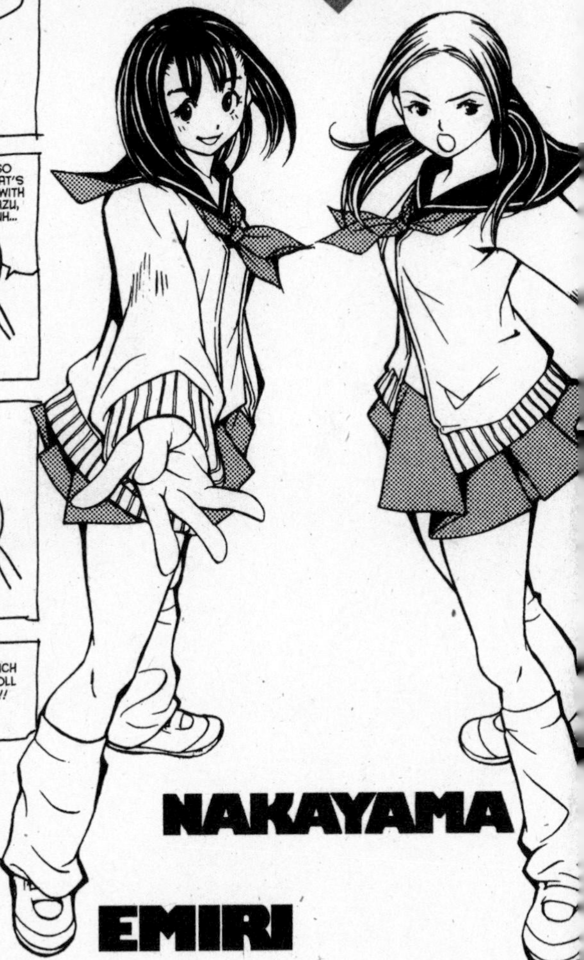
NAKAYAMA
EMIRI

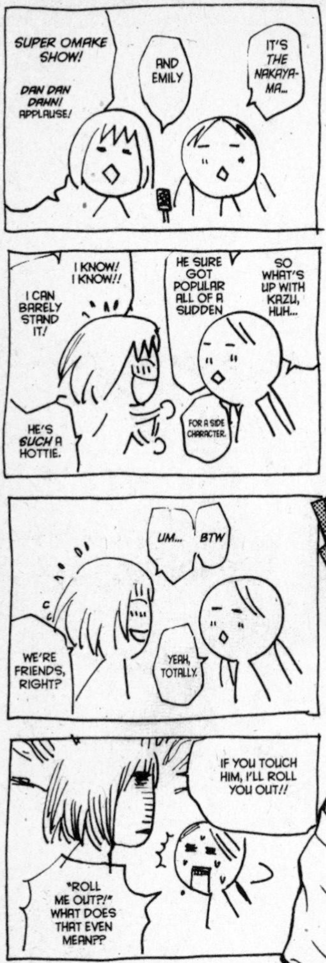
IT'S THE NAKAYAMA...
AND EMILY
SUPER OMAKE SHOW!
DAN DAN DAHN! APPLAUSE!
SO WHAT'S UP WITH KAZU, HUH...
HE SURE GOT POPULAR ALL OF A SUDDEN
FOR A SIDE CHARACTER.
I KNOW! I KNOW!!
I CAN BARELY STAND IT!
HE'S *SUCH* A HOTTIE.
BTW
UM...
YEAH, TOTALLY.
WE'RE FRIENDS, RIGHT?
IF YOU TOUCH HIM, I'LL ROLL YOU OUT!!
"ROLL ME OUT?!" WHAT DOES THAT EVEN MEAN??

• YAYOI NAKAYAMA: She's got some appeal...although "some" can still equal almost none. Still she's my favorite of the incidental characters.

Height: 157 cm (5' 1") Bust: 79 cm (31 in)
Waist: 55 cm (21 in) Hips: 77 cm (30 in)

She has a strong sense of morals and I guess if you compare her to the rest of the characters, she's probably the most honest and good. But that's just because the rest of the characters have issues.

• EMILY ADACHI: She's a cute girl with a nice figure, and yet not much appeal. Appeal = O, in fact. Must be because she has a bad personality.

Height: 152 cm (4' 11") Bust: 89 cm (35 in)
Waist: 63 cm (24 in) Hips: 83 cm (33 in)

A big fan of Kazu-sama. Although Onigiri fought just as much as Kazu, Emily didn't remember him. Or even care that she didn't remember. That's the kid of person she is.

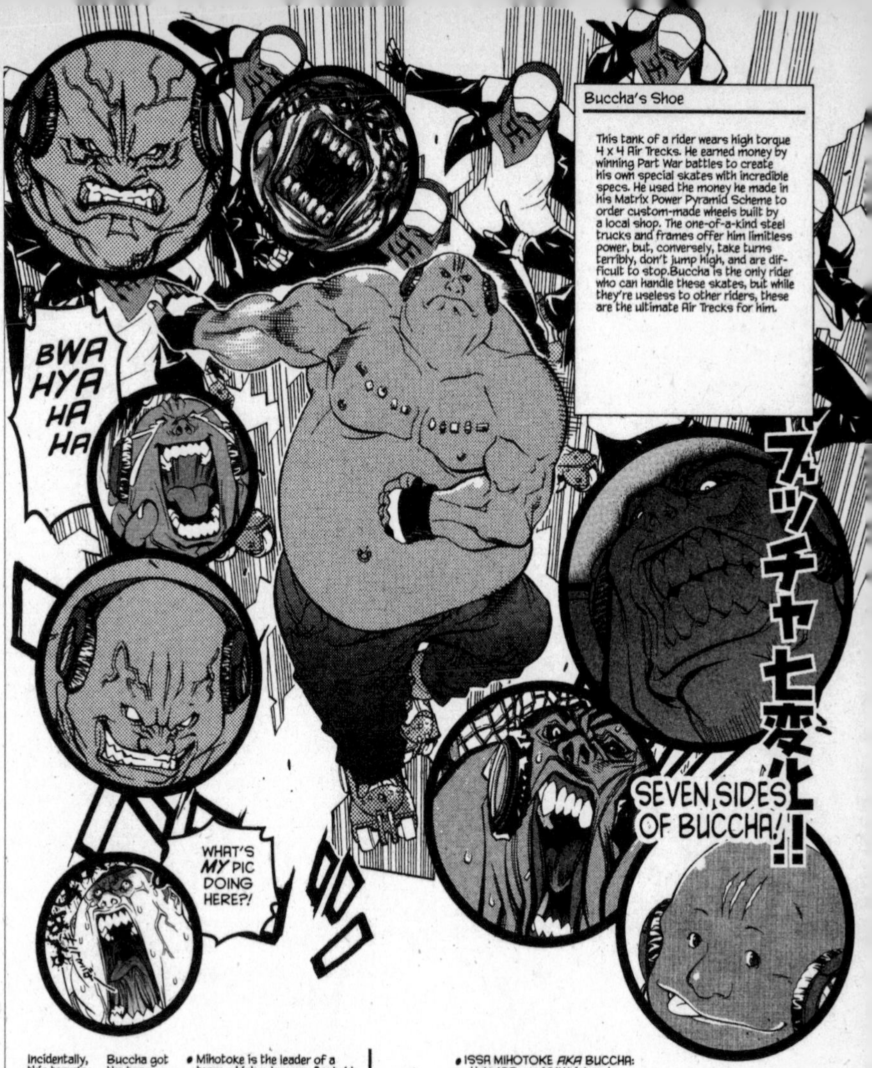
Buccha's Shoe
This tank of a rider wears high torque 4 x 4 Air Trecks. He earned money by winning Part War battles to create his own special skates with incredible specs. He used the money he made in his Matrix Power Pyramid Scheme to order custom-made wheels built by a local shop. The one-of-a-kind steel trucks and frames offer him limitless power, but, conversely, take turns terribly, don't jump high, and are difficult to stop. Buccha is the only rider who can handle these skates, but while they're useless to other riders, these are the ultimate Air Trecks for him.
ブッチャ七変化!!
SEVEN SIDES OF BUCCHA!
BWA HYA HA HA
WHAT'S MY PIC DOING HERE?!

Incidentally, this team's sticker is one of my favorites! It's too bad that now they've been defeated... I won't have an excuse to use it anymore.

Buccha got the team together with bigs plans to advance, but since everyone he recruited was F Class, he was never able to get higher than E. He probably figured that a one-man powerhouse was enough to offset the rest of his weak team.

- Mihotoke is the leader of a team, which rules over Eastside JHS at night, earning him the name "Eastside's Greatest Heel." The team is made up of twenty-two students, including Buccha's right hand man called "Yanz," but in effect none of the other team members are really that strong. No one else at the school knows who is a member of Team Yaou, so everyone stays quiet. Since the team was first started two years ago, Buccha has used that to his advantage, as he rules from the shadows—no one knowing who is on his side.

TEAM YAOU:

- ISSA MIHOTOKE *AKA* BUCCHA: He's 192 cm (6'4" in) and weighs about 907 kg (448 lbs). But his body fat percentage is only about 10%. He was born the son of a Buddist priest, and his family was pretty wealthy. He puts mayonnaise on absolutely everything he eats. His favorite food is mayo rice. Incidentally, people who put, not mayo, but SAUCE on everything are the pinnacle of macho! (I know I've checked for myself!)

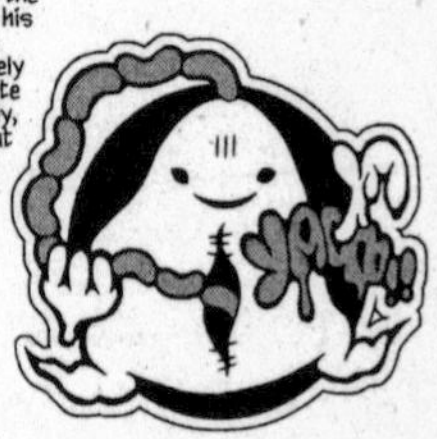

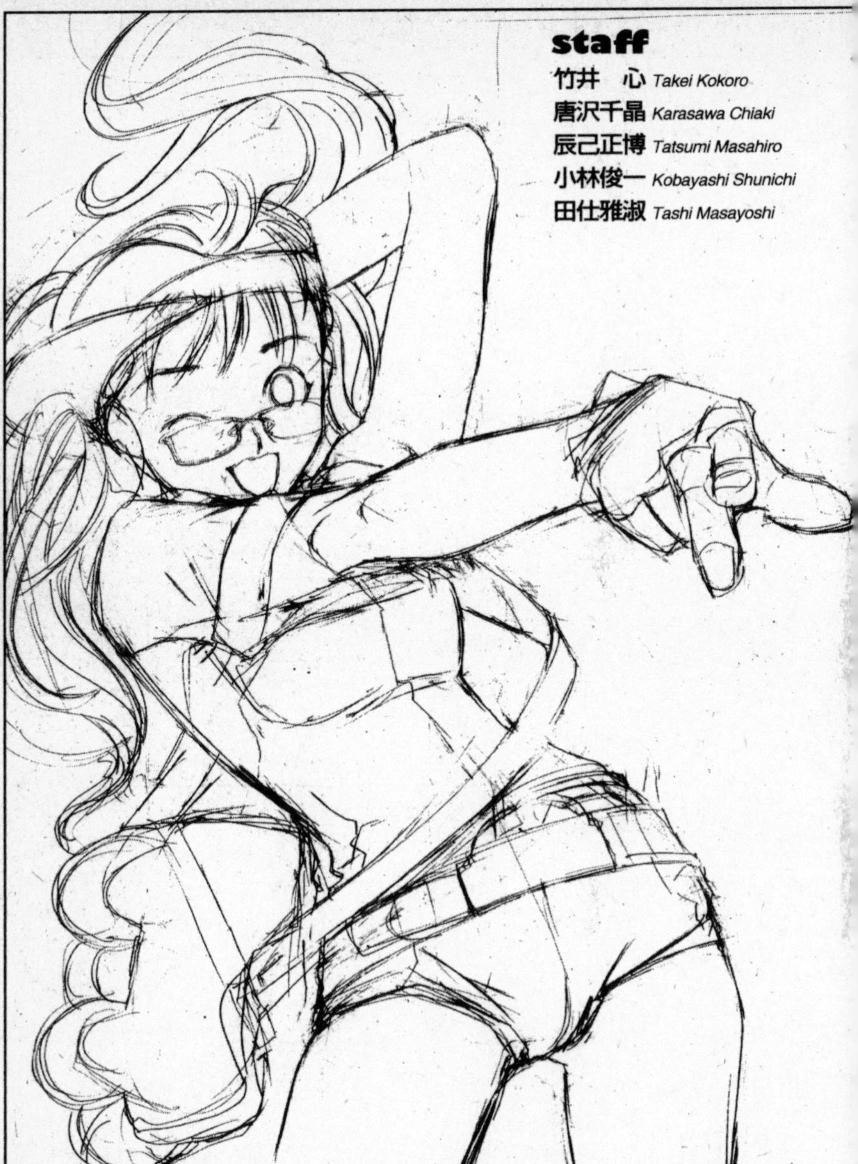

staff

竹井　心 *Takei Kokoro*
唐沢千晶 *Karasawa Chiaki*
辰己正博 *Tatsumi Masahiro*
小林俊一 *Kobayashi Shunichi*
田仕雅淑 *Tashi Masayoshi*

special thanks

石神由紀子 *Ishigami Yukiko*
pacific
屋代川隆史 *Yashirogawa Takashi*
青木　優 *Aoki Yu*

Translation Notes

Japanese is a tricky language for most Westerners, and translation is often more art than science. For your edification and reading pleasure, here are notes on some of the places where we could have gone in a different direction in our translation of the work, or where a Japanese cultural reference is used.

Nova Usagi-chan, page 26

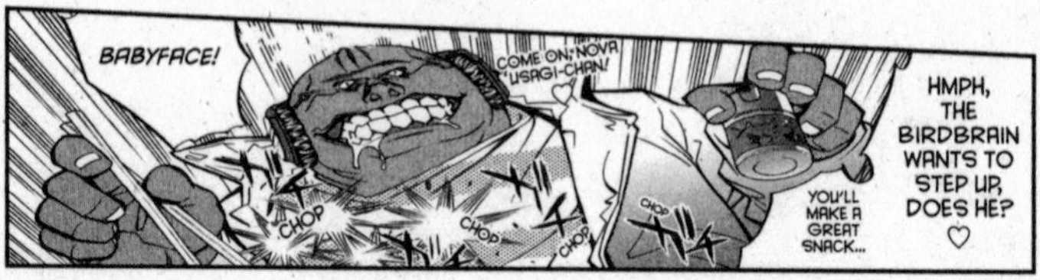

HMPH, THE BIRDBRAIN WANTS TO STEP UP, DOES HE? ♡
YOU'LL MAKE A GREAT SNACK...
CHOP
COME ON, NOVA USAGI-CHAN! ♡
BABYFACE!
CHOP
CHOP
CHOP

During Emily's recollection of the fight, she quotes Mihotoke saying "Come on, Nova Usagi-chan!"...The Nova Usagi-chan is a mascot for a very large chain of English Conversation schools in Japan and their commercials feature the bunny reciting grammatically perfect, but nevertheless random English sentences, such as "Headphones go on your ears." Non-English speakers sometimes quote the Nova Usagi-chan to sound exotic. And everyone knows English is the language of Hollywood-style brawling.

Megumi-class, page 30

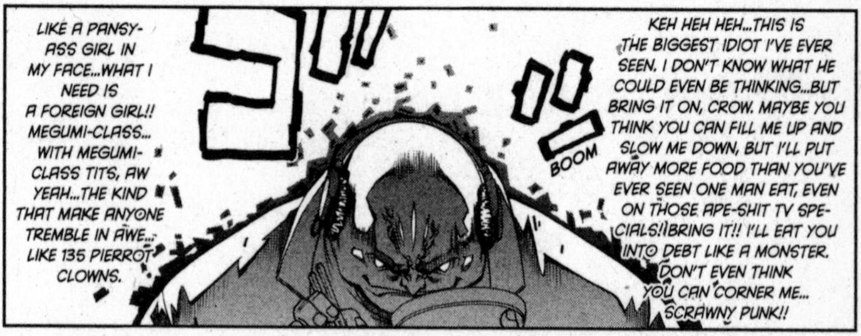

KEH HEH HEH...THIS IS THE BIGGEST IDIOT I'VE EVER SEEN. I DON'T KNOW WHAT HE COULD EVEN BE THINKING...BUT BRING IT ON, CROW. MAYBE YOU THINK YOU CAN FILL ME UP AND SLOW ME DOWN, BUT I'LL PUT AWAY MORE FOOD THAN YOU'VE EVER SEEN ONE MAN EAT, EVEN ON THOSE APE-SHIT TV SPE-CIALS!!BRING IT!! I'LL EAT YOU INTO DEBT LIKE A MONSTER. DON'T EVEN THINK YOU CAN CORNER ME... SCRAWNY PUNK!!
BOOM
LIKE A PANSY-ASS GIRL IN MY FACE...WHAT I NEED IS A FOREIGN GIRL!! MEGUMI-CLASS... WITH MEGUMI-CLASS TITS, AW YEAH...THE KIND THAT MAKE ANYONE TREMBLE IN AWE... LIKE 135 PIERROT CLOWNS.

In this panel, we get to overhear Mihotoke's thoughts in a long, stream-of-consciousness ramble...but one thing that might be unclear if you aren't into Japanese supermodels is the term "Megumi-Class." Megumi is a Japanese model and pop idol who's famous for having large, attractive breasts and guys like Mihotoke believe that *all* Western women are built the same way. What he means by "135 pierrots," and how it's connected with nice breasts, is up to your imagination.

Road to Tropaeum, page 58

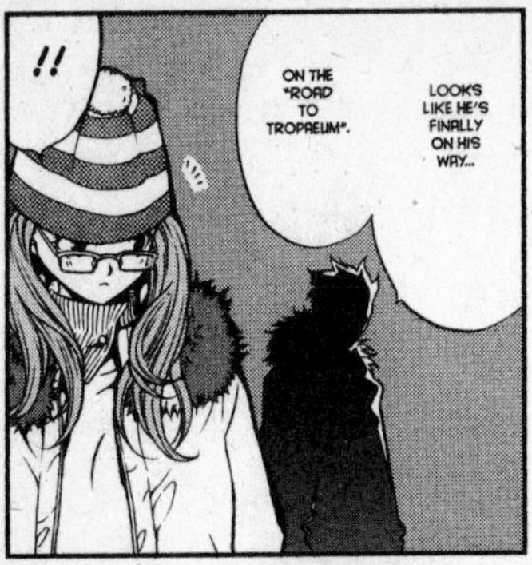

!!
LOOKS LIKE HE'S FINALLY ON HIS WAY...
ON THE "ROAD TO TROPAEUM".

Spitfire's reference to the "Road to Tropaeum" is an allusion to Ikki's new destination. A *tropaeum* is an ancient Greek or Roman monument commemorating a military victory. Details about what kind of *tropaeum* that Itsuki might eventually find remain to be seen.

Garandoo, page 97

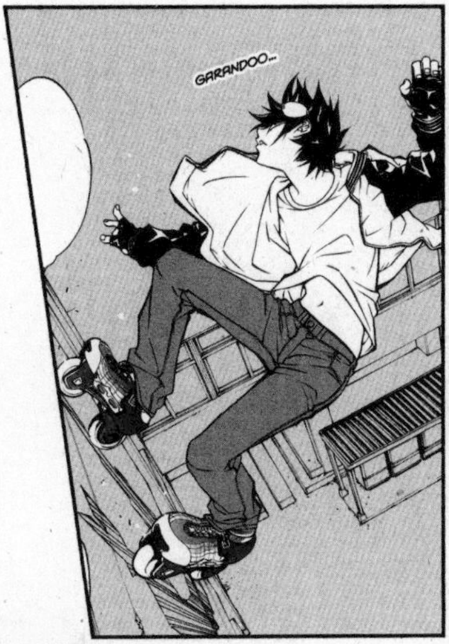

GARANDOO...

Oh!great has written above the falling Itsuki "Garandoo." That's the title of a song made famous by Saijou Hideki and though the word had no meaning in Japanese before that, it's since been adopted for common use. Since Saijou's wardrobe decisions allowed viewers to see his midriff easily, the term "Garandoo" is used to describe the same area of hair that some Westerners might call the "Happy Trail." Itsuki doesn't even have any hair there (yet? Do manga characters ever?) but the joke is that you can see where it *would* be.

"You feeling good tonight?!" page 142

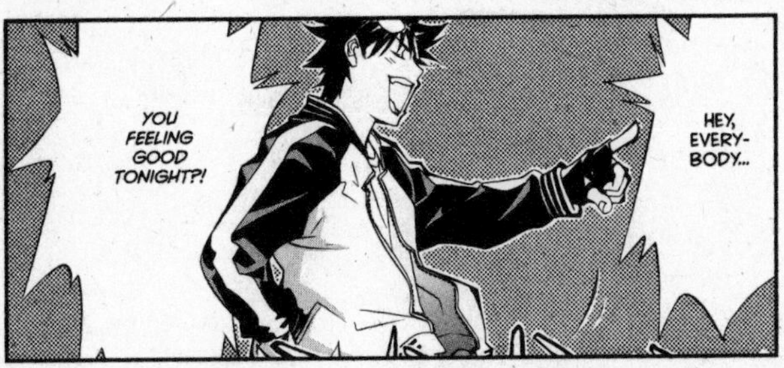

HEY, EVERY-BODY...
YOU FEELING GOOD TONIGHT?!

Itsuki shouts to his classmates "You feeling good tonight?!" with the same feeling as a rockstar at a concert or a DJ at a club. In the original Japanese, he says "Genki desuka–!!," which is meant to recall the great Japanese pro wrestler Antonio Inoki's famous catchphrase. (Later, when he finishes his speech on page 143, Itsuki's face even changes shape to match Inoki's—you can tell by the terrifyingly large chin!)

Salamander, page 162

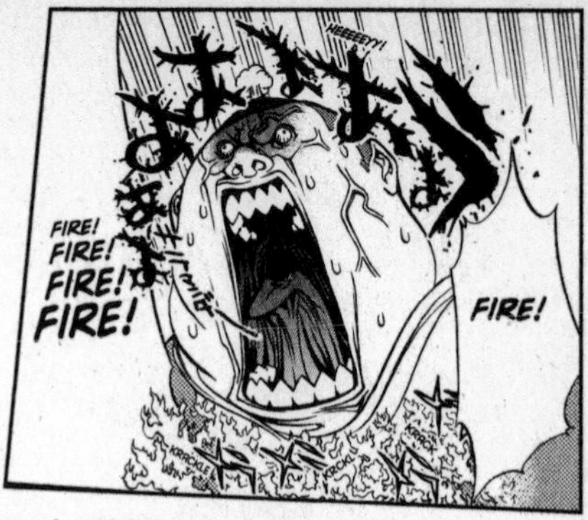
HEEEEEYY!
FIRE!
FIRE! FIRE! FIRE! FIRE!

Onigiri yells for "Salamander" when the trails of flames start to catch the school shrubbery. "Salamander" is the name of an Eastern Fire Spirit. It's unclear whether Onigiri is pleading with, or cursing at, the Salamander spirit.

Dera Beppin and Shining Wizard Attack, page 171

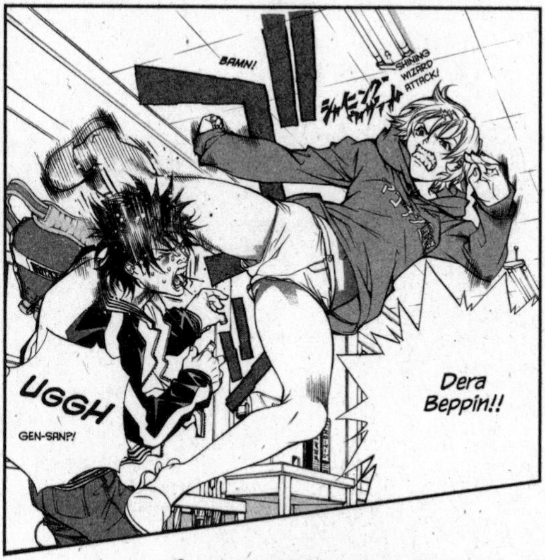
SHINING WIZARD ATTACK!
BAMN!
Dera Beppin!!
UGGH
GEN-SAN?!

As Itsuki returns home, Mikan attacks him at the door with the pro wrestling move "Shining Wizard Attack," on top of which, she shouts *"Dera Beppin!!"* which is the name of a naughty magazine in Japan. In the manga *Agonashi Gen to Ore,* Gen-san's character is known for smacking enemies with *Dera Beppin* magazine.

Galaxy Express 999 train, page 176

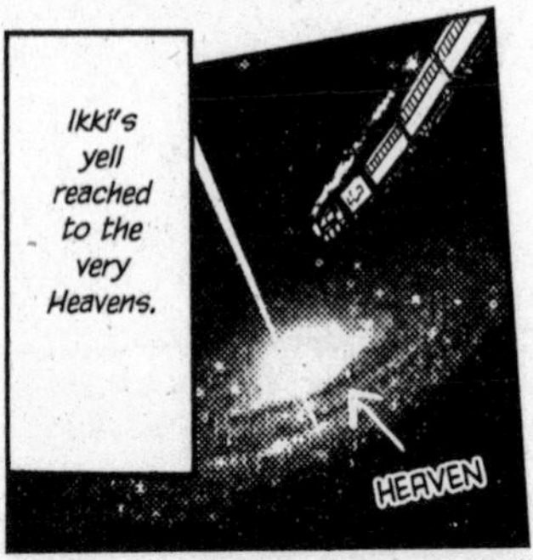
Ikki's yell reached to the very Heavens.
HEAVEN

Look closely at this panel and you'll see a train orbiting the Earth. This is a reference to the very same train from the series *Galaxy Express 999.*

Tsukkomi, page 182

In classic Japanese comedy duos, one person is "the idiot" and the other is "the straight man" who reacts to the idiot. When the straight man or *tsukkomi* tries to converse with the idiot or bokke, comedy ensues. Ringo realizes that trying to out-geek Simca when it comes to 8-bit games puts her in the role of the *tsukkomi.*

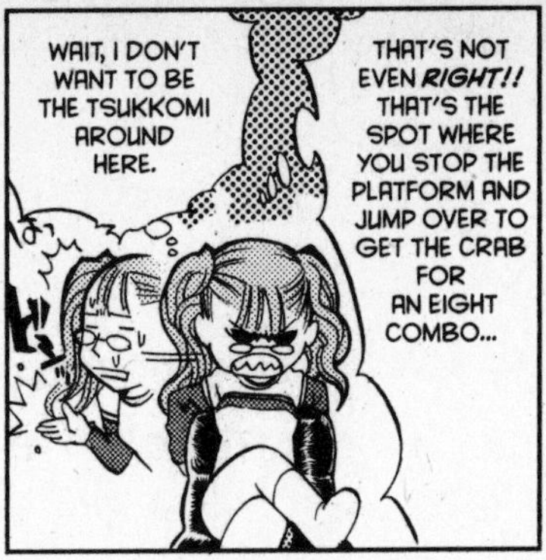
THAT'S NOT EVEN RIGHT!! THAT'S THE SPOT WHERE YOU STOP THE PLATFORM AND JUMP OVER TO GET THE CRAB FOR AN EIGHT COMBO...
WAIT, I DON'T WANT TO BE THE TSUKKOMI AROUND HERE.

Iskandar, page 189

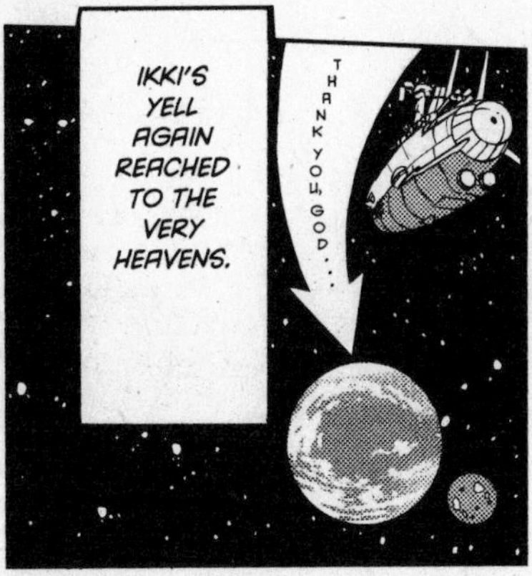
THANK YOU, GOD...
IKKI'S YELL AGAIN REACHED TO THE VERY HEAVENS.

The planet is marked Iskandar, a celestial destination from the series *Space Battleship YAMATO.*

Star Platinum, page 198

Surfacing behind Ringo in her moment of fury is Star Platinum, from the series *JoJo's Bizarre Adventure.*

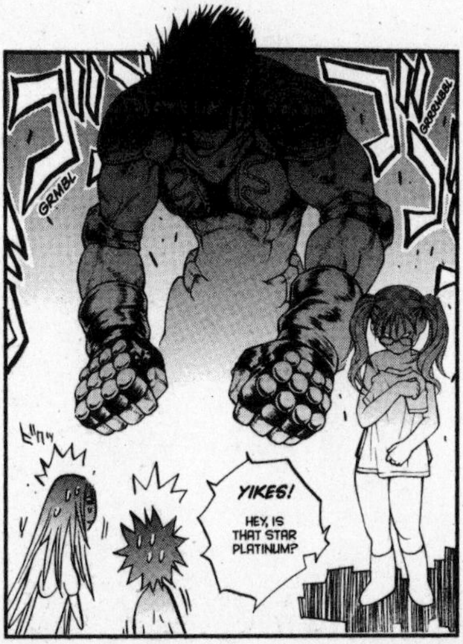
GRRRMBL
GRMBL
YIKES!
HEY, IS THAT STAR PLATINUM?

We're pleased to present you a preview from Volume 4. This volume will be available in English on April 24, 2007, but for now, you'll have to make do with Japanese.

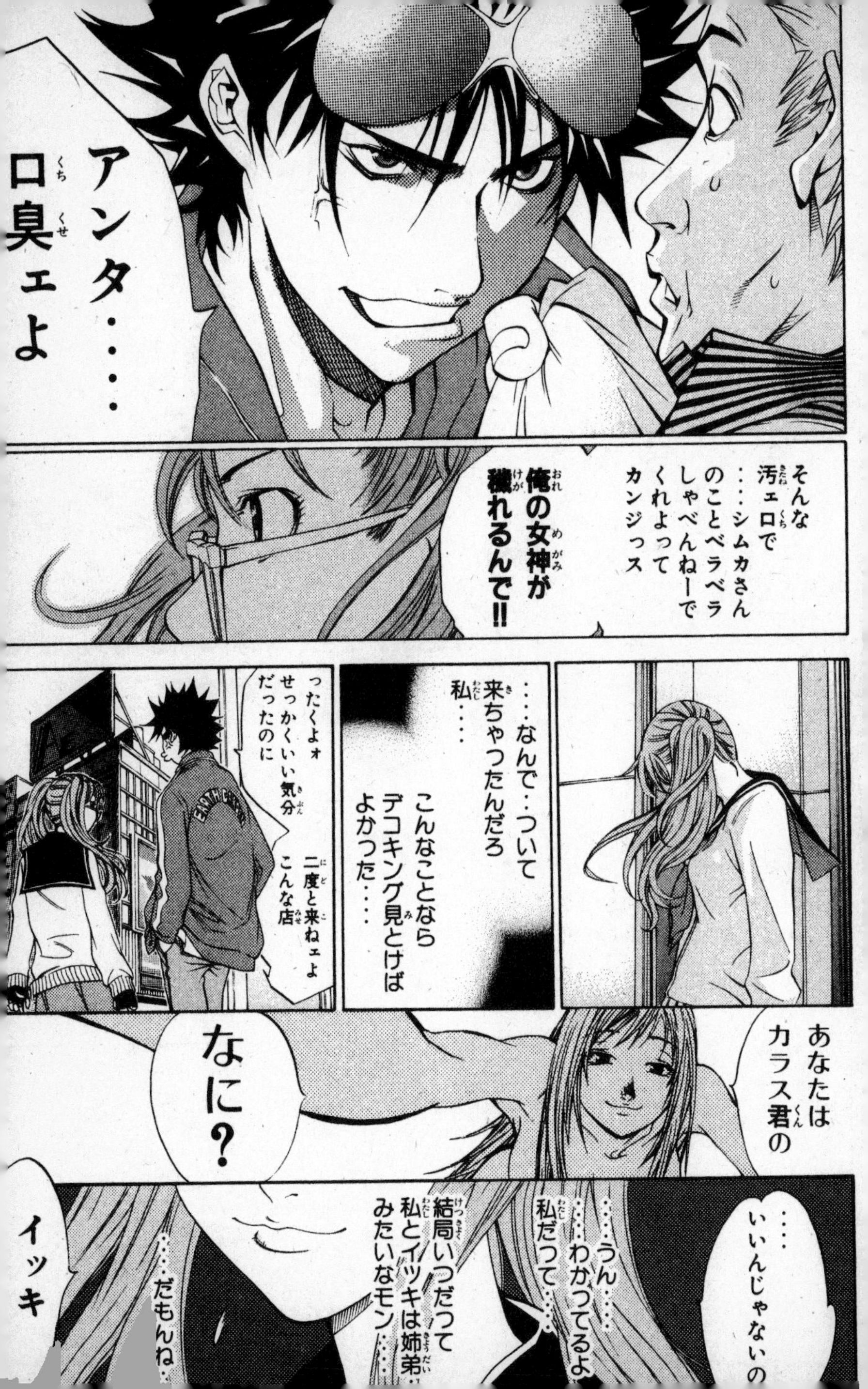

アンタ……口臭ェよ
そんな汚エロで……シムカさんのことベラベラしゃべんねーでくれよってカンジっス
俺の女神が穢れるんで!!
……なんで…ついて来ちゃったんだろ私……
こんなことならデコキング見とけばよかつた……
ったくよォせっかくいい気分だったのに
二度と来ねェよこんな店
あなたはカラス君の
なに?
……いいんじゃないの
うん……わかってるよ……私だって……
結局いつだって私とイッキは姉弟みたいなモン……
……だもんね…
イッキ

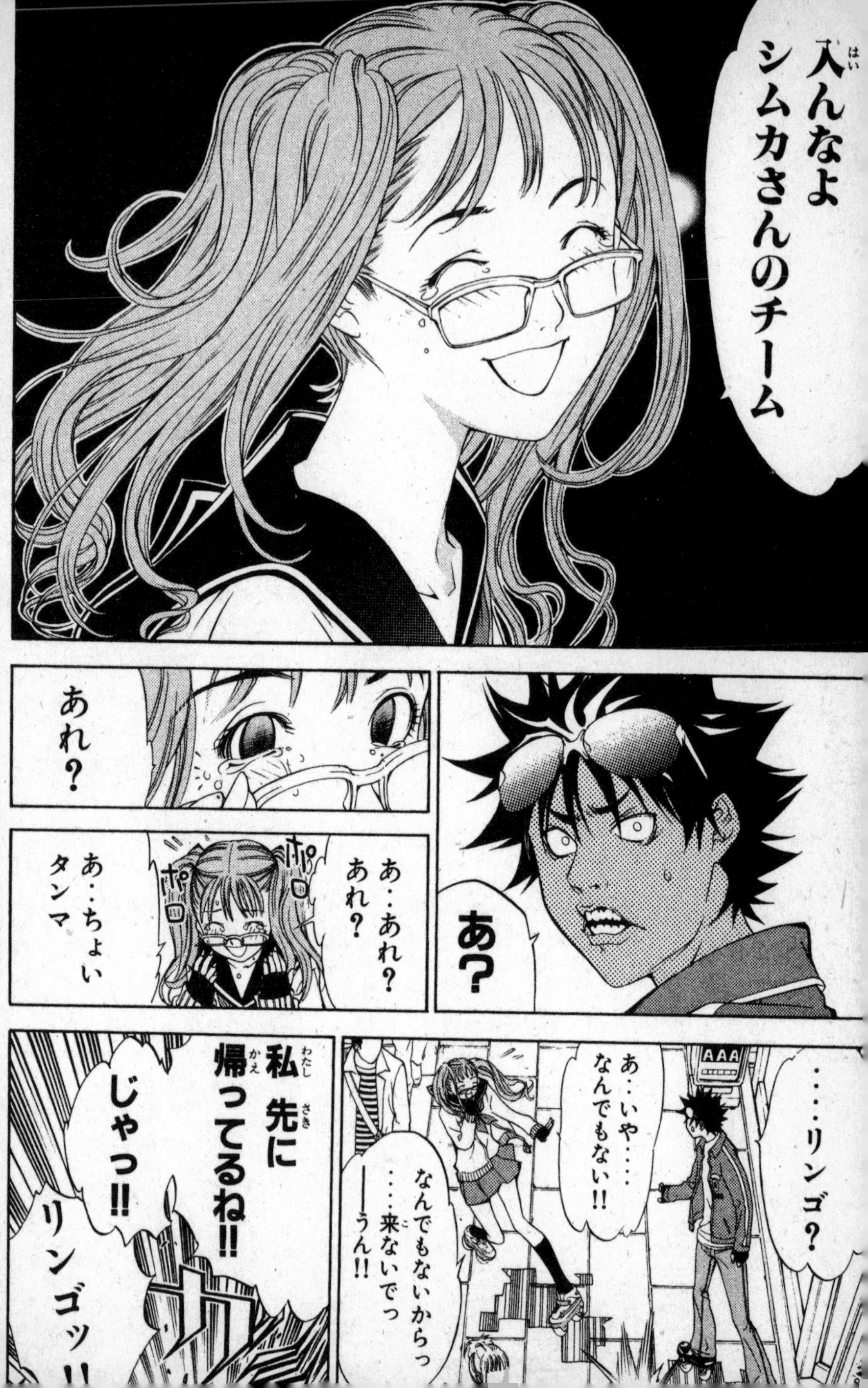
入んなよ
シムカさんのチーム
あ?
あれ?
あ…あれ?
あれ?
ポロ
ポロ
あ…ちょい
タンマ
……リンゴ?
あ…いや……
なんでもない!!
なんでもないからっ
……来ないでっ
——うん!!
私
先に
帰ってるね!!
じゃっ!!
リンゴッ!!

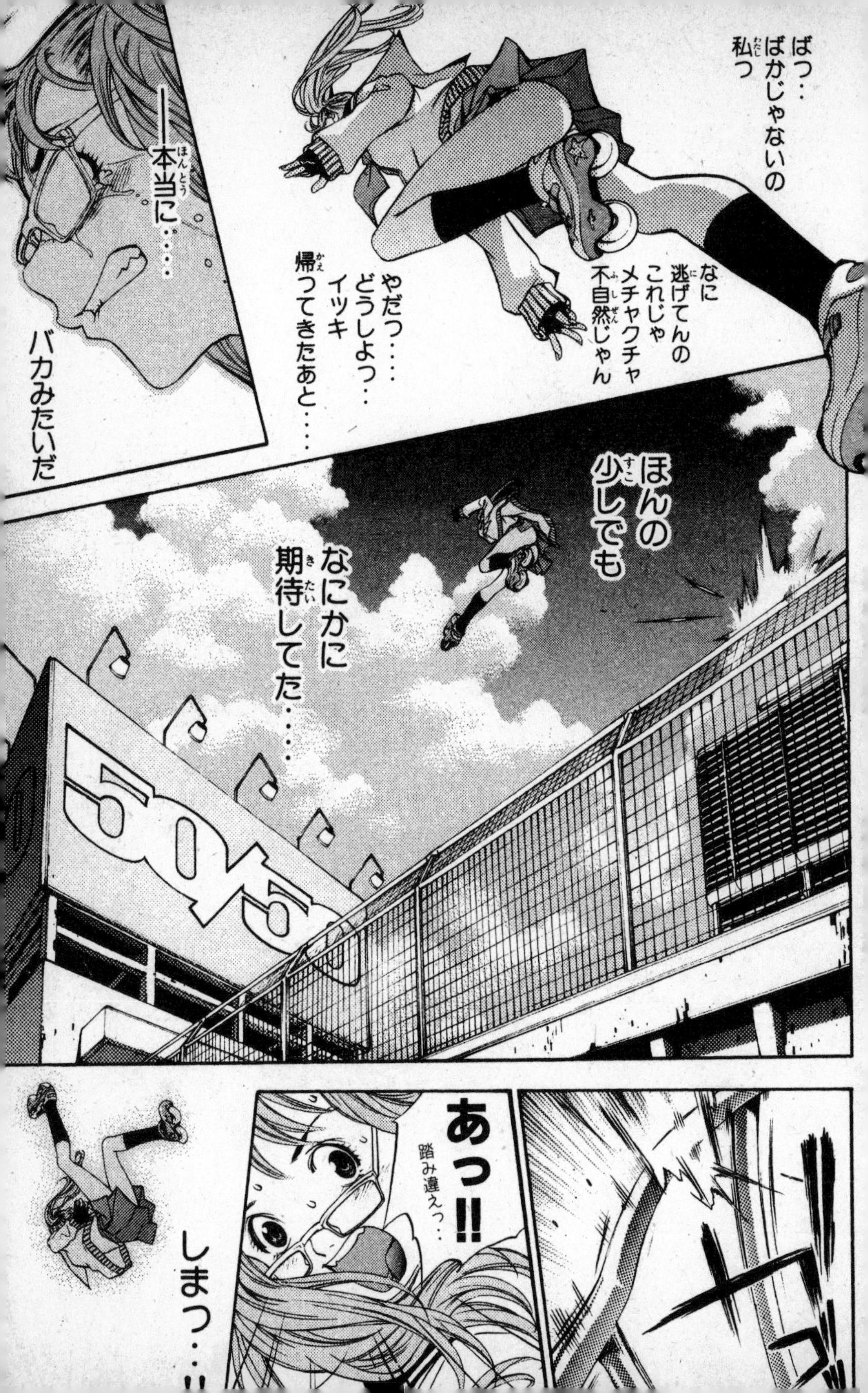
ばつ…ばかじゃないの私つ
なに逃げてんのこれじゃメチャクチャ不自然じゃん
やだつ……どうしよつ…イッキ帰つてきたあと……
──本当に……
バカみたいだ
ほんの少しでも
なにかに期待してた……
あっ!!
踏み違えっ…
しまっ…!!

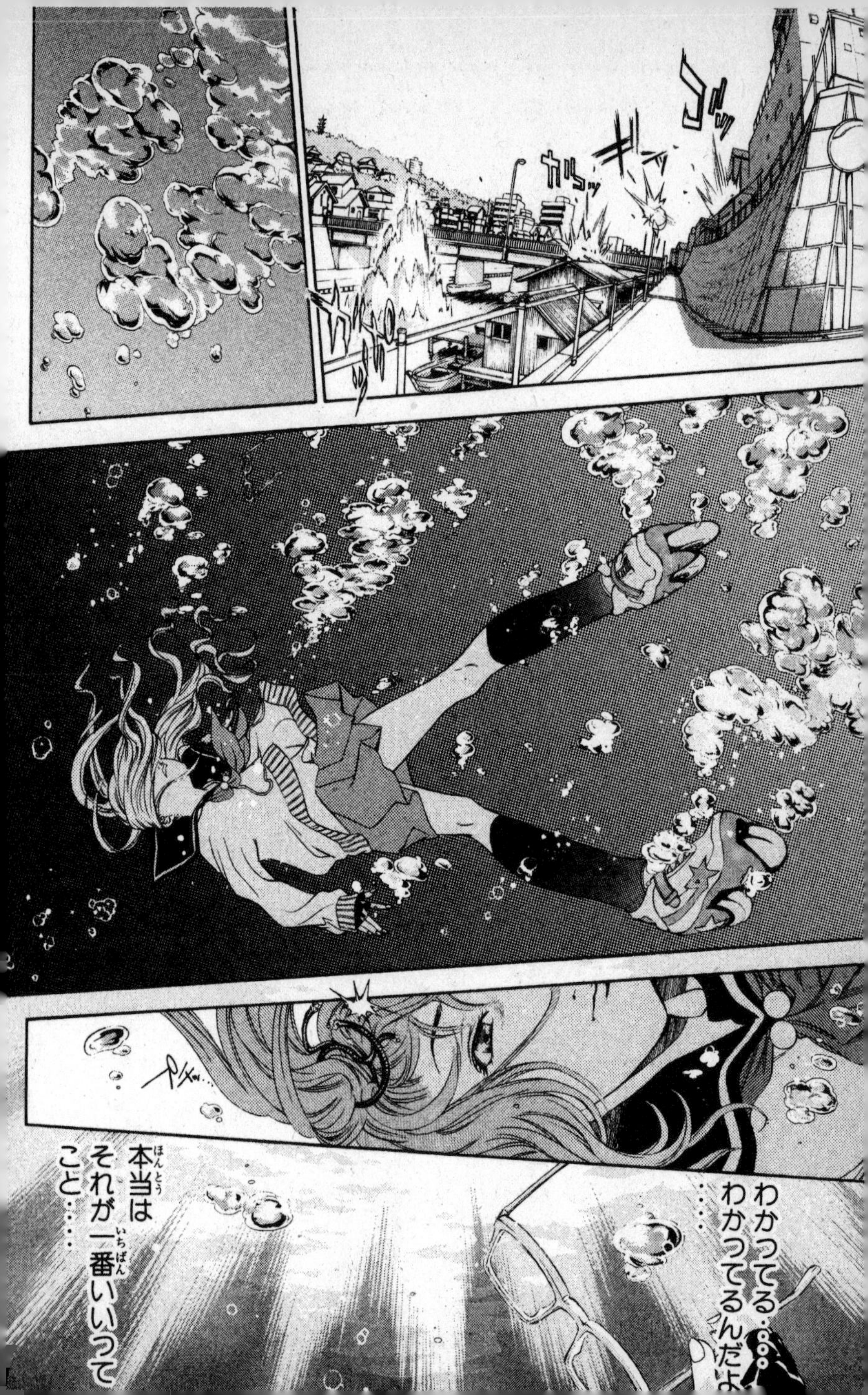
ゴッ
ギシャッ
カランッ
わかってる・・・・
わかってるんだよ・・・・
本当はそれが一番いいってこと・・・・

FREE COLLARS KINGDOM

フリーカラーズキングダム

TAKUYA FUJIMI

THOSE FEISTY FELINES!

1
FREE COLLARS
フリーカラーズキングダム
KINGDOM
TAKUYA FUJIMA

It's hard to resist Cyan: He's an adorable catboy, whose cute ears and tail have made him a beloved pet. But then his family abandons him, leaving the innocent Cyan to fend for himself.

Just when Cyan thinks he's all alone in the world, he meets the Free Collars, a cool gang of stray cats who believe that no feline should allow a human to imprison his Wild Spirit. They invite Cyan to join them, and the reluctant housecat has to decide fast, because a rival gang of cats is threatening the Free Collars' territory! Can Cyan learn to free his Wild Spirit—and help his new friends save their home?

Special extras in each volume! Read them all!

VISIT WWW.DELREYMANGA.COM TO:

- Read sample pages
- View release date calendars for upcoming volumes
- Sign up for Del Rey's free manga e-newsletter
- Find out the latest about new Del Rey Manga series

RATING OT AGES 16+

DEL REY DEL REY MANGA デルレイ

The Otaku's Choice

BY JIN KOBAYASHI

SUBTLETY IS FOR WIMPS!

She . . . is a second-year high school student with a single all-consuming question: Will the boy she likes ever really notice her?

He . . . is the school's most notorious juvenile delinquent, and he's suddenly come to a shocking realization: He's got a huge crush, and now he must tell her how he feels.

Life-changing obsessions, colossal foul-ups, grand schemes, deep-seated anxieties, and raging hormones—School Rumble portrays high school as it really is: over-the-top comedy!

Ages: 16 +

Special extras in each volume! Read them all!

TOMARE!
[STOP!]

You are going the wrong way!

Manga is a completely different type of reading experience.

To start at the *beginning*, go to the *end*!

That's right! Authentic manga is read the traditional Japanese way—from right to left. Exactly the *opposite* of how American books are read. It's easy to follow: Just go to the other end of the book, and read each page—and each panel—from right side to left side, starting at the top right. Now you're experiencing manga as it was meant to be.

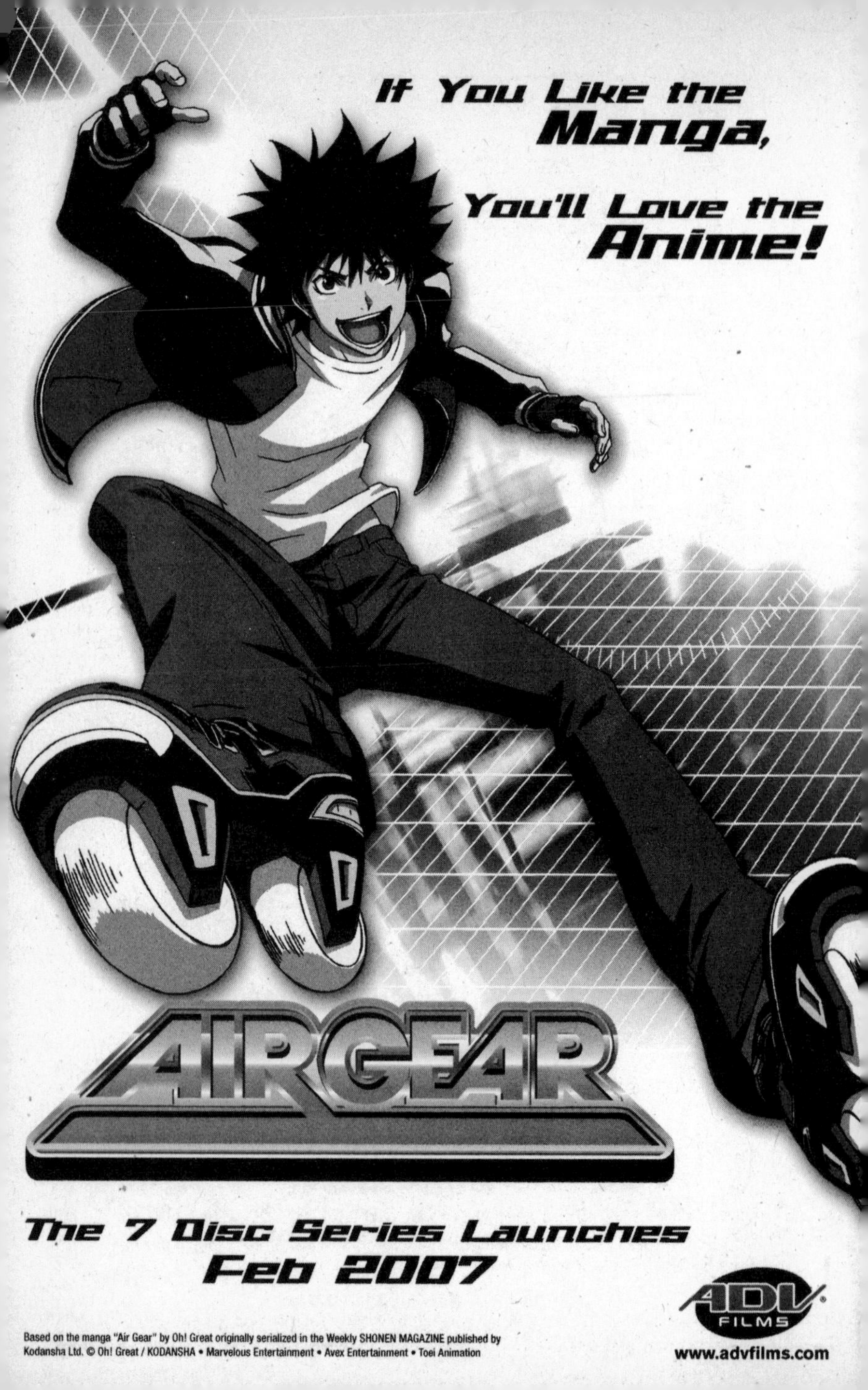

If You Like the Manga,
You'll Love the Anime!
AIR GEAR
The 7 Disc Series Launches Feb 2007
ADV FILMS
Based on the manga "Air Gear" by Oh! Great originally serialized in the Weekly SHONEN MAGAZINE published by Kodansha Ltd. © Oh! Great / KODANSHA • Marvelous Entertainment • Avex Entertainment • Toei Animation
www.advfilms.com